FORENSIC FINGERPRINTS

FORENSIC FINGERPRINTS

Advanced Forensic Science Series

MAX M. HOUCK, PhD, FRSC

Managing Director, Forensic & Intelligence Services, LLC, St. Petersburg, FL, USA

ELSEVIER

Amsterdam • Boston • Heidelberg • London • New York • Oxford
Paris • San Diego • San Francisco • Singapore • Sydney • Tokyo

Academic Press is an imprint of Elsevier

Academic Press is an imprint of Elsevier
125 London Wall, London EC2Y 5AS, UK
525 B Street, Suite 1800, San Diego, CA 92101-4495, USA
50 Hampshire Street, Cambridge, MA 02139, USA
The Boulevard, Langford Lane, Kidlington, Oxford OX5 1GB, UK

ISBN: 978-0-12-800573-6
ISSN: 2352-6238

British Library Cataloguing-in-Publication Data
A catalogue record for this book is available from the British Library

Library of Congress Cataloging-in-Publication Data
A catalog record for this book is available from the Library of Congress

For information on all Academic Press publications visit our website at www.elsevier.com

Publisher: Sara Tenney
Acquisitions Editor: Elizabeth Brown
Editorial Project Manager: Joslyn Chaiprasert-Paguio
Production Project Manager: Lisa Jones
Designer: Matthew Limbert

Typeset by TNQ Books and Journals
www.tnq.co.in

CONTENTS

SENIOR EDITOR: BIOGRAPHY

Max M. Houck is an internationally recognized forensic expert with research interests in anthropology, trace evidence, education, and the fundamentals of forensic science, both as a science and as an enterprise. He has worked in the private sector, the public sector (at the regional and federal levels), and in academia. Dr Houck has published in a wide variety of areas in the field, in books, book chapters, and peer-reviewed journals. His casework includes the Branch Davidian Investigation, the September 11 attacks on the Pentagon, the D.B. Cooper case, the US Embassy bombings in Africa, and the West Memphis Three case. He served for 6 years as the Chair of the Forensic Science Educational Program Accreditation Commission (FEPAC). Dr Houck is a founding coeditor of the journal Forensic Science Policy and Management, with Jay Siegel; he has also coauthored a major textbook with Siegel, *Fundamentals of Forensic Science*. In 2012, Dr Houck was in the top 1% of connected professionals on LinkedIn. Dr Houck is currently the Managing Director of Forensic and Intelligence Services, LLC, St. Petersburg, FL.

LIST OF CONTRIBUTORS

E Burton
Greater Manchester Police Forensic Services Branch, Manchester, UK

M Carter
Las Vegas Metropolitan Police Department Forensic Laboratory, Las Vegas, NV, USA

C Champod
University of Lausanne, Lausanne, Switzerland

F Crispino
Université du Québec à Trois-Rivières, Trois-Rivières, QC, Canada

J Epstein
Widener University School of Law, Wilmington, DE, USA

AA Frick
Curtin University, Perth, WA, Australia

P Fritz
Curtin University, Perth, WA, Australia

I Hamilton
Glasgow Fingerprint Unit, Forensic Services, Scottish Police Services Authority, Glasgow, UK

MM Houck
Consolidated Forensic Laboratory, Washington, DC, USA

LA Hutchins
US Government, Washington, DC, USA

K Inman
California State University, Hayward, CA, USA

D Johnson
Las Vegas Metropolitan Police Department, Las Vegas, NV, USA

RB Kennedy
Orleans, ON, Canada

T Kent
University of Lincoln, Lincoln, UK

SW Lewis
Curtin University, Perth, WA, Australia

A Loll
Phoenix Police Crime Laboratory, Phoenix, AZ, USA

A Maceo
Las Vegas Metropolitan Police Department Forensic Laboratory, Las Vegas, NV, USA

SL Massey
Campbell River, BC, Canada

DL Ortiz-Bacon
US Army Criminal Investigation Laboratory – Expeditionary Forensic Division, Forest Park, GA, USA

K Ramsey
Greater Manchester Police Forensic Services Branch, Manchester, UK

M Reznicek
Federal Bureau of Investigation – Latent Print Units, Quantico, VA, USA

N Rudin
Forensic DNA Consultant, Mountain View, CA, USA

RM Ruth
Federal Bureau of Investigation – Latent Print Units, Quantico, VA, USA

B Saw
Australian Federal Police, Canberra, ACT, Australia

DM Schilens
Federal Bureau of Investigation – Latent Print Units, Quantico, VA, USA

N Scudder
Australian Federal Police, Canberra, ACT, Australia

B Stromback
Las Vegas Metropolitan Police Department Forensic Laboratory, Las Vegas, NV, USA

CL Swanson
US Army Criminal Investigation Laboratory – Expeditionary Forensic Division, Forest Park, GA, USA

L Tierney
Gaithersburg, MD, USA

Ted Vosk
Criminal Defense Law Firm, Kirkland, WA, USA

FOREWORD

> "The best thing for being sad", replied Merlin, beginning to puff and blow, "is to learn something. That's the only thing that never fails. You may grow old and trembling in your anatomies, you may lie awake at night listening to the disorder of your veins, you may miss your only love, you may see the world about you devastated by evil lunatics, or know your honor trampled in the sewers of baser minds. There is only one thing for it then — to learn. Learn why the world wags and what wags it. That is the only thing which the mind can never exhaust, never alienate, never be tortured by, never fear or distrust, and never dream of regretting. Learning is the only thing for you. Look what a lot of things there are to learn". — T.H. White, *The Once and Future King*

Forensic science has much to learn. The breadth of the discipline alone should render any reasonably learned person dizzy with expectations; insects, explosives, liver functions, DNA, firearms, textiles, adhesives, skeletons, and so on the list goes on forever. That is because anything, truly *anything*, can become evidence, from a single fiber to an entire ocean liner. Forensic science does not lack for specialized knowledge (some might stay too specialized), but what it is wanting is knowledge that is comprehensive, integrated, and foundational. Introductions to forensic science abound, and many highly specialized texts are also available, but a gap exists between the two: a bridge from novice to practitioner. As the 2009 NRC report noted:

> Forensic science examiners need to understand the principles, practices, and contexts of scientific methodology, as well as the distinctive features of their specialty. Ideally, training should move beyond apprentice-like transmittal of practices to education based on scientifically valid principles. NRC (2009, pp. 26–27).

The *Advanced Forensic Sciences Series* seeks to fill that gap. It is a unique source, combining entries from the world's leading specialists who contributed to the second edition of the award-winning *Encyclopedia of Forensic Sciences* and organizing them by topic into a series of volumes that are philosophically grounded yet professionally specialized. The series is composed of 12 volumes that cover the breadth of forensic science:

1. Professional Issues
2. Biology
3. Chemistry
4. Fingerprints
5. Firearms
6. Materials Analysis
7. Pathology

8. Anthropology
9. Engineering
10. Behavioral
11. Digital and Documents
12. Toxicology and Drugs

Each volume contains sections common to all forensic sciences, such as professionalism, ethics, health and safety, and court testimony, and sections relevant to the topics in that particular subdiscipline. Pedagogy is included, providing review questions, discussion questions, the latest references in additional readings, and key words. Thus, each volume is suitable as a technical reference, an advanced textbook, or a training adjunct.

The *Advanced Forensic Science Series* provides expert information, useful teaching tools, and a ready source for instruction, research, and practice. I hope, like learning, it is the only thing for you.

M.M. Houck, PhD, FRSC
Series Editor

Reference

National Research Council, 2009. Strengthening Forensic Science in the U.S.: A Path Forward. National Academies of Science, Washington, DC.

PREFACE

One of the first evidence types people think of when they hear "forensic" is fingerprints. Fingerprints have been noted and used for millennia, but around 1880, a 25-year surge in activity and popularity secured their use for government identification. Used for over 100 years by police, fingerprinting is a stalwart of forensic science: quick, cheap, and reliable. In fact, fingerprint experts claimed 100% reliability, a 0% error rate. Not long ago, fingerprint testimony sounded much like Mark Twain's character, Pudd'nhead Wilson, a lawyer who touted the power of fingerprints:

> Every human being carries with him from his cradle to his grave certain physical marks which do not change their character, and by which he can always be identified—and that without shade of doubt or question. These marks are his signature, his physiological autograph, so to speak, and this autograph cannot be counterfeited, nor can he disguise it or hide it away, nor can it become illegible by the wear and the mutations of time... This signature is each man's very own. There is no duplicate of it among the swarming populations of the globe!

The concept of absolute individualization was broad-sided by a case in Philadelphia which questioned the validity of fingerprints as a science, *U.S. v. Byron Mitchell*. In the admissibility hearing, the judge heard testimony that the FBI had never misidentified anyone. This was the party line for many years ("Of all the methods of identification, fingerprinting alone has proved to be both infallible and feasible".) (FBI, 1985). Legal challenges aside, fingerprinting had its validity questioned scientifically in spotlight cases, like Shirley McKie's, Stephan Cowans', and Brandon Mayfield's, among others (Cole, 2005). These cases have shown that fingerprinting is as fallible as any method or science and more susceptible to undue influence. A culture of resistance, refutation, and rebuttal grew around the myth that fingerprints were perfect (Cole, 2005). Accepting its flaws and moving on to improve the profession would have been sensible but that is not what happened. Arguments, name calling, and personal attacks were hurled at those who questioned the infallibility of fingerprints (Russell, 2009).

The community finally pulled itself together and began to make headway with a reasoned plan of improvement, created collaboratively with critics and stakeholders. A sourcebook was written in a project shepherded by the West Virginia University Forensic Science Initiative in collaboration with the International Association for Identification through an award from the National Institute of Justice (2011). Research began slowly from a variety of sources but led to more enlightened and professional discussions of error rates, bias, accuracy, and methodology. With much more work to be done, fingerprints has become a bellwether for the rest of traditional forensic science: Change or be changed, it is up to you.

Additional Readings

Cole, S.A., 2005. More than zero: accounting for error in latent fingerprint identification. Journal of Criminal Law & Criminology 95, 985 (2004–2005).

Cole, S.A., 2014. Individualization is dead, long live individualization! Reforms of reporting practices for fingerprint analysis in the United States. Law, Probability and Risk. http://dx.doi.org/10.1093/lpr/mgt014 (online January 21, 2014).

Cole, S.A., 2014. The innocence crisis and forensic science reform. In: Zalman, M., Currano, J. (Eds.), Wrongful Conviction and Criminal Justice Reform: Making Justice. Routledge, New York, pp. 167–185.

Champod, C., 2015. Fingerprint identification: advances since the 2009 National Research Council report. Philosophical Transactions of the Royal Society B 370 (1674), 20140259.

Edmond, G., Cole, S.A., 2014. Identification technologies in policing and proof. In: Encyclopedia of Criminology and Criminal Justice. Springer, New York, pp. 2407–2419.

Federal Bureau of Investigation, 1985. The Science of Fingerprints: Classification and Uses. U.S. Department of Justice, Washington, DC.

Ludwig, A., Fraser, J., 2014. Effective use of forensic science in volume crime investigations: identifying recurring themes in the literature. Science & Justice 54 (1), 81–88.

McCartney, C., Walker, C., 2014. Forensic identification and miscarriages of justice in England and Wales. In: Mallett, X., Blythe, T., Berry, R. (Eds.), Advances in Forensic Human Identification. CRC Press, Boca Raton, FL, pp. 391–405.

Mnookin, J., Cole, S.A., Dror, I., Fisher, B.A., Houck, M., Inman, K., Kaye, D., Koehler, J., Langenburg, G., Risinger, D., Rudin, N., Siegel, J., Stoney, D.A., 2011. The need for a research culture in the forensic sciences. UCLA Law Review 58, 725.

National Institute of Justice, 2011. Fingerprint Sourcebook. U.S. Department of Justice, Washington, DC.

Russell, S., June 18, 2009. Bias and the big fingerprint dust-up. Pacific Standard. Online at: http://www.psmag.com/politics-and-law/bias-and-the-big-fingerprint-dust-up-3629.

Specter, M., May 27, 2002. Do fingerprints lie? The New Yorker.

Section 1. Introduction

Forensic science is about 100 years old, depending on how the accomplishments are counted. That is relatively young, for a science; chemistry goes back to at least 1661 with the publication of Boyle's *The Sceptical Chymist*, for example. Forensic science is only now beginning to delve into its methods and history to construct the scaffolding of a guiding philosophy. This foundation will be critically important as forensic research and operation moves forward but it will take several generations of forensic scientists before it becomes sturdy and robust.

Principles of Forensic Science

F Crispino, Université du Québec à Trois-Rivières, Trois-Rivières, QC, Canada
MM Houck, Consolidated Forensic Laboratory, Washington, DC, USA

Glossary

Abduction Syllogism in which one premise is certain whereas the other one is only probable, generally presented as the best explanation to the former. Hence, abduction is a type of reasoning in which we know the law and the effect, and we attempt to infer the cause.
Deduction Process of reasoning which moves from the general to the specific, and in which a conclusion follows necessarily from the stated premises. Hence, deduction is a type of reasoning in which, knowing the cause and the law, we infer the effect.
Forensic intelligence Understanding on how traces can be collected from the scene, processed, and interpreted within a holistic intelligence-led policing strategy.
Heuristic Process of reasoning by rules that are only loosely defined, generally by trial and error.
Holistic Emphasizing the importance of the whole and the interdependence of its parts.
Induction Process of deriving general principles from particular facts or instances, i.e., of reasoning that moves from the specific to the general. Hence, induction is a type of reasoning in which, knowing the cause and the effect (or a series of causes and effects), we attempt to infer the law by which the effects follow the cause.
Linkage blindness Organizational or investigative failure to recognize a common pattern shared on different cases.
Science The intellectual and practical activity encompassing the systematic study of the structure and behavior of the physical and natural world through observation and experiment. It is also defined as a systematically organized body of knowledge on a particular subject.

Given that it identifies and collects objects at crime scenes and then treats them as evidence, forensic science could appear at first glance to be only a pragmatic set of various disciplines, with practitioners adapting and developing tools and technologies to help the triers of fact (juries or judges) interpret information gained from the people, places, and things involved in a crime. The view could be—and has been—held that forensic science has no philosophic or fundamental unity and is merely the application of knowledge generated by other sciences. Indeed, many working forensic scientists regard themselves mainly as chemists, biologists, scientists, or technicians and rarely as practitioners of a homogeneous body of knowledge with common fundamental principles.

Even the 2009 National Academy of Sciences National Research Council Report failed to recognize such a concept, certainly blurred by a semantic gap in the terminology itself of

 http://dx.doi.org/10.1016/B978-0-12-800573-6.00001-X

field practitioners, who confuse words like "forensic science(s)," "criminalistic(s)," "criminology," "technical police," "scientific police," and so on, and generally restrict the scientific debate on analytical techniques and methods. An independent definition of forensic science, apart from its legal aspects, would support its scientific status and return the expert to his domain as scientist and interpreter of his analyses and results to assist the lay person.

What Is Forensic Science?

In its broadest sense, forensic science describes the utility of the sciences as they pertain to legal matters, to include many disciplines, such as chemistry, biology, pathology, anthropology, toxicology, and engineering, among others. ("Forensic" comes from the Latin root *forum*, the central place of the city where disputes and debates were made public to be solved, hence, defining the law of the city. Forensic generally means of or applied to the law.) The word "criminalistics" was adopted to describe the discipline directed toward the "recognition, identification, individualization, and evaluation of physical evidence by application of the natural sciences to law-science matters." ("Kriminalistik" was coined in the late nineteenth century by Hans Gross, a researcher in criminal law and procedure to define his methodology of classifying investigative, tactical, and evidential information to be learned by magistrates at law schools to solve crimes and help convict criminals.) In the scheme as it currently stands, criminalistics is part of forensic science; the word is a regionalism and is not universally applied as defined. Difficulties in differentiating the concepts certainly invited the definition of criminalistics as the "science of individualization," isolating this specific epistemologically problematic core from the other scientific disciplines. Individualization, the concept of determining the sole source of an item, enthroned a linear process—identification or classification on to individualization—losing sight of the holistic, variable contribution of all types of evidence. Assessing the circumstances surrounding a crime, where the challenge is to integrate and organize the data in order to reconstruct a case or propose alternative propositions for events under examination, requires multiple types of evidence, some of which may be quite nuanced in their interpretation. This is also true in the use of so-called forensic intelligence, which feeds investigative, police, or security needs, where one of the main reasons for failures is linkage blindness. Nevertheless, it seems that the essence of the forensic daily practice is hardly captured within the present definitions of both terms.

Forensic science reconstructs—in the broadest sense—past criminal events through the analysis of the physical remnants of those activities (evidence); the results of those analyses and their expert interpretation establish relationships between people, places, and objects relevant to those events. It produces these results and interpretations through logical inferences, induction, abduction, and deduction, all of which frame the hypothetico-deductive method; investigative heuristics also play a role. Translating scientific information into legal information is a particular domain of forensic science; other sciences must (or at least should) communicate their findings to the public, but forensic science is often required by law to communicate their findings to public courts. Indeed, as the Daubert hearing stated, "[s]cientific conclusions are subject to perpetual revision as law must resolve disputes finally and quickly." This doubly difficult requirement of communicating to the public and to the law necessitates that forensic scientists should be better communicators of their work and their results. Scientific inferences are not necessarily legal proofs, and the forensic scientist must recognize that legal decisions based, in part, on their scientific work may not accord with their expert knowledge. Moreover, scientists must think in probabilities to explain evidence given possible causes, while jurists must deal in terms of belief beyond reasonable doubt. As Inman and Rudin state: "Because we [the scientists] provide results and information to parties who lack the expertise to independently understand their meaning and implications, it is up to us to furnish an accurate and complete interpretation of our results. If we do not do this, our conclusions are at best incomplete, at worst potentially misleading."

The Trace as the Basic Unit of Forensic Science

The basic unit of forensic science is the trace, the physical remnant of the past criminal activity. Traces are, by their very nature, semiotic: They represent something more than merely themselves; they are signifiers or signs for the items or events that are its source. A fiber is not the sweater it came from, a fingerprint is not the fingertip, soot in the trachea is not the victim choking from a fire, blood droplets are not the violence against the victim, but they all point to their origin (source and activity) to a greater or lesser degree of specificity. Thus, the trace is a type of proxy data, that is, an indicator of a related phenomenon but not the phenomenon itself. Traces come from the natural and manufactured items that surround us in our daily lives. Traces are, in essence, the raw material available at a crime scene which becomes forensic intelligence or knowledge. Everyday items and their traces become evidence through their involvement in criminal activities; the activities add meaning to their existing status as goods in the world; a fireplace poker is transformed into "the murder weapon" by its use as such. The meaning added should also take into account the context of the case, the circumstances under which the criminal activities occurred, boarding the trier of fact mandate.

Traces become evidence when they are recognized, accepted as relevant (if blurred) to the past event under investigation, and collected for forensic purposes. Confusing trace, sign, and evidence can obscure the very process of trace "discovery," which lies at the root of its interpretation. Evidence begins with detection by observation, which is possible because of the available knowledge of the investigator or scientist; unrecognized traces go undiscovered and do not become evidence. When the investigator's or scientist's senses are extended through instrumental sensitivity, either at the scene or in the laboratory, the amount of potential evidence considerably increased. Microscopes, alternate light sources, instrumental sensitivity, and detection limits create increases in the number of traces that can be recognized and collected. More evidence, and more evidence types, inevitably led to increases in the complexity not only of the search for traces but also to their interpretation. Feeding back into this system is the awareness of new (micro)traces that changed the search methods at scenes and in laboratories, with yet more evidence being potentially available.

Traces are ancillary to their originating process; they are by-products of the source activity, an accidental vestige of their criminal creation. To be useful in the determination of associations, traces whose ultimate sources are unknown must be compared to samples from a known source. Comparison is the very heart of the forensic science process; the method is essentially a diagnostic one, beginning with Georges Cuvier, and is employed by many science practitioners, including medical professionals. (Including, interestingly, Arthur Conan Doyle, a medical doctor and author, whose Sherlock Holmes character references Cuvier's method in *The Five Orange Pips*.) Questioned traces, or items, may have a provenance (a known location at the time of their discovery) but this is not their originating source; a few examples may help:

Trace (questioned)	Source (known)
Fiber on victim	Sweater
Gunshot residue	Ammunition discharge
Blood droplet	Body
Toolmarks in door jamb	Pry bar used to open door
Shoeprint in soil	Shoe from suspect
Fingerprint on glass	Finger from suspect

The collection of properly representative known samples is crucial to accurate forensic analyses and comparisons. Known samples can be selected through a variety of legitimate schemes, including random, portion, and judgment, and must be selected with great care. Thus, traces are accidental and known samples are intentional.

Some of the consequences of what has been discussed so far induce the capacities and limitations of a forensic investigation based on trace analysis. A micro- to nanolevel existence allows forensic scientists to plan physical and chemical characteristics in their identifications and comparisons with other similar data. This allows forensic science to be as methodologically flexible as its objects of study require. Because time is asymmetric and each criminal action is unique, the forensic investigation and analysis in any one case is wedded, to a certain degree, to that case with no ambition to issue general laws about that event ("In all instances of John Davis being physically assaulted with a baseball bat..."). Inferences must be drawn with explicit uncertainty statements; the inferences should be revised when new data affect the traces' relevancy. Therefore, the search for traces is a recursive heuristic process taking into account the environment of the case at hand, appealing to the imagination, expertise, and competency of the investigator or scientist to propose explicative hypotheses.

Two Native Principles

With this framework, two principles can be thought of as the main native principles that support and frame philosophically forensic science. In this context, principles are understood as universal theoretical statements settled at the beginning of a deduction, which cannot be deduced from any other statement in the considered system, and give coherence to the area of study. They provide the grounds from which other truths can be derived and define a paradigm, that is, a general epistemological viewpoint, a new concept to see the natural world, issued from an empiricist corroborated tradition, accepted by the community of practitioners in the field. Ultimately, this paradigm can even pilot the perception itself.

Although similar but nonequivalent versions are used in other disciplines, Locard's exchange principle exists as the central tenant of forensic science. The principle that bears his name was never uttered as such by Locard, but its universal statement of "every contact leaves a trace" stands as a universally accepted short-hand phrasing. Locard's principle embraces all forms of contact, from biological to chemical to physical and even digital traces, and extends the usual perception of forensic science beyond dealing only with physical vestiges.

One of its corollaries is that trace deposition is continual and not reversible. Increases in the number of contacts, the types of evidence involved, and cross-transfers (A–B and B–A) also increase the complexity of determining the relevance of traces in short duration and temporally close actions.

Even the potentially fallacious rubric of "absence of evidence is not evidence of absence" leads to extended discussions on the very nature of proof, or provable, that aims to be definitive, notwithstanding the explanations for the practical aspects of the concept (lack of sensitivity, obscuring of the relevant traces, human weakness, actual absence, etc.). Applying Locard's principle needs to address three levels. First, the physical level, which deals with ease of transfer, retention, persistence, and affinity of materials, which could better support the exchange of traces from one source to another. Second is the situational or contextual level, which is the knowledge of circumstances and environments surrounding criminal events and sets the matrix for detection, identification, and proximate significance of any evidence. Third, the intelligence level, which covers the knowledge about criminal behavior in single events or series, specific problems related to current trends in criminal behavior, and communication between relevant entities (police, scientists, attorneys, etc.); these components help the investigator in the field to focus on more meaningful traces that might otherwise go undetected.

The second, and more debated, principle is Kirk's individuality principle; again, Kirk did not state this as such beyond saying that criminalistics is the science of individualization. In its strongest form, it posits that each object in the universe can be placed demonstratively into a set with one and only one member: Itself. It therefore asserts the universal statement, "every object in our universe is unique." Philosophers like Wittgenstein have argued that without defined rules or limits, terms such as "the same" or "different" are essentially meaningless. There is little question that all things are unique—two identical things can still be numerically differentiated—but the core question is, can they be distinguished at the resolution of detection applied? Simply saying "all things are unique" is not useful forensically. For example, each fingerprint left by the same finger is unique, but to be useful, each print must also be able to be traced back to its source finger. Uniqueness is therefore necessary to claim individualization, but not sufficient. Thus, it is the degree of association that matters, how similar, how different these two things being compared are. Referring to Cole, "What distinguishes...objects is not 'uniqueness'; it is their diagnosticity: our ability to assign traces of these objects to their correct source with a certain degree of specificity under certain parameters of detection and under certain rules governing such assignments," or as Osterburg stated, "to approach [individualization] as closely as the present state of science allows." Statistics, typically, is required to accurately communicate levels of comparison that are reproducible. In fact, Kirk noted that individualization was not absolute. ("On the witness stand, the criminalist must be willing to admit that *absolute identity is impossible to establish*. ...The inept or biased witness may readily testify to an identity, or to a type of identity, that does not actually exist. This can come about because of his confusion as to the nature of identity, his inability to evaluate the results of his observations, or because his general technical deficiencies preclude meaningful results" (Kirk, 1953; emphasis added).)

Nonnative Principles

Numerous guiding principles from other sciences apply centrally to forensic science, several of which come from geology, a cognate historical science to forensic science. That these principles come not from forensic science but from other sciences should not imply that they are somehow less important than Locard's or Kirk's notions. The first, and in many ways the most important, of the external principles is that of uniformitarianism. The principle, proposed by James Hutton, popularized by Charles Lyell, and coined by William Whewell, states that natural phenomena do not change in scope, intensity, or effect with time. Paraphrased as "the present is the key to the past," the principle implies that a volcano that erupts today acts in the same way as volcanoes did 200 or 200 million years ago and, thus, allows geologists to interpret proxy data from past events through current effects. Likewise, in forensic science, bullets test-fired in the laboratory today do not change in scope, intensity, or effect from bullets fired during the commission of a crime 2 days, 2 weeks, or 2 years previously. The same is true of any analysis in forensic science that requires a replication or reconstruction of processes in play during the crime's commission. Uniformitarianism offers a level of objectivity to historical sciences by posing hypotheses or relationships generally and then developing tests with respect to particular cases.

Three additional principles from geology hold as applicable to forensic science. They are as follows:

- *Superposition*: In a physical distribution, older materials are below younger materials unless a subsequent action alters this arrangement.
- *Lateral continuity*: Disassociated but similar layers can be assumed to be from the same depositional period.
- *Chronology*: It refers to the notion of absolute dates in a quantitative mode (such as "10:12 a.m." or "1670–1702") and relative dates in a relational mode (i.e., older or younger).

These three principles are attributed to Nicolaus Steno but were also formalized and applied by William Smith. A forensic example of applying the principle of superposition would be the packing of different soils in a tire tread, the most recent being the outermost. A good case of lateral continuity would be the cross-transfer of fibers in an assault, given that the chances of independent transfer and persistence prior to the time of the incident would be improbable. An example of absolute chronology in forensic science would be the simple example of a purchase receipt from a retail store with a time/date stamp on it. Examples of relative chronology abound but could range from the *terminus post quem* of a product no longer made to something hotter or colder than it should be.

See also: **Foundations:** Forensic Intelligence; History of Forensic Sciences; Overview and Meaning of Identification/Individualization; Semiotics, Heuristics, and Inferences Used by Forensic Scientists; Statistical Interpretation of Evidence: Bayesian Analysis; The Frequentist Approach to Forensic Evidence Interpretation; **Foundations/Fundamentals:** Measurement Uncertainty; **Pattern Evidence/Fingerprints (Dactyloscopy):** Friction Ridge Print Examination – Interpretation and the Comparative Method.

Further Reading

Cole, S.A., 2009. Forensics without uniqueness, conclusions without individualization: the new epistemology of forensic identification. Law, Probability and Risk 8, 233–255.

Crispino, F., 2006. Le principe de Locard est-il scientifique? Ou analyse de la scientificité des principes fondamentaux de la criminalistique. Editions Universitaires Européennes No. 523, Sarrebrücken, Germany, ISBN 978-613-1-50482-2 (2010).

Crispino, F., 2008. Nature and place of crime scene management within forensic sciences. Science and Justice 48 (1), 24–28.

Dulong, R., 2004. La rationalité spécifique de la police technique. Revue Internationale de Criminologie et de Police Technique 3 (4), 259–270.

Egger, S.A., 1984. A working definition of serial murder and the reduction of linkage blindness. Journal of Police Science and Administration 12, 348–355.

Giamalas, D.M., 2000. Criminalistics. In: Siegel, J.A., Saukko, P.J., Knupfer, G.C. (Eds.), Encyclopedia of Forensic Sciences. Academic Press, London, pp. 471–477.

Good, G. (Ed.), 1998. Sciences of the Earth, vol. 1. Garland Publishing, New York.

Houck, M.M., 2010. An Investigation into the Foundational Principles of Forensic Science (Ph.D. thesis). Curtin University of Technology, Perth.

Inman, N., Rudin, K., 2001. Principles and Practice of Criminalistics: The Profession of Forensic Science. CRC Press, Boca Raton, FL, pp. 269–270.

Kirk, P.L., 1953. Crime Investigation: Physical Evidence and the Police Laboratory. Interscience, New York, p. 10.

Kirk, P.L., 1963. The ontogeny of criminalistics. Journal of Criminal Law, Criminology and Police Science 54, 235–238.

Kuhn, T., 1970. La structure des révolutions scientifiques. Flammarion, Paris.

Kwan, Q.Y., 1976. Inference of Identity of Source (Ph.D. thesis). Berkeley University, Berkeley.

Mann, M., 2002. The value of multiple proxies. Science 297, 1481–1482.

Masterman, M., 1970. The nature of a paradigm. In: Lakatos, I., Musgrave, A. (Eds.), Criticism and the Growth of Experimental Knowledge. Cambridge University Press, Cambridge, pp. 59–86.

Moriarty, J.C., Saks, M.J., 2006. Forensic Science: Grand Goals, Tragic Flaws, and Judicial Gatekeeping. Research Paper No. 06-19. University of Akron Legal Studies.

National Research Council Committee, 2009. Identifying the Needs of the Forensic Science Community, Strengthening Forensic Science in the United States: A Path Forward. National Academy of Sciences Report. National Academy Press, Washington, DC.

Osterburg, J.W., 1968. What problems must criminalistics solve. Journal of Criminal Law, Criminology and Police Science 59 (3), 431.

Schuliar, Y., 2009. La coordination scientifique dans les investigations criminelles. Proposition d'organisation, aspects éthiques ou de la nécessité d'un nouveau métier (Ph.D. thesis). Université Paris Descartes, Paris; Université de Lausanne, Lausanne.

Sober, E., 2009. Absence of evidence and evidence of absence: evidential transitivity in connection with fossils, fishing, fine-tuning, and firing squads. Philosophical Studies 143, 63–90.

Stephens, C., 2011. A Bayesian approach to absent evidence reasoning. Informal Logic 31 (1), 56–65.

US Supreme Court No. 92–102, 1993. William Daubert, et al., Petitioners v. Merrell Dow Pharmaceuticals, Inc. Certiorari to the US Court of Appeals for the Ninth Circuit. Argued 30 March 1993. Decided 28 June 1993.

Wittgenstein, L., 1922. Tractacus Logico-Philosophicus. Gallimard Tel 311, Paris.

Relevant Websites

http://www.all-about-forensic-science.com—All-About-Forensic-Science.com, Definition of Forensic Science.

http://www.forensic-evidence.com—Forensic-Evidence.com.

http://library.thinkquest.org—Oracle ThinkQuest—What Is Forensics?

Forensic Classification of Evidence

MM Houck, Consolidated Forensic Laboratory, Washington, DC, USA

Glossary

Set Any group of real or imagined objects.

Taxonomy The science of identifying and naming species with the intent of arranging them into a classification.

Taxon (pl. taxa) A group of one or more organisms grouped and ranked according to a set of qualitative and quantitative characteristics; a type of set.

Introduction

Evidence is accidental: Items are transformed into evidence by their involvement in a crime regardless of their source or mode of production. By becoming evidence, their normal meaning is enhanced and expanded. Evidence is initially categorized much as the real world; that is, based on the taxonomy created by manufacturers. Forensic science adds to this classification to further enhance or clarify the meaning of evidence relevant to the goals and procedures of the discipline.

Methods of Classification

Set Theory

Any collection of objects, real or imagined, is a set; set theory is the branch of mathematics that studies these collections. Basic set theory involves categorization and organization of the objects, sometimes using diagrams, and involves elementary operations such as set union and set intersection. Advanced topics, including cardinality, are standard in undergraduate mathematics courses. All classification schemes are based on set theory, to a greater or lesser degree.

The notion of "set" is undefined; the objects described as constituting a set create the definition. The objects in a set are called the members or elements of that set. Objects belong to a set; sets consist of their members. The members of a set may be real or imagined; they do not need to be present to be a member of that set. Membership criteria for a set should be definite and accountable. The set, "All people in this room are over 5′5″ tall," is a well-defined, if currently unknown, set—the height of the people in the room would have to be measured to accurately populate the set. If the definition is vague, then that collection may not be considered a set. For example, is "q" the same as "Q"? If the set is, "The 26 letters of the English alphabet," then they are the same member; if the set is, "The 52 uppercase and lowercase letters of the English alphabet," then they are two separate members.

Sets may be finite or infinite; a set with only one member is called a single or a singleton set. Two sets are identical if and only if they have exactly the same members. The cardinality of a set is the number of members within it, written $|A|$ for set A. A set X is a subset of set Y if and only if every member of X is also a member of Y; for example, the set of all Philips head screwdrivers is a subset of the set of all screwdrivers. Forensic scientists would term this a "subclass" but that is a terminological and not a conceptual difference. Two more concepts are required for the remainder of our discussion. The union of X and Y is a set whose members are only the members of X, Y, or both. Thus, if X were (1, 2, 3) and Y were (2, 3, 4), then the union of X and Y, written $X \cup Y$, would contain (1, 2, 3, 4). Finally, the intersection of two sets contains only the members of both X and Y. In the previous example, the intersection of X and Y would be (2, 3), written $X \cap Y$.

Taxonomy

Natural items, such as animals, plants, or minerals, often occur as evidence. These items are classified according to schemes used in other sciences such as biology, botany, or geology. It is incumbent on the forensic scientist to be knowledgeable about the classification of naturally occurring items.

In biology, taxonomy, the practice and science of classification, refers to a formalized system for ordering and grouping things, typically living things using the Linnaean method. The taxa (the units of a taxonomic system; singular "taxon") are sufficiently fixed so as to provide a structure for classifying living things. Taxa are arranged typically in a hierarchical structure to show their relatedness (a phylogeny). In such a hierarchical relationship, the subtype has by definition the same constraints as the supertype plus one or more additional constraints. For example, "macaque" is a subtype of "monkey,"

 http://dx.doi.org/10.1016/B978-0-12-800573-6.00002-1

so any macaque is also a monkey, but not every monkey is a macaque, and an animal needs to satisfy more constraints to be a macaque than to be a monkey. In the Linnaean method of classification, the scientific name of each species is formed by the combination of two words, the genus name ("generic" name), which is always capitalized, and a second word identifying the species within that genus. Species names (genus species) are either italicized or underlined; for example, *Homo sapiens* (humans), *Sus scrofa* (pigs), *Canis familiaris* (domesticated dogs), and *Rattus rattus* (rats).

The term "systematics" is sometimes used synonymously with "taxonomy" and may be confused with "scientific classification." However, taxonomy is properly the describing, identifying, classifying, and naming of organisms, while "classification" is focused on placing organisms within groups that show their relationships to other organisms. Systematics alone deals specifically with relationships through time, requiring recognition of the fossil record when dealing with the systematics of organisms. Systematics uses taxonomy as a primary tool in understanding organisms, as nothing about the organism's relationships with other living things can be understood without it first being properly studied and described in sufficient detail to identify and classify it correctly.

In geology, rocks are generally classified based on their chemical and mineral composition, the process by which they were formed, and by the texture of their particles. Rocks are classified as igneous (formed by cooled molten magma), sedimentary (formed by deposition and compaction of materials), or metamorphic (formed through intense changes in pressure and temperature). These three classes of rocks are further subdivided into many other sets; often, the categories' definitions are not rigid and the qualities of a rock may grade it from one class to another. The terminology of rocks and minerals, rather than describing a state, describes identifiable points along a gradient.

Manufacturing

Manufactured evidence is initially categorized by the in-house or market-specific system created by one or more manufacturers. Manufacturers of economic goods create their classifications through product identity or analytical methods. Set methods of production ensure a quality product fit for purpose and sale; the classification is based on the markets involved, the orientation of the company production methods, and the supply chain. Explicit rules exist on categories recognized by manufacturers and consumers, as either models or brands. Materials flow downstream from raw material sources through to a manufacturing level. Raw materials are transformed into intermediate products, also referred to as components or parts. These are assembled on the next level to form products. The products are shipped to distribution centers and from there on to retailers and customers.

Forensic Approaches to Classification

The supply network of raw materials, intermediate steps, production methods, intended consumer end use, and actual end use all contribute to the characteristics available for forensic taxonomic classification. While the forensic taxonomies are unique to that discipline, they are based on the production taxonomies used in manufacturing. These characteristics form the basis for statements of significance; that is, the relative abundance or rarity of any one particular item in a criminal context. Some objects are common but have a short-entrance horizon (e.g., iPods), but are essentially identical at the outset while others are common with long-entrance horizons (denim blue jeans), but have a high variance (regular, stonewashed, acid-washed, etc.). It is in the best interest of forensic scientists to understand the fundamental manufacturing processes of the items that routinely become evidence. This understanding can form the basis for statistical significance statements in courts and may provide the foundations for a more quantitative approach to testimony.

Forensic analytical methods create augmented taxonomies because the discipline uses different sets of methods and forensic scientists have different goals. Their taxonomies are based on manufactured traits, but also aftermarket qualities, and intended end use, but also "as used." The "as used" traits are those imparted to the item after purchase through either normal or criminal use. Forensic science has developed a set of rules through which the taxonomies are explicated. For example, forensic scientists are interested in the size, shape, and distribution of delustrants, microscopic grains of rutile titanium dioxide incorporated into a fiber to reduce its luster. The manufacturer has included delustrant in the fiber at a certain rate and percentage with no concern for shape or distribution (but size may be relevant). The forensic science taxonomy is based on manufacturing taxonomy but is extended by incidental characteristics that help us distinguish otherwise similar objects.

Natural, manufacturing, and forensic classifications lead to evidentiary significance because they break the world down into intelligible classes of objects related to criminal acts. Forensic science has developed an enhanced appreciation for discernment between otherwise similar objects but has yet to explicate these hierarchies to their benefit.

Class Level Information

Identification is the examination of the chemical and physical properties of an object and using them to categorize it as a member of a set. What the object is made of, its color, mass, size, and many other characteristics are used to identify an object and help refine that object's identity. Analyzing a white powder and concluding that it is cocaine is an example of identification; determining that a small translucent chip is bottle glass or yellow fibrous material and determining that they are dog hairs are also examples of identification. Most identifications are inherently hierarchical, such as classification systems themselves: In the last example, the fibrous nature of the objects restricts the following possible categories:

- Hairs
- Animal hairs
- Guard hairs
- Dog hairs
- German shepherd hairs

As the process of identification of evidence becomes more specific, it permits the analyst to classify the evidence into successively smaller classes of objects. It may not be necessary to classify the evidence beyond dog hairs if human hairs are being looked for. Multiple items can be classified differently, depending on what questions are asked. For example, the objects in **Figure 1** could be classified into "fruit" and "nonfruit," "sports related" and "nonsports related," or "organic" and "inorganic."

Sharing a class identity may indicate two objects that come from a common source. Because forensic science reveals and describes the relationships among people, places, and things involved in criminal activities, this commonality of relationship may be critical to a successful investigation. Commonality can show interactions, limitations in points of origin, and increased significance of relationships. What is meant by a "common source" depends on the material in question, the mode of production, and the specificity of the examinations used to classify the object. For example, the "common source" for an automotive paint chip could be the following:

- the manufacturer (to distinguish it from other similar paints),
- the factory (to determine where it was made),
- the batch or lot of production (to distinguish it from other batches at the same factory),
- all the vehicles painted with that color paint, or
- the vehicle painted with that color paint involved in the crime in question?

All of these options, and they are not exhaustive, could be the goal in an investigation of determining whether two objects had a "common source."

Uniqueness and Individualization

If an object can be classified into a set with only one member (itself), it can be said to be unique. An individualized object is associated with one, and only one, source: It is unique. Uniqueness is based on two assumptions. The first assumption is that all things are unique in space and, thus, their properties are nonoverlapping. The assumption of uniqueness of space is considered axiomatic and, therefore, an inherently nonprovable proposition for numerous reasons. The population size of "all things that might be evidence" is simply too large to account. In addition, conclusive evidence is not readily available in typical forensic investigations. Because of this, as Schum notes, statistics are required:

> Such evidence, if it existed, would make necessary a particular hypothesis or possible conclusion being entertained. In lieu of such perfection, we often make use of masses of inconclusive evidence having additional properties: The evidence is incomplete on matters relevant to our conclusions, and it comes to us from sources (including our own observations) that are, for various reasons, not completely credible. Thus, inferences from such evidence can only be probabilistic in nature (Schum, 1994, p. 2).

Figure 1 A range of objects may be classified in a variety of ways, depending on the question being asked. For example, given the objects in this figure, the sets would differ if the question was, "What is edible?" rather than, "What is sporting equipment?"

A statistical analysis is therefore warranted when uncertainty, of either accounting or veracity, exists. If an absolutely certain answer to a problem could be reached, statistical methods would not be required. Most evidence exists at the class level, and although each item involved in a crime is considered unique, it still belongs to a larger class. In reality, the majority of forensic science works at a class level of resolution. Indeed, even DNA, the argued "gold standard" of forensic science, operates with classes and statistics.

It has been argued that the concept of uniqueness is necessary but not sufficient to support claims of individualization. If it is accepted that uniqueness is axiomatic, then

> What matters is whether we have analytical tools necessary to discern the characteristics that *distinguish* one object from all others or, in the forensic context, distinguish *traces* made by each object from traces made by every other object ... Every object is presumably unique at the scale of manufacture. The question is whether objects are distinguishable at the scale of detection. Since all objects in the universe are in some respects "the same" and in other respects "different" from all other objects in the universe, according to Wittgenstein, what really matters is not uniqueness but rather what rules we articulate by which we will make determinations of "sameness" and "difference" (Cole, 2009, pp. 242–243).

Although things may be numerically unique at the point of *production*, this does not help to distinguish between otherwise similar objects at the point of *detection* or *interpretation*. This is where forensic science adds value to the investigative and legal processes.

Relationships and Context

The relationships between the people, places, and things involved in crimes are central to deciding what items to examine and how to interpret the results. For example, if a sexual assault occurs and the perpetrator and victim are strangers, more evidence may be relevant than if they live together or are sexual partners. Strangers are not expected to have ever met previously and, therefore, would have not transferred evidence before the crime. People who live together would have some opportunities to transfer certain types of evidence (e.g., head hairs and carpet fibers from the living room) but not others (semen or vaginal secretions). Spouses or sexual partners, being the most intimate relationship of the three examples, would share a good deal of more information (**Figure 2**).

Stranger-on-stranger crimes beg the question of coincidental associations, that is, two things that previously have never been in contact with each other have items on them, which are analytically indistinguishable at a certain class level. Attorneys in cross-examination may ask, "Yes, but could not [insert evidence type here] really have come from anywhere? Are not [generic class level evidence] very common?" It has been proven for a wide variety of evidence that coincidental matches are extremely rare. The enormous variety of mass-produced goods, consumer choices, economic factors, biological and natural diversity, and other traits create a nearly infinite combination of comparable characteristics for the items involved in any one situation.

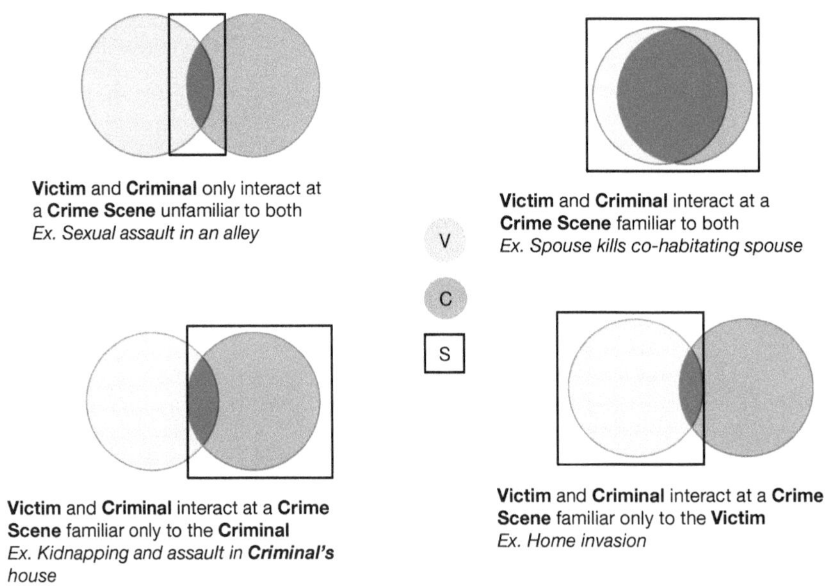

Figure 2 The relationships between suspect, victim, and scene influence what evidence is collected, and what its significance is.

See also: **Foundations:** Evidence/Classification; Statistical Interpretation of Evidence: Bayesian Analysis; The Frequentist Approach to Forensic Evidence Interpretation.

Further Reading

Cole, S., 2009. Forensics without uniqueness, conclusion without individualization: the new epistemology of forensic identification. Law, Probability, and Risk 8 (3), 233–255.

Devlin, K., 1993. The Joy of Sets. Springer, Berlin.

Haq, T., Roche, G., Parker, B., 1978. Theoretical field concepts in forensic science. 1. Application to recognition and retrieval of physical evidence. Journal of Forensic Sciences 23 (1), 212–217.

Houck, M.M., 2006. Production Taxonomies as the Foundation of Forensic Significance. European Academy of Forensic Sciences, Helsinki, Finland.

Johnson, P., 1972. A History of Set Theory. Weber & Schmidt, New York.

Kwan, Q.Y., 1977. Inference of Identity of Source (Ph.D. thesis). University of California.

Schum, D.A., 1994. Evidential Foundations of Probabilistic Reasoning. John Wiley & Sons, New York.

Thornton, J., 1986. Ensembles of class characteristics in physical evidence examination. Journal of Forensic Sciences 31 (2), 501–503.

Underhill, P., 2000. Why We Buy: The Science of Shopping. Simon & Schuster, New York.

Interpretation/The Comparative Method

MM Houck, Consolidated Forensic Laboratory, Washington, DC, USA

Glossary

Alignable differences Differences that are connected to the hierarchical system of relatedness of two or more things.
Analogous trait A characteristic that is similar between two things that is not present in the last common ancestor or precedent of the group under comparison.
Analogy A cognitive process that transfers information or meaning from one subject (the analog or source) to another subject (the target).
Diagnosticity The degree to which traits classify an object.
Homologous trait A characteristic shared by a common ancestor or precedent.
Nonalignable differences Differences with no correspondence at all between the source and the target.

Introduction

Analogy, and its more specific relative comparison, is a central component of human cognition. Analogy is the process behind identification of places, objects, and people and plays a significant role in many human mental operations, like problem solving, decisions, perception, memory, and communication. Some researchers, including Hofstadter, have even argued that cognition is analogy. Likewise, the cognitive process of analogy and the method of comparison lie at the heart of the forensic sciences. The ability to compare is predicated on some sort of classification (more properly, a taxonomy) that results in classes, groups, or sets.

Aristotle is considered the first to approach comparison as a way to arrange the world. His attempt to codify the process raised, however, an intractable problem that would only be addressed later: the classification of living things. Comparison, by itself, is a minimal technique, at best. A classification system—a taxonomy—is a prerequisite to a fuller comparative methodology. Comparative anatomy, one of the earliest formal applications of the method, goes beyond mere representation (mere comparison, that is) to explain the nature and properties of each animal.

The French naturalist Pierre Belon (1517–1564) compared the skeletal structures of birds to humans in his book *L'Histoire de la Nature des Oiseaux* (*History of the Nature of Birds*, 1555; **Figure 1**), and, along with the Flemish naturalist Andreas Vesalius (1514–1564), was one of the first naturalists to explicitly apply the comparative method in biology. Georges Cuvier (1769–1832) was the first to use comparative anatomy and taxonomy as a tool, not an end in itself, in his studies of animals and fossils. Cuvier was frustrated that biological phenomena could not be reconfigured into experimental conditions that would allow controlled testing, a difficulty common to many sciences (e.g., see Diamond). The intimate integration of a living organism's physiology with its anatomy created obstacles in teasing out and relating function to structure: Once an organism was dead and prepared for dissection, its function had ceased, thus confounding the relationship of form to function. Cuvier considered that careful examinations and the interrelating of structures between specimens might also prove to be useful in revealing principles of observation and comparison. Perhaps the original scientist-as-detective, Cuvier, used scattered, fractured bits of information to reconstruct the prehistory of the Earth and its animals. In a 1798 paper, Cuvier wrote on his realization of the form and function of bones as it relates to the overall identifiable anatomy of an animal, leading to the recognition of the creature from which the bone originated:

> This assertion will not seem at all astonishing if one recalls that in the living state all the bones are assembled in a kind of framework; that the place occupied by each is easy to recognize; and that by the number and position of their articulating facets one can judge the number and direction of the bones that were attached to them. This is because the number, direction, and shape of the bones that compose each part of an animal's body are always in a necessary relation to all the other parts, in such a way that – up to a point – one can infer the whole from any one of them, and vice versa. (Rudwick, 1997, p. 36)

This has been called "Cuvier's principle of correlation of parts" and is a central tenet in biology and paleontology. It is

 http://dx.doi.org/10.1016/B978-0-12-800573-6.00003-3

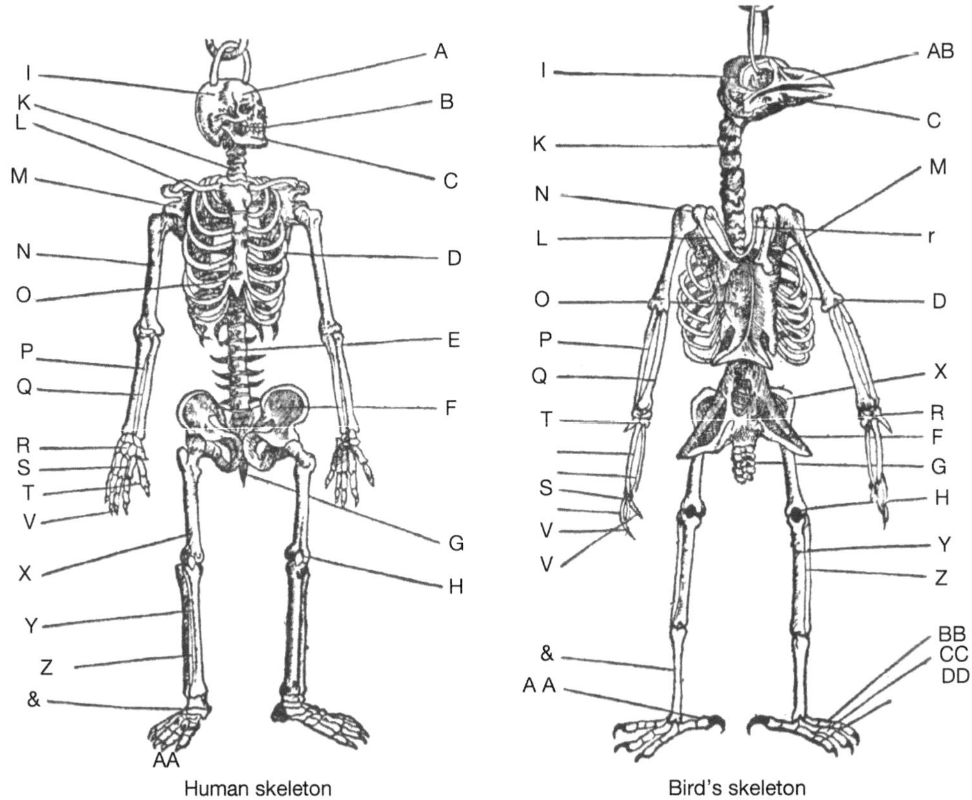

Figure 1 A drawing from Pierre Belon's 1555 book, *History of the Nature of Birds*, comparing the skeletal anatomy of birds to humans which is one of the first books using the science of comparative anatomy. Source: Wikimedia Commons, open source.

important to note that Cuvier claimed to be able to *identify* an animal taxonomically from a single bone, but not completely *reconstruct* it, as the above quote might imply. The reconstruction would only be possible with a sufficient number of bones representing the animal in question. The comparative method has been a successful cornerstone of science ever since, with new or emerging sciences, such as ecology, moving from the purely observational or descriptive approach to that of comparison through experimental or analytical methods.

A short discussion of terms in biology will help clarify concepts used in biological comparisons. The concept of homology, the same structure under every variety of form found in different animals, is the organizing foundation for comparative anatomy. Animals share homologous traits because they also share a common ancestor with the same or related trait. By contrast, analogous traits are similarities found in organisms that were not present in the last common ancestor of the group under comparison; that is, the traits evolved separately. The canonical example of the difference between homologous and analogous traits is the wings of birds and bats: They are homologous as forearms but analogous as wings; the latter structures evolved their functions separately. A homologous trait is termed a homolog. In biology, evolution and natural selection formed the system within which these relationships developed and were maintained, homogenized, or differentiated.

In manufacturing, other external and internal constraints form the basis for homologous and analogous traits through design, function, form, and costs. Design follows from the product's intended end use, aesthetic concerns, and cost limitations. The function and form of an object tend to correlate and variances in design cluster around necessary and sufficient criteria. In **Figure 2**, for example, although the hammer heads, opposite sides, handles, materials, weight, shape, and components all vary, they are nonetheless identifiable as hammers. If **Figure 2** were finches, as Darwin studied in the Galapagos in his historic voyage with the *Beagle*, the base process of taxonomy would be the same but the criteria and foundations—the history and causes—would obviously vary because of the vastly different processes that produce hammers and finches.

Broadly speaking, the supply chains and distribution networks of material goods are like the phylogenetic trees

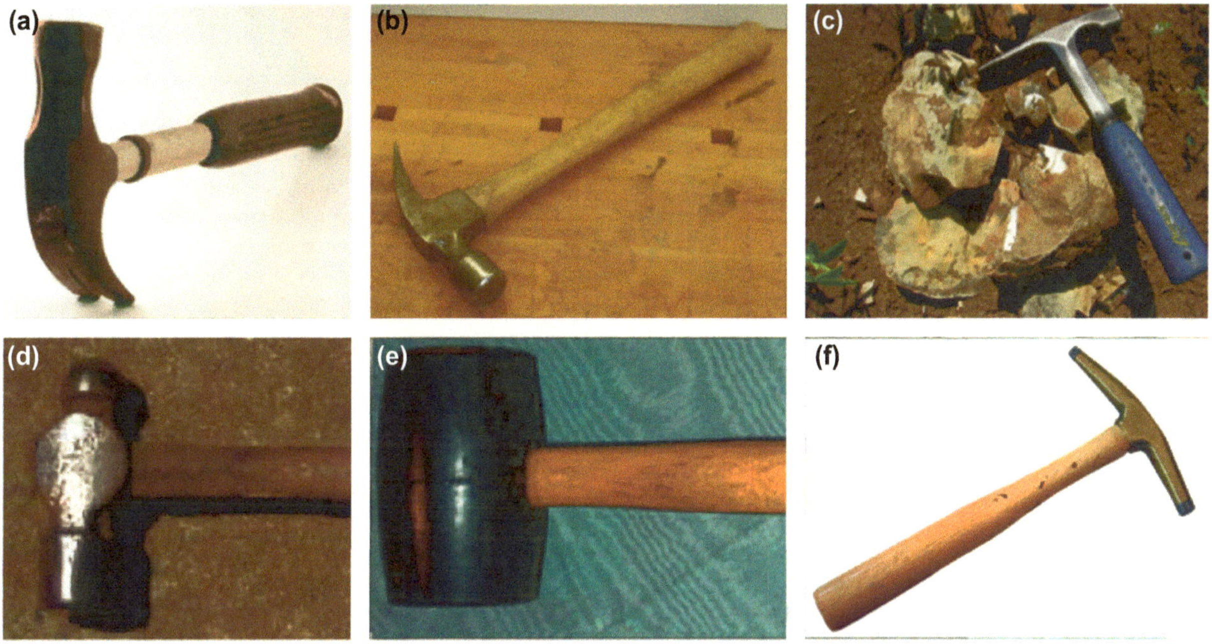

Figure 2 Hammers. All of the objects (a–f) are recognizable as hammers even though their components vary. (a) Claw hammer; (b) framing hammer; (c) geological hammer; (d) ball-peen hammer; (e) rubber mallet; and (f) upholstery hammer. Source: Wikimedia Commons, open source.

based on evolutionary descent. Regardless of whether the items are biological or manufactured, the independence of traits should not be assumed. Comparative studies that do not control for historical relationships through phylogeny or supply chains may imply spurious relationships (coincidences). Forensic science is unique in its use of the comparative method to reconstruct past criminal events and sourcing of evidence, either biological or manufactured (in essence, reverse engineering to a level of distribution or manufacturing resolution).

Analogy and Comparison within a Forensic Process

Analogy is a cognitive process that transfers information or meaning from one subject (the analog or *source*) to another subject (the *target*); it thus implies at least two things: situations or events. The source is considered to be the more complete and more complex of the two and the target is thus less informative and incomplete in some way. The incompleteness may be due to any of several factors, alone or combined, such as damage, fracture, deterioration, or size. The elements or traits—including their relationships, such as evolutionary or supply chains—between the source and the target are mapped or aligned in a comparison. The mapping is done from what is usually the more familiar area of experience and more complete repository of information, the source, to the typically more problematic target.

Salience of the elements or traits is of prime importance: there are an innumerable number of arbitrary differences in either elements or relations that could be considered but are not useful given the question at hand ("Are both items smaller than the Empire State Building? Are they redder than a fire truck?"). Ultimately, analogy is a process to communicate that the two comparators (the source and the target) have *some* relationship in common despite any arbitrary differences. Some notion of possible or hypothetical connection must exist for the comparison to be made. As a forensic example, consider trace debris removed from the clothing of a suspect and the body of a victim: Although there may be no physical evidence (hairs, fibers, glass, soil, etc.) in common, the suspect's clothing and the victim's body have, at least prima facie, a common *relationship* (the victim is the victim and the suspect is a person of interest in the crime) until proven otherwise. Thus, common relations, not common objects, are essential to analogy and comparison.

The comparison process as a method makes several assumptions. First, the space in which the comparators are mapped is assumed to be Euclidean. Second, the method embeds the comparators in a "space of minimum dimensionality" (Tversky) based on all observed salient similarities. Each object, a, is detailed and described by a set of elements or traits, A. Any observed similarities between a and another object b, denoted as $s(a, b)$, are expressed as a function of the salient traits they are determined to have in common. The comparison

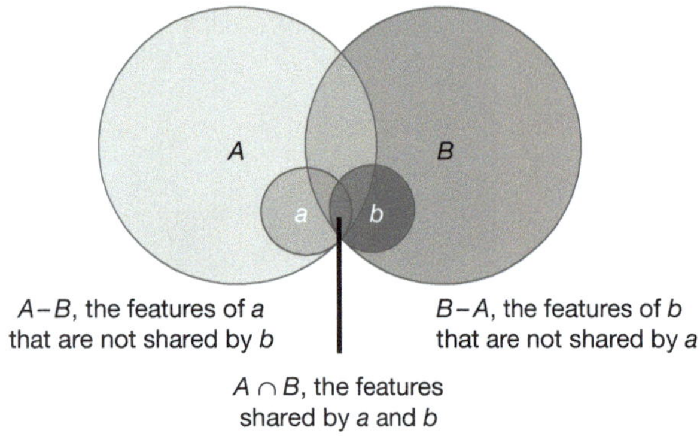

Figure 3 A comparison of observed familiarities can be expressed as a function of three arguments; visualized here.

and any observed familiarity can be expressed as a function of three arguments (**Figure 3**):

- *A* ∩ *B*, the features shared by *a* and *b*
- *A–B*, the features of *a* that are not shared by *b*
- *B–A*, the features of *b* that are not shared by *a*

Psychological studies show that people tend to pay more attention to the target (the comparator with less information) than to the source. In forensic science, this means that analysts would pay more attention to the samples from the crime scene or actors than to the known samples collected. This is true even though the known has more salience, because arguably it has more information and a documented provenance than the questioned sample. For example, a toy ship is quite similar to a real ship because most of the main features of the real ship are expressed in the toy (otherwise it might not be recognized as a simulacrum of its referent). A real ship, however, is not as similar to the toy ship because many of the features of a real ship are not expressed in the toy (due to function, scale, or safety, among other factors). The reason for paying more attention to the target is, first and foremost, to determine if there is sufficiency of salient information in the target for the comparative process to occur (see Vanderkolk for a discussion on this).

The main determinant of feature salience for comparative purposes is the degree to which they classify an object, that is, their diagnosticity. A feature that serves as the basis to reassign an object from one class to another class with fewer members is more salient than one that does not. Salience is hierarchical and is based on how many members of a class share that feature; the goal is thus to place an object, by successive comparative features, into classes with increasingly fewer members. Salience of a feature, therefore, should increase inversely with the number of members of a class into which it places an object; *A* ∩ *B* increases and may be thought of as an expression of diagnosticity. A comparative process that does not maximize diagnosticity or exploit features that do so will have low forensic utility.

The Comparative Method within Forensic Science

The comparative method involves the aligning of the relational structures between one or more targets (items of questioned source; Qs) and one or more sources (items of known provenance or source; Ks). This alignment, to work as a method, has three constraints or requirements:

- The alignment has to be *structurally consistent*; that is, it has to observe a one-to-one correspondence between the comparators in an argumentative structure that is the same between the comparisons (*parallel connectivity*). One point of comparison can be aligned with at most one other point of comparison in the target or source. Similarly, matching relationships must have matching arguments to support them (the reason for the proposed relationship cannot be based on an unrelated argument).
- The comparison has to involve *common relations* but does not have to involve common object descriptions. All the evidence that came from the crime scene, for example, need not have originated from only one source.
- Finally, comparisons are not made merely between the objects at hand but also include all of the higher order "constraining relations" that they may share (*systematicity*). In biology, this would relate to the evolutionary and genetic connections; for manufactured materials, this would be the design factors and the supply chain of raw materials and intermediate processes that lead to a finished consumer good. The deeper the relational history, the more higher order classes that two objects share, the stronger the relationship they share, and, therefore, the greater is the chance of a shared origin. This obviates the significance of coincidental matches between otherwise similar but unrelated objects: A series of coincidences between two objects are not a salient relationship, no matter how many of them exist. Type I and type II errors stem from these coincidences.

A comparison results in a type of cross-mapping of analogous traits or phenomena that have differential relational roles in two situations (e.g., victim's clothing and crime scene). A systematic mapping between source and target is a natural method for differentiating potentially ambiguous relationships. This relates to the classification of the target and source, the identification of traits or features each has that place them in one or more sets (classes) of items. The cross-mapping is of these traits within a class. Once a source has been aligned to a target, *candidate inferences*, based on the source, can be projected onto the target, such as a shared source or history. A handgun with blood on it, for example, can be compared to a bullet removed from a victim (through test firings of similar ammunition) and determined to have been the source (to some degree of certainty) of the bullet while the blood can be tested through DNA typing with the victim's known sample and be shown to have the victim as its source (again, to some degree of certainty); the fact that the victim's blood is on the handgun indicates a shared history of occurrence (lateral contemporaneity).

Comparison is selective. The requirement of systematicity is predicated on the idea that classes or sets are flexible and hierarchical. Higher-order connections predict lower-order relations, and commonalities that are not a part of the aligned system of relationships are considered inconsequential: A blue shoe and a blue car have little in common other than the stated color category; likewise, the fact that the source shoe and the target print might have the same kind of outsole design recedes in importance to the fact that none of the individual traits on the sole appears in the print. Differences that are connected to the hierarchical system of relatedness are called *alignable differences*; those differences with no correspondence at all between the source and the target are called *nonalignable differences*. Alignable differences are more meaningful and salient than nonalignable ones because they exist within the same relationship system making them more relevant to each other. The strange conclusion this observation leads to is that there should be more meaningful differences for comparators that are very similar (*toy train–real train*) than for ones that are less similar (*toy train–toy ship*) because the more similar comparators will have or be derived within more common systems of relationships and will have more alignable differences. As an example, consider all the possible differences for the pair *automobile–truck* and for the pair *duck–baseball*. More alignable differences could be found for the first pair than the second: After a few differences ("You don't play sports with a duck. You don't hunt baseballs."), the list seems pointless because the two are not aligned. The details that could be elicited by comparing *automobile* with *truck*, however, could go on for some time, depending on the level of detail desired. Most sets of comparators in the world are dissimilar (which is why forensic comparisons tend to be stronger in exclusion than inclusion) and this "nonconsideration" heuristic makes sense given humans' cognitive load: "Intuitively, it is when a pair of items is similar that their differences are likely to be important" (Genter and Markman). Psychological experiments support this statement and it seems to be an integral part of human cognition. Related to this idea is Wittgenstein's proposal 5.5303 in his work *Tractatus Logico-Philosophicus*: "Roughly speaking, to say of two things that they are identical is nonsense, and to say of one thing that it is identical with itself is to say nothing at all." This points to the need for a statistical evaluation of the *strength* of a comparison, either inclusive or exclusive.

See also: **Foundations:** Forensic Intelligence; Overview and Meaning of Identification/Individualization; Semiotics, Heuristics, and Inferences Used by Forensic Scientists.

Further Reading

Diamond, J., Robinson, J.A. (Eds.), 2010. Natural Experiments of History. Cambridge University Press, Cambridge, MA.
Gentner, D., Markman, A.B., 1997. Structure mapping in analogy and similarity. American Psychologist 52 (1), 45–56.
Hofstadter, D., 2001. Analogy as the core of cognition. In: Gentner, D., Holyoak, K., Kokinov, B. (Eds.), The Analogical Mind: Perspectives from Cognitive Science. MIT Press/Bradford Book, Cambridge, MA, pp. 499–538.
Markman, A.B., Genter, D., 2000. Structure mapping in the comparison process. American Journal of Psychology 113 (4), 501–538.
Pellegrin, P., 1986. Aristotle's Classification of Living Things. University of California Press, Berkeley, CA.
Rudwick, M., 1997. Georges Cuvier, Fossil Bones, and Geological Catastrophes. University of Chicago Press, Chicago.
Tversky, A., 1977. Features of similarity. Psychological Review 84, 327–352.
Vanderkolk, J., 2009. Forensic Comparative Science. Academic Press, New York.
Wittgenstein, L., 1922. Tractatus Logico-Philosophicus. Routledge, London. Translated by Ogden, C.K., 1922, prepared with assistance from Moore, G.E., Ramsey, F.P., and Wittgenstein.

Fingerprints

I Hamilton, Glasgow Fingerprint Unit, Forensic Services, Scottish Police Services Authority, Glasgow, UK

Introduction

Fingerprint identification is one of the oldest forensic tools used by police forces to investigate crime. The concept of identifying individuals using their fingerprints began in Asia, and the spread of the British Empire allowed observation and development of the process by civil servants in India who then publicized the practice in the United Kingdom. Initially, fingerprints were used to sign documents, but their use was expanded and developed before being adopted by the police in England at the turn of the twentieth century both as a means to identify repeat offenders and also to link individuals to crimes. It became accepted as one of the best forms of evidence available, a definitive way to identify an individual or to connect them to a crime scene. When DNA evidence was first introduced, it was called "DNA fingerprinting" in an attempt to link it to the perceived strength of fingerprint identification. The field has enjoyed almost a century of high regard, but, in recent times, a small number of highly publicized errors coupled with developments in other forensic sciences have meant that it is no longer universally viewed as the "gold standard" of evidence.

What Is a Fingerprint?

A fingerprint is an impression left behind by the skin found on the inner surface of the fingers. The skin on this area is called friction ridge skin and is found on the palms of the hands, as well as on the toes and soles of the feet. Its main evolutionary use is for gripping, which is why it is only found in these areas; the same type of skin is found on the hands and feet of primates. Friction ridge skin comprises many tiny ridges and furrows, covering the surface. The ridges do not flow continuously but bend and curve, stop and start, come together and split apart, creating patterns and unique arrangements of features. The ridges form before birth, as the fetus develops in the womb, and barring a deep-seated injury which penetrates through the epidermal layer of skin, their arrangement will remain unchanged until after death. Their configuration is a combination of many factors including the stresses and strains on the skin in the womb as it develops, hormones, and genetics.

Each ridge contains many sweat pores, which run along the crest of the ridge. These are always exuding sweat, and when a receptive surface is touched this sweat is left behind, leaving an impression of the ridge pattern. An impression in sweat will be left on every surface touched, but the impression is only of use if the surface is smooth and receptive. Flat plastic and glass are excellent surfaces to recover fingerprints from; rough surfaces like wood are more difficult. Recovering a print from a rough, textured, powdery surface like stone is unachievable. A mark left in sweat can be almost invisible, hence the name latent print, derived from the Latin "latere" meaning hidden. Fingerprints can also be left after touching contaminants such as paint, oil, or blood and in malleable substances such as putty.

Fingerprint examiners study the features of friction ridge skin, which can be divided into three areas or levels: level 1 is the pattern type and ridge flow, level 2 is the ridge characteristics, and level 3 is pores and ridge edge shapes. Each of these levels represents a more minute level of detail; the following sections will describe each of these in more detail.

Pattern Type and Ridge Flow

The topographical surface of the hand will determine the general pattern formed by the ridges. As they develop, they take the path of least resistance, and so will flow over flat areas, and around raised areas. The three main pattern types are known as arches, loops, and whorls, shown in **Figure 1**, but there are many variations and combinations within these pattern types.

Looking at the patterns, it is possible to imagine the arch pattern being formed by ridges flowing over a flat area of skin; the whorl pattern resulting from ridges flowing around a raised area of skin; and a loop pattern being the result of a raised area on the right or left side which the ridge flow curves away from.

Ridge Characteristics

The ridges themselves do not flow in unbroken lines across the skin. They can come to a stop, making a feature called a ridge ending, or they can split apart, making a feature called a bifurcation. These features are known as ridge characteristics. These two basic characteristics can combine to form others, as shown in **Figure 2**.

It is the appearance and relative position of ridge characteristics that comprise the main area of comparison for fingerprint examiners.

 http://dx.doi.org/10.1016/B978-0-12-800573-6.00004-5

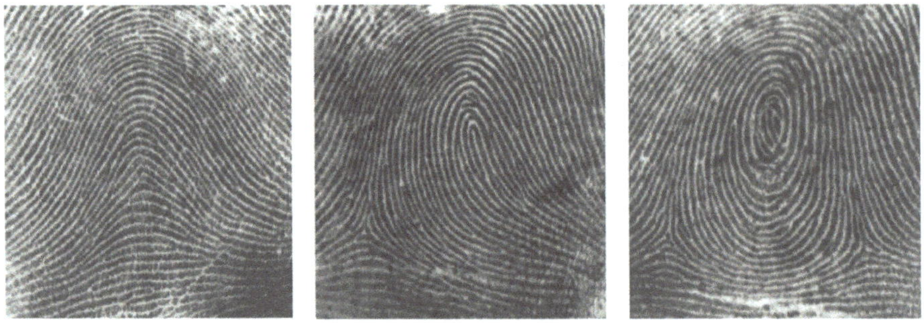

Figure 1 Three main pattern types.

Pores and Ridge Edge Shapes

On many prints, the ridges may appear to the naked eye to be solid lines, but on magnification, the pores which run along the crest of each ridge may be visible. They will appear as white dots inside the black of the ridge. The pores themselves are not evenly spaced or of uniform size, and so their size and location can also be used as a comparison feature.

The ridges are undulating and bumpy in places. On a fingerprint of good quality, the shape of the ridge edges can also be used as part of the comparison process. **Figure 3** shows a magnified section of a fingerprint, showing the pores and ridge edge shapes.

The appearance of pores and ridge edge shapes is affected by several factors: the quality of the print, pressure used, the smoothness of the surface the print has been left on, and the type of ridges an individual has. Some individuals will have thick ridges, making pores and edge shapes more apparent, while others will have fine ridges making these features less apparent.

Other Discriminating Features

All of the features described above are biological features which develop before birth and are permanent. There are other features of the skin on the hands and feet which can be used for identification purposes. The friction ridge skin on the hands and feet is marked by creases, some permanent, where the joints bend; for example, and others which may change and develop over time, depending on how the skin is used, and as the skin ages.

If the skin is damaged badly enough to penetrate through to the dermal layer of the skin and affect the layer which holds the "blueprint" for the ridge pattern, the layout of the ridges will be affected. This will result in the formation of a scar. Although this will alter the fingerprint, the scar becomes an identifying feature itself as once the scar pattern is set, it will become part of the regenerating pattern of the ridges. **Figure 4** shows a fingerprint with a large permanent scar.

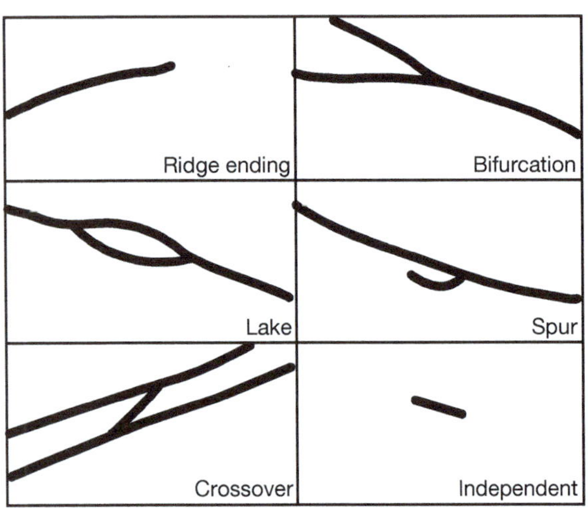

Figure 2 Ridge features.

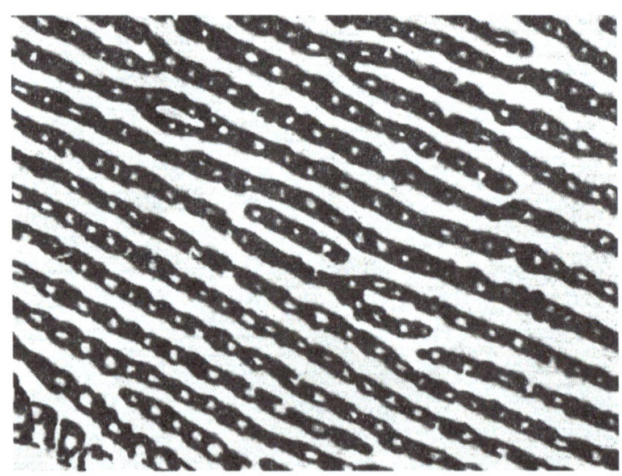

Figure 3 Enlargement of fingerprint showing pores and ridge edge shapes. Reproduced from Duncan, J.H., 1942. An Introduction to Fingerprints. Butterworth and Co., London.

Figure 4 Fingerprint showing permanent scar.

Marks and Prints

In fingerprint identification, two terms are often used to distinguish between the two different types of fingerprint which are analyzed. Fingerprint identification consists of a comparison between an unknown fingerprint recovered at a crime scene and a known fingerprint from a fingerprint form. The fingerprint from a crime scene is commonly known as a "mark" and can vary greatly in quality. It may be a very high-quality reproduction of the skin's surface, showing a high level of detail including ridge flow, pattern, ridge characteristics, and even pore and ridge edge shape detail, or it may be of very poor quality, with details obscured by dirt, the texture of the surface, movement, pressure, smudging, or overlapping fingerprints.

In contrast, the fingerprint from a fingerprint form, known as a "print," is almost always of good quality in comparison to the unknown mark. These fingerprints are taken in controlled circumstances, usually by a police officer. These prints can be taken by two different means: by coating the finger in ink and rolling it smoothly across paper, or using an electronic device known in the United Kingdom as Live Scan, which uses a computer scanning device to scan the surface of the skin and then prints this onto paper. Although these are usually of very good quality, this is not guaranteed; prints can still be of poor quality due to dirt or sweat on the hands, too much pressure, or if the finger is moved while being printed.

Recovery of Fingerprints from Scenes

Crime scene examiners will examine every scene to attempt to recover fingerprints. Some marks may be visible to the naked eye; others may need some form of development.

Generally, marks left in sweat are invisible and will need to be developed in order to be recovered. The most common method used is dusting powder. The crime scene examiner will lightly brush a fine powder over an object or surface area, and the powder will adhere to any fingerprints left there. Any marks are then recovered by a process known as "lifting"; a piece of adhesive tape is smoothed over the mark and then carefully peeled away and adhered to a clear acetate sheet. The powder is transferred to the tape, and the mark is then visible on the acetate.

This method is generally used for smooth, clean surfaces. There are a range of powders available, the most commonly used being aluminum and magnetic metal flake powders; granular powders are also available in a variety of colors. The type of powder and the color used are dependent on the surface being examined; granular powders are often photographed rather than lifted, and colors can help contrast with the color of the underlying surface.

Chemical Development

Articles are often removed from a crime scene to be treated at a lab. There are a wide range of treatments available to develop fingerprints on different surfaces; many of these require chemical processes not possible at the crime scene. Liquid chemical treatments such as ninhydrin and 1,8-diazafluoren-9-one are used to develop prints on porous surfaces such as paper and are probably the most common chemical treatments. Cyanoacrylate (superglue) vapor can develop prints on smooth nonporous surfaces, and vacuum-metal deposition employs vacuum-coating technology, which uses thermal evaporation of gold and zinc to coat surfaces such as plastic bags and reveal fingerprints on the surface. Different chemical treatments will react with different constituent components of sweat, and some can be used in sequence to get the best possible results.

Fingerprint Practice

Fingerprint Comparison Methodology

Once fingerprints have been recovered, either by the crime scene examiner or at the lab, they will be sent to the fingerprint department to be worked on. A fingerprint examiner will use a methodology known as analysis, comparison, evaluation, and verification (ACE-V) to conduct their analysis of a fingerprint. In most cases, when fingerprints arrive at a fingerprint department, they will be accompanied by a list of individuals to be compared against the crime scene prints. These individuals may be quoted as suspects: people suspected of committing the crime, or as eliminations: people with legitimate access to the scene or property and whose prints might therefore be expected to be found. ACE-V describes the various stages of the comparison process.

During the first stage, analysis, the unknown mark is studied. Details such as the surface the mark has been left on,

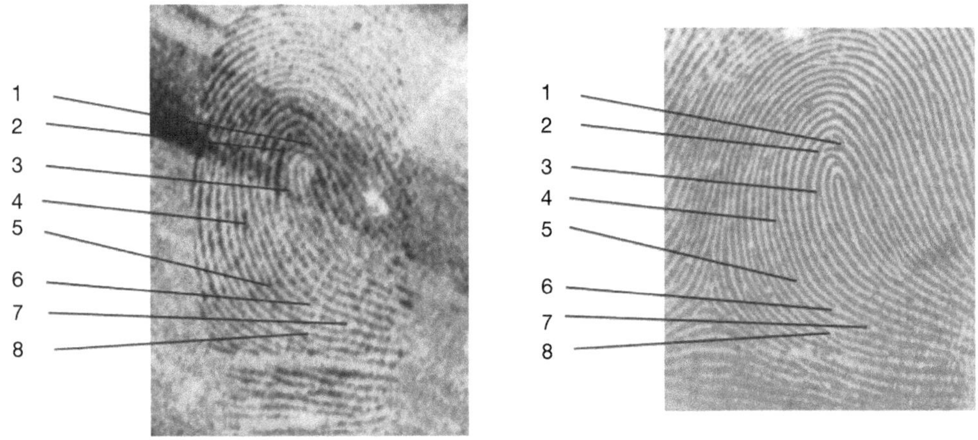

Figure 5 Mark and print showing eight corresponding ridge features.

the substance it has been left in, and the development medium used will be noted where possible. The mark itself will be analyzed to determine the quantity and quality of information contained within it, such as pattern type, ridge flow, presence of scars, creases, ridge features, and pores. Using all of this information, the examiner will use his/her judgment to best determine which area of skin, finger, or palm left the mark.

If there is too low a level of information contained within the mark, the examiner will deem it insufficient; there is not enough information present to make an identification.

The second stage is comparison; the unknown mark is compared against a known print. The examiner is looking for features in sequence and agreement, with none in disagreement, unless there is an explanation for such disagreement.

Once the mark and print have been compared, the next stage is evaluation. All of the information found is weighed up in the examiner's mind, and a conclusion is reached. Current practice, based on professional culture, allows for three different conclusions:

1. Identified: the mark was left by that individual.
2. Not identified: the mark was not left by that individual.
3. Insufficient: there is not enough information to reach one of the above conclusions.

Some jurisdictions allow for a fourth finding: inconclusive. This is used in situations where features are found in agreement, but there is not enough information to identify.

The final stage of the process is verification. Practices vary in different jurisdictions, but all identifications are verified by at least one other fingerprint examiner, working independently, before the result is passed out to the police. The verifier will carry out his/her own analysis, comparison, and evaluation of the mark and determine whether the mark is identified. An identification is only passed out as a result by the fingerprint department if it is agreed by all examiners who have examined it.

Figure 5 demonstrates the comparison process. The points highlighted can be seen on the mark and found in the same location on the print. For example, points 1 and 2 form a lake and are seen on the mark and the print. Looking at the mark, we can follow the ridge down and move one ridge to the right and find point 3, a bifurcation. Counting five ridges to the left from point 3, we find another bifurcation, point 4. Again, these points are found on the print. It is possible to work through all the points in this manner, finding them all in both mark and print, in the same relationship to each other.

Numeric Standards

Until recently, it was common for jurisdictions to work to a numeric standard in order to determine whether a mark was identified. In the United Kingdom, this standard was 16 points in common and in the United States of America, it was 12 points, although the Federal Bureau of Investigation (FBI) worked with a standard of 8 points.

In 1973, the International Association for Identification (IAI) declared that "no valid basis exists at this time for requiring that a predetermined minimum number of friction ridge characteristics must be present in two impressions in order to establish positive identification." The decision to require a minimum number of points in agreement for an identification arose as a way of ensuring commonality within a country between regions and police forces. The numbers decided upon were not the result of scientific research but rather on a need for safety and perceived objectivity.

The IAI announcement in 1973 prompted a move away from numeric standards, and many countries have now adopted a nonnumeric system. This development did create a problem; up until this point, an identification was easily explained by confirming that the required number of points had been found. Now something else was needed to replace it.

A new explanation of fingerprint identification was developed by David Ashbaugh, a Canadian fingerprint examiner, and given the name "ridgeology." Ashbaugh concentrated on the way the skin is formed, and its uniqueness, to explain that scientifically there could never be an arbitrary quantity of points required; instead, it depended on the mark itself and the quality, quantity, and clarity of available information. He coined the term ACE-V as a way to describe the identification procedure, taking into account all available information and the unique formation of the skin to reach a conclusion.

Although many countries have been using a nonnumeric system for many years (e.g., the United Kingdom, the United States, Canada, Australia, and Norway), there are still countries that prefer to work to a numeric standard. Some examples of these would be Holland, Greece, Finland, and Spain, which use a 12 point standard, as well as Germany and Sweden, which use an 8–12 point standard.

Computer Technology

If after the comparison process has been carried out the mark has not been identified, or if there are no individuals quoted to be compared, marks can be searched against a computer database. In the United Kingdom, this database is called Ident 1, and in the United States, it is the Automated Fingerprint Identification System. In 2011, the UK fingerprint database contained prints for 8.45 million individuals. When a set of fingerprints is taken for an individual, it is loaded onto the fingerprint database. Fingerprint examiners can then scan a mark from a crime scene, encode it with visible features, and search it against the database. These searches can be local, regional, or national searches and provide an excellent investigative tool, frequently providing "cold" hits against unsuspected individuals. A computer search is, however, by no means perfect; it does not provide unverified matches and all results must be checked by a fingerprint examiner to be confirmed.

The latest development in computer technology is direct transfer of marks from recovery at the locus to the fingerprint department. At present, marks from a crime scene are generally printed and sent in a hard copy or lift form to the fingerprint department, and this can result in a long processing time. Some areas of the United Kingdom are now beginning to use a form of electronic transfer, where fingerprints recovered from a scene can be photographed or scanned by a computer and sent directly to the fingerprint department, meaning that a delivery which might have taken days can now be conducted in seconds.

The Role of the Tenprint

Much of the public awareness about the uses of fingerprints relates to the recovery of fingerprints at crime scenes and their comparison to prints from a suspect. Within criminal justice, fingerprints play another important role. On arrest, an individual's fingerprints are taken and immediately searched on a computer against all held fingerprint forms. By this method, it can be established whether the individual already has a criminal record and can also confirm identity if a record is held. This ensures databases such as the Scottish Criminal History System and the Police National Computer in the United Kingdom remain accurate.

Current Issues in the Field

Recent developments in fingerprint practice and forensic science as a whole have opened up fingerprint identification to new discussion, debate, and criticism in the past decade. The profession developed in the Victorian era, when the public were very open and accepting of new scientific advancements, and little has changed in the way the profession conducts its work since those early days. Critics have argued that there are weaknesses in the foundation of fingerprint identification as well as concerns regarding the methods used to reach conclusions. Many of these issues have arisen due to a greater awareness of scientific practice within the legal system.

Daubert hearings in courts in the United States, regarding admissibility of evidence, have resulted in a desire within the fingerprint profession for scientific credibility, and this appears to have grown in strength since the removal of a numeric standard. Without a seemingly objective numeric standard, the concept of "science" has been used to convey the authority and objectivity of fingerprint practice. This has led to heated debate: critics have been quick to argue that it is not a science, and, as a result, the implication has been made that if it is not science, then it is useless. The fingerprint professionals have denied this and say that it is a science, and therefore valuable. These arguments revolve around a misconception: value and utility are not restricted to science.

Uniqueness

The uniqueness of friction ridge skin is seen as one of the key premises of fingerprint practice. However, an identification is made on an examination of a mark left behind, which can be of widely varying quality, rather than the skin on the finger itself. The biological uniqueness applies to the finger, not the print left behind, and by asserting that a print is as unique as the skin which made it, the profession has ignored investigation into how similar two prints from different people can be. Most examiners will have seen areas of similarity between fingerprints from different people, but this has not been empirically studied. Although biological uniqueness is important, it is the ability to perceive this information which is crucial.

Infallibility and Certainty

Fingerprinting is synonymous with absolute certainty and absolute identification. This type of reporting arose in the early days of fingerprint identification, and early texts show that fingerprint examiners were not seen to be giving an opinion, but reporting a fact. It is unusual that, although fingerprint identification is viewed as expert opinion evidence, the notion of conclusions as fact has not shifted. This view can still be found in recent publications, stating that the conclusions of fingerprint experts are absolute and final. Irrespective of whether or not this is "scientific," it is irrational to make claims of absolute certainty and therefore eliminate all other possible donors in the world. No matter how much experience an examiner may have, they will only have viewed a tiny percentage of the fingerprints in the world, and of those which they have examined, they will not be able to retain in memory all of the other prints they may have examined.

The McKie case in Scotland, the subject of the Scottish Fingerprint Inquiry, is an example of the inherent problems of attempting to be certain about a conclusion which can only be an inference. This case was the first time disagreements between experts was brought to the attention of the general public and demonstrated that not all fingerprint examiners agree all of the time. The report, published in December 2011, concluded that fingerprint examiners cannot report their findings with 100% certainty and that it should be recognized as opinion evidence rather than fact. This will have far-reaching effects on the profession.

Probabilistic Evaluation

One possible solution for fingerprint practice would be to adopt a probabilistic model for reporting their findings, rather than a categoric one. Although statistics were discussed by some of the founding fathers of fingerprints, it has until recently been rejected outright by the fingerprint profession. There are three common reasons given for the rejection of a probabilistic approach: the first is that friction ridge skin is unique. Suggesting the possibility of commonality between different prints would suggest the possibility of duplication, which is not deemed possible. The second is that there is currently no model which could be used to calculate a probability. This, however, is changing; at the present time, there are models under development and these will only continue to be refined and become more accurate. The final reason given is that a probabilistic approach would weaken fingerprint evidence. The fingerprint profession views the certainty of its conclusions as its main strength, but as questions accumulate about the logic of such conclusions, this is no longer the case.

Currently, it is difficult to determine the reliability of the conclusions of a fingerprint examiner as they are based purely on observations made by the examiner, using their personal experience, training, and ability. A probabilistic model may be a way to add a more objective verification of an examiner's opinion.

Error Rate

It has been stated that the error rate of fingerprint examination is zero. As errors within the field have been discovered, this has been altered to claim that the methodological error rate is zero; that is, any error is not with the methodology, but with the examiner. These arguments were made most widely by fingerprint examiners in the United States, attempting to defend fingerprint identification against criticism in Daubert hearings, when they were asked about the error rate of their field. More recently, it has become widely accepted that such statements are not valid; the examiner is a key component of the process of fingerprint identification and it is illogical to discount their input.

Bias

Confirmation bias can be defined as "the tendency to confirm an initial theory or preconception and avoid disconfirming information" and is an unconscious aspect of how our minds function.

The concept of confirmation bias in the comparison process of fingerprint identification can take various forms:

- Being unconsciously affected by extraneous information, such as police case information
- Being affected by the known conclusions of others about the mark in question
- Rationalizing (explaining away) discrepancies because of a subjective confidence in the identification
- Being led by the known print to find features in the unknown, and poorer quality, mark
- Being more likely to observe features in agreement and not notice areas of disagreement

Fingerprint examiners are trained to look for discrepancies as well as similarities, but the human brain is programmed to weight positive instances more heavily than negative ones, so it can be quite possible to dismiss negative factors. A small amount of research has been done in this area; some studies have suggested that bias has a strong effect on fingerprint conclusions, while others have suggested the opposite.

Conclusion

From the issues mentioned above, it is clear that fingerprint practice is at the beginning of a new era, with many issues to be resolved over the coming years. Currently, the main collection of knowledge used by fingerprint examiners is accumulated through their own experience, and "common sense" explanations, passed down from one examiner to another. The future of fingerprint identification will likely see this knowledge supplemented by empirical research. Fingerprint analysis must be seen to be logical and its processes transparent, its findings able to be demonstrated. It provides a highly valuable tool to police forces, giving fast and economical results. The current debates do not discredit fingerprint evidence, but they highlight areas for improvement to ensure the field maintains its position as a significant part of forensic science.

See also: **Foundations:** History of Forensic Sciences; Overview and Meaning of Identification/Individualization; Principles of Forensic Science; **Management/Quality in Forensic Science:** *Sequential Unmasking*: Minimizing Observer Effects in Forensic Science; **Pattern Evidence:** Analysis, Comparison, Evaluation, and Verification (ACE-V); Bare Footprint Marks; Palm Prints; **Pattern Evidence/Fingerprints (Dactyloscopy):** Automated Fingerprint Identification Systems (AFIS); Friction Ridge Skin Impression Evidence – Standards of Proof; Identification and Classification; **Pattern Evidence/History:** Fingerprint Sciences; **Professional:** National Academy of Sciences (NAS).

Further Reading

Ashbaugh, D.R., 1999. Quantitative-Qualitative Friction Ridge Analysis: An Introduction to Basic and Advanced Ridgeology. CRC Press, Boca Raton, FL.

Campbell, A., 2011. The Fingerprint Inquiry Report. APS Group Scotland, Edinburgh, Scotland.

Champod, C., Lennard, C.J., Margot, P., Stoilovic, M., 2004. Fingerprints and Other Ridge Skin Impressions. CRC Press, Boca Raton, FL.

Cole, S.A., 2001. Suspect Identities: A History of Fingerprinting and Criminal Identification. Harvard University Press, Cambridge, MA.

Dror, I.E., Charlton, D., 2006. Why experts make errors. Journal of Forensic Identification 56 (4), 600–616.

Mnookin, J.L., 2008. The validity of latent fingerprint identification: confessions of a fingerprinting moderate. Law, Probability and Risk 7, 127–141.

National Research Council, 2009. Strengthening Forensic Science in the United States: A Path Forward. The National Academies Press, Washington, DC.

Neumann, C., Champod, C., Puch-Solis, R., Egli, N., Anthonioz, A., Bromage-Griffiths, A., 2007. Computation of likelihood ratios in fingerprint identification for configurations of any number of minutiae. Journal of Forensic Science 52 (1), 54–64.

Peterson, P.E., et al., 2009. Latent prints: a perspective on the state of the science. Forensic Science Communications 11 (4). Available from: http://www.fbi.gov/hq/lab/fsc/backissu/oct2009/review/2009_10_review01.htm (accessed 16.06.10.).

Saks, M.J., Koehler, J.J., 2008. The individualization fallacy in forensic science evidence. Vanderbilt Law Review 61 (1), 199–219.

Scientific Working Group on Friction Ridge Analysis, Study and Technology, 2011. The Fingerprint Sourcebook. US Department of Justice Office of Justice Programs, Washington, DC.

Zabell, S.L., 2005. Fingerprint evidence. Journal of Law and Policy 13, 143–179.

Key Terms

Analogy, Bifurcation, Classification, Comparison, Crime, Epistemology, Evidence, Fingerprints, Forensic, Friction ridge skin, Kirk, Latent print, Locard, Marks, Method, Paradigm, Pores, Science, Set, Taxon, Taxonomy.

Review Questions

1. How do Crispino and Houck define forensic science?
2. What is the basic unit of forensic science? How is it defined?
3. What are the native principles of forensic science?
4. What are the nonnative principles—that is, borrowed—of forensic science?
5. What are the two types of chronology? How could they be used in forensic science?
6. How could fingerprints be considered "transfer evidence"?
7. If, as Houck states, "two sets are identical if and only if they have exactly the same members," what does this mean for fingerprint identification? Name three sets that would have exactly the same members.
8. What are some of the criteria for the taxonomy of fingerprints? Name at least 10.
9. What is the basis for the classification criteria used in fingerprints; that is, what processes form the taxonomy?
10. What is the difference between uniqueness and individualization? Is that difference meaningful in forensic science? Is either a scientifically provable concept?
11. Why has fingerprinting found itself at the center of discussion and debate as of late?
12. Is ACE-V a true scientific method, like chromatography? Why or why not?
13. What problem did moving to a nonnumeric system create?
14. How does Cuvier's Correlation of Parts apply to fingerprint examination?
15. What is the role of classification in creating a "space of minimum dimensionality"? How does this support or assist comparisons?

16. Using a partial latent as an example, why would an examiner want to pay more attention to this "target" (the comparator with less information)? How does this help or hurt the comparison process?
17. What is diagnosticity?
18. What does parallel connectivity have to do with comparisons?
19. When would one or more traits be inconsequential to a comparison?
20. Why are alignable differences more significant than nonalignable ones?

Discussion Questions

1. Are statistical interpretations of fingerprint evidence possible? Why or why not? If so, what might be the benefits? If not, why not and where does that leave fingerprinting as a science?
2. Consider a burglary of a home. Using the principles offered by the previous entries, what evidence might be useful in the investigation, what principles are relevant, and what could or could not possibly be compared?
3. Fingerprints is one of the disciplines that is almost wholly within forensic science. Without a relevant cognate in the academic world (biometrics is more about the engineering of the identification devices), the question remains: Is forensic fingerprinting examination a science? Is it merely a technique? Argue both sides of the issue, using pros and cons with references from the literature.
4. How accurate are fingerprint examinations? How could you tell? Is absolute identification supportable?
5. What is the difference between biometrics and fingerprinting? Is there one?

Additional Readings

Champod, C., Espinoza, M., 2014. Forgeries of fingerprints in forensic science. In: Handbook of Biometric Anti-Spoofing. Springer, London, pp. 13–34.
Forbes, P.G., 2014. Quantifying the Strength of Evidence in Forensic Fingerprints (Doctoral dissertation). University of Oxford.
Kellman, P.J., Mnookin, J.L., Erlikhman, G., Garrigan, P., Ghose, T., Mettler, E., Charleton, D., Dror, I.E., 2014. Forensic comparison and matching of fingerprints: using quantitative image measures for estimating error rates through understanding and predicting difficulty. PLoS One 9 (5), e94617.

Section 2. Chemistry and Visualization

Forensic science makes the absent present; it brings history into the "now" by reconstructing past events through the physical remnants of the criminal activity. Fingerprint traces are the canonical example of this: They must be visualized to be useful and, in doing so, what was perceived as absent becomes visible in the present. The arsenal of chemical processes available to visualize latent prints is vast and complicated. Interestingly, this aspect of fingerprinting has not been challenged, probably because it is so heavily based in chemistry.

Chemistry of Print Residue

AA Frick, P Fritz, and SW Lewis, Curtin University, Perth, WA, Australia

This article is a revision of the previous edition article by S.K. Bramble and J.S. Brennan, volume 2, pp. 862–869, © 2000, Elsevier Ltd.

Glossary

Apocrine glands Sweat glands associated with hair follicles around the axillary regions; that is, the armpits, groin, and chest.
Eccrine glands Sweat glands found in all skin areas.
Eccrine sweat Aqueous mixture of salts and amino acids secreted by the eccrine glands.
Sebaceous glands Secretory glands associated with hair follicles.
Sebum Mixture of lipids secreted by the sebaceous glands.

Abbreviations

DESI-MSI Desorption electrospray ionization mass spectrometry imaging
GC-MS Gas chromatography–mass spectrometry
MALDI-MSI Matrix-assisted laser desorption/ionization mass spectrometry imaging
SIMS Secondary ion mass spectrometry

Introduction

The impressions left by friction ridge skin on the grasping surfaces of the hands (and feet) not only demonstrate contact, but are also sufficiently discriminating to allow personal identification. They are thus extremely important in criminal investigations to establish links between the objects, victims, and suspects. The most common forms of these impressions are latent (hidden) fingerprints, and successful recovery from a scene or object relies on their detection. A range of physical and chemical methods have been developed over the years for the visualization of latent fingerprints. These methods target differences between the latent fingerprint and the substrate on which it is laid and are based either on physical attraction or a chemical reaction. Knowledge of the chemistry of latent fingerprints is critically important in understanding the detection methods.

Latent fingerprints are considered to be an emulsion of aqueous and lipid components derived from natural skin secretions, contaminants, and other skin debris such as dead skin cells. At deposition, they typically comprise a thin film of residue

 http://dx.doi.org/10.1016/B978-0-12-800573-6.00005-7

approximately 0.1 μm thick and less than 10 μg in weight. The chemistry of the latent fingerprint on deposition may be affected by a number of donor factors such as age, gender, diet, disease state, medication, and the presence of exogenous contaminants on the surface of the skin. Over time, the chemical nature of the deposit will change through evaporation of components, microbial action, and exposure to the air. The rate of change will be dependent on the chemistry of the original deposit and the surrounding environment. Donor variability and aging of the deposit will have a significant effect on the successful detection of latent fingerprints. However, most fingerprint detection procedures have been developed from the knowledge of human skin secretions without regard to these factors.

Since most chemical reagents used in fingerprint recovery procedures are developed on this theoretical model of latent fingerprint residue, there is an incentive to pursue a more accurate understanding of fingerprint composition if researchers are to develop new and more effective reagents. The degradation of fingerprints presents a significant setback for criminal investigations, as many visualization techniques are ineffective on latent fingerprints more than a few months old. In addition to the discovery of new reagents, there is still a need for further research to gain a better understanding of the reaction mechanisms associated with established reagents and those still under development.

Over the past few years, there have been several studies on fingerprint composition, namely, to establish if any compositional variations can be attributed to traits such as age or gender and to characterize the changes in fingerprint composition that occur with degradation under various conditions. This would enable the optimization of latent fingerprint development techniques currently used by forensic laboratories, as well as the development of new, more effective methods, thus providing improved fingerprint detection.

The most commonly used analytical technique is gas chromatography–mass spectrometry (GC-MS). Other techniques employed in recent years include Fourier transform infrared spectroscopy, Raman spectroscopy, desorption electrospray ionization MS imaging (DESI-MSI), matrix-assisted laser desorption/ionization MS imaging (MALDI-MSI), and secondary ion MS (SIMS). These methods are advantageous over GC-MS, as they require little or no sample preparation and are nondestructive of fingerprints, allowing changes over time to be monitored.

A major problem in analyzing the chemical composition of a latent fingerprint is overcoming the problem of sampling. Some studies analyze fingerprints prepared by having the donor rub a fingertip on the skin to collect sebum, whereas others clean the fingertip with a solvent and allow perspiration to accumulate before fingerprint deposition. Earlier studies have not used latent fingerprints at all but have collected material directly from the fingertip via solvent extraction. This creates some problems in making comparisons between studies, considering the solubilities of the various compounds in certain solvents, as these results will unsurprisingly only report compounds amenable to the solvent extraction procedure used. Due to the complex nature of fingerprints, most studies thus far have investigated only certain groups of components rather than the entire known range of compounds. Amino acids, fatty acids, and sebaceous lipids have been studied most often, as these compounds are of greatest forensic relevance.

To date, the results of the analysis of recently deposited fingerprints are consistent with those expected from the analysis of sweat and sebum. It has also been established that there are significant differences in the lipid content of latent fingerprints deposited by prepubescent children and adults, with children's fingerprints containing a greater proportion of volatile compounds. While many current fingerprint development methods are unable to detect the nonvolatile portion of children's fingerprints, potential target compounds in children's fingerprints for future detection techniques have recently been identified. Studies regarding the effects of time and environment on deposited fingerprints indicate a general trend of loss of material, especially within the first 3 months, attributed to bacterial action, oxidation, and evaporation of volatiles. Further studies are required to determine the effects that factors such as an individual's age, gender, ethnic background, or health may have on latent fingerprint composition.

This article provides an overview of the chemical composition of latent fingerprints and a discussion of recent approaches to investigate the factors affecting fingerprint composition. This overview by necessity is limited in length, and for a comprehensive review of the chemical composition of latent fingerprint residues, readers are directed to the chapter by Robert Ramotowski listed in the Further Reading.

Sources of Fingerprint Residue

The endogenous substances found in latent fingerprints are derived from the secretions of the eccrine (sweat), sebaceous, and apocrine glands located within the dermis, as well as the constant sloughing of dead cells by the epidermis (**Table 1**). Current models of latent fingerprint composition are based on medical research on the secretions of the skin glands, although this does not provide an exhaustive list of the hundreds of compounds that may be present. For the purpose of latent fingerprint detection, the most important sources of material are the secretions of the eccrine and sebaceous glands, as secretions from the apocrine glands are rarely a significant component of latent fingerprint residue due to their location in the body.

Eccrine glands serve to dissipate body heat through the evaporation of sweat from the skin surface and to excrete excess water, electrolytes, and waste products such as urea. These

Table 1 Human skin secretory glands

Types of glands	*Secretion types*	*Body distribution*	*Role of gland*
Sebaceous	Sebum (lipids)	Typically localized to regions containing hair follicles	Inhibits the growth of bacteria, lubricates and protects the keratin of the hair shaft, and conditions the surrounding skin
Sweat (sudiferous) glands			
Eccrine (merocrine)	Sweat (aqueous)	Entire body, highly concentrated on the palms of the hands and soles of the feet	Cooling the surface of the skin to reduce body temperature; excretion of water, electrolytes, and metabolites; and protection from environmental hazards
Apocrine	Sweat (aqueous)	Associated with hair follicles around the axillary regions. In particular, the armpits, groin, and chest	Scent glands (pheromones)

Reproduced from Jelly, R., Patton, E.L.T., Lennard, C., Lewis, S.W., Lim, K.F., 2009. The detection of latent fingermarks on porous surfaces using amino acid sensitive reagents: a review. Analytica Chimica Acta 652, 128–142, with permission from Elsevier.

glands, located within the dermis, are coiled, tubular structures, which lead directly to the skin surface. As the eccrine glands are the sole type of secretory gland on the palms of the hands, located along the skin ridges, latent fingerprints always contain at least some eccrine sweat components. Eccrine sweat is an aqueous mixture consisting primarily of salts, amino acids, and some lipids. The response of the eccrine glands to elevated temperatures is gradual and weak but is much stronger and more immediate when stimulated by stress; the latter is thought to be an important factor in the deposition of latent fingerprints at crime scenes.

Sebaceous glands are found all over the body, except for the palms of the hands and soles of the feet. The sebaceous glands consist of one or several lobes, encapsulated by highly vascularized connective tissue. The oily mixture produced by these glands, known as sebum, is usually secreted into hair shaft canals and is present in greatest density on the forehead and scalp. The main functions of sebum are thought to include lubricating the skin and hair, waterproofing the epidermis, transporting antioxidants, and providing individuals with a unique scent signature. The production of sebum is largely under the control of androgens, in particular, testosterone. These hormones cause an increase in sebaceous gland size, which has a direct effect on the production rate of sebum. Changes in androgen levels that occur with age therefore impact sebum production over the course of an individual's lifetime. Sebum is incorporated into latent fingerprints through the individual touching his/her face or hair, and it provides the majority of the lipid content in fingerprint deposits.

As eccrine glands are the only glands present on the grasping surfaces of hands, they contribute greatly to the aqueous component of latent fingermarks. However, due to activities such as touching the face or hair, hands will often be contaminated with sebaceous secretions. Thus, while one type of secretion may predominate in a latent fingerprint, there can be no purely eccrine or purely sebaceous fingerprint (**Table 2**).

Table 2 Summary of main constituents of eccrine and sebaceous skin secretions

	Constituents	
Secretion	*Organic*	*Inorganic*
Eccrine sweat	Amino acids	Water (>98%)
	Proteins	Chloride
	Urea	Metal ions (Na^+, K^+, Ca^{2+})
	Uric acid	Sulfate
	Lactic acid	Phosphate
	Sugars	Hydrogen carbonate
	Creatinine	Ammonia
	Choline	
Sebum	Glycerides	
	Fatty acids	
	Wax esters	
	Squalene	
	Sterol esters	

Reproduced from Jelly, R., Patton, E.L.T., Lennard, C., Lewis, S.W., Lim, K.F., 2009. The detection of latent fingermarks on porous surfaces using amino acid sensitive reagents: a review. Analytica Chimica Acta 652, 128–142, with permission from Elsevier.

The most abundant compounds in eccrine sweat include salts and amino acids. Sodium chloride is the most abundant compound present in eccrine secretions and makes up the majority of the inorganic salt content, together with potassium chloride. Lactate salts are the second most abundant component of eccrine sweat and are thought to be one of the target molecules for cyanoacrylate fuming. The presence of lactate is indicative of eccrine gland activity, as it is derived from glucose utilization; however, lactate concentration decreases as sweat rate increases over time. Eccrine sweat also contains trace amounts of various metals such as zinc, copper, and manganese, as well as drugs and hormones and their metabolites, which diffuse into the eccrine glands from blood plasma.

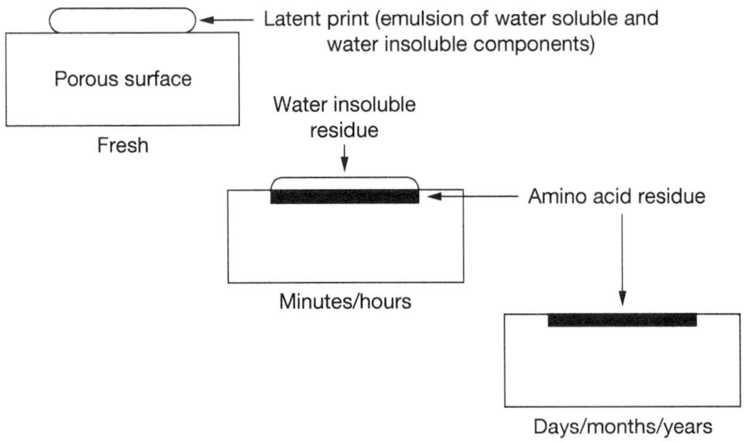

Figure 1 Schematic cross section of a latent fingermark on a paper substrate at various stages after deposition. Reproduced from Lewis, S.W., 2011. Chemical Sensing and Detection in Forensic Science. Chemosensors: Principles, Strategies, and Applications. John Wiley & Sons, Hoboken, NJ, pp. 475–496 (Chapter 22).

Table 3 Summary of main constituents of eccrine and sebaceous skin secretions

Amino acid	*Amount (μmol)*
Serine	0.106
Glycine	0.071
Ornithine	0.034
Alanine	0.029
Aspartic acid	0.023
Threonine	0.018
Histidine	0.018
Valine	0.013
Proline	0.011
Leucine	0.011

Reproduced from Jelly, R., Patton, E.L.T., Lennard, C., Lewis, S.W., Lim, K.F., 2009. The detection of latent fingermarks on porous surfaces using amino acid sensitive reagents: a review. Analytica Chimica Acta 652, 128–142, with permission from Elsevier.

Table 4 The major lipids present on the skin surface

Lipid	*Surface (%)*
Squalene	10
Sterol esters	2.5
Sterols	1.5
Wax esters	22
Triglycerides	25
Mono- and diglycerides	10
Fatty acids	25
Unidentified	4

The presence of amino acids in human sweat has been widely reported in the biomedical literature, with a wide range of amino acids identified (**Table 3**). Up to 22 amino acids may be present in eccrine sweat, including those involved in the urea cycle. The most abundant amino acids include serine, glycine, ornithine, alanine, and aspartic acid, although the types and concentrations of amino acids present will depend on a variety of factors including general health, diet, gender, and age. It has also been reported that the abundance of amino acids may be up to 18 times higher in sweat produced during exercise than from thermal stimulation.

Amino acids are of particular interest when considering the detection of latent fingerprints on paper. When transferred to such a substrate, the amino acids bind strongly without significant migration, provided the paper does not get wet or exposed to high levels of humidity (see **Figure 1**). Latent fingerprints formed this way can be developed decades after deposition.

Sebum consists of a mixture of lipid compounds including triglycerides, fatty acids, wax esters, cholesterol, and squalene (**Table 4**). As with eccrine sweat, the composition of sebum can be affected by various factors such as age, health, genetics, and diet. The lipids secreted by the sebaceous glands are unusual compared to other lipids found in the human body, in that they consist of a higher proportion of unsaturated and branched-chain molecular structures, allowing sebum to remain as a liquid film on the skin surface due to its low melting point of 30 °C. Some components of sebum, such as wax esters and some fatty acids, are produced exclusively by the sebaceous glands, and so their concentration is correlated directly to gland activity. Squalene is produced in all tissues, but it is usually rapidly metabolized to cholesterol. It is only in the skin that squalene reaches significant levels, but the reason for this is unknown. Sebum cholesterol itself is thought to be actually of epidermal origin. Free fatty acids are not produced in the sebaceous glands but on the skin surface, as epidermal and bacterial lipases hydrolyze triglycerides to fatty acids, diglycerides, monoglycerides, and glycerol. The durable nature of the nonvolatile sebaceous materials such as triglycerides and wax esters provides a means to detect latent fingerprints that have been exposed to water; for example, with physical developer.

Factors Affecting Fingerprint Composition

Substrate

For the purpose of latent fingerprint development, surfaces are broadly categorized into porous and nonporous, based on their ability to absorb fingerprint residue. Paper and cardboard typify the former; glass and metals, the latter. There is also a third, intermediate category of semiporous surfaces, which encompass any substrate with a combination of porous and nonporous surface properties, such as painted surfaces and some polymers. The surface type will largely determine the development techniques to be used, based on the interactions between certain fingerprint compounds and the surface, as well as the compatibility between the reagent and the surface.

Substrates with greater porosity will absorb fingerprint residue to some degree during deposition, with the end result that fingerprints on porous substrates typically contain more material than those on nonporous surfaces. For instance, it has been shown that up to three times more amino acid material is found in fingerprints on porous surfaces than those on nonporous surfaces. Eccrine sweat is more readily absorbed than sebum; therefore, the former is more efficiently transferred onto porous surfaces, while the latter will remain on the surface of the substrate for up to several years following deposition.

Deposition

The physical contact of the fingertip with a surface is clearly important in determining the initial composition of fingerprint residue. Not all substances on a fingertip are transferred on contact, which is easily demonstrated by the production of a depletion series of fingerprints. Parameters involved in the deposition process include duration of contact, contact angle, electrostatic forces, surface temperature, and pressure. For example, applying excessive pressure during deposition leads to a greater amount of residue being deposited but will cause the ridges of the fingertip to distort, reducing the clarity of the resulting fingerprint.

It is difficult to determine the precise influence of these parameters in isolation from the nature of the surface itself. Studies have indicated that both the quantity and type of material transferred are dependent on substrate type. Currently, it is not clear whether this transfer process is due to physical or chemical interactions and represents an important unexplored area of scientific study.

Donor

The chemical composition of material found on the fingertips of individuals is known to differ between people but it also varies over time with a single individual. There are numerous factors that affect perspiration rates and material secreted. It has been suggested that should a fingerprint be of insufficient clarity to provide identification, the composition of the fingerprint residue could provide important clues about an individual, such as age, gender, or personal habits.

There is a significant difference in fingerprint composition between prepubescent children and adults due to the marked increase in sebaceous gland activity that occurs at the onset of puberty. Anecdotal evidence has suggested that fingerprints deposited by young children evaporate within a relatively short time frame, whereas adults' fingerprints are rather more durable under the same conditions. This presents a great difficulty to the investigation of crimes involving children, such as abduction, as the victim's fingerprints will evaporate within a few days following deposition. It has since been established that children's fingerprints contain a greater proportion of volatile lipids, which accounts for their short-lived nature.

As sebum production is under the influence of androgen levels, males tend to produce more sebum than females across all age groups. However, attempts to distinguish between genders based on fingerprint composition have thus far failed to find any significant differences. Other factors known to affect the composition of eccrine and sebaceous secretions include health, diet, and medication, with xenobiotics and their metabolites excreted by the eccrine glands.

To date, no other significant compositional differences have been linked to donor traits apart from pre- and post-pubescence. Rather, many studies have commented on the significant variation found between individuals, indicative of the combined influences of several factors contributing to fingerprint composition.

Contaminants

Incidental contact with a wide range of materials through everyday activity can introduce a significant amount of exogenous contamination onto the fingertips, which are then incorporated into latent fingerprints. Such contaminants include commonplace substances such as food residues and cosmetic products; however, compounds of forensic relevance may also be present in fingerprints in detectable levels. To this effect, various studies have been conducted that have successfully identified contaminants from recently handled items, such as legal and illicit drugs (including metabolites, which indicate use rather than just handling), explosive residues, and fibers, from latent fingerprints.

Ambient Conditions and Time

Apart from the factors that affect the initial composition of fingerprint residue, there are a number of potential parameters that affect the chemical composition of latent fingerprints after deposition. Fingerprint residue begins to degrade almost immediately after deposition by processes including evaporation of volatile components, oxidation, environmental factors, and bacterial activity. The rate of degradation is dependent on the initial chemical composition of the residue, as well as the environmental conditions. Exposure to UV light, temperature, and humidity has some effect on degradation and thus on the ability of forensic personnel to recover latent fingerprints. In recent years, there has been increased interest on the factors affecting the degradation of fingerprint residue over time.

One of the first stages of fingerprint degradation is the evaporation of water and volatile lipid constituents, leaving an increasingly viscous, waxy residue. Up to 85% of a latent fingerprint may evaporate within 2 weeks following deposition; however, children's fingerprints evaporate much faster due to their higher proportion of eccrine and volatile compounds. The salts present in eccrine sweat are nonvolatile and crystallize on the surface becoming subject to degradation by both exposure to UV light and erosion by airflow. On porous surfaces, substances such as chloride and urea begin to diffuse through porous surfaces approximately 1 week following deposition, and the rate of diffusion will be hastened by humidity.

It has been observed that fingerprint lipids undergo a gradual breakdown to their constituent fatty acids and that fingerprints stored in the dark degrade less rapidly than those stored under direct light. Over a period of 60 days, there is an initial increase in the level of shorter chain fatty acids, followed by a subsequent decrease. This is possibly due to oxidation or bacterial degradation of long-chain fatty acids, wax esters, and triglycerides, generating short-chain fatty acids, which later evaporate or are degraded further. Squalene, being a highly unsaturated compound, is readily oxidized to hydroperoxides and squalene epoxide, which themselves degrade to volatile compounds such as aldehydes and ketones, in a process accelerated by exposure to UV light and deposition on a nonporous substrate. Children's fingerprints degrade differently than those left by adults because of the lower lipid content in their fingerprints.

Other factors that can affect the detectability of a fingerprint include immersion and fire damage. As many amino acids and inorganic salts are water soluble, exposure to rain or high humidity has detrimental effects on these constituents. Lipid-specific reagents have proven effective on substrates submerged under laboratory conditions, although documents recovered from water sources may be less successful due to the presence of contaminants or degradation by microbial action.

Several studies have investigated the effect of pyrolysis (as may be encountered in cases involving arson or firearms) on fingerprint constituents, indicating that excessive temperature can cause new pyrolytic products to form, which could be used as targets for development reagents. Exposure to temperatures in excess of 100 °C is a known cause of thermal degradation of some amino acids and urea fingerprints. Lactate is also subject to both thermal and photodegradation.

It has been suggested that knowledge of fingerprint degradation could be used to date fingerprints, thereby placing an individual at, or excluding them from, the scene of a crime at the time it occurred. More research is needed in this area to fully understand the factors affecting degradation with evidence to suggest that substrate type may influence some processes.

Future Directions and Conclusions

Given the value of fingermark evidence in law enforcement, improvements in their detection will have a significant effect on successful investigation of terrorism and crime. However, the ability to make future improvements to current fingermark detection methods and the development of new approaches to the visualization of latent fingermarks depend critically on a greater understanding of the chemistry of the fingermark residue.

A major challenge is the development of a "standard" latent fingermark, vital for establishing the effectiveness of new detection methods and for quality assurance and quality control in fingermark detection. The lack of suitable analytical standards for research on the development and optimization of novel and existing formulations is a significant ongoing issue. Quality control tests of reagents and comparisons between different formulations and application methods are often performed using latent fingerprints collected from a small, local sample population. Due to variation in fingerprint composition, reproducibility thus becomes difficult, especially when comparing results across several studies. The absence of standard methodologies introduces additional variation, as some tests may collect "charged" fingerprint samples containing sebum, whereas others use "natural" fingerprints, further complicating objective comparisons.

Attempts have been made to address this problem by spotting solutions of the relevant target compounds in serial dilutions onto strips of paper or using a modified ink-jet printer. In this way, "fingerprints" of consistent, uniform quality may be printed on paper for subsequent treatment with reagents such as ninhydrin and physical developer. However, as these test strips only contain the target compounds of specific development reagents, they are applicable to only a few techniques at best and cannot replicate any interactions between compounds, which may also affect development. A more realistic approach would be to use a standard more closely modeled on actual fingerprint composition.

The studies currently underway around the world on the fundamental chemistry of latent fingermarks will provide a platform for the development of the next generation of latent fingermark detection methods. They will also provide a step toward the development of a "standard" latent fingermark that may be used as an analytical standard, thereby ensuring experimental reproducibility and enabling comparisons between different laboratories by removing variables derived from natural fingerprint variation.

See also: **Investigations:** Fingerprints; **Pattern Evidence/Fingerprints (Dactyloscopy):** Sequential Treatment and Enhancement; Visualization or Development of Crime Scene Fingerprints; **Pattern Evidence/History:** Fingerprint Sciences.

Further Reading

Almog, J., Azoury, M., Elmaliah, Y., Berenstein, L., Zaban, A., 2004. Fingerprints' third dimension: the depth and shape of fingerprints penetration into paper-cross section examination by fluorescence microscopy. Journal of Forensic Science 49, 981–985.

Antoine, K.M., Mortazavi, S., Miller, A.D., Miller, L.M., 2010. Chemical differences are observed in children's versus adults' latent fingerprints as a function of time. Journal of Forensic Sciences 55, 513–518.

Becue, A., Eglie, N., Champod, C., Margot, P.A., 2010. Fingerprints and other impressions left by the human body. Review: 2007–2010. In: Daeid, N.N. (Ed.), Proceedings of 16th International Forensic Science Symposium Interpol. Interpol, Glasgow, pp. 222–319.

Bhargava, R., Perlman, R.S., Fernandez, D.C., Levin, I.W., Bartick, E.G., 2009. Non-invasive detection of superimposed latent fingerprints and inter-ridge trace evidence by infrared spectroscopic imaging. Analytical and Bioanalytical Chemistry 394, 2069–2075.

Bond, J.W., 2009. Imaging fingerprint corrosion of fired brass shell casings. Review of Scientific Instruments 80, 075108.

Champod, C., Lennard, C., Margot, P., Stoilovic, M., 2004. Fingerprints and Other Ridge Skin Impressions. CRC Press, Boca Raton.

Girod, A., Ramotowski, R., Weyermann, C., 2012. Composition of fingermark residue: a qualitative and quantitative review. Forensic Science International. http://dx.doi.org/10.1016/j.forsciint.2012.05.018 (Epub ahead of print).

Grant, A., Wilkinson, T.J., Holman, D.R., Martin, M.C., 2005. Identification of recently handled materials by analysis of latent human fingerprints using infrared spectromicroscopy. Applied Spectroscopy 59, 1182–1187.

Jelly, R., Patton, E.L.T., Lennard, C., Lewis, S.W., Lim, K.F., 2009. The detection of latent fingermarks on porous surfaces using amino acid sensitive reagents: a review. Analytica Chimica Acta 652, 128–142.

Jones, N.E., Davies, L.M., Russell, C.A.L., Brennan, J.S., Bramble, S.K., 2001. A systematic approach to latent fingerprint sample preparation for comparative chemical studies. Journal of Forensic Identification 52, 504–515.

McRoberts, A. (Ed.), 2011. The Fingerprint Sourcebook. Department of Justice, Washington, DC.

Ramotowski, R., 2001. Composition of latent print residue. In: Lee, H., Gaensslen, R. (Eds.), Advances in Fingerprint Technology. CRC Press, Boca Raton, pp. 63–104.

Thomas, G.L., 1978. The physics of fingerprints and their detection. Journal of Physics E: Scientific Instruments 11, 722–731.

Sequential Treatment and Enhancement

T Kent, University of Lincoln, Lincoln, UK

Glossary

Eccrine sweat It is exuded by the eccrine glands which are located over most of the body but the highest concentration is on the palmar surfaces of the hands, the soles of the feet, and on the scalp.

Sebaceous sweat It is exuded by sebaceous glands which are located in various concentrations over most parts of the body with the exception of the palmar surfaces of the hands and the soles of the feet.

Unfortunately terminology in this area is not consistent. The "undeveloped" deposit of chemicals on a surface delineating the shape of the ridges of a finger will be referred to here as a "fingermark" or a "latent fingerprint." These are sometimes referred to as "fingerprints," "latent impressions," or "latent fingermarks" or just, or sometimes simply as "marks" or "prints." When they are visible but have not been enhanced they are sometimes referred to as "patent prints."

When they have been rendered visible by chemical or physical means they will be referred to here as fingerprints.

If papillary ridges have left visible impressions in soft materials such as putty or wax they may be referred to as "plastic prints."

Record fingerprints of offenders or suspects taken by law enforcement agencies are commonly also referred to as "prints" or sometimes "10 prints."

Introduction

Development of latent fingerprints is a vital part of the forensic examination of crime scenes and produces important evidence for the effective prosecution of offenders. As indicated elsewhere in this encyclopedia, there are many techniques that may be used on the various types of surface encountered at crime scenes.

With the advent of DNA as a powerful crime-scene investigation tool, it has become increasingly important that fingerprint development techniques do not compromise other aspects of the examination of the crime scene.

In addition to detecting DNA in body fluids and latent fingerprints, the range of forensic examination procedures which may be necessary at typical crime scenes includes handwriting, indented impressions, ballistics, blood pattern analysis, explosive or drug detection, footwear impressions, examination for fibers, and other trace evidence and other specialisms.

In principle, the application of, for example, even fingerprint powder or a solvent-based fingerprint reagent solution, could compromise many of these other forensic procedures. Sequence is therefore all important, with care it is usually possible to extract maximum value from all of the potential evidence. On rare occasions, one may have to compromise one type of evidence if it is judged that there is an interaction with treatment procedures and another should take precedence. This decision should be taken by a senior officer with responsibility for the investigation who has been fully briefed on the situation.

As various types of fingerprint development techniques detect several different classes of chemical compounds, there is considerable benefit in using several techniques one after the other. One therefore needs to consider which techniques are most appropriate for the surface; what sequence they will be applied in; and what other forensic examinations need to be incorporated into this overall protocol. Experts should work together to sequence examination procedures in a way that minimizes the loss of any type of forensic information. This can become quite a complex issue and the final sequence chosen will be dependent on a number of factors. These include the nature of the crime, the surfaces involved, any obvious contamination, the environmental conditions, and the time which has elapsed since the crime is believed to have been committed.

Sequencing protocols must be regularly reviewed as techniques change and in major cases a meeting between appropriate experts is advisable before starting any treatments. When new procedures are introduced, controlled experiments should be carried out to establish what interactions may be occurring and how any damaging effects can be minimized.

 http://dx.doi.org/10.1016/B978-0-12-800573-6.00006-9

In addition to the obvious contamination by materials such as powders and the chemical effects of some developer solutions, it is also necessary to consider the effects of high-intensity visible or ultraviolet light, which will form part of many normal examination protocols for fingerprints.

Sequential Application of Fingerprint Development Techniques

The classes of compound present in natural latent fingerprints originating primarily from sebaceous and eccrine sweat glands are dealt with elsewhere in this encyclopedia. It also describes the types of reagent and the classes of compounds with which these reagents, in general terms, are believed to react. It also describes procedures for use when the deposit from a suspect's fingers may be wholly, or in part, some other known material such as blood or grease.

Usually, the investigator will know nothing about the chemical distribution of sweat constituents on the hands of a suspect. The application of several techniques targeting different classes of compound and used sequentially is very likely, therefore, to increase the chances of obtaining useful fingerprints. Even different reagents that target the same classes of compound will sometimes develop different fingerprints for reasons, which are currently unclear. There is therefore merit, in important cases, in applying several techniques, if sequences can be established which minimize interference with subsequent processes.

Any sequence of techniques should therefore incorporate one or more methods which

- detect visible deposits on the surface; or impressions in soft materials such as wax or putty;
- detect eccrine sweat secretions, water, inorganic salts, amino acids, etc.
- detect sebaceous, fatty, or greasy deposits; or if appropriate,
- detect known or suspected, contaminants such as grease or blood.

Sometimes a subsequent technique will improve fingerprints developed by a previous method, sometimes it may develop completely new fingerprints; and sometimes it will destroy or degrade those already developed.

A process of logic, experimental trials, and operational trials has lead to sequences which have been generally agreed to maximize fingerprint yields. Flow charts have then been constructed for most types of surface. The first detailed recommendations for these sequences were published by the UK Home Office in 1986. These have been updated by the same team and researchers elsewhere have devised some variations to them.

Process Compatibility

Some techniques are almost completely compatible with one another if used in a particular sequence. An example of this is the use of physical developer after ninhydrin when treating paper. Ninhydrin reacts primarily with amino acids and if a suitable solvent system is used, it has little or no effect on the heavier fats, waxes, or esters which are probably developed by the aqueous physical developer solution.

If physical developer solution were to be applied first, the aqueous constituent would wash out any amino acid present eliminating the possibility of subsequently detecting any fingerprints with ninhydrin.

Other interactions are less obvious and many are not well understood but have been established pragmatically. The use of DFO (1,8-diazafluoren-9-one) before ninhydrin yields significant numbers of extra fingerprints although both are reacting with amino acids. If, however, ninhydrin is used first virtually no extra fingerprints are found by subsequent treatment with DFO.

Other Factors to Be Considered

When planning a sequence of fingerprint treatments some other issues need to be considered:

- What is the likely age of fingermarks of interest?
- What is known about environmental conditions to which the article has been subjected?
- Which forensic examination procedures are also necessary?
- How important is the crime and what resources can be allocated to it?

Some fingerprint treatments will not develop fingermarks which have been wetted. Some are ineffective on older fingermarks and some conversely show some improvement with older fingermarks.

Some surfaces are so frequently touched by hands, for example door handles, handrails, and credit cards, that the surface has a very high background content of fingerprint constituents which will cause considerable problems for the detection of fresher fingerprints superimposed onto this background deposit. Some techniques are more likely to detect fresher fingerprints but none can be relied on as a method of estimation of the age of a fingerprint.

In serious crimes, the investigators will want to explore all possible sources of evidence. It must be appreciated, however, that a full implementation of all viable techniques to all exhibits in a case is rarely possible. Examining, for example, an entire house or business premises, in a kidnapping or terrorist case, could take many months of work. In reality, most examination procedures are a compromise.

In particular, examination using high-intensity light sources or lasers is very time-consuming and demanding on the examiner due to the number of possible excitation wavelengths and viewing filter combinations and the very faint fluorescence sometimes observed.

Photographic Recording of Developed Fingerprints

Since subsequent processes may degrade fingerprints revealed by a previous process developed fingerprints on exhibits must be photographed between each stage of a sequential examination. All the usual protocols for photographic evidence must be implemented. The image must be in sharp focus, taken perpendicular to the surface, incorporate an accurate scale, and be captured at sufficiently high resolution for all identification purposes. Any digital imaging audit trail procedures, as required by local jurisdictions, must be complied with so that images may be presented in evidence at court.

The various development techniques result in different types of fingerprint and may require very different illumination and photographic procedures. If sequential processing is to be implemented routinely in a laboratory there are considerable advantages in establishing photographic workstations, which can be readily configured for the various types of image recording. Various light sources and filters will be needed and facilities for the use of various geometries of scattered, reflected, and transmitted light.

Fingerprints in Contaminants

If fingermarks are found at a scene of a violent crime where there is a considerable amount of blood, and it is believed that some articles have been handled by a bloody hand, special sequences may be more effective.

None of the techniques used for the development of fingerprints in blood is specific to blood so none can be used as presumptive tests for blood.

Similarly, at some crime scenes there may be obvious fatty or greasy contamination as, for example, in a kitchen or from the consumption of fast food. This may make conventional techniques such as powdering ineffective and inappropriate.

Examples of other fingerprint contamination may be oils and greases from industrial or automotive premises, accelerants at scenes of attempted arson, lubricants from condoms, and drugs or explosives, or their precursors, in drug- or terrorist-related crime. Some of these may require specialist advice from chemists on likely interactions with reagents.

Contaminated Exhibits

In many cases, articles may have been exposed to contamination subsequent to latent fingerprints being deposited. Examples include water either from rain or immersion, soaking in accelerants such as gasoline in failed attempts at arson or other materials.

Most agreed protocols cover situations where the article has been wetted, some other contamination may require specialist advice. Most accelerants do not prevent fingerprints being developed with amino acid reagents or physical developer.

Packaging and Handling of Evidence

It must be understood that any handling of exhibits from crime scenes, whether or not while wearing gloves, carries a serious risk of damaging latent fingerprints. Even superimposing, folding, or sliding surfaces together will have some effect on the fingerprint deposit, if it is on a smooth, nonporous, surface such as polythene.

Handling nonporous exhibits during treatment and photography through a sequence of processes, therefore, requires considerable care.

Porous surfaces such as paper absorb much of the deposit and handling is much less likely to cause damage.

Preliminary Procedures

If exhibits are wet in most cases it is advisable to allow to dry before any examination. Moderate temperature, usually no higher than 30 °C in a drying cabinet with a gentle forced draft may be used for such drying.

Investigators tasked with searching for fingerprints must have good eyesight and should be able to focus clearly on exhibits at a distance of 200 mm or less at low brightness levels. If necessary, spectacles must be worn to achieve sharp focus at this distance otherwise faint fluorescent fingerprints and some others may be missed.

Sequence Selection and Complex Exhibits

After drying there should be an initial assessment of the exhibit and a number of questions need to be asked which will assist in the selection of an appropriate sequence of treatments.

1. What materials are the main surfaces of the exhibit?
2. Which areas are most likely to bear fingerprints?
3. If the exhibit is made of more than one material, can it easily be separated into constituent materials for separate treatment?

4. Are there indications that any fingermarks are likely to be contaminated with significant amounts of materials such as blood or grease which may influence the choice of reagent?
5. What colors are the surfaces to be treated?

If the article has more than one surface type which cannot easily be separated, for example a paper label on a wine bottle, methods of treating areas separately need to be considered, or a sequence of compatible processes established.

Initial Visual Examination—All Exhibits

The first step for most exhibits is a thorough visual examination with a source of uniform white light illumination. Reflective or textured surfaces may require manipulation of the light source to achieve high-angle and low-angle illumination which can considerably affect contrast and visibility of latent fingerprints.

There is some advantage in using relatively powerful sources but great care should be taken with light sources equipped with arc lamps. Some of these exceed the eye damage threshold, even for short period use, if looked at directly.

Visible fingerprints are most likely to be observed if:

1. the surface is particularly smooth,
2. dirt or blood or some other colored contaminant has been deposited from the fingers,
3. the surface was dusty in which case the finger ridges may have removed dust, leaving an image of the finger, and
4. the surface is soft such as wax or putty and an impression of the ridges has been left.

Initial Fluorescence Examination—All Exhibits

Some latent fingerprints may fluoresce, as a result of either natural constituents or more likely contamination. In serious cases, a fluorescence examination should be carried out before chemical or physical treatments are applied. The background substrate color and fluorescence may influence the range of excitation and emission wavelengths, which are likely to be most effective.

In practice, relatively small numbers of fingermarks are usually detected during initial examination although on some surfaces such as polythene wrappers and bags; however, significant numbers may be detected if high-power sources such as lasers of appropriate wavelength are used. Currently, it would seem that solid-state lasers emitting several watts of light at around 532 nm are among the most practical and effective for preliminary searching.

There is a greater possibility of fluorescent fingermarks being detected at certain types of crime scenes. In particular, in kitchens or other areas where food is prepared and there may be contamination with vegetable oils, greases, and fats. Similarly, at some types of industrial premises such as garages where mineral oils and greases may be common. Many printing inks fluoresce so premises involved in, for example, forgery of currency may yield fluorescent fingerprints. Some of the precursors to drug and explosive manufacture also fluoresce so again fluorescence examination may be more productive in these cases but it will be necessary to use a number of excitation and viewing wavelengths as the characteristics of the chemicals will not normally be known.

Surface Compatibility and Performance

If we simply look at which processes will develop some fingerprints on a particular type of surface, we find that for smooth nonporous surfaces, powders, powder suspensions, small particle reagent, superglue, and vacuum metal deposition are all possible methods.

If one considers porous surfaces, ninhydrin, indanedione, DFO, silver nitrate, and physical developer are possible methods.

Looking in more detail at the nature of the surface and examining the actual performance of these processes in substantial operational trials, significant variations are found.

The performance of dry powdering on low- or high-density polyethylene wrappings, a very commonly occurring substrate, for example, is generally poor. On the same surfaces, it has been found that superglue develops considerably more fingerprints than powders. Vacuum metal deposition will find even very old light fingermarks on some types of polythene but on recycled polythene bags, and some thick new low-density polythene the performance is poor.

Some of the recently developed powder suspension formulations based on special grades of iron oxide or titanium dioxide, however, perform well on many types of polythene surface.

Adhesive tapes can present particular problems, if they are stuck down we must decide whether to treat the back of the tape, before removing it and treating the adhesive side. If, for example, the tape is around a package of drugs in polythene wrappers it may be that a process such as superglue could be used to treat both surfaces before the tape is removed.

Some types of adhesive are incompatible with most powder suspension formulations so testing a small corner may be advisable before treating a whole batch of exhibits.

Operational Performance

Ultimately, the analysis of actual operational performance over hundreds or thousands of cases is the most effective way of determining optimum process selection and sequencing procedures.

Keeping records of the numbers of useful fingerprints developed on exhibits assists in improving future process selection but can also highlight problems with equipment, chemicals, or staff training. As packaging materials and technology change keeping accurate records can identify changes in substrates which require alternative methods or further research. Materials such as paper and more particularly plastics are evolving technologies which can significantly impact on fingerprint reagent performance.

Process Selection Charts

The sequences in the example charts in the section below have been developed by the UK Home Office. Large-scale laboratory trials were carried out on carefully constituted donor panels depositing depletion sequences of fingerprints repeatedly from the same finger. These were followed up by substantial operational trials in police forces of all major techniques. There are still, however, areas of uncertainty due to insufficient operational data.

The principle of these charts is that the most productive processes are on the main, wide routes but in important cases the additional techniques on the smaller side routes may be incorporated and sometime will lead to additional fingerprints being developed (**Figures 1 and 2**).

Recent indications are that some combined indanedione–zinc salt formulations could be used in place of DFO and subsequent ninhydrin treatment, in the sequence for paper and cardboard with similar overall results.

Sequences have also been established for the following other classes of surface:

- Rough nonporous
- Plastic packaging material
- Vinyl, rubber, and leather
- Wood
- Metal
- Adhesive tapes
- Blood-contaminated surfaces

Difficult Surface Types

Some of the surfaces listed above present particular problems for fingerprint development and for some there are no methods with significant success rates. The particular reasons for such difficulties are indicated below:

Rough surfaces—the ability of the surface to retain sufficient information transfer from the fingerprint ridges. An additional problem, however, is that some techniques such as powdering will tend to enhance the surface topology rather than the fingerprint.

Vinyl (plasticized PVC)—particular problems are encountered with plasticized PVC, as used in imitation leathers for bags, etc. The plasticizers used are generally fatty materials which interfere with the development process.

Adhesive tapes—many fingerprints are developed on tapes but they can present problems because it is usually desirable to develop fingerprints on both sides of the tape. There are many backing materials used for tapes and different types of adhesive. Establishing a treatment protocol in such cases can be difficult; some techniques such as superglue or powder suspension may develop fingerprints on both sides of some tapes.

Adhesive tapes commonly have either acrylic or rubber-based adhesives which react very differently and sometimes adversely with methods such as powder suspensions. Testing on a small area before treating whole exhibits is recommended to determine whether background uptake is excessive.

Freezing or solvents may be used to assist separating adhesive tapes from substrates, although removal from porous surfaces such as paper is difficult. Solvents need to be used with care and most have some detrimental effects on some adhesives.

Metal Surfaces

Some specific metal items present problems for fingerprint detection and result in generally poor success rates. Firearms may be oily due to cleaning, or rusty, when secreted in damp conditions and much of the surface handled is often grooved or textured. These factors all mitigate against successful fingerprint development. Success rates on cartridge cases both unfired, and particularly fired, is low. This may be due to their limited size, method of handling, surface treatment, mechanical abrasion, and other factors.

Fabrics

There is no general technique for developing latent fingerprints on fabrics with a significant degree of success. Various workers have proposed osmium tetroxide, vacuum metal deposition, radioactive sulfur dioxide, and superglue. Some of these have shown some promise in laboratory experiments. Experimental results are usually significantly better on synthetic fabrics than natural fibers probably due to issues associated with absorption of sweat by the latter. Clothing items not in contact with the skin appear more likely to bear deposits which might be developed. Some ridge detail has been developed in a small number of cases by radioactive sulfur dioxide and a combination of the latter with a pretreatment with superglue. Trials by the UK Home Office in the 1980s indicated that a minimum

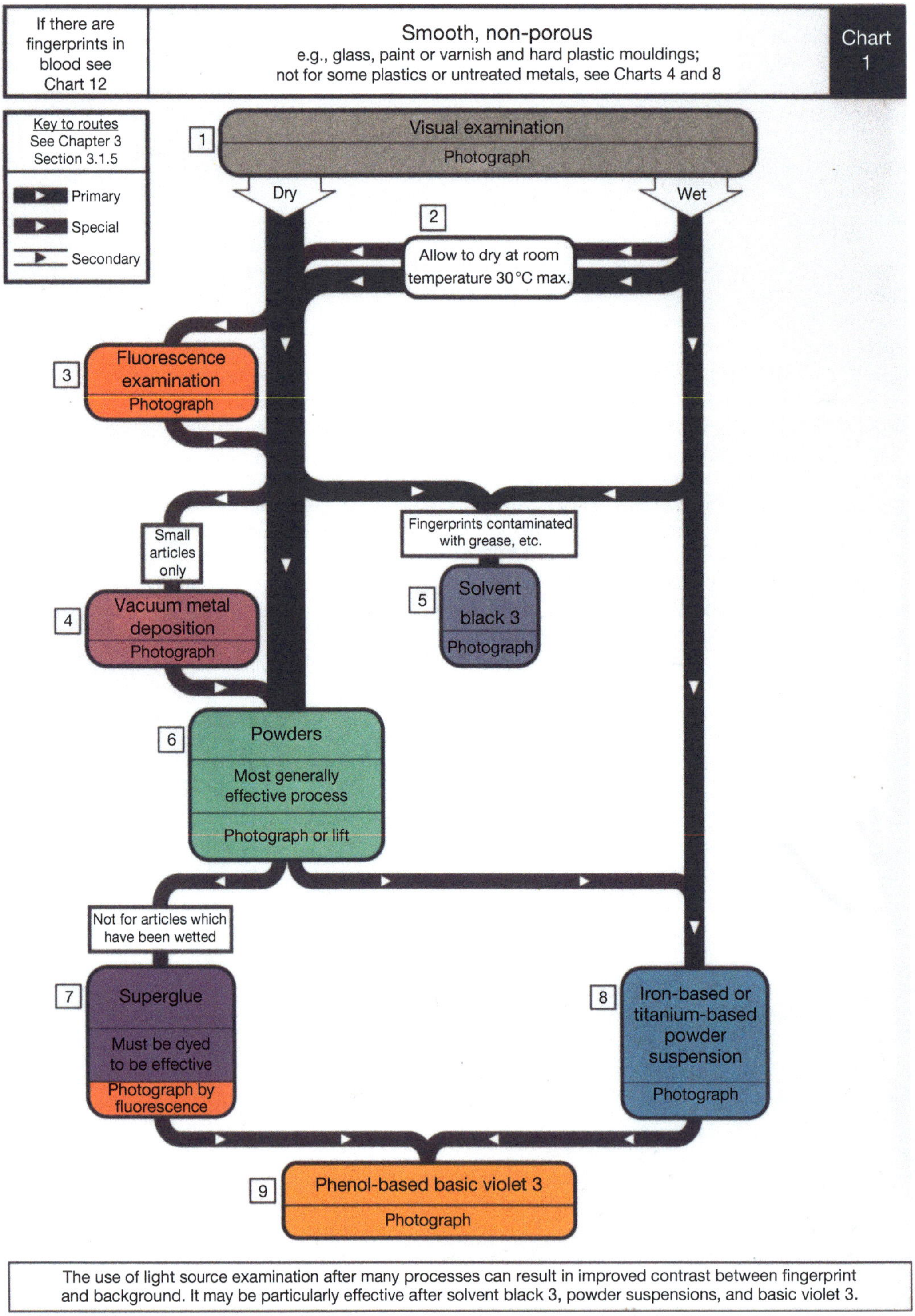

Figure 1 Process selection chart for smooth, nonporous surfaces. From Bowman, V. (Ed.), Updated 2009. Manual of Fingerprint Development Techniques, second ed. Home Office, London.

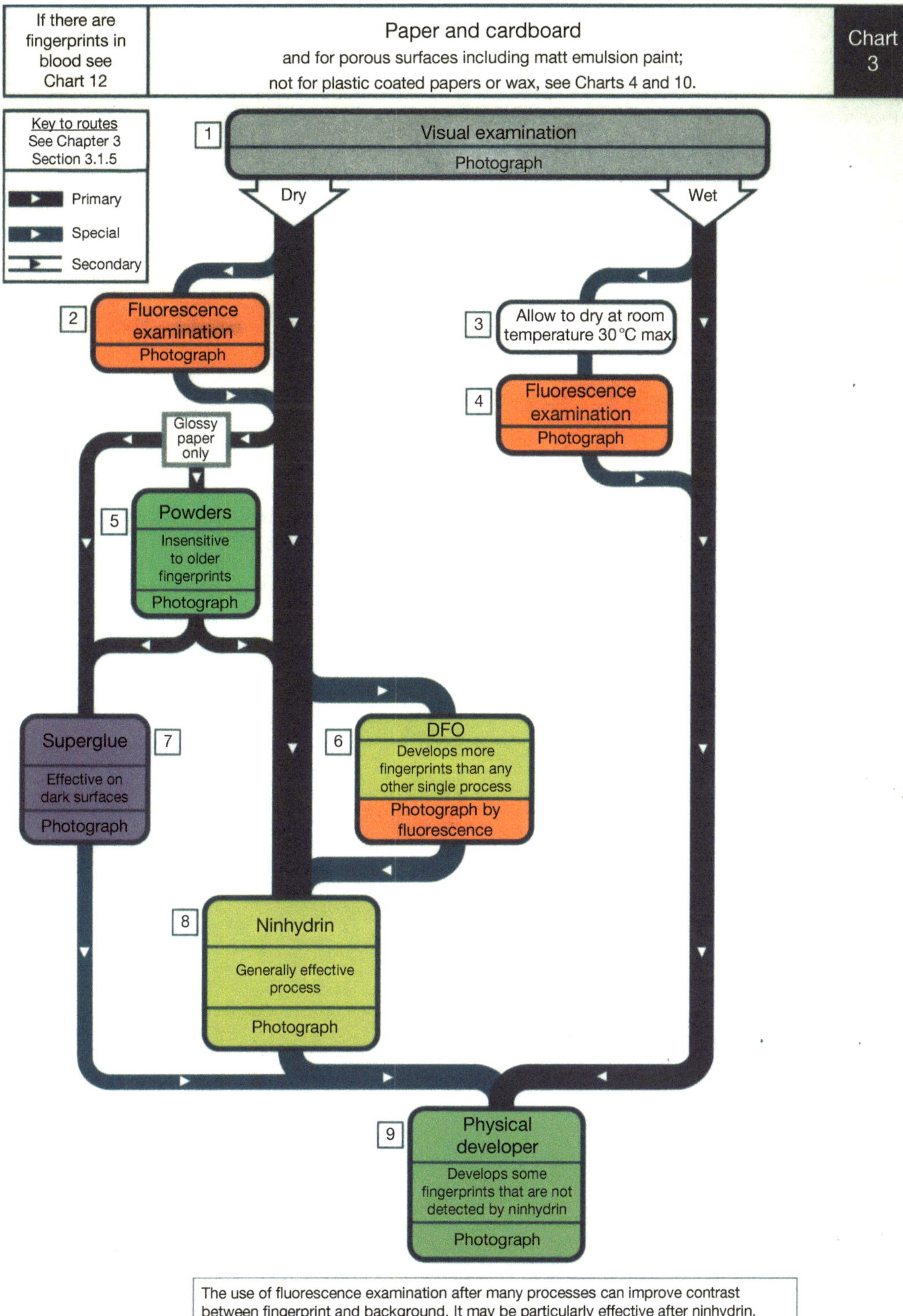

Figure 2 Process selection chart for paper and cardboard surfaces. From Kent, T. (Ed.), 1998. Manual of Fingerprint Development Techniques, second ed. Home Office, London.

thread density of around three threads per millimeter is necessary to have any chance of recording sufficient information for characteristics in a fingerprint to be resolved.

If hands or fingers are contaminated with dirt, blood, or other materials there may be more chance of usable fingerprints being developed and there are significant numbers of cases of fingerprints in blood on fabrics being of operational value (e.g., Washington v. Hayden, 1995).

Skin

There is no generally accepted effective method for developing latent fingerprints on live or recently dead skin. There have been a number of trials of techniques for the detection of latent fingerprints on cadavers, recently Trapecar and Balazic in Slovenia examined a number of methods. There have been similar trials in Canada, the United Kingdom, and Germany. Techniques tried have included lifting and transfer methods with silver plates and iodine, glossy paper and magnetic black powder, and direct powdering techniques. Treatment with superglue has also been tried. The few-claimed successes are not well documented and in at least one case, reports indicated that this was due to contamination of the suspect's hands with oil.

In principle, fingerprints in blood on skin could be potentially of value although there are no generally available reported cases.

See also: **Pattern Evidence/Fingerprints (Dactyloscopy):** Visualization or Development of Crime Scene Fingerprints.

Further Reading

Bowman, V. (Ed.), 2004. Manual of Fingerprint Development Techniques, second ed. Home Office, Police Scientific Development Branch, London, ISBN 1 85893 972 0.
Kent, T., 2010. Standardizing protocols for fingerprint reagent testing. Journal of Forensic Identification 60 (3), 371.
Merrick, S., Gardner, S., Sears, V., Hewlett, D., 2002. An operational trial of ozone-friendly DFO and 1,2-indanedione formulations for latent fingerprint detection. Journal of Forensic Identification 52 (5), 595–605.
Olsen Sr., R.D., 1978. Scott's Fingerprint Mechanics. Charles C. Thomas, Springfield, IL.
Ramatowski, R. (Ed.), 2009. Lee and Gaensslen's Advances in Fingerprint Technology, third ed. CRC Press, Boca Raton. ISBN-13:9781420088342.
Stoilovic, M., Lennard, C., Wallace-Kunkel, C., Roux, C., 2007. Evaluation of a 1,2--indanedione formulation containing zinc chloride for improved fingermark detection on paper. Journal of Forensic Identification 57 (1), 4–18.

Relevant Websites

http://www.enfsi.eu—European National Forensic Institute Site.
http://www.fbi.gov—FBI Website.
http://onin.com—Fingerprints/Biometrics: Everything You Ever Wanted to Know About Fingerprints, Palmprints and Other Means of Identifying Persons by Physical Traits.
http://www.latent-prints.com—Latent Prints: home page.
http://www.nij.gov—Scientific Working Group on Friction Ridge Analysis, Study and Technology (SWGFAST) (2011).
http://www.fpsociety.org.uk—The Fingerprint Society.
http://www.theiai.org—The International Association for Identification.
http://www.nij.gov—US National Institute of Justice SWGFAST Fingerprint Sourcebook.
http://www.nij.gov—US National Institute of Justice Website.

Visualization or Development of Crime Scene Fingerprints

T Kent, University of Lincoln, Lincoln, UK

Glossary

Automatic fingerprint recognition (AFR) and automatic fingerprint identification systems (AFIS) These systems encode fingerprint images, generally by locating the positions, relative angles, and ridge counts between fingerprint minutiae or characteristics. This enables database searching for likely matches.

CCD and CMOS These are two types of solid-state digital imaging sensors with subtly different characteristics and are used in modern digital cameras.

Eccrine sweat This is exuded by the eccrine glands which are located over most of the body, but the highest concentration is on the palmar surfaces of the hands, the soles of the feet, and the scalp.

Minutiae, characteristics, or Galton details These are ridge endings and bifurcations, or forks.

Sebaceous sweat This is exuded by sebaceous glands which are located in various densities over most parts of the body with the exception of the palmar surfaces of the hands and the soles of the feet.

Introduction

Fingerprints are widely associated with the identification of offenders in many types of major and minor crimes; although in recent years, DNA trace evidence has made an increasingly important and high-profile contribution to criminal identifications.

This increasing use of DNA analysis of swabs from crime scenes, while important, has not diminished the need for fingerprint examination. Generally, DNA analysis is still significantly more expensive, and does not necessarily prove actual contact between suspect and object. DNA is, however, capable of providing crucial identification evidence in some circumstances when there are no suitable surfaces available for fingerprint examination. The two techniques are therefore complementary, although generally in most countries fingerprints currently still produce more identifications.

Increased usage of forensic databases and crime-linking and data analysis tools allows combinations of fingerprints, DNA, footwear, toolmarks, and other data such as modus operandi to link multiple crime scenes with offenders.

Efficient and effective visualization, referred to more commonly as development or enhancement, of latent fingerprints, is therefore a vital part of the forensic examination of a crime scene and of exhibits removed from crime scenes. It is important that it is carried out in a careful and methodical manner with due regard to preserving DNA and other evidence.

Origins of Fingerprint Deposits

The papillary ridges of the fingers, the palms, and the soles of the feet have located in them rows of sweat pores linked to eccrine sweat glands and they exude aqueous eccrine sweat in varying amounts. The fingers and palms are naturally in intermittent contact with other parts of the body, due to normal human behavior patterns, including the hair and face of an individual. These areas have traces of oily or greasy sebaceous sweat originating from sebaceous glands which are found in greatest abundance on the face and the scalp, some of this sebaceous sweat transfers to the fingers and palms resulting in these surfaces bearing a mixture of sebaceous and eccrine sweat. There may also be material from apocrine glands, which are restricted to the axillae, areola, and genitoanal regions. Although the division of aqueous and fatty deposit into clearly separate phases, or droplets, may often be observed microscopically, it is likely that some of the deposit is actually in the form of an emulsion.

This mixture, or emulsion, does not have any particular, fixed distribution and will contain hundreds of compounds in various concentrations, which depend on the climatic conditions, an individual's biochemistry, habits, lifestyle, and recent behavior such as hand washing.

Sometimes, the fingers and hands of a suspect may be contaminated with materials which do not have a bodily origin such as foodstuffs, soaps, cosmetics, industrial chemicals, and other materials from the environment.

 http://dx.doi.org/10.1016/B978-0-12-800573-6.00007-0

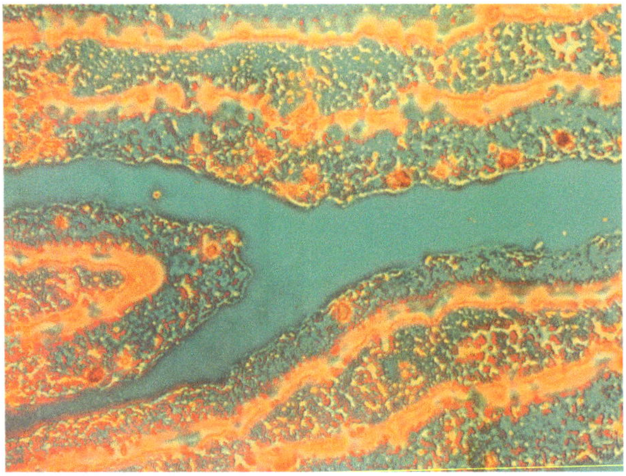

Figure 1 Enlargement of part of an interference micrograph of a fingerprint on a glass surface—colors are created within the microscope. Courtesy: UK Home Office.

When the ridges of the fingers, palms, or feet touch a surface, they will transfer some of this mixture of chemicals to that surface—an example of Locard's exchange principle that "every contact leaves a trace." Depending on the pressure and direction of contact, and the nature of the surface, some of the deposit may be in the form of a pattern reproducing the ridges on the skin surface.

These deposits are not usually in simple continuous lines but on smooth nonporous surfaces are usually in the form of a distribution of retracted droplets of various sizes on a thin film which may be only a few molecules thick. On porous surfaces, such as paper, wicking action results in the more mobile constituents being absorbed into the surface (**Figures 1 and 2**).

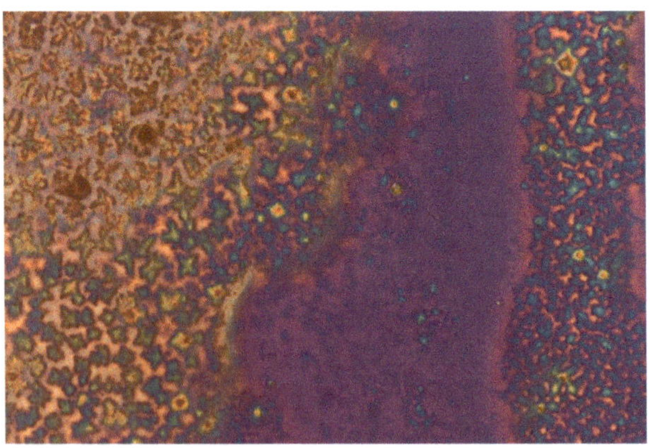

Figure 2 Enlargement of part of an interference micrograph of a fingerprint with a very high eccrine sweat content which has dried out on a glass surface showing salt crystals—colors are created within the microscope. Courtesy: UK Home Office.

Fingermarks may also contain solid matter such as dead skin cells shed from the hands and dust from the environment.

At some crime scenes, there may be gross contamination resulting in most of the fingerprint deposit being blood, grease, oil, drugs, explosives, and so on.

Fingerprint Patterns, Characteristics, and Details

When fingermarks are to be developed or enhanced, in order that identifications may be made for judicial purposes, they must contain sufficient detail for comparison with record prints. This usually necessitates sufficient area of two or more of the following levels of details:

1. the overall ridge flow pattern, namely loop, arch, whorl, and so on,
2. characteristics, also known as Galton details or minutiae, essentially the patterns left by papillary ridge terminations and bifurcations, and
3. the so-called third-level details which may encompass finer details of pore distribution, ridge width, ridge shape, and minor papillary ridge irregularities.

The development technique chosen may affect the amount or quality of information produced at these three levels.

Imaging of Developed Fingerprints

Until the end of the twentieth century, fingerprints would normally be photographed using film cameras of various formats. The resulting negatives would then be used to produce "life-size" hard copy prints on black-and-white photographic paper. Usually, the procedure was to produce such prints so that the ridges were black and the inter ridge spaces white; for detailed comparison and court presentation work, five times life-size enlargements would usually be printed.

Now, imaging, or recording, is virtually entirely carried out using digital cameras or scanners. The capture systems may then download the digital image into an automatic fingerprint identification system (AFIS); when necessary, life-size, or enlarged, prints can be produced, normally still in black and white.

Image quality is important and in digital systems is controlled by a number of factors:

1. the quality of the charged coupled device (CCD) or complementary metal-oxide semiconductor (CMOS) imaging chip;
2. the effective pixel count per millimeter in the image plane;
3. the quality of the optical system; and
4. correct exposure and focus.

Lossy image compression techniques will also reduce the amount of information in the image and algorithms must be carefully assessed before adoption.

Image scale is also important, different AFIS may tolerate varying amounts of distortion, but images should generally be captured within a linear tolerance of 1% or 2% to maximize hit rates.

It is good practice always to incorporate a scale into captured images unless fixed-focus camera systems are used.

Development or Visualization of Latent Fingerprints

Many fingerprints are still retrieved at crime scenes with simple powdering techniques, which have changed little over several decades. There are, however, an increasing number of more sophisticated and sensitive processes which may sometimes be used at crime scenes, but which are more commonly applied in specialist fingerprint enhancement laboratories to which articles are sent. Studies in some law enforcement agencies have shown that half, or more, of the operationally useful fingerprints are now produced in such laboratories.

The wide range of chemicals which are likely to be present in fingermarks provides scope for many different chemical and physical reactions to be exploited. The amounts of material present, however, are very small, usually nanogram quantities, and some individuals leave exceptionally small amounts of deposit. Developing such latent fingerprints is a difficult technical challenge and presents problems which are at the extremes of current methods of detection.

Not only do we want to detect the components on a variety of surfaces but we need to map them so that we produce a high-quality image of their distribution on a surface.

Latent Fingerprint Chemical Constituents

While many studies have been carried out into the chemical constitution of sebaceous and eccrine sweat there are rather fewer of the actual deposits left by a finger on a surface. This is due partly to the technical challenges in analyzing the sub-nanogram quantities of components. One significant early review was carried out by Cuthbertson in the 1960s; he also carried out some early measurements of chloride content. More recently, Croxton in 2008 analyzed the content of actual fingerprints rather than sweat.

From our knowledge of sebaceous and eccrine sweat, we would expect some of the materials in **Table 1** to be in a fingerprint.

Amounts of deposit vary widely within and between donors. A significant proportion of the original mass of some eccrine-rich fingermarks is actually thought to be water, which on a nonporous surface may evaporate over the first few hours or days depending on ambient temperature. Trapping of the aqueous component in a fatty matrix or emulsion may be responsible for some observed differences in evaporation rates.

Table 1 Latent fingerprint constituents—after Cuthbertson

Gland type	*Inorganic constituents*	*Organic constituents*
Eccrine	Chlorides	Amino acids
	Sodium	Urea
	Potassium	Lactic acid
	Ammonia	Sugars
	Sulfates	Creatinine
	Phosphates	Choline
		Uric acid
Apocrine	Iron	Proteins
		Carbohydrates
		Cholesterol
Sebaceous	–	Fatty acids
		Glycerides
		Hydrocarbons
		Alcohols

On a porous surface such as paper, this water will assist in the diffusion of some of the constituents into the surface. Studies in the early 1970s by Thomas indicated that on nonporous surfaces, many fingerprints lost significant volume by evaporation over the first few days after deposition (**Figure 3**).

Operational Methods of Visualizing Fingerprints

There are published papers on hundreds of chemical reagents and other techniques which are claimed to visualize latent fingerprints. Operational trials and experience have shown, however, that only around 15 basic techniques produce significant numbers of usable fingerprints under realistic crime scene conditions. We will not therefore include here the wide spectrum of possible techniques but rather focus on those which have so far been developed to the stage of being operationally of significant value and implemented successfully.

Some reagents have been used in dozens, or even hundreds, of formulations and it is important that optimum formulations and treatment protocols are established and adhered to. Much of the research effort expended has been in refining formulations and procedures to optimize techniques. Subtle changes in solvent systems, humidity, or heating regimes can make substantial differences to the numbers of fingerprints developed with some methods.

When new techniques are discovered, it is important that they are compared against existing techniques in a thorough manner using realistic sample fingermarks from a range of donors.

Some researchers have used "groomed" or "enhanced" fingermarks by touching the nose or forehead before depositing test prints. This procedure cannot be relied upon to give an indication of operational performance. Recent research has

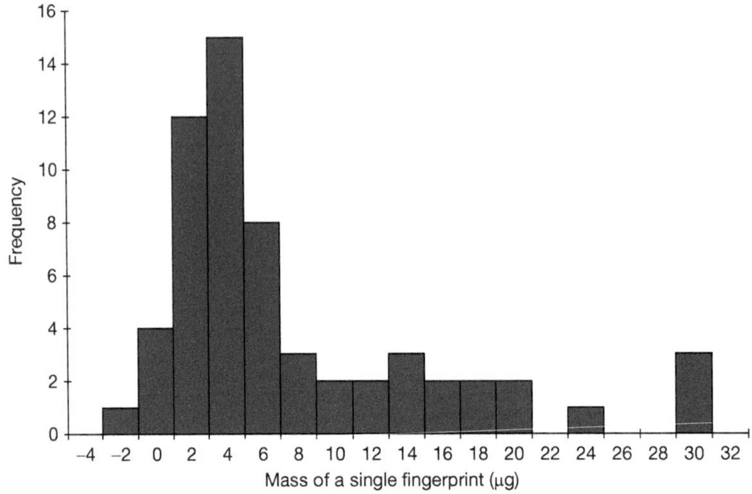

Figure 3 Distribution of the mass (μg) of a single latent fingerprint. Reproduced from Croxton, R.S., 2008. Analysis of Latent Fingerprint Components by Gas Chromatography-Mass Spectrometry (Ph.D. thesis). University of Lincoln, UK.

shown that the lipid content of such groomed fingerprints may be many times that of a typical operational fingerprint (**Table 2**).

Fingerprint development or enhancement techniques fall into five broad categories:

1. Chemical reagents which react with a known constituent or class of constituents of latent fingerprints stoichiometrically; with these techniques, the intensity of the reaction is quantitative and directly proportional to the amounts of the specific compounds in the latent fingerprint.
2. Chemical or physical agents which are absorbed, or adhere to, or undergo some other nonspecific interaction with a class of compounds in the fingermark. Generally speaking, the reaction is approximately proportional to the amount of deposit present.
3. Chemical reagents which rely on a component of the fingermark to catalyze a chain reaction, which leads to a nonlinear enhancement or amplification of the fingerprint.
4. Chemical or physical agents which are designed to target known contaminants such as blood or grease and used if these are seen on the surface under examination.
5. Optical techniques which rely on the absorption, scattering, polarization, or fluorescence effects on radiation, which we can speak of as light, but which may be anywhere in the spectrum from the far ultraviolet (200 nm) to near the infrared (2 μm).

Some developmental procedures are actually multistep, involving development and enhancement techniques where the initial reaction produces a low visibility product, which is then enhanced by a further step or steps.

Table 2 Fatty acid and squalene composition of latent fingerprint samples (nanograms per single fingerprint)

Constituent	*"Natural" fingerprint (mean (s.d.))*	*"Groomed" fingerprint (mean (s.d.))*
Dodecanoic acid	14.96 (11.26)	51.09 (41.75)
Tetradecanoic acid	33.77 (9.72)	124.77 (115.24)
Pentadecanoic acid	16.08 (6.71)	89.27 (85.82)
Hexadecanoic acid	141.26 (43.64)	468.46 (340.73)
Octadecanoic acid	46.47 (27.68)	122.11 (65.94)
Octadecenoic acid	66.71 (27.96)	229.84 (175.78)
Squalene	125.08 (80.52)	1426.31 (1236.49)

$n = 18$ donors aged between 18 and 57 and consisting of 9 males and 9 females.
Source: Croxton, R.S., 2008. Analysis of Latent Fingerprint Components by Gas Chromatography-Mass Spectrometry (Ph.D. thesis). University of Lincoln, UK.

Choice of Technique

Generally, the most significant factor influencing the choice of process will be the surface to be examined. Smooth, solid, essentially nonporous surfaces such as glass retain a "sticky" latent fingerprint residue on the surface which may be detected by careful application of powders, although there are other techniques which may be more sensitive.

Porous surfaces such as paper or cardboard absorb varying amounts of the sebaceous and eccrine deposit and visualization may be best achieved by more specific chromogenic reagents; for example, those which react with amino acids.

Some plastic surfaces present problems which are midway between the nonporous and porous classes.

Some surfaces which are frequently handled can prove difficult for the investigator due to the buildup over time of a background level of the constituents of eccrine and sebaceous sweat; examples are door handles and credit cards.

Other factors which can affect choice of process are as follows:

1. Facilities available.
2. Importance of the case.
3. Possible age of the fingerprints of interest—days, weeks, or months.
4. Ambient conditions and the likely exposure to sun and rain and contamination from the environment.
5. Presence of contaminants in the fingerprint such as grease or blood which may make up a significant part of the deposit.
6. The need to carry out other forensic examinations including sampling for DNA, explosives, fibers, drugs, and so on. Documents may require examination of handwriting or indented writing. Some fingerprint development techniques can interfere with some of these procedures, so the correct sequence of examination is important.

Packaging and Handling of Evidence

It must be understood that any handling of exhibits from crime scenes, whether or not while wearing gloves, carries a risk of damaging latent fingerprints. Even superimposing, folding, or sliding surfaces together will have some effect on the fingerprint deposit if it is on a smooth, nonporous surface such as polythene or a weapon such as a gun or knife. Porous surfaces such as paper absorb much of the deposit into the surface, so careful handling is much less likely to cause damage. Hard, smooth items should preferably be tied, or wired down into boxes, and never carried in evidence bags.

Operational Fingerprint Development Processes

The processes that will be described here include most of the methods currently considered to be most productive and operationally effective. Brief details of each process, and where known, some details of the possible reactions and materials detected are given. Other similar variants are also listed but detailed formulations are available elsewhere, so no specific formulations are given here.

Most are reagents for the usual constituents of latent fingerprints where the material on the fingers is primarily eccrine and sebaceous sweat.

Four additional reagents—amido black, acid yellow 1, acid violet 17, and solvent black 3—are included, of which the first three are used for enhancing blood and the last for greases or fats from nonsweat sources. These are used when there is an indication that any fingerprints present may be significantly contaminated with such materials.

Optical techniques, which may be used before or after chemical treatments, are described separately.

Health and Safety Procedures

Some constituents of some reagent formulations present significant health and safety issues, including high flammability and toxicity by ingestion, by inhalation, or in some cases by skin absorption; for example, methanol. Safe working practices have been developed for most reagents but competent expert advice must be sought before implementing any chemical enhancement technique.

There are potentially serious eye safety considerations with many light sources used for fluorescence examination and even some used for white light examination. Hardwick and others published the only significant study of these sources in 1990; users should never look into the beam of such sources.

Local regulations and standard operating procedures must be complied with.

1,8-Diazafluoren-9-one

1,8-Diazafluoren-9-one (DFO) is a very effective reagent for amino acids in fingermarks and was proposed in 1990 by Grigg, although the chemical had been synthesized by CIBA in 1950. It reacts with amino acids from eccrine sweat, usually producing only a faintly pink-colored visible reaction product. The reaction product is, however, strongly fluorescent and, overall, the method is more sensitive than ninhydrin if exhibits are examined and photographed with the correct combination of excitation and viewing wavelengths.

The absorption and emission maxima are close with only a small Stoke's shift. Exhibits are usually best illuminated between 525 and 550 nm and viewed or photographed with a short-wave cutoff filter transmitting above about 560 nm.

Articles are dipped into a solution containing DFO, acetic acid, and a carrier solvent mixture. They are then heated in a dry oven at 100 °C for 20 min. As with most amino acid reagents, the precise combination of solvents dramatically affects the operational success rates observed.

DFO is generally used on the same types of porous substrates as ninhydrin, primarily paper, and cardboard. It does not develop all of the fingermarks detected by the latter, so additional fingerprints may be produced by subsequent treatment with ninhydrin.

If humidified conditions are used during the heating of DFO-treated articles, no fingerprints are detected (cf. ninhydrin).

As amino acids are soluble in water, reagents such as DFO, ninhydrin, or indanedione are ineffective on surfaces which have been wetted or exposed to very high humidities.

DFO is not usually used at scenes of crime as it is difficult to generate sufficient heat in a room to produce an acceptable rate of fingermark development although local heating can be used for small areas. It is similar in performance to some indanedione formulations which incorporate zinc and is widely used.

Gun Bluing and Similar Metal-Toning Treatments

Latent fingerprints usually have a significant proportion of sebaceous, or oily or fatty, components. This can provide a protective layer on some surfaces such as metals, and chemical toning techniques can be used to discolor the areas not protected by the fingerprints, thus rendering the latter visible. A number of commercial gun-bluing solutions have been used on cartridge cases and some other surfaces with variable success. Similar methods using selenic acid or sulfides or other metal toners or etching solutions have been reported and some are in operational use.

Iodine Vapor Fuming

The observation that iodine fumes could be used to both detect handwriting alterations and develop latent fingerprints was reported by Coulier in 1863; methods of application were described in the literature in 1891 and 1912.

A temporary faint purple to brown stain is created which fades in minutes or hours although it may be enhanced, or fixed, by a number of techniques including starch powder or alpha-naphthoflavone applied in solution. Various iodine fuming chambers or "guns" have been used to treat paper or other porous or nonporous exhibits. It is most effective on fresh fingermarks that are hours or days old.

The vapor process is little used now partly due to the intensely corrosive and toxic nature of iodine but also because several techniques have generally surpassed it in terms of sensitivity.

The mechanism is not fully understood and may involve more than one reaction. It appears to be readily reversible and it has been proposed that it may be a reaction with unsaturated fats, a physical absorption by lipids, or a reaction with aqueous components.

Indanedione

In the late 1990s, the reaction of fingermark amino acids with indanedione was explored by researchers at the University of Pennsylvania. It is similar in application to DFO and reacts to form a faintly colored, but fluorescent, product. The original formulations were found to be operationally less effective than DFO during substantial trials in 2002 in the United Kingdom by West Midlands Police.

If treated subsequently with zinc, or other heavy metal-toning solution, a substantial increase in fluorescence is achieved with a resulting increase in numbers of fingerprints of value detected.

Recently, incorporation of zinc salts into the indanedione primary reagent solution, by Stoilovic and others in Australia, and use as a single treatment, has produced a very effective reagent with a performance comparable to DFO followed by ninhydrin.

The treatment protocol is similar to ninhydrin or DFO, involving briefly dipping exhibits in the solution followed by heating either in an oven or a press; the former is more controllable. Various solvent formulations have been proposed and as with most amino acid reagents they have a critical effect on operational performance.

Some workers have recorded improved results in a humidified oven if the ambient humidity is low but more research is probably needed.

There are a number of published spectra for reaction with specific amino acids but there are few data on optimum excitation and emission for typical fingerprints although most workers illuminate in the green/yellow region and observe in the orange/red.

It is now quite widely used as an alternative to DFO and, as a single treatment, can replace the DFO–ninhydrin combination.

Ninhydrin

Ninhydrin was proposed by Oden in the 1950s as a reagent for detecting fingermarks. After the publication of the Crown formulation in 1969, and others, it became the most widely used reagent on paper, cardboard, and some other porous materials such as raw smooth wood. It is chromogenic, producing a purple reaction, Ruhemann's purple, with some amino acids. Various formulations have been developed with a range of solvents from flammable petroleum ether and chlorofluorocarbons to the more recently introduced hydrofluoroethers. The solvent system and pH significantly affect the operational performance, and the most effective formulations incorporate acetic acid. Where written documents are to be processed, it is important to consider the effects of solvents and possible ink running and loss of indented impressions.

Articles are dipped into a solution containing ninhydrin, acetic acid, and the carrier solvent mixture and allowed to dry. For best results, they should then be heated at 80 °C for 3–4 min at 65% relative humidity (**Figure 4**).

The developed purple-colored fingerprints can be easily photographed in white light but a green filter is often used to improve contrast on some colored backgrounds.

Ninhydrin can be very effectively used at scenes of crime, with the same formulation being brushed onto the surfaces. Sealing

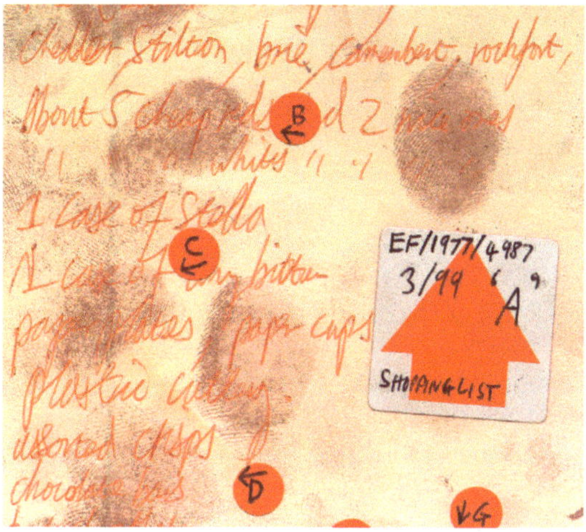

Figure 4 Document with a number of ninhydrin-developed fingerprints. Courtesy: UK Home Office.

the room and raising the temperature with domestic heaters will assist fingerprint development but it may take several days as it is difficult to control the temperature and humidity.

When ninhydrin develops fingermarks on dark nonfluorescent backgrounds, or when the background is a very similar color to the fingerprint, zinc chloride toning solution can be applied and the exhibit gently heated to produce fluorescent fingerprints, which can then be photographed.

Physical Developer

This is essentially a stabilized silver-plating solution, which may be used on porous surfaces such as paper, cardboard, and wood. Jonkers and others at the Philips Eindhoven Laboratory published details of a solution for depositing silver onto printed circuit boards. Morris and others at the UK AWRE laboratory found that some long-lasting and persistent constituents of latent fingerprints would trigger the deposition of silver microspherules although there is still speculation as to which materials these are. It was found that as a fingerprint reagent it was capable of developing fingermarks on articles which have been soaked in water or exposed to rain.

It is a relatively slow multibath treatment but it has shown considerable operational success on old and wetted paper items. Items must be soaked in distilled water and washed in dilute acids such as maleic, to reduce background reaction, before carefully controlled treatment with the silver solution.

The reagent is an aqueous solution of silver nitrate containing an Fe(II)/Fe(III) redox couple and two detergents. Subsequently, excess silver salts must be thoroughly washed out before drying. All glassware must be extremely clean to prevent triggering of the silver deposition.

The developed fingerprints are a light to medium gray in color and can be recorded using conventional photography. The exact reaction mechanism is unknown; it was thought that it was developing some of the heavier fats and waxes although it is possible that trapped chloride ions in sebaceous deposits could play a part.

Fingerprints developed by the physical developer may be enhanced by conversion to a radioactive sulfide and autoradiography, or X-ray mapping in an electron beam instrument.

Powders

Powders are probably the oldest and most common techniques for the enhancement of latent fingerprints; Forgeot and others were experimenting with different powders in the latter part of the nineteenth century. In the early decades of the twentieth century, many powder combinations were in use including toxic mercury and chalk mixtures (hydrargyrum–cum–creta), and oxides of lead, and many other less toxic materials such as carbon and natural materials such as *Lycopodium* and dragon's blood.

Many types of powders and brushes have been used over the intervening years and hundreds of combinations are commercially available.

Powders with a flat, flake-like, structure, such as milled aluminum or brass, for example molybdenum disulfide, are among the more sensitive and are generally quite effective at developing fingerprints on smooth, clean surfaces. Stearic acid or similar fats are commonly added during the milling process of aluminum and it is thought that this may contribute to the sensitivity of the technique. A milled iron flake powder was developed at the University of Swansea in the late 1990s for application with a magnetic "wand" and is quite effective particularly on unplasticized polyvinyl chloride window frames. Other magnetic powders based on iron or nickel have been available for many years.

Aluminum and some other flake powders can be applied effectively with glass fiber or fine synthetic brushes. Fine black carbon-based powders are best applied with soft synthetic or animal hair brushes and trials have indicated that some of the fine carbon black powders are of similar sensitivity to flake powders.

Flake powders are usually lifted with transparent adhesive tape or commercial tacky "lifters," for scanning or photography, this assists with the removal of background and simplifies recording. Other powders may be lifted or photographed in situ.

If sensitive flake powders are used on surfaces which are dirty or contaminated, sometimes too much will deposit obscuring any fingerprints. In such cases, granular black or white powders may be more suitable, even if slightly less sensitive. Rough or grained surfaces may sometimes be treated using iron, cobalt, or nickel-based powders used with a magnetic applicator although other processes may be more suitable.

Many fluorescent powders have been proposed for use with suitable light sources, and is referred to in several books on fingerprinting techniques, including that by Bridges in 1942, many of which are currently marketed. Although these may improve contrast between fingerprint and multicolored surfaces, some fluorescent powders are less sensitive than established nonfluorescent powders, probably due to their physical shape and size.

Powders may be used on surfaces which have been wetted, but only after the articles have been thoroughly dried at temperatures not exceeding 30 °C.

The performance of powders generally deteriorates with the age of the latent fingerprint but occasionally very old ones are detected by this means; they are therefore not a reliable indicator of time since a latent fingerprint was deposited.

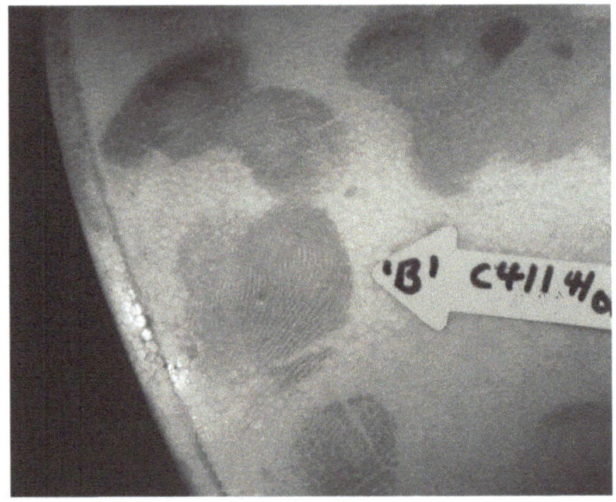

Figure 5 Fingermarks on a polystyrene cup developed with small particle reagent. Courtesy: UK Home Office.

Powder Suspensions

Although commonly referred to as suspensions, they are actually rather viscous mixtures of fine nontoxic powders such as iron oxide, carbon black, or titanium dioxide with a surfactant and various proportions of water. Bratton and others reported the use of a viscous mixture of black fingerprint powder and detergent for the development of fingermarks on the adhesive side of tapes in the mid-1990s.

Several such powder suspensions or pastes were proposed or marketed under various names including "Sticky-Side Powder™" for use on the adhesive side of adhesive tapes. They were usually based on mixtures of black fingerprint powder with surfactant and water. A fairly thick paste of the powder is applied to the adhesive side of the tape, either by dipping or careful brushing. The solution is left in contact with the tape for 10–15 s and then washed off under running water, resulting in gray to black images, which can be recorded using conventional photography.

Subsequently, it has been found that such suspensions can be very effective on many smooth surfaces but particle size and shape are critical, as is the surfactant. Formulations using white and other colored or fluorescent powders have also been developed.

The process is becoming more widely used although further research is needed. They are easily applied in a laboratory where exhibits can be washed in a sink but more difficult at crime scenes where they cause gross contamination and require considerable cleanup.

Small Particle Reagent

Small particle reagent was developed by Morris and others at the Aldermaston Weapons Research Establishments in the United Kingdom in 1978, the original formulation being based on gray molybdenum disulfide flake in water and surfactant. Concentrations of powder and surfactant were much lower than the more recently developed powder suspensions, so the reagent has a very low viscosity, similar to water. It is most effectively applied in a tank in which the powder is agitated prior to immersion of the object to be treated. The main surface of interest should be uppermost, on which the powder is allowed to settle, then excess powder is carefully rinsed off and the exhibit is allowed to dry (**Figure 5**).

The grade of molybdenum disulphide is critical to its effectiveness. The Forensic Science Service in the United Kingdom promoted a spray version of the molybdenum disulphide version for use on wet cars, but it proved to be far less sensitive than the immersion process. Other researchers have developed white and fluorescent versions although in tests none has matched the original formulation for sensitivity.

Basic Violet 3 (Gentian Violet, Crystal Violet, CI 42555)

The use of aniline dyes for staining latent fingerprints was patented in the United States by Bock in 1917. A very effective formulation of Basic Violet 3 in phenol and ethanol solution was reported by the Italian Police in the late 1960s and has been used widely since the 1970s for the detection of latent fingerprints on the adhesive side of tapes. The reagent stains latent fingerprints purple and is usually applied by floating the tape on the surface of the solution with the adhesive side down. The tape is then washed in running water and dried. Fingerprints may then be photographed if the tape is light in color.

Increasing usage of black electrical tapes on improvised explosive devices resulted in the development of a technique by

Kent in 1978 for transferring the image onto fixed, washed, and dried photographic paper.

Low concentrations of Basic Violet 3 in fingerprint deposits will fluoresce in the far red if illuminated with yellow light.

Concerns over the toxicity of phenol by skin absorption have resulted in the development of a number of surfactant-based formulations omitting phenol. Some of these, particularly those using aerosol OT surfactant, show similar or better performance than the original. Recent developments of powder suspensions have, however, reduced the usage of dye techniques on adhesive tapes.

Superglue

The reaction of the vapor of ethyl or methyl cyanoacrylate with latent fingerprint deposits appears to have been noticed independently in Japan in around 1977, and in subsequent years in Canada and the United Kingdom, as the Japanese discovery was not initially revealed in the West.

Fingermarks exposed to the vapor were observed to produce a white deposit of cyanoacrylate polymer, usually after a few hours although sometimes extended development times of up to 24 h were used. Kendall and others reported heating superglue to speed up the reaction in the early 1980s (**Figure 6**).

Research by the UK Home Office established that by raising the humidity to 80% and the glue temperature to around 120 °C, fingerprints development was much more rapid and even older fingermarks would often develop in about 20 min. These conditions were recommended in the Home Office Fingerprint Manual of 1986 after microscopic studies and extensive trials (**Figure 7**).

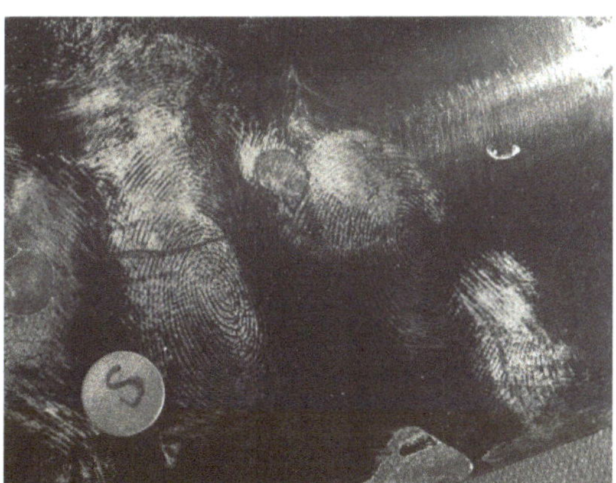

Figure 6 Plastic molding with a number of superglue-developed fingerprints. Courtesy: UK Home Office.

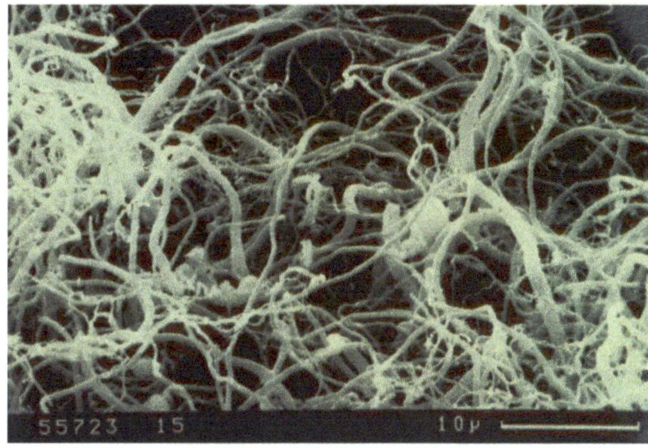

Figure 7 Electron micrograph of superglue-developed fingerprints. Courtesy: UK Home Office.

Elevation of the relative humidity to around 80% causes sodium chloride in latent fingerprints to take up water, forming minute droplets along the lines of the deposit. Other components in the deposit may be responsible for raising the pH and accelerating the reaction, which usually results in a white growth of "cotton wool" or "noodle-like" growth of microscopically fine fibers. Use of an aluminum container reduces the amount of cyanoacrylate, which polymerizes in the source vessel.

On many surfaces, the white deposit may simply be photographed by scattered light but enhancement with fluorescent dyes such as Rhodamine 6G was soon introduced by Menzel and others in 1983 with methanol as a solvent, and has been widely used since although methanol should not be used due to its high toxicity. In 1986, the UK Home Office introduced the use of Basic Yellow 40 in ethanol as a nontoxic extremely efficient fluorescent dye for superglue-developed fingerprints. Brief immersion followed by gentle washing in water and drying results in strongly fluorescent fingerprints which may be illuminated in the blue region and observed in the yellow region, making photography easier on some surfaces.

The exact nature of the initiation and growth process of the polycyanoacrylate is not well understood although several studies have examined possible mechanisms and initiators.

The technique has been exploited widely since its discovery with several types of commercial cabinets available, and several incorporating facilities to raise the humidity. It is a quick simple method for many types of plastic film, plastic moldings, and polystyrene foam and has been used on a wide range of other surfaces experimentally and operationally.

Fingermark development is also observed under vacuum conditions and was first reported by Watkins in 1989, although the fingerprints developed do not show the characteristic "noodle-like" growth, instead appearing as transparent glassy deposits which must then be enhanced with fluorescent dyes. It is generally agreed that this method is significantly less effective operationally as it has lower sensitivity with less uptake of dyes by the glassy deposits.

Several researchers, including Weaver in 1993, have attempted, so far unsuccessfully, to synthesize a modified cyanoacrylate which is inherently fluorescent.

Vacuum Metal Deposition

This method is derived from a commercial process for coating surfaces with thin layers of metal or dielectric materials. It is carried out under vacuum and involves the thermal evaporation of metals onto the surface to be examined.

The process had been known for many years to be susceptible to fingerprint contamination, and in industry, degreasing procedures are used before glass or plastic items are coated with materials such as aluminum or chrome.

In 1964, Tolansky suggested that this technique might be of operational forensic value; in 1968, Theys in France proposed its use for detection of fingerprints on paper. Hambley, in 1972 at Royal Holloway College, investigated the behavior of a wide range of single metal and metal combinations. The use of gold followed by cadmium was then developed by Kent in the UK Home Office initially as an operational technique for the fingerprint treatment of low-density polyethylene bags and wrappings; due to health and safety concerns, cadmium was replaced by zinc in the early 1980s (**Figure 8**).

It is extremely sensitive, sometimes too sensitive, and it has been shown that a monolayer of fatty acid can sometimes inhibit metal film growth. It has found fingerprints in cases where polythene wrappings have been underwater for long periods of time.

The object being treated is placed inside a large metal chamber, most of the air is evacuated reducing the pressure to between 2 and 4×10^{-4} mbar, and metals are evaporated sequentially onto the surface. The generally recommended method for fingermarks on polythene is the evaporation of a few milligrams of gold from a molybdenum filament heated to a bright yellow to white heat, at about 1000 °C. A larger quantity of zinc is then evaporated from a molybdenum trough heated to a dull red at about 450 °C; the evaporated zinc deposits onto available gold nuclei and produces a gray image. Any developed fingerprints may appear as positive or negative images as the film growth is modified by surface contamination. The differential rates of film growth on substrate and fingerprint may be due to differences in gold nuclei size or penetration of the nuclei into the surface.

Figure 8 Vacuum metal deposition-developed fingerprints using gold and zinc on low-density polyethylene. Courtesy: UK Home Office.

The process has been used very effectively operationally on polythene packaging. Experiments to apply the method on fabrics in the 1980s yielded some results with fresh fingerprints on finely woven fabrics but no operational successes during limited trials.

Silver can be used as a single metal treatment and may be effective on some types of cling film. Coating of some types of recycled plastics is difficult and some other techniques such as powder suspensions are more effective.

Development of Contaminated Fingermarks

Fingermarks in Blood

If a fingermark on a porous surface looks as if it may consist of some eccrine sweat and some blood, amino acid reagents such as ninhydrin, DFO, and indanedione may be very effective. On nonporous surfaces, acid black, acid yellow 7, or acid violet 17 are most effective for detection of the bloody component.

Many tests and dyes for blood have been reported in the literature.

Acid black 1 (amido black)

Acid black 1 or amido black, CI 20470, is a dye which has long been used to stain protein. It will bind to proteins present in blood or other body fluids to give a blue-black stain. It will not detect normal eccrine and sebaceous sweat components of natural fingerprints and is therefore used when it is believed that the fingermark consists largely or wholly of blood. Porous surfaces will take up the dye and often cause a high background coloration and alternative reagents may be preferable on such surfaces. It is usually used in an aqueous ethanolic solution but the bloody deposits must first be "fixed" either by heating or more commonly by application of solutions such as sulphosalicylic acid. This fixing prevents diffusion of the deposit during the staining stage and was reported by Faragher and others in 1981.

Fingerprints developed by amido black are dark blue-black in color and can be recorded using conventional photography.

Acid yellow 7

This has been introduced more recently as an extremely sensitive technique to enhance fingerprints in blood but is a fluorogenic reagent which must be examined and photographed using an appropriate combination of excitation and viewing filters. It is recommended in the UK Home Office *Fingerprint Manual*, which suggests excitation in the green region, between 445 and 478 nm and recording the emission in the green–yellow region between 485 and 500 nm.

Fingermarks in Grease

Light fingermarks contaminated with grease from, for example foodstuffs, or as may be encountered in engineering workshops, may be developed with conventional processes such as fingerprint powders. It is recommended that small areas be tested first, and if gross contamination resulting in substantial take-up on the background is observed, the following alternative reagents may prove more effective.

Solvent black 3 (Sudan black 3)

Proposed as a fingerprint reagent by Mitsui and others in 1980, this method was investigated for developing latent fingermarks on surfaces such as polythene by Pounds in the UK Forensic Science Service but it was found to be less effective than established techniques. It was subsequently found to be of value in circumstances where there is a significant amount of fatty or greasy contamination. These surfaces can be difficult to treat with powders due to a high uptake across the surface. Treatment with fat dyes can selectively indicate areas of thicker or thinner deposit sometimes revealing fingerprints (**Figure 9**).

In the laboratory, articles are usually immersed in an ethanolic solution of solvent black 3 followed by careful washing. A less-flammable methoxypropanol (propylene glycol methyl ether) formulation has been proposed by the UK Home Office for use at crime scenes.

Solvent black 3 has been suggested by Castello of the University of Valencia as a method of enhancing lip prints.

Optical Techniques

Visual examination with white light

Visual examination in white light has the advantage of being nondestructive with regard to both the fingerprint deposit and any other forensic evidence. Sometimes on smooth surfaces, visible fingerprints will be seen that can be photographed by means of reflected or scattered light.

It is important to experiment with the angles of illumination and observation. In particular, reflective or textured surfaces may require manipulation of the light source to achieve high- and low-angle illumination, which can considerably affect contrast and visibility of latent fingerprints. On porous surfaces, only contaminated fingerprints are likely to be seen visually.

Sometimes on badly contaminated surfaces, such as where there is a substantial deposit of grease from foodstuffs and such application of chemical or physical development techniques may actually obscure fingerprints which can be seen visually.

Epitaxial white light visual examination

On some surfaces, illumination and viewing coaxially, usually normal to the surface, can be effective in detecting untreated fingerprints (**Figure 10**).

Viewing devices have been marketed which incorporate white light sources in combination with prisms or other types of beam splitter to carry out such epitaxial, or coaxial illumination, and observation. This technique is probably most useful on smooth, flat, shiny surfaces when latent fingerprint

Figure 9 Fingermarks in greasy contamination on food packaging developed with solvent black 3. Courtesy: UK Home Office.

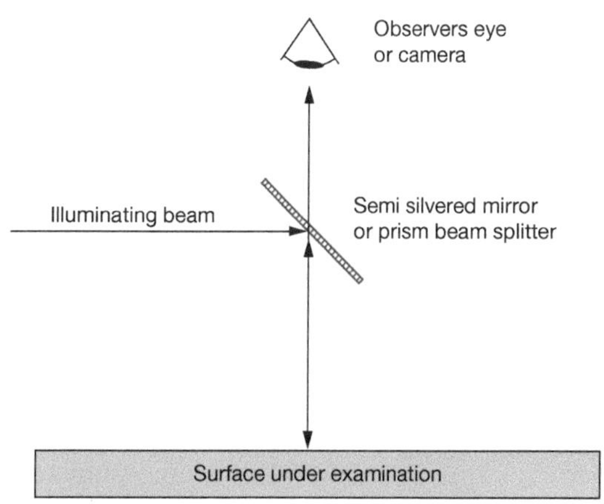

Figure 10 Schematic showing optical path for epitaxial viewing.

ridges may appear dark against a light background; the method is, however, not widely used.

Reflected short-wave ultraviolet imaging

Reflected short-wave ultraviolet imaging (RUVIS) was proposed in the 1980s and several types of prototype or commercial systems have been built. Surface reflection characteristics in the ultraviolet can be very different to those in the normal visible spectrum. The shorter wavelengths are scattered more than in the visible spectrum so that, for example, superglue-developed fingerprints can often be easily separated from the background with good contrast and no use of fluorescent dyes.

As the eye is not capable of imaging UV light, special image converter tubes are used, usually in conjunction with 254 nm mercury light sources. This wavelength is potentially damaging for eyes and skin and full protective equipment is essential.

Some fresh latent fingerprints on smooth surfaces are visible by short UV scattering by careful manipulation of illumination angle. After a few days, this effect is dramatically reduced and generally powdering or other techniques are more productive.

Fluorescence examination

Although there were some earlier experiments using ultraviolet lamps to attempt to detect latent fingerprints, the most significant step was that by Duff and Menzel in 1976. They reported seeing latent fingerprints in their laboratory using a high-power argon ion laser operating at 488 or 514.5 nm. Such lasers were expensive and the procedure was time-consuming and not very productive, but this triggered the development of a variety of detection and enhancement systems based on fluorescent processes.

Work in the early 1980s in the United Kingdom, Australia, and Canada resulted in the introduction of various high-power nonlaser light sources. All these used focused arc lamps and dichroic filter combinations, giving relatively narrow bands of visible light which could be used to excite fluorescence. These were considerably cheaper and more portable than the argon ion lasers of the day and were capable of producing illumination over a wider wavelength range. Several light sources available today for forensic fluorescent examination are based on this technology although recent developments in light-emitting diode (LED) and solid-state lasers are also utilized in some systems.

The requirements of fluorescent examination are that the light source should provide a relatively uniform divergent or parallel beam capable of illuminating a few hundred square centimeters with a relatively narrow range of wavelengths, perhaps 20–200 nm bandwidth depending on the application. Effective light power in the incident beam, not lamp power consumption, should be between 0.5 and 5 W in the band of interest; higher powers can be used but great care must be taken not to melt or damage substrates. Commonly, wavelength selection from arc lamp sources is by insertion of dichroic filters in the path of the lamp. Delivery of light to the surface under examination is usually by liquid light guide for higher powered systems although lasers will normally use optical fibers and LED sources may be simply handheld devices.

Fluorescent compounds have unique excitation and emission spectra and can require widely different excitation and viewing wavelengths. Absorption of a photon of short wavelength radiation usually results in an almost immediate release of a photon of lower energy, and hence longer wavelength: Stoke's law q.v.

Light sources must have sharp cutoffs at the longer wavelength end of the power band and be used with viewing filters or camera filters which have a sharp cut-on close to the light source cut-off and transmit less than one part in 10^4 of the "excitation" range of wavelengths (**Figures 11 and 12**).

Fluorescence examination for fingerprints falls into two major categories:

1. Initial examination of untreated, or latent, fingerprints for any inherent fluorescence which may be of natural or foreign origin.
2. The enhancement of development fingerprints that have been treated with reagents which may or may not produce a fluorescent product.

Fluorescence—initial examination

This requires slow methodical careful examination under darkroom conditions by staff with good close vision and who are fully dark-adapted. Usually, any fluorescence of untreated fingerprints is very faint and easily missed. Most natural components of latent fingerprints do not fluoresce. There are three amino acids which fluoresce in the visible region: tryptophan, tyrosine, and phenylalanine. Some workers have reported measurable levels of phenylalanine in fingerprint deposits. It is extremely unlikely, however, that these materials are being detected during initial fluorescence examination procedures.

It may be more likely that when untreated fingerprints are found by fluorescence, they are contaminated with fluorescent materials from the environment. No reliable data are available in this area but many greases, creams, cosmetics, industrial chemicals, and even environmental dust, among others fluoresce.

Operationally, it has been found that with suitable powerful light sources and correct viewing and camera filters, fluorescent fingerprints can be more frequently found on some polythene packaging, in kitchens and industrial premises, at illicit drug factories, in printing industry premises, and so on.

A difficulty with effective initial fluorescence examination is that as the chemicals which may be detected are unknown, there is no single combination of excitation and viewing filter which will detect all materials. The wrong combination of wavelengths will not result in visible fluorescence. In a major

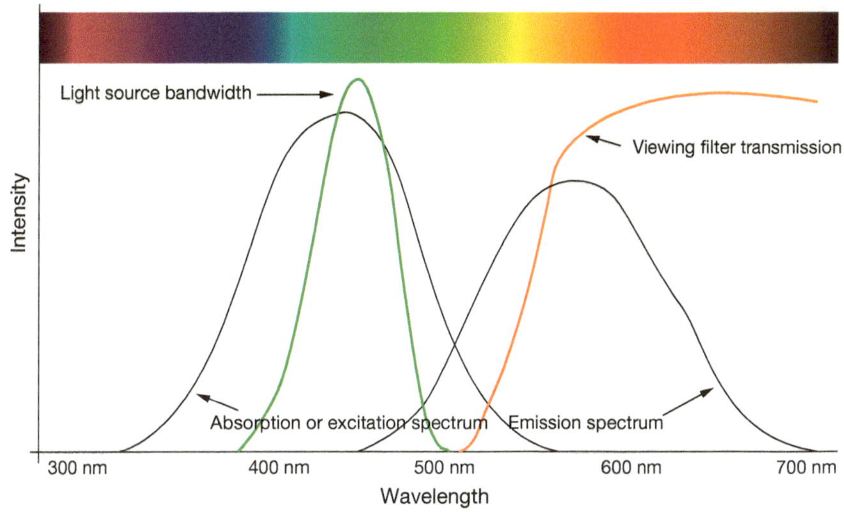

Figure 11 Schematic showing absorption and emission bands of a fluorescent material and the relative light source and viewing filter characteristics necessary for detection of fluorescence.

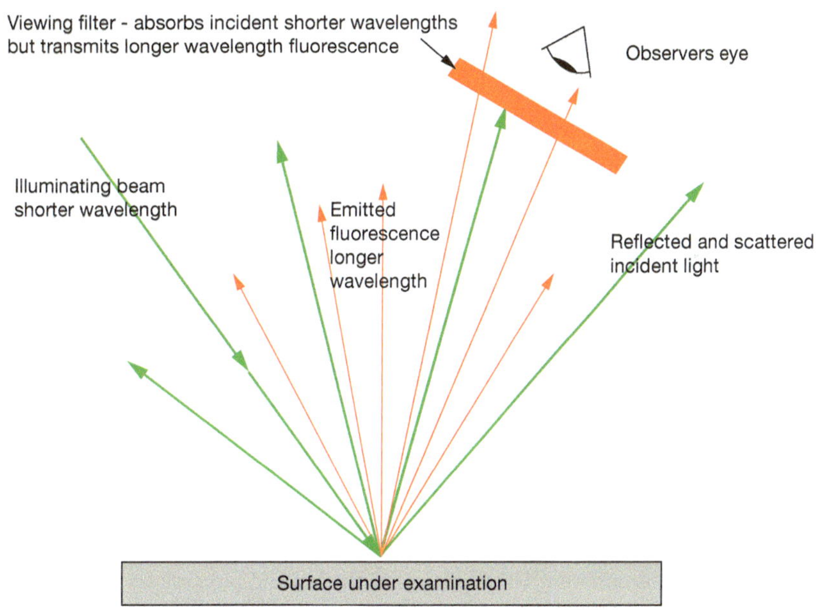

Figure 12 Schematic showing effect of correct viewing filter for the detection of fluorescence.

investigation, it is therefore necessary to use a number of light source and filter combinations. Comprehensive detection can only be achieved by sequential examination with a range of excitation wavelengths from the violet to the yellow region that should be used with appropriate viewing filters. There is some evidence that excitation around 530 nm is particularly productive. This may be due in part to the fact that it is above the primary excitation range for most artificial brighteners which are incorporated into many man-made materials such as paper, plastic, and paint.

Fluorescence—enhancement of developed fingerprints

Several of the established fingerprint development processes either produce a fluorescent product, such as DFO, or have

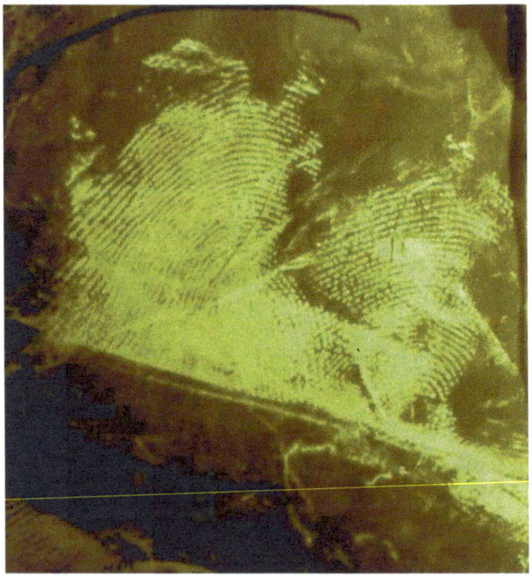

Figure 13 Superglue-developed fingerprints which have been dyed with basic yellow 40 and photographed by fluorescence. Courtesy: UK Home Office.

supplementary treatment steps which produce a fluorescent result, such as superglue-enhanced with basic yellow 40, or indanedione with zinc salts.

Fluorescent viewing and photography of such fingerprints can be very effective if the correct excitation and emission wavelengths are used (**Figure 13**).

Fluorescence examination can also be used to enhance some nonfluorescent-developed fingerprints by causing the background to fluoresce; for example, ninhydrin-developed fingerprints on colored paper surfaces may sometimes be enhanced in this way.

Ultraviolet and infrared fluorescence and imaging

UV fluorescence between 300 and 400 nm excited by UV at 277 nm was reported by Okhi in 1970. Long-wave and short-wave fluorescence were investigated and used by Creer in the UK Metropolitan Police in the late 1980s and 1990s. Some fingermarks on smooth papers were detected by background fluorescence of the paper with local absorption of UV by the fingermarks.

Some natural constituents, such as phenylalanine, or contaminants, such as greases, may absorb light in the near ultraviolet and emit in the blue part of the spectrum. Some may absorb in the ultraviolet and emit in the ultraviolet, requiring specialist UV-sensitive imaging devices as used for reflected ultraviolet imaging, RUVIS, see earlier.

Many inks and some oils absorb in the yellow–red part of the spectrum and emit in the infrared region. To detect fingermarks in such contamination requires the use of infrared-sensitive viewing devices or cameras. Such procedures are not currently common although there is increasing interest in imaging outside of the visible part of the spectrum, referred to variously as chemical imaging, or hyperspectral or multispectral imaging.

Silicon-based CCD and CMOS cameras have inherent sensitivity in the near infrared but many have internal blocking, which can make them unsuitable unless they can be removed.

Other Reported Techniques

The following techniques are not in widespread use but have either been reported to be worthy of investigation or have been used, or are used, in special circumstances, or are currently under development and assessment.

Radioactive sulfur dioxide has been used to detect and image latent fingerprints on adhesive tape and experimentally to image them on some types of finely woven fabrics. First reported by Grant in 1963 and investigated at AERE Harwell, small quantities of a sulfur-containing compound are ignited and the exhibits after exposure are autoradiographed.

The use of bromine, iodine, or iodine monochloride incorporating radioactive isotopes was investigated in similar treatment protocols to the use of sulfur dioxide.

Various electron beam imaging methods are being investigated.

Modified physical developers and multimetal deposition techniques have been investigated by several workers including Saunders at Los Alamos, Cantu of the US Secret Service, Becue of the University of Lausanne, and others.

Nanoparticle methods in solution are being investigated by various research groups.

The use of sulfur nitride polymerization is a recent development by Kelly and King at the University of Loughborough.

Electrostatic imaging methods for revealing fingerprint-induced corrosion on metals, such as cartridge cases, are under investigation.

Silver nitrate solution, reported in the 1890s, reacts with chloride in the fingerprint to form insoluble silver chloride, which goes black on exposure to light. This was used for many years on porous surfaces such as paper and raw wood but has generally been superceded by amino acid reagents such as ninhydrin and physical developer.

Osmium or ruthenium tetroxide has been used either in the vapor phases or in solution to develop latent fingerprints by their reaction with unsaturated fats, which results in gray deposits of the reduced metals. These have been used experimentally on fabrics but with limited success.

Dimethylaminocinnamaldehyde in solution was investigated by Morris and others at AWRE Aldermaston for fingerprints on paper but it proved less successful than ninhydrin. It has recently been used by a number of workers for developing fingerprints on thermal printing papers and has been applied in the vapor phase.

Many authors have referred to heating paper at temperatures between 150 and 200 °C, which will eventually often result in fingermarks becoming visible as the deposit initiates local carbonization resulting in brown fingerprints. This method is not used operationally due to availability of other methods.

See also: **Pattern Evidence/Fingerprints (Dactyloscopy):** Chemistry of Print Residue; Identification and Classification; Sequential Treatment and Enhancement.

Further Reading

Archer, N.E., Yannis, C., Elliott, J.A., Jickells, S., 2005. Changes in the lipid composition of latent fingerprint residue with time after deposition on a surface. Forensic Science International 154 (2–3), 224–239.

Bowman, V. (Ed.), 2004. Manual of Fingerprint Development Techniques, second ed. Home Office, Police Scientific Development Branch, London, UK.

Croxton, R.S., 2008. Analysis of Latent Fingerprint Components by Gas Chromatography-Mass Spectrometry (Ph.D. thesis). University of Lincoln, UK.

Cuthbertson, F., Cripps, F.W., 1965. SSCD SAC/2/65 Report. Atomic Weapons Research Establishment, Aldermaston, Berkshire, UK.

Hardwick, S.A., Kent, T., Sears, V.G., 1990. Fingerprint Detection by Fluorescence Examination – A Guide to Operational Implementation. PSDB Publication No. 3/90, Sandridge, UK.

Jones, N.E., Davies, L.M., Brennan, J.S., Bramble, S.K., 2000. Separation of visibly-excited fluorescent components in fingerprint residue by thin-layer chromatography. Journal of Forensic Sciences 45 (6), 1286–1293.

Merrick, S., Gardner, S., Sears, V., Hewlett, D., 2002. An operational trial of ozone-friendly DFO and 1,2-indanedione formulations for latent fingerprint detection. Journal of Forensic Identification 52 (5), 595–605.

Mong, G.M., Petersen, C.E., Clauss, C.R.W., 1999. Advanced Fingerprint Analysis Project, Final Report – Fingerprint Constituents. Pacific Northwest Laboratory Report PNNL-13019, Richland, WA.

Olsen Sr., R.D., 1978. Scott's Fingerprint Mechanics. Charles C. Thomas, Springfield, IL.

Ramatowski, R. (Ed.), 2009. Lee and Gaensslen's Advances in Fingerprint Technology, third ed. CRC Press, London.

Stoilovic, M., Lennard, C., Wallace-Kunkel, C., Roux, C., 2007. Evaluation of a 1,2-indanedione formulation containing zinc chloride for improved fingermark detection on paper. Journal of Forensic Identification 57 (1), 4–18.

Thomas, G.L., 1978. The physics of fingerprints and their detection. Journal of Physics E; Scientific Instruments 11 (8), 722–731.

Wilshire, B., Hurley, N., 1995. Development of latent fingerprints on paper using magnetic flakes. Journal of Forensic Sciences 40 (5), 837–841.

Relevant Websites

http://www.enfsi.eu—ENFSI.
http://www.theiai.org—International Association for Identification.
http://www.nij.gov—National Institute of Justice.
http://onin.com/fp—The History of Fingerprints.
http://www.nij.gov—US National Institute of Justice SWGFAST Fingerprint Sourcebook.
http://en.wikipedia.org—Wikipedia, Fingerprints.

Key Terms

Characteristic, Composition, Contaminants, Degradation, Development, Donor effect, Eccrine, Eccrine sweat, Enhancement, Fingermark, Fingerprint, Fluorescence, Latent, Latent fingerprints, Minutiae, Print, Ridges, Sebaceous, Sebum, Sweat.

Review Questions

1. What factors influence the ability to render and quality of latent mark visualization?
2. What methods have been used to analyze the composition of fingerprint residue?
3. What is fingerprint residue composed of?
4. What produces fingerprint residue? Where does it come from?
5. How does the substrate affect the visualization of prints?
6. What other methods used at a crime scene might interfere with the processing of fingerprints?
7. How could processing for latent prints affect other crime scene methods? What steps can be taken so evidence is not compromised?
8. How could the necessities of a "major case" change the sequencing of processing?
9. A sequence of techniques should incorporate methods that do what?
10. What are some of the considerations necessary for photographing latents going through sequential processing?
11. Can any of the techniques used for the development of fingerprints in blood be used as a presumptive test for blood?
12. Do accelerants prevent fingerprint development?
13. Under what conditions would fingerprints be found visible?
14. Lasers of what wavelength are the most practical for preliminary screening for latents?
15. What solid matter may be found in a latent print?
16. List the factors that control image quality for digital imaging systems.
17. What is a "lossy image compression technique"?
18. List at least five factors which can affect the choice of visualization process.

19. When was ninhydrin first proposed for fingerprint development?
20. How does vacuum metal deposition work? What are some of its strengths and weaknesses?

Discussion Questions

1. Why must examiners avoid over-interpreting class characteristics that display only slight differences? What are two examples of these "slight differences"?
2. How is the photographing and viewing of patent prints different from latent prints (besides being immediately visible)?
3. What are some factors that might effect the visualization of a latent print? How can protocols mitigate these issues?
4. What factors in visualizing a latent print might effect its interpretation?
5. What are the main quality concerns for a fingerprint examiner? What might reduce or prohibit quality work on fingerprint cases? How can these concerns be addressed?

Additional Readings

King, R.S., Hallett, P.M., Foster, D., 2015. Seeing into the infrared: a novel IR fluorescent fingerprint powder. Forensic Science International 249, e21–e26.

Merritt, D., Morgan Jr., J.P., Houlgrave, S., Ramotowski, R., Brock, A., Shelar, K., 2015. Development of latent prints on Tyvek Large Pak and Padded Pak shipping envelopes. Journal of Forensic Identification 65 (5), 828.

Ramotowski, R., 2012. Lee and Gaensslen's Advances in Fingerprint Technology, third ed. CRC Press, Boca Raton, FL.

Williams, S.F., Pulsifer, D.P., Shaler, R.C., Ramotowski, R.S., Brazelle, S., Lakhtakia, A., 2015. Comparison of the columnar-thin-film and vacuum-metal-deposition techniques to develop sebaceous fingermarks on nonporous substrates. Journal of Forensic Sciences 60 (2), 295–302.

Williams, S.F., Pulsifer, D.P., Lakhtakia, A., Shaler, R.C., 2015. Visualization of partial bloody fingerprints on nonporous substrates using columnar thin films. Canadian Society of Forensic Science Journal 48 (1), 20–35.

Section 3. Fingerprints

The utility of fingerprints was born of a time when people became more mobile, cultural and social norms were changing, and populations were growing. Crime expanded with these opportunities (what we would now call "transnational crime") as it has always done. It was no longer supportable to know everyone in your neighborhood or village—there were too many "new" people coming through too often for authorities to keep track of. What could be more useful for personal identification than fingerprints? Easy to collect, examined with little to no equipment requirements, and (once a classification scheme was devised) eminently searchable. Note that the usefulness of fingerprints was not fully realized until they could be organized and searched. Without a systematic approach to searching, they were a research curiosity.

While the friction ridges on an individual's fingertips are assumed to be unique (testing everyone is a practical impossibility), the prints or marks those ridges leave are not. That fingerprints that are unique was a leap of faith that became an article of faith in the forensic profession. Galton, the first of many to do so in different ways by varying criteria, calculated the chance of two people having the "same" friction ridge pattern to be 1 in 64 billion.[1] Whether that number or another is adopted, is still a *statistical calculation based on the sampling of a population* and cannot be assumed to be "too big to fail" (to borrow a recent term). Fingerprints—the marks—are fallible and cases like McKie, Mayfield, and others have unequivocally demonstrated this.

Does this mean fingerprints are not useful? The question is not whether they work but *how well do they work*—a very different question that requires a new perspective. Research into how well fingerprints and fingerprint examiners work is ongoing and should lead the profession to a far better place with statistical interpretations than the so-called "good old days" of absolutism.

Fingerprint Sciences

DL Ortiz-Bacon and CL Swanson, US Army Criminal Investigation Laboratory – Expeditionary Forensic Division, Forest Park, GA, USA

Glossary

Anthropometry Relating to measurements of the human body; Bertillonage was a classification system based on a number of these measurements.

Chiridium Hand or foot.

Dactyloscopy Comparison of fingerprints for purposes of identification.

Friction ridge skin Specialized skin found on the palmar and plantar surfaces; characterized by raised ridges which assist with traction and increase tactile stimulation.

LASER Light amplification by stimulated emission of radiation; a device that emits a single wavelength of light and is employed as a forensic light source.

Minutiae Characteristics or events along a ridge which are considered during the comparison of fingerprints; also referred to as Galton details.

Papillary ridges Orderly rows of peglike structures emerging from the dermis.

Spectroscopic Referring to the interaction between matter and radiated energy.

[1] Galton, F., 1892. Fingerprints. MacMillan & Co., London.

 http://dx.doi.org/10.1016/B978-0-12-800573-6.00008-2

Introduction

For over 100 years, fingerprints have provided a reliable and efficient means of identification, proving its value in criminal investigations. The biological principles of permanence and uniqueness along with the capability to be classified have made fingerprints a fundamental tool in forensic science. A reproduction of the arrangement of the ridges present on the fingers can be deposited on an object or surface when the finger comes into contact with it. Recognition of this tendency as far back as the late 1800s has led to continued research and development of fingerprint visualization, detection, and recovery techniques to further their potential use for identification. Despite the established application of fingerprint identification over the past century, fingerprint science has recently faced challenges within the legal system regarding the legitimacy of individualizations. The information presented here is by no means an exhaustive review of the research performed nor are the scientists involved in unfolding the biological basis and classification methods of friction ridge skin comparison and identification, but it is the authors' intent to present a concise and sequential development of the science of dactyloscopy.

Early History (221 BC–AD 220)

The first known evidence of the recognition of friction ridge patterns has been linked back to Kejimkujik Lake, Nova Scotia, Canada, where a tracing of the hand was found etched into slate rock. This is believed to be the first documented anthropological illustration depicting the friction ridges and flexion creases of the hand. Impressions of the hands have also been found in Altamira, Spain, and Lascaux, France, and are estimated to be over 17 000 years old. Similar impressions have been found in clay as far back as 5000 years ago. In addition to these findings, fingerprints are known to have been used as a form of signature and identification on the seals of contracts in China as early as 206 BC. Fingerprints were not scientifically researched until many years later during the seventeenth century.

Recognition of Friction Ridge Skin (1684–1858)

The first scientist to recognize and comment on friction ridge formations was the English Botanist Nehemiah Grew in 1684. In his publication *Philosophical Transactions,* Grew described friction ridge skin in detail to include the papillary ridges, the patterns they form, and the pores they contain. Grew is recognized as the first scientist to document his findings on friction ridge skin. In 1686, Marcello Malpighi, an Italian anatomist, mentioned the patterns of friction ridge skin while studying the skin using the recently invented microscope. Malpighi gathered his observations and formally published on the function, form, and structure of friction ridge skin in an article entitled *Concerning the External Tactile Organs.* A layer of the skin, the Malpighian layer, was later named after him in honor of his contribution to dactyloscopy.

For almost a century and a half after the work of Grew and Malpighi, little advancement was made in the science of friction ridge skin. Eventually, in 1823, Johan-Evangelist Purkinje classified nine principal configuration groups of fingerprints and assigned each a name. His work was the first published research to describe and attempt to classify fingerprint patterns; however, Purkinje did not research the subject any further. Years later in 1853, while serving with the British Civil Service in Bengal, India, Sir William Herschel noticed a great number of natives were receiving pensions from the government by impersonation. While Herschel held the position of Magistrate and Collector at Hooghly, near Calcutta, he was in charge of the criminal courts, the prisons, the registration of deeds, and the payment of government pensions, all of which he controlled through the collection of finger and palm prints. This marks the first use of friction ridge skin as a signature by a European. Throughout his career, Herschel continued to collect fingerprints and study them as a hobby. Eventually, Herschel realized fingerprints remain unchanged over time and differ from person to person. Herschel wrote a letter in 1877, later to be called the "Hooghly Letter," explaining his belief that fingerprints should be used as the new system of identification in prisons in England. At the time, however, he received no response. Herschel continued empirical studies of permanence by publishing prints he took of himself in 1859, 1877, and 1916, demonstrating their persistence, echoing a previous study published by Hermann Welcker in 1898.

Criminal Applications and as a Means of Identification (1880–1905)

Shortly after Herschel wrote the "Hooghly Letter," Dr Henry Faulds became interested in friction ridge skin after seeing ridge detail on pottery found on a Japanese beach while working there as a medical missionary from Scotland. In October 1880, he became the first ever to publish about friction ridge skin in a scientific journal. In his letter to the editor *On the Skin-Furrows of the Hand,* published in the journal *Nature,* Faulds discusses the value of friction ridge skin and its application in criminal investigations. Faulds provided two examples of how prints can be used to identify a person at a crime scene within the article. The first example involved a greasy print found on a drinking glass that helped Faulds discover who had been drinking distilled spirits in his lab, and the second described sooty fingerprints left on a white wall which resulted in the exoneration of an accused individual. On November 25, 1880, Herschel responded to Faulds' letter stating that he had already been using fingerprints for 20 years, since he first took the prints of Rajyadhar Konai in an attempt to prevent denial of his signature on a business contract and then, later, by recording the fingerprints of natives to prevent impersonation offering the "Hooghly Letter" as proof. Years later, in 1917 Herschel would acknowledge the difference between his and Faulds' use of fingerprints during their debate in 1880, giving credit to Faulds as the first to suggest the use of fingerprints for the identification of criminals from impressions left at crime scenes.

Prior to publishing in *Nature,* Faulds had written a letter to Charles Darwin detailing his research and soliciting his aid in continued studies into the topic. Darwin's health at the time would not allow him to pursue the proposal but he forwarded the letter to his cousin, Francis Galton. Galton developed an interest in fingerprints at approximately the same time that Faulds and Herschel were researching the topic. Galton began correspondence with Herschel and eventually compiled his research into the first textbook on fingerprints, published in 1892, titled *Finger Prints.* In this book, Galton established that fingerprints are never duplicated and the arrangement of the ridges persists throughout the life of an individual. Galton was also the first to name and describe friction ridge minutiae which in recognition of his work are often referred to as "Galton details."

Around the same time Galton was publishing his work, the first working fingerprint classification system was being designed in Argentina by Juan Vucetich. Vucetich provided a viable filing system which he referred to as "icnofalangometrica." Vucetich is credited with creating and implementing the first classification system leading to earliest replacement of anthropometric methods for filing criminal records.

In 1892, Inspector Eduardo Alvarez, a former student under Vucetich, played a crucial role in the investigation of the Rojas murders, a case in which a bloody fingerprint found at the crime scene was matched to the right thumb of Francisca Rojas, ultimately leading to her confession of the crime. This case was the first homicide to be solved by fingerprint evidence and, soon after, Argentina became the first country to rely solely on fingerprints as a method of identification.

The next working classification system came in 1897. This system was developed by Sir Edward Henry, Inspector General of Police for the Lower Provinces in Bengal, India. Henry developed this system with the help of two Indian police officers, Azizul Haque and Chandra Bose, who created a method of separating fingerprint records into a large number of groupings that were based on Galton's fingerprint pattern types and specific characteristics in those patterns such as ridge counts in loop patterns and tracings in whorl patterns. Soon after its development, the Henry system was introduced in Britain and for long was the most widely used classification system in the world eventually being replaced by the computerized systems in use today.

Prior to implementation of the Henry system, Anthropometry was the practical identification and classification method in use. Introduced by Alphonse Bertillon, Anthropometry, also referred to as Bertillonage, was based on 11 body measurements meticulously taken using calipers. Bertillon was a clerk at the Prefecture of Police in Paris, France, and his system was originally put into use in 1882. Anthropometry was replaced by the Henry system in most countries by the early 1900s; however, its use continued in France until Bertillon's death in 1914.

In 1898, Sir Henry made an identification in a criminal case in Bengal, India, in which the fingerprint evidence was used to secure a conviction for the first time and in 1900, recognizing the superiority of fingerprints as a means of identification. As a result, the Belper Committee in England established that all criminal identification records would be classified by the Henry system. Ironically, in 1902, Alphonse Bertillon was responsible for the first use of fingerprints in Europe to solve a murder in Paris, France.

Shortly after the Henry system was put into use in Europe, fingerprint science was introduced to the United States by Detective John K. Ferrier in 1904 at the St Louis World's Fair. Det. Ferrier of New Scotland Yard was sent to guard the Crown's Jewels of the British Empire, which were on loan for exhibition. During the fair, New Scotland Yard set up an exhibition in which Ferrier demonstrated the use of fingerprints as a method of identification and how they were being used in England. It was here that the science of fingerprints was taught to the first group of Americans, eventually leading to the incorporation of the Henry system in prisons throughout the country and the utilization of fingerprint evidence in criminal investigations. Just a year later, in 1905, the Deptford murder trial in England became the first case in which fingerprint evidence was used to secure a conviction within the English court system.

Developments in Comparison and Identification (1914–1973)

Inevitably, the science of fingerprints continued to progress. In 1914, Edmond Locard, a former student of Alphonse Bertillon and the Director of the Laboratory of Police at Lyons, France, further promoted the use of fingerprints as powerful forensic evidence and he also introduced the theory of poroscopy. Locard explained how the study of pores and their locations on the ridges could be used to supplement fingerprint comparisons. In 1915, the International Association for Identification (IAI) was established and would grow to become the primary professional organization and governing body for practitioners of fingerprint science. A significant event occurred in 1924 when images of two fingerprints from different individuals exhibiting 16 points in agreement surfaced at New Scotland Yard. The images were originally published in a 1912 paper by Bertillon. Presented with the chance that the fingerprints from two different individuals could be so similar it was decided that the 12-point standard was not sufficient and 16 points became the new standard. Since that decision, examination of the prints in their original publication revealed that the images received by New Scotland Yard had been doctored. In 1953, a meeting was held between the then Deputy Director of Public Prosecutions, officials from the Home Office, and officers from several police forces, for the purpose of agreeing on a common standard in fingerprint identifications. As a result, the National Fingerprint Standard was created, which required 16 separate similar ridge characteristics. Also in 1924, under the direction of J. Edgar Hoover, the Federal Bureau of Investigation (FBI) developed its Identification Division bringing together the International Chiefs of Police fingerprint records and the records housed at the Federal Penitentiary at Ft. Leavenworth, Kansas—a compilation that would become the master criminal file housed by the FBI.

One of the first cases of fingerprint fabrication occurred in 1943. On July 8, Harry Oakes was found murdered in his mansion in Nassau, Bahamas. Alfred de Marigny, Oakes' son-in-law, was accused of the crime. A fingerprint recovered at the scene and identified as de Marigny's was the major piece of evidence against him at trial. Police claimed that the print been developed on a Chinese screen in Oakes's bedroom where the body was found. Following a trial which lasted several weeks, he was eventually acquitted, after it was discovered that the print said to have been lifted from the screen had actually been lifted from a water glass that de Marigny had used during questioning by police and that the detectives had fabricated the evidence against him. Heightened awareness of the consequence of fingerprint identification was also evident outside of the realm of investigators and scientists with criminals such as Jack Klutas and Donald Darling Roguerre carving into their fingers to mutilate the patterns thus precluding identification. John Dillinger went as far as applying corrosive acid to what he must have learned were "key areas"—the deltas and cores—in order to destroy his fingerprints. Possibly the most infamous case of mutilation was Roscoe Pitts. With the assistance of a doctor, Pitts cut strips from the sides off his torso and removed as much skin as possible from his fingers. He then bound his hands to the skin strips for 3 weeks after which the edges of the torso skin strips were severed and the torso skin, which is absent of friction ridge detail, became grafted to the fingertips. Pitts was later identified from friction skin impressions of the second joints of the fingers.

Throughout the 1930s and 1940s, interest in dermatoglyphics grew within the universities as well. Furthering studies endeavored by Harris H. Wilder and Inez Whipple at Smith College in Massachusetts, and Harold Cummins, from Tulane University in Louisiana, conducted research on volar pad development. In 1952, a colleague of Cummins at Tulane University, Alfred Hale, published further research on volar skin development in the human fetus. These researches are discussed in further detail later in this article. In 1962, Salil K. Chatterjee described the use of the ridge edges and shapes and how they could be used to supplement fingerprint comparisons—which he termed edgeoscopy. Edgeoscopy along with poroscopy, described previously, would become what we refer to today as third-level details.

Shortly after Chatterjee introduced edgeoscopy, Andre Moenssens published the books *Fingerprints & the Law* and *Fingerprint Techniques*, in 1969 and 1971, respectively, which became authoritative textbooks in the training and teaching of fingerprint science for many decades. In 1973, the IAI passed a resolution stating that there is no need to require a predetermined minimum number of characteristics to make an identification. This assertion would become fundamental in the shift toward ridgeology—a term introduced in 1991 by David Ashbaugh of the Royal Canadian Mounted Police (RCMP) in his paper *Ridgeology*. After the publication of his book *Quantitative-Qualitative Friction Ridge Analysis* in 1996, ridgeology or the study of ridges quickly became the philosophy and approach for latent print comparisons. Till today, this is the prevailing philosophy behind fingerprint comparison.

Recent (1990–Present)

At the International Symposium of Fingerprint Detection and Identification in June 1995, the Ne'Urim Israeli Declaration was presented stating that "No scientific basis exists for requiring that a pre-determined minimum number of friction ridge features must be present in two impressions in order to establish a positive identification." This declaration was unanimously accepted by all present at the time, and later, signed by 28 persons from the following 11 countries: Australia, Canada, France, Holland, Hungary, Israel, New Zealand, Sweden, Switzerland, the United Kingdom, and the United States of America.

Two recent cases which have brought attention and challenges to the question of the reliability of fingerprint science are the Shirley McKie trial and the Madrid train bombing incident. In 1997, Shirley McKie, a detective with a Scotland Police Department, was identified by several Scottish Criminal Record Office (SCRO) latent print examiners as having been present and entered upon a crime scene she claimed to have never entered. External experts reviewing the case believed the identifications were erroneous while the local experts, and others associated with the case, maintained that the identifications were accurate. Debate and controversy persisted for over a decade, with neither side shifting on their position. This precipitated a major public judicial inquiry and on December 14, 2011 the report put the controversy to rest. The report sided with the external experts stating that both McKie's and the victim's fingerprints had been misidentified by the examiners involved. The report concluded that the identifications were a result of human error and that no impropriety had been committed by the SCRO examiners.

Another highly publicized error in fingerprint examination occurred in 2004 during the Madrid train bombing in which the FBI erroneously identified a latent fingerprint from the crime scene to Brandon Mayfield, an American living in Portland, Oregon, at the time of the incident. The case incited a tremendous amount of negative publicity for the fingerprint community and is used to challenge the soundness of fingerprint identifications in courts today.

The National Research Council (NRC) formed a committee through the National Academy of Sciences (NAS) to identify the needs of the forensic science community in the United States. The 2009 report emphasized the need for establishing an error rate and measuring the discriminability of features in latent print comparison work. It also addressed the lack of standardized training and procedures across agencies and practitioners in the fingerprint field. The national attention the report has received has stimulated the fingerprint community to critically evaluate the foundation of their science, fostering additional research in the field.

In 2010, the IAI passed a significant resolution (Resolution 2010–2018) which allows the use of mathematically based models to assess the associative value of latent print evidence to provide a numerical basis for supporting an examiner's opinion. This resolution was monumental because prior to it, latent print examiners were not permitted to offer qualifying statements regarding the likelihood or probability of an identification. Interest in statistical models began as early as the probative value of fingerprints as a means of identification was realized. Historically, scientists and mathematicians such as Galton, Balthazard, Roxburgh, Amy, and Osterburg have all attempted to describe a probabilistic estimate of fingerprint individuality. Most recently, computer-assisted models and statistical tools to provide likelihood ratios in fingerprint comparisons have been developed by Champod, Egli, and Neumann. The continued development of these models will offer the fingerprint community further support for their conclusions.

Early Scientific Foundation

As major advances were being made on the classification and comparison front of fingerprint science, study of the biological aspects of ridge development continued as well (**Figure 1**). Expanding on the external examinations of friction ridge skin described thus far, Arthur Kollmann was the first to publish, in 1883, concerning the embryological development of ridges and went on to describe the presence and location of the volar pads on the hands and feet. It was not until 1897 that Harris H. Wilder put forward that the centers of disturbances—the core of the patterns—corresponded with the location of the volar pads as opposed to earlier propositions basing the location of the pads on topographical observations which often confused the pads with muscle structure. Wilder also suggested an association between the location of the volar pads and the epidermic ridges that developed upon them. As a fellow professor in the Department of Zoology at Smith College in Massachusetts, Inez Whipple came to share his interest in dermatoglyphics and in 1904 published a landmark treatise describing the arrangement of the volar pads on the mammalian chiridium and their influence on the formation of ridges and patterns upon these elevated surfaces. Wilder also collaborated with American Police Commissioner Bert Wentworth and in 1918 they published research on the uniqueness and persistence of incipient ridges and pores. Our current understanding of the formation and development of the papillary ridges has built upon the pioneering work of these early researchers.

In 1946, Harold Cummins and Charles Midlo published the authoritative work entitled *Finger Prints, Palms, and Soles* (1946), which included many of Cummins' earlier papers and the body of knowledge established by their forerunners on the subject of dactyloscopy. Cummins described in detail the development of the volar pads on fetuses and concluded that the onset of friction ridge development coincides with the regression of the volar pads and that the stage of regression along with the location, size, and shape of the pads influences the overall pattern configuration. Another major advancement in establishing the scientific premises for the uniqueness and persistence of friction ridge skin was the research presented by Alfred Hale describing differential growth. In summary, development of the friction ridges of the palmar surfaces begins around 13–16 weeks of gestation, which corresponds with volar pad regression. Differential growth explains how stresses resultant from differences in growth rate of the ridge units influence their arrangement into lines. Although the overall pattern of friction ridge skin is influenced by heredity, the minutiae ensue from both localized surface tensions across the pads as ridges proliferate and pads regress, as well as, from environmental influences within the womb resulting in the randomized formation of ridge characteristics on which fingerprint identification is based.

Further Scientific Research

Research into both the morphological and embryological development of friction ridge skin has expanded the foundation laid previously. In 1976, Michio Okajima presented his research on incipient ridges and described the comparable double-row arrangement of the papillae under these smaller ridges to the double-row arrangement under normal ridges. Okajima's observations suggested that incipient ridges are primary ridges that were not completely matured at the cessation of ridge proliferation during differential growth. In 1984,

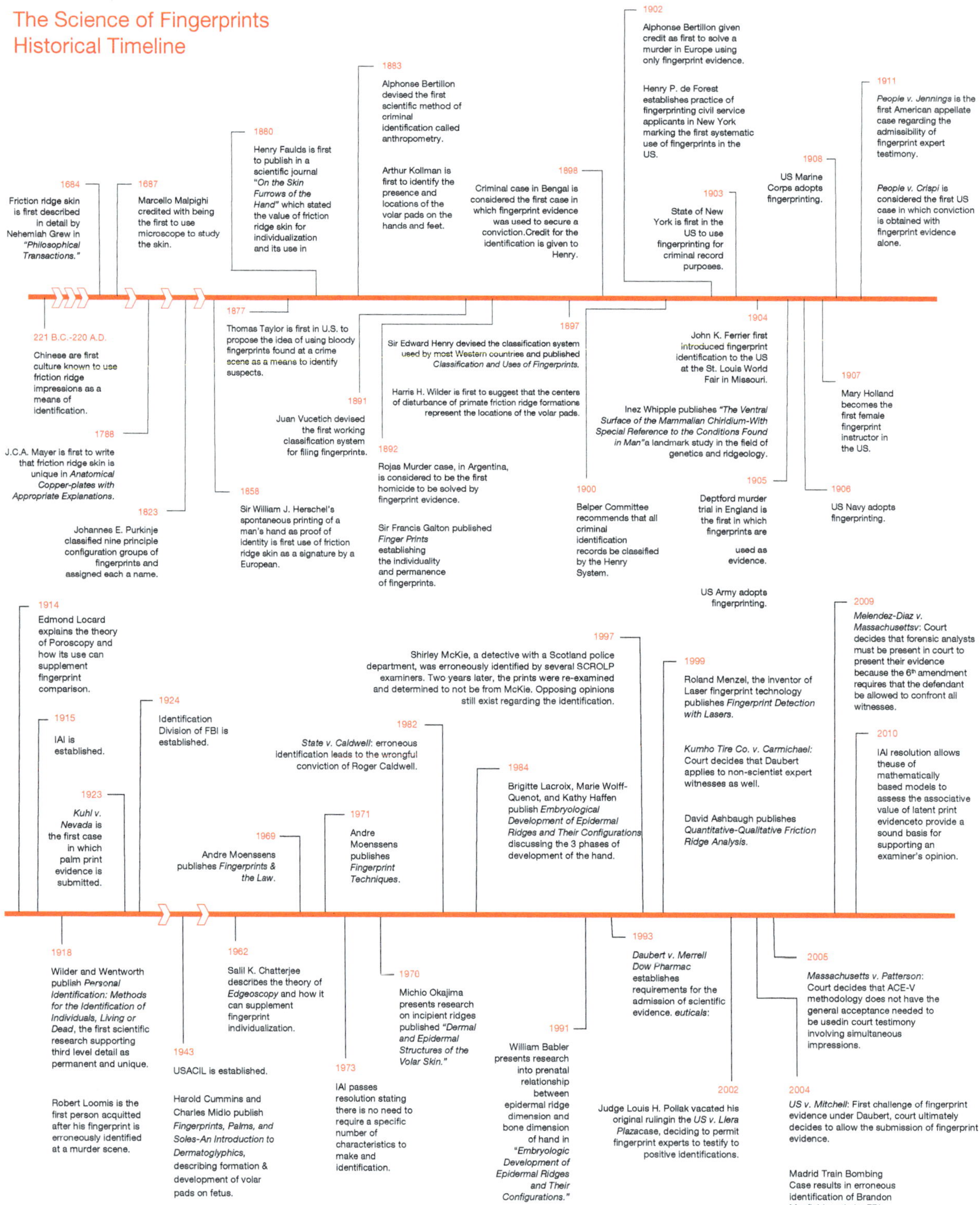

Figure 1 The science of fingerprints: historical timeline.

Brigitte Lacroix et al. published the paper *Early Human Hand Morphology: An Estimation of Fetal Age* in which the authors used scanning electron microscopy to examine the development of pads and ridges on the hand. Their analysis confirmed original observations made by Katherine Bonnevie that development of the volar pads precedes the proliferation of ridges and also corroborated with the histological studies of Alfred Hale demonstrating the appearance of ridges as early as 13 weeks of gestation. Most recently (1991), William Babler has shown that not only the pattern formed by ridges is dependent on the shape and size of the volar pads, the timing of volar pad regression, and ridge proliferation but also prenatal bone dimension influences ridge configuration.

Fingerprint Detection and Enhancement

Visualization and, often, preservation of fingerprints is fundamental in their exploitation as a means of identifying individuals in contact with an object or crime scene. A plethora of methods are available for the enhancement of latent impressions on different surfaces each targeting different compounds—inorganics, amino acids, lipids and fats, moisture, etc.—in latent print residue. Traditional methods include powder dusting for nonporous surfaces, iodine fuming as a nondestructive method for porous surfaces, and physical developer for porous surfaces which may have been previously wetted. A major advancement in the development of latent impressions on porous surfaces came with the introduction of ninhydrin by the Swedish scientists Oden and von Hofsten in 1954. Ninhydrin, which forms a purple product upon reaction with amino acids, offered a nonfleeting method (as opposed to iodine fuming) for developing prints on papers and other porous surfaces. Analogous methods have since been developed which offer greater sensitivity and contrast by employing forensic light sources such as LASERs to visualize the developed prints. These include 1,8-diazafluoren-9-one developed by Tony Pounds (1990) and 1,2-indanedione synthesized by R.S. Ramatowski (1997).

In 1978, the Criminal Identification Division of the Japanese National Police Agency took notice of cyanoacrylate, or superglue, fuming and its ability to develop and preserve latent print residue on nonporous surfaces, a method that remains the workhorse of most forensic laboratories today. Superglue fuming techniques work through the polymerization of cyanoacrylate esters with the eccrine and sebaceous components in fingerprint residue forming a readily visible white polymer in the areas where friction ridge skin came into contact with the surface. Almost simultaneously, Roland Menzel, Brian Dalrymple, and J.M. Duff were considering LASERs as a means of detecting latent impressions. Photoluminescence was first exploited as a latent fingerprint visualization technique in 1976 when the Canadian researchers took notice of the inherent luminescence in fingerprint residue and employed an argon laser to induce the substance to luminesce. By 1980, Menzel had implemented the process of dye staining nonporous evidence with Rhodamine-6-G after superglue fuming as a means of making the fingerprint residue luminesce more intensely and to overcome background fluorescence and permit for optical filtering. Other detection techniques which expanded detection of latent impressions to more challenging surfaces and items exposed to varying environmental conditions have been introduced by the Home Office in Great Britain and include physical developer for the enhancement of impressions on previously wet items, vacuum metal deposition for developing prints on polyethylene bags, and radioactive labeling for developing prints on adhesive tapes. Most recently, methods employing spectroscopic techniques utilizing visible and infrared absorption and reflectance are being investigated as rapid and nondestructive methods to visualize latent impressions on a variety of surfaces. The arsenal from which fingerprint examiners can draw to detect, develop, and capture latent impressions will continue to grow as research continues.

See also: **Anthropology/Odontology:** Identification of the Living; Personal Identification in Forensic Anthropology; **Foundations:** Overview and Meaning of Identification/Individualization; **Investigations:** Fingerprints; **Methods:** Spectroscopy: Basic Principles; **Pattern Evidence/Fingerprints (Dactyloscopy):** Automated Fingerprint Identification Systems (AFIS); Automated Methods, Including Criminal Records Administration; **Professional:** National Academy of Sciences (NAS).

Further Reading

Ashbaugh, D.R., 1991. Ridgeology. Journal of Forensic Identification 41, 16–64.

Ashbaugh, D.R., 1996. Quantitative-Qualitative Friction Ridge Analysis. CRC Press, Boca Raton.

Berry, J., 1991. The history and development of fingerprinting. In: Lee, H.C., Gaensslen, R.E. (Eds.), Advances in Fingerprint Technology. Elsevier, New York.

Campbell, A., 2011. The Fingerprint Inquiry Report. APS Group Scotland, Edinburgh.

Champod, C., Lennard, C., Margot, P., Stoilovic, M., 2004. Fingerprints and Other Ridge Skin Impressions. CRC Press, Boca Raton.

Cowger, J.F., 1983. Friction Ridge Skin. Elsevier, New York.

Cummins, H., Midlo, C., 1943. Finger Prints, Palms and Soles. The Blakiston Company, Philadelphia, PA.

Home Office Scientific Development Branch, 2005. Fingerprint Development Handbook. Heanor Gate Printing Limited, Derbyshire.

Langenburg, G., Champod, C., Genessay, T., 2010. Informing the judgments of fingerprint analysts using quality metric and statistical assessment tools. Forensic Science International 219, 183–198.

National Research Council of the National Academies, 2009. Strengthening Forensic Science in the United States: A Path Forward. National Academies Press, Washington, DC.

Wertheim, K., Maceo, A., 2002. The critical stage of friction ridge and pattern formation. Journal of Forensic Identification 52, 35–85.

Whipple, I., 1904. The ventral surface of the mammalian chiridium, with special reference to the conditions found in man. Zeitschrift fur Morphologie und Anthropologie VII, 261–368.

Relevant Websites

http://clpex.com/—Complete Latent Print Examination.
http://www.theiai.org/—International Association for Identification.
http://onin.com—Latent Print Examination: Fingerprints, Palmprints, and Footprints.
http://www.thefingerprintinquiryscotland.org.uk—The Fingerprint Inquiry of Scotland.

Friction Ridge Print Examination—Interpretation and the Comparative Method

RM Ruth, M Reznicek, and DM Schilens, Federal Bureau of Investigation – Latent Print Units, Quantico, VA, USA

Glossary

Analysis Analysis is the first step of ACE-V, and it is the step used to determine if a print is suitable for comparison.

Applied science Application of trusted scientific theories to real-life situations.

Bias Effect that perception and/or mental processes may have on the reliability or validity of one's observations and conclusions. See also confirmation bias and contextual bias.

Blind verification The independent application of ACE to a friction ridge print by another qualified examiner who does not know the conclusion(s) of the previous examiner(s) and has limited or no knowledge of case information.

Comparison The examination of two friction ridge prints to detect similarities and differences. This is the second step of ACE-V but may require return to analysis.

Confirmation bias Seeing what one expects to see and rationalizing any information that disagrees with a preconceived notion.

Contextual bias The possible influence on the examiner of information that is not directly related to a friction ridge print examination.

Distortion Variances in the reproduction of friction ridge arrangements of the skin caused by pressure, movement, force, contact surface, etc.

Evaluation The formulation of a conclusion based on the interpretation of all the data gathered during analysis and comparison. This is the third step of ACE-V.

Exclusion A decision by a qualified examiner that there are sufficient features in disagreement to conclude that two areas of friction ridge prints do not originate from the same source, where source refers to the area of friction ridge skin that produced the latent print in question.

Identification (individualization) A decision by a qualified examiner that there are sufficient features in agreement to conclude that two friction ridge prints come from the same source.

Inconclusive A decision by a qualified examiner that means a conclusive decision (identification or exclusion) could not be reached. Inconclusive means that more information is required to come to a conclusive decision. The meaning of the inconclusive decision varies based on the definition of suitability for comparison that is used by the reporting agency.

Latent print (mark) Unintentional or uncontrolled deposition of the friction ridge arrangements of the skin onto a substrate. These are often fragmentary and may require forensic light sources, chemicals, or powders to visualize.

Level I detail Overall ridge flow and print morphology.

Level II detail Individual friction ridge paths and friction ridge events (e.g., dividing ridges, ending ridges, and dots).

Level III detail Dimensional attributes of individual friction ridges (e.g., width, ridge shapes, and pores).

Premises The knowledge that friction ridge arrangements are unique and persistent has been supported through study; therefore, the premises of uniqueness and persistency are used as a given allowing examiners to conduct friction ridge print examinations.

Quality The clarity and the discriminating strength of the data contained in a friction ridge print.

Quantity The amount of information contained in an area of a friction ridge print.

Suitability Determination that a friction ridge print contains enough quantity and quality of information to be used for comparison. Some agencies use a suitable for identification standard, while others use a suitable for identification or exclusion standard. The terms of value and of no value are commonly used interchangeably with suitability.

Verification Independent application of analysis, comparison, and evaluation by a qualified examiner. This fourth step of ACE-V may include a peer review of the data used to reach a conclusion.

 http://dx.doi.org/10.1016/B978-0-12-800573-6.00009-4

Friction Ridge Print Examination—Interpretation and the Comparative Method

The examination of friction ridge prints is a scientific endeavor that involves the application of information learned from many fields of science. A qualified examiner must have an understanding of the embryological development and biological regeneration of friction ridge skin in order to fully understand how it might appear when recorded. The understanding of the development and structure of skin gives qualified, trained examiners the ability to interpret the data left in two-dimensional (2D) recordings of the 3D surface of the skin.

Due to the pliability of the skin, features may appear slightly different in each recording, but a qualified examiner will recognize that these features will move in concert as they are locked together in their arrangement. This means that while each recording of an area of friction ridge print will appear slightly different, the examiner must be trained to recognize the limitations of the movement of the skin.

The qualified examiner must also know, by understanding the development of the skin as well as through empirical review of friction ridge prints, the discriminating strengths of different features and how the discriminating strength changes in different areas of the friction ridge skin. An understanding of pattern force development will assist the examiner in recognizing that certain areas of the skin may require more features to have the same discriminating strength as fewer features in another area. This will also be evident when examining prints, and this is why a large amount of friction ridge prints should be studied before an examiner is considered qualified to conduct friction ridge print examinations.

In order to apply this knowledge in a systematic manner and properly interpret the data available in friction ridge print examinations, examiners apply ACE-V. ACE-V stands for analysis, comparison, evaluation, and verification and is the standard process used by friction ridge print examiners.

Analysis, Comparison, Evaluation, and Verification

ACE-V is a holistic process used in comparative sciences, such as friction ridge print examinations. ACE-V is a systematic way of conducting examinations. When following ACE-V, an analyst takes into account the quality (clarity of the features and the discriminating strength of those features) and quantity (amount of features in an area) of information present in a latent print. These quality and quantity are assessed during the analysis step.

Analysis is the information-gathering step of the ACE-V process. The prints are analyzed independently, usually beginning with the lower-quality print. Analysis serves to identify tolerance, classify and orient friction ridge prints, and reduce contamination, or bias, from information in the known print. During analysis, the expert assesses factors (distortions) that affect the appearance of the print. These factors include, but are not limited to, matrix (the substance the friction ridge print is left in, such as sweat or oil), substrate (the material the friction ridge print is left on), development medium (the chemical, forensic light source, or powder used to make a latent print visible), and pressure and movement. The three levels of detail, as detailed in **Figure 1**, contained within a print are also assessed.

Once all of the information contained in a print has been assessed, a determination of suitability for comparison is made. Suitability is the determination that a print has an adequate quality and quantity of information. This determination is based

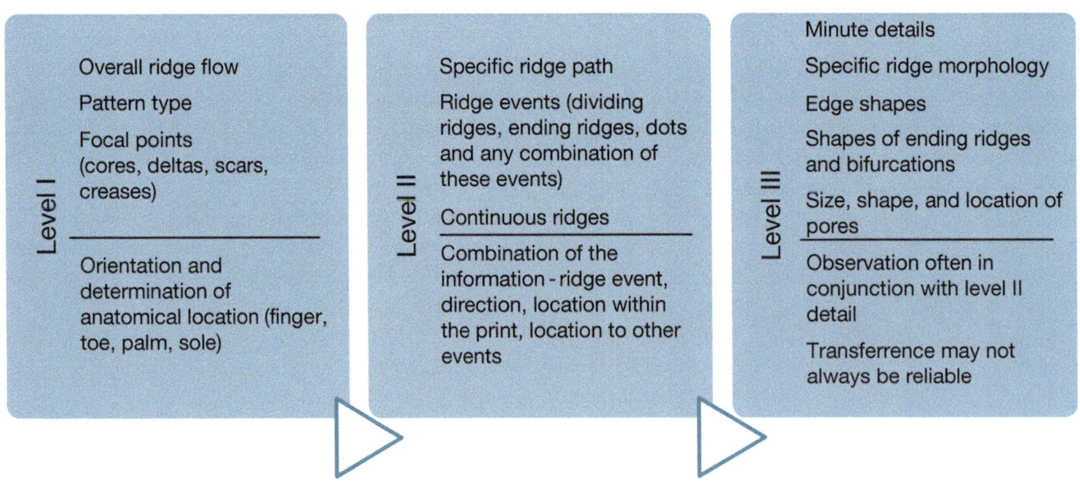

Figure 1 Three levels of detail.

on the assessment of the discriminating strengths of the features and their arrangement within the print. There are two approaches to determining suitability for comparison. Some agencies determine that a print is suitable for comparison if it contains sufficient reliable information in order to determine that the print can be identified to a source, given the corresponding known print. Other agencies determine that a print is suitable for comparison if the print can be excluded or identified.

Comparison begins after a determination of suitability for comparison is made. During comparison, additional information is gathered in the form of a side-by-side examination of the latent, or unknown, print and the known print to determine agreement and disagreement. An examiner is not looking for the prints to be identical but is using the information gathered in analysis to determine whether areas of agreement or differences between the friction ridge arrangements exist. To ensure that examiners are properly interpreting data, strong quality assurance measures, including thorough documentation, are essential for transparency.

Analysis and comparison are not completely distinct steps. A thorough analysis must be conducted and documented prior to beginning comparison; however, once comparison has begun, it may be necessary to reanalyze information that was interpreted differently prior to comparison. It is imperative that any new data interpretation developed after the beginning of the comparison should be documented thoroughly to ensure a proper recording of the interpretive steps of the examination.

During the evaluation phase, all the information gathered during analysis and comparison is used to generate a conclusion. The information is evaluated, and it is determined whether the prints come from different sources, the same source, or there is not sufficient information to render a conclusive decision. There are three corresponding decisions that can be reached: exclusion, identification, or inconclusive.

Exclusion is a decision made by a qualified examiner that there are sufficient features in disagreement to conclude that two areas of friction ridge impressions do not originate from the same source, where source refers to an area of friction ridge skin.

Identification (individualization) is a decision made by a qualified examiner that there are sufficient features in agreement to conclude that two friction ridge prints come from the same source. The identification of a friction ridge print to a source is the decision that the likelihood the impression was made by another (different) source is so remote that it is considered as a practical impossibility.

An inconclusive decision means that more information is required to reach a conclusive decision. The meaning of an inconclusive decision varies based on the definition of suitability for comparison that is used by the reporting agency.

If an agency is using the suitability for identification standard, then an inconclusive decision means that a latent print contains sufficient reliable information to be identified and more information is needed in the known print. This can happen if the comparable areas are not available for comparison. An example of this is if the latent print is from the tip area of the finger and this information is not available on the corresponding known print. More information is needed from the known print before an exclusion or identification decision can be made. This can also occur if the corresponding areas are recorded but are not of sufficient quality for comparison.

If an agency is using the suitability for exclusion and identification standard, then an inconclusive decision is rendered when there are features that are noted to be different, but there is not enough information to generate an exclusion decision. Alternatively, there may be some information in agreement but not enough to render an identification decision. This may include situations where more information is required in the known print.

In all cases where an inconclusive decision is rendered, regardless of the suitability standard, there is not enough information present between the prints being compared in order to generate either an exclusion or an identification decision.

Verification is the final step in the ACE-V process. In verification, another qualified examiner performs an independent analysis on and comparison and evaluation of the two prints to verify the examination of the original examiner. It is a quality measure built into the process. It is a standard practice that all identification decisions must be verified, but in other instances when verification must be performed, it should be built into the quality system of an agency. Verification of an erroneous decision is equivalent to making the erroneous decision and is treated with the same gravity.

Each step of ACE-V, as described above, involves interpretation of data. Because all the data interpretation is conducted and known only to the examiner's brain, thorough documentation is imperative.

ACE-V as an Applied Science

ACE-V is an applied process using information determined through studies previously conducted in other sciences. ACE-V is applied by a human being, so the risk of error must be mitigated through quality control measures. Verification, the quality control measure built directly into the process, is automatic for identifications but applicable to all conclusions (SWGFAST), but it should not be the only form of quality control used when conducting ACE-V.

Blind Verification

Blind verification functions as a quality control measure, testing the reproducibility of decisions made during ACE-V by limiting the bias introduced into the examinations.

Blind verification is the independent application of ACE to a friction ridge print by another qualified examiner who does not know the conclusion(s) of the previous examiner(s) and has limited or no knowledge of the case information. It should be used to eliminate confirmation bias and limit contextual bias in the examinations of friction ridge prints. Blind verification may be used at any step of the ACE process where a decision is made.

Bias is a term that can be used for any number of outside influences that may affect the cognitive decision process during the examination. Two types of bias are most commonly discussed in relation to the comparative sciences—confirmation and contextual bias.

Confirmation bias, in general terms, is seeing what one expects to see, and disregarding or minimizing any information that disagrees with a preconceived notion. There is concern that this type of bias may enter friction ridge print examination during verification or any peer review because the verifying/reviewing examiner knows the conclusion of the original examiner.

Contextual bias is the potential influence exerted on the examiner by the details in the case that are not directly related to the print. Contextual bias may occur; for example, if the examiner knows specific details of the criminal activity or the investigative steps leading up to the submission of the evidence being examined.

Consultation

In any scientific endeavor, consultation may be necessary. At times, an examiner may need to consult someone with more experience, whether counted in number of years or prior exposure to a particular type of evidence, or a trusted colleague for their view of the evidence. This may occur if there are distortions affecting the appearance of a print, the surface that the print is on is unusual, or an examiner wants to ensure that he or she is interpreting the data correctly. Consultation is always encouraged, as it allows examiners to objectively discuss the information present in the friction ridge prints. Consultation should be documented, and it must not be substituted for verification. Verification must be conducted independently by a qualified examiner who has not been consulted in the examination process.

Complex Prints

At times, an examiner may determine that a print is complex. This may occur when a more in-depth analysis is needed due to the presence of distortion (i.e., extreme pressure, extreme movement, unusual matrix, and unusual development). More detailed documentation is required when examining complex prints.

Conflict Resolution

Opinions may vary from expert to expert; therefore, agencies should have a process in place to attempt to resolve these technical conflicts. It is possible to develop multiple ways to resolve conflict. Some agencies may use a discussion-based approach where the experts attempt to resolve the conflict through documented discussion, possibly in conjunction with a third-party arbiter. Other agencies may adopt policies that involve reaching a consensus through a group, and still other agencies may choose to use blind verification as a means to resolve conflict. Conflicts may occur in multiple areas throughout the ACE-V process.

The key to a conflict resolution policy is that there should also be an attempt to determine if a corrective action is appropriate through review of the data and the interpretations generated using that data.

Documentation

Documentation of friction ridge print examinations must be such that another qualified examiner can determine what examinations were conducted and can interpret the data. It may also be helpful for the documentation to make clear specifically which data were used to generate the conclusions that were reached. This transparency not only helps the courts understand which data were used and how, but also helps in any quality review process should an error occur.

All relevant information that is available to the examiner should be documented. However, the extent of detail of the documentation may be different, depending on the complexity of the examination. The print alone is not enough documentation since it provides no understanding of how a conclusion was reached. The print must be accompanied by annotations or notes. An attempt should be made to thoroughly document all steps in the process where interpretation of data occurs.

Analysis is the initial data-gathering phase and should be documented prior to comparison to avoid any contamination of the brain by information from the known print. The minimum documentation that should be required for analysis is the anatomical source (fingerprint, palm print, toe print, footprint, impression), level I detail present (orientation, distal direction, etc.), and level II detail present. If they are known, the substrate, development medium, and preservation method (lift, photograph, etc.) should be documented as well. Other things that may need documentation could be the matrix, pressure, movement, level III detail (if reliably recorded), and any other features of the print that may affect a decision (creases, scars, etc.).

After analysis, two or more prints are compared to each other. This comparison should also be documented. A legible copy of the known exemplar (or the original known exemplar) should be kept in the case record for any future verification uses, or the exemplar should be retrievable. The known exemplar should have some form of a unique identifier tying it to the individual being compared and separating it from anyone else. It should also be documented if the known exemplar is not suitable for comparison. Along with this documentation, any information that is used during the comparison that was not originally documented in analysis should be documented, and it should be clear what information was detected during the comparison versus what was detected during the analysis. This will provide transparency as to what data were interpreted at which phase of ACE.

Proper documentation is required in order to clearly state the conclusions reached in the evaluation phase. When documenting identifications, it must be made clear which friction ridge print has been identified. The individual identified must be documented as well as the anatomical origin (finger position, right/left palm, etc.). It must be clear which examiner reached the conclusion and when he or she reached it. An exclusion should be documented in a similar manner. It must be clear from the case file which known print was compared to which latent print and which examiner reached a conclusion and when. Documentation for an inconclusive decision should contain all the same information, who reached the conclusion, when the conclusion was reached, the known print(s) used, the latent print examined, and the anatomical area(s) compared. Due to the different possible meanings of inconclusive decision based on the type of suitability for comparison standard used, an inconclusive decision needs more documentation for transparency. It must be made clear why this examination has been deemed inconclusive. If the print was compared under the suitable for identification standard, better known prints would be required, and this should be documented. If the print was compared under the suitable for exclusion and identification standard, it must be made clear if better known prints are required for conclusive comparisons, or if there was insufficient ridge detail in agreement based on the latent print alone. This allows investigators to know if they need to retrieve more known exemplars. All conclusions must be documented before having a conclusion verified. Documentation of a verification or blind verification must include all the same information as that of the original evaluation documentation.

Consultations should also be documented for transparency. This should include which print was reviewed or discussed, what the consultation entailed, and what results were generated, along with an indication of which examiner was consulted and the date of the consultation.

Ownership of the documentation is also imperative. All documentation should be dated and initialed, signed, or the equivalent, by the individual(s) who participated in each specific activity. This documentation will allow for transparency, ownership, and peer review.

Acknowledgment

This is publication number 11-2 of the Laboratory Division of the Federal Bureau of Investigation. Names of commercial manufacturers are provided for identification only, and inclusion does not imply endorsement by the FBI.

See also: **Pattern Evidence/Fingerprints (Dactyloscopy):** Automated Fingerprint Identification Systems (AFIS); Automated Methods, Including Criminal Records Administration; Chemistry of Print Residue; Friction Ridge Skin Impression Evidence – Standards of Proof; Identification and Classification; Sequential Treatment and Enhancement; Visualization or Development of Crime Scene Fingerprints.

Further Reading

Ashbaugh, D.R., 1999. Quantitative – Qualitative Friction Ridge Analysis: An Introduction to Basic and Advanced Ridgeology. CRC Press, Boca Raton, FL.

Ashbaugh, D.R., 2005. Basic Forensic Ridgeology. FBI Training Seminar, Quantico, VA.

FBI Laboratory, 2011a. Latent Print Unit Operations Manual. Standard operating procedures for examining friction ridge prints. Revision 5.

FBI Laboratory, 2011b. Latent Print Unit Quality Assurance Manual. Procedures for blind verification. Revision 1.

Huber, R.A., 1959–1960. Expert witness. Criminal Law Quarterly 2, 276–295.

Interpol European Expert Group on Fingerprint Identification II (IEEGFI II), 2004. Method for Fingerprint Identification Part 2: Detailing the Method Using Common Terminology and through the Definition and Application of Shared Principles, p. 12. Available from: www.interpol.int/public/Forensic/fingerprint.WorkingParties/IEEGFI2/default.pdf (accessed 01.07.11.).

Langenburg, G., 2009. A performance study of the ACE-V process: a pilot study to measure the accuracy, precision, reproducibility, repeatability, and biasability of conclusions resulting from the ACE-V process. Journal of Forensic Identification 59 (2), 219–257.

Langenburg, G., Champod, C., Wertheim, P., 2009. Testing for potential contextual bias effects during the verification stage of the ACE-V methodology when conducting fingerprint comparisons. Journal of Forensic Sciences 54 (3), 571–582.

Maceo, A., 2009. Qualitative assessment of skin deformation: a pilot study. Journal of Forensic Identification 59 (4), 390–440.

National Research Council of the National Academies, 2009. Strengthening Forensic Science in the United States: A Path Forward. The National Academies Press, Washington, DC, pp. 8, 9, 123, 142.

Pankanti, S., Prabhakar, S., Jain, A.K., 2002. On the individuality of fingerprints. IEEE Transactions on PAMI 24 (8), 1010–1025. http://biometrics.cse.msu.edu/publications.html.

Peterson, P., et al., 2009. Latent prints: a perspective on the state of the science. Forensic Science Communications 11 (4). www.fbi.gov/hq/lab/fsc/current/indes.htm (accessed 01.07.11.).

Raven, P.H., Johnson, G.B., 1992. Biology, third ed. Mosby, St. Louis, MO, p. 7.

Reznicek, M., Ruth, R.M., Schilens, D.M., 2010. ACE-V and the scientific method. Journal of Forensic Identification 60 (1), 87–103.

Scientific method, 1992. Academic Press Dictionary of Science and Technology. Academic Press, San Diego, CA, p. 1996.

Stoney, D.A., 2001. Measurement of fingerprint individuality (Chapter 9). In: Lee, H., Gaensslen, R.E. (Eds.), Advances in Fingerprint Technology, second ed. CRC Press, Boca Raton, FL, pp. 327–387.

SWGFAST, 2002. Friction Ridge Examination Methodology for Latent Print Examiners. Ver. 1.01. www.swgfast.org (accessed 01.07.11.).

SWGFAST, 2004. Standards for conclusions, ver. 1.0. Journal of Forensic Identification 54 (3), 358–359.

SWGFAST, 2006. Quality Assurance Guidelines for Latent Print Examiners. Ver. 3.0. www.swgfast.org (accessed 01.07.11.).

SWGFAST, 2010. Standard for the Documentation of Analysis, Comparison, Evaluation, and Verification (ACE-V) (Latent). Ver. 1.0. www.swgfast.org (accessed 01.07.11.).

SWGFAST, 2011a. Standards for Examining Friction Ridge Impressions and Resulting Conclusions. Draft for comment. Ver. 1.1. www.swgfast.org (accessed 01.07.11.).

SWGFAST, February 11, 2011b. Standard for the Application of Blind Verification of Friction Ridge Examination. Ver. 1.0. www.swgfast.org (accessed 01.07.11.).

SWGFAST, February 11, 2011c. Standard Terminology of Friction Ridge Examination. Ver. 3.0. www.swgfast.org (accessed 24.02.12.).

SWGFAST Guidelines & Standards. www.swgfast.org.

Ulery, B.T., Hicklin, A.R., Buscaglia, J., Roberts, M.A., 2011. Accuracy and reliability of forensic latent fingerprint decisions. Proceedings of the National Academy of Sciences 108 (19), 7733–7738.

Wertheim, K., Maceo, A., 2002. The critical stage of friction ridge and pattern formation. Journal of Forensic Identification 52 (1), 35.

Relevant Websites

www.clpex.com—Complete Latent Print Examination.

www.onin.com—Onin.com. homepage.

www.swgfast.org—Scientific Working Group on Friction Ridge Analysis, Study and Technology.

Analysis, Comparison, Evaluation, and Verification (ACE-V)

L Tierney, Gaithersburg, MD, USA

Introduction

As viewed in many television shows such as CSI, The Mentalist, and Bones, forensic evidence has created a large impact in American society. This is due to the fact that forensic evidence has made an even larger impact on the criminal justice system. Determining the source of items, whether they may be carpet fibers, toolmarks, shoeprints, or fingerprints, has assisted law enforcement in solving many crimes. There are a great many items that can be linked to a source, helping to tell the chain of events that transpired, whether in criminal activities or everyday life. The essential component of using forensic evidence to identify a source is making a comparison between the evidence (or unknown) and a known sample of the source. One way this can be achieved is by comparing the item with a potential source using ACE-V process.

ACE-V is an acronym that stands for analysis, comparison, evaluation, and verification and is a systematic, careful approach for the examination and comparison of forensic evidence. It is used as a framework to maintain a maximum amount of objectivity and guide the forensic examiner through the comparison process in a thorough and orderly manner, requiring that all visible information be taken into account and weighed before reaching a conclusion. Several branches of forensic science follow ACE-V either formally or informally, including fingerprints, footwear/tire tracks, and questioned documents.

History and Etiology

The concept of ACE-V as a process by which some forensic practitioners compare two or more items of evidence appears to have first been introduced by Roy Huber, a questioned document examiner with the Royal Canadian Mounted Police (RCMP) in 1959. It was at this time that Huber published an article entitled "Expert Witnesses – In Defence of Expert Witnesses in General and of Document Examiners in Particular" in *Criminal Law Quarterly* in which he laid out analysis, comparison, and evaluation as the stages used to compare and identify a person or thing. At this time, no mention of the verification stage of the process was made.

In 1962, Huber presented this same information at an International Association for Identification (IAI) Document Seminar in St. Louis, Missouri. During this presentation, he stated that the scientific method "…insists on verification as the most reliable form of proof" but did not include verification as one of the stages in the comparison process. In 1972, Huber published a reiteration of the concept of ACE with the same quote regarding verification without the addition of a verification stage in the July–August edition of the *Royal Canadian Mounted Police Gazette* in an article entitled "The Philosophy of Identification."

At some point in the 1970s, the Ontario Police College adopted the concept of ACE-V but only for physical evidence. David Ashbaugh (at present, renowned as a major innovator in the field of friction ridge examination) trained at the Ontario Police College under Harold Tuthill. Tuthill believed that fingerprints did not fall under the category of physical evidence and thus ACE-V did not apply. Ashbaugh disagreed. He felt that ACE-V was relevant and began using it as a method for the examination of friction ridge impressions.

In 1979, Ashbaugh (then with the RCMP) began putting ACE-V forward as a process for the examination of friction ridge impressions. While initially ACE-V was resisted by the community, after years of Ashbaugh presenting material to support ACE-V one concept at a time, it is with friction ridge examiners that the process has been most fully fleshed out and adopted.

At about the same time when Ashbaugh was introducing friction ridge examiners to ACE-V, Michael Cassidy (also of the RCMP) wrote and published a book entitled *Footwear Identification* in which he espoused ACE (with a reexamination and confirmation of identification work for all inexperienced examiners) as the process for comparing footwear evidence.

While ACE-V has been adopted by individual examiners or scientific working groups in several forensic sciences, including footwear identification, tire track identification, questioned documents, forensic photographic comparison, and forensic podiatry, only in the field of friction ridge identification has the adoption of the process (while not universal) been formal and widespread enough to result in numerous publications, testing, and extensive training.

 http://dx.doi.org/10.1016/B978-0-12-800573-6.00010-0

The Process

Each branch of forensic science using this process has its own definition for the steps of ACE-V, but they can be summed up generally as follows:

Analysis A thorough assessment during which the available and relevant discriminating features are assessed for class characteristics and accidental/individual characteristics (if applicable), quantity, clarity (quality), and reliability.

Comparison Details of the unknown and known are comparatively measured for similarities and dissimilarities.

Evaluation Similarities and dissimilarities between the unknown and known are weighed and a conclusion is reached.

Verification A quality check during which an independent ACE examination by a second, qualified examiner is completed.

An important aspect of the analysis phase is the determination of suitability to continue on to the comparison and evaluation phases of ACE. The determination of suitability is based on the assessment of the quality and quantity of the detail present and the discriminating strength of that detail. Any evidence that is determined not to possess enough detail with strong specificity of features will be determined to be unsuitable or not of value for comparison (or identification).

While ACE is described as a three-step process and each step is followed through to its completion, the steps are not discrete and cannot be completely isolated from each other. Instead, a blending of the steps often takes place. For example, during the comparison of the unknown and known images, data regarding the similarities and/or dissimilarities between them is gathered, and the examiner begins to see support for one conclusion over another and a tentative conclusion is reached. This is particularly apparent in the case of an exclusion or elimination where there is little or no similarity between the unknown and the known.

For simplicity sake, ACE is described as a linear process, but the steps do not always follow a linear progression and steps often recur. Just as noted above that blending of the steps may occur, an examiner may reenter the analysis phase during comparison or may reenter the comparison phase during evaluation. For example, during the comparison phase as the examiner notes a dissimilarity, he or she may be forced to reanalyze the known or unknown to determine if a true difference exists or if an error was made during analysis.

A note should be made that successful use of the ACE-V process requires that experts have an in-depth understanding of the manufacturing processes, biological/physiological aspects, etc., which go into making the relevant impression. Without this knowledge, a full analysis cannot be completed and the appropriate weight of different characteristics utilized during the evaluation phase cannot be determined. In fact, Huber, in his 1959 publication, stated that the true value of the expert lies in his ability to conduct a "more efficient analysis" by ignoring less valuable information and to use his "knowledge, training, experience, and skill" to make more accurate decisions during the evaluation phase.

Quality and Quantity of Detail

The pattern evidence disciplines (fingerprints, footwear/tire tracks, firearms/toolmarks, and questioned documents), in particular, have been the subject of much criticism in regards to quantitative thresholds for decision making. One point these criticisms miss is that the quantity of detail in an impression does not stand alone. A Galton feature or an accidental characteristic by itself is almost meaningless and cannot be given a discrete quantity on its own. The quality, reliability, and specificity of that detail also need to be considered and weighed (considerations made during the analysis phase). As an example, an unclear and thus potentially unreliable Galton feature in a friction ridge impression can certainly not be given the same weight or quantity as a very clear and reliable Galton feature. The result is a strong relationship between quality and quantity of detail, so that as the quality of the detail increases, the need for quantity of detail decreases. The inverse is true as well in that as the quality of the detail decreases, the need for quantity of detail increases.

The relationship between quality and quantity is best illustrated in **Figure 1**, depicting John Vanderkolk's quality–quantity curve. In this illustration of the interplay between quality and quantity in reaching a conclusion of agreement or disagreement, the *X*- and *Y*-axis represent quality and quantity of detail present in the items to be compared. The right side depicts agreement and the left side depicts disagreement. The white areas above the curves represent a combination of quantity and quality of information sufficient to determine agreement or disagreement between the items compared, while the black areas below the curves represent a combination of quantity and quality of information insufficient to determine agreement or disagreement between the items compared. The gray area represents an area of doubt where the examiner will not be able to make a determination because of insufficient information observed during the examination. If this area of doubt is where an examiner remains at the conclusion of the ACE process, a determination of insufficiency (or inconclusive) must be made.

An integral part of quality/quantity relationship is the setting of tolerances by the examiner. Tolerance refers the acceptable allowance in variation in appearance of the detail present in the evidence examined. When the detail is unclear or of low quality, the examiner may allow for a higher tolerance

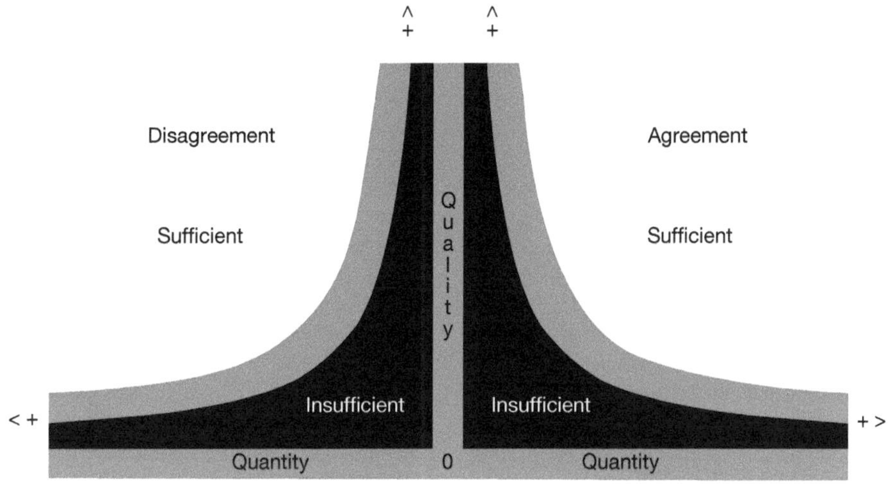

Figure 1 Quality–quantity curve. Reprinted from Vanderkol, J.R., 2001. Levels of quality and quantity in detail. Journal of Forensic Identification 51 (5), 461–468.

for acceptable variations in appearance of the same detail in the corresponding item. When the detail is clear or of high quality, the examiner can only allow minor tolerance for acceptable variations in appearance of the same detail in the corresponding item. These tolerances are established during the analysis phase and taken into consideration during both the comparison and evaluation phases of ACE.

Testing

Testing of a process such as ACE-V is undertaken to determine if the conclusions reached using the process are accurate and reproducible. Accurate meaning that an expert using the ACE-V process can be expected to reach the correct conclusion and reproducible meaning that all experts will reach the same conclusions.

Studies that indicate in some way the accuracy and/or reproducibility of the ACE-V process appear to primarily be limited to friction ridge identification. While several studies, each with their own limitations (found in the full publications), have been conducted which give results on the accuracy and reproducibility of friction ridge comparisons, only a few specifically reference the ACE-V process.

In 2004, Glenn Langenburg published "Pilot Study: A Statistical Analysis of the ACE-V Methodology – Analysis Stage" in the *Journal of Forensic Identification*. In this study, 24 fingerprint examiners and trainees in the state of Minnesota and 50 novices were asked to mark the minutiae (ridge endings, bifurcations, and dots) in a total of 12 latent and inked prints. The results showed that there was no statistically significant difference for the average number of minutiae marked by trainees, examiners, and certified examiners; there was a statistically significant difference in the average number of minutiae marked by experts and novices in 8 of the 10 life-sized (1:1) latent prints; experts correctly marked more minutiae than novices in the enlarged latent print; and both the experts and the novices marked more minutiae on average in the enlargement of the latent print than in the life-sized version of the same print.

In the 2006 article "The potential (negative) influence of observational biases at the analysis stage of fingermark individualization" published by Beatrice Schiffer and Christophe Champod in *Forensic Science International*, forensic science students were asked to mark and determine the type of minutiae in latent prints and assess the usefulness of the prints ("exploitable" or "identifiable"). Test I was conducted in an effort to determine whether exposure to specific theoretical and practical knowledge in forensic identification would alter the number of minutiae marked. The students were given 12 latent prints to analyze—once before completing training in forensic identification and once after. Schiffer and Champod determined that after completing training, the students found more minutiae in the latents (especially in those with background noise or low contrast), and they considered nearly twice as many of the prints "exploitable" and more than twice as many prints "identifiable." Test II was conducted to observe possible differences in the number of minutiae marked when a known print is presented with the latent and with differing background case information. They found that neither the presence of a known print nor the background case information made a significant difference to the number or type of minutiae marked or to whether the prints were determined to be "exploitable" or "identifiable."

In 2006, Kasey Wertheim, Glenn Langenburg, and Andre Moenssens published an article entitled "A Report of Latent Print Examiner Accuracy during Comparison Training Exercises" in the *Journal of Forensic Identification*. While it may be safe to infer that, because the comparison exercises reported on in the main body of the article took place in the United States (where ACE-V is widely accepted and taught) not long after friction ridge identification came under heavy attack by critics, the ACE process was being taught and therefore used for the comparison exercises, the authors do not explicitly state this. Therefore, we will focus on the report of the "follow-up experiment" in which the authors state that the verification stage of ACE-V was tested. For this portion of the study, the authors prepared verification packets each containing two errors for 25 participants. Participants were given the conclusions of previous students and were then asked to indicate whether they agreed or disagreed with the answers. Of the 50 errors present, 49 were detected by the participants with the one error that was not detected being missed by a trainee with less than 1 year of experience, who was not yet performing unsupervised casework. This shows that verification as a quality assurance measure in the ACE-V process is effective for catching erroneous identifications. The authors also noted that not all of the correct identification answers given by previous students were agreed upon by the participants. In fact, nine of the participants with more than 1 year of experience disagreed with at least one of the correct identifications. While the exact reason for their "disagreement" was not noted on participant worksheets, the authors surmised that examiners serving in the quality assurance role as verifier "assume a more critical and conservative opinion…." The authors also suggest that because the verifiers were not just willing to just go along with all of the previous students' answers, criticism that the verification stage of the ACE-V is simply "ratification" was not supported by the observations made in the experiment.

In the 2009 "Testing for Potential Contextual Bias Effects During the Verification Stage of the ACE-V Methodology when Conducting Fingerprint Comparisons" by Glenn Langenburg, Christophe Champod, and Pat Wertheim published in the *Journal of Forensic Sciences*, an experiment involving 43 fingerprint experts and 86 novices and the effects of contextual bias was conducted. The experts and novices (tested separately) were divided into three groups, each exposed to differing levels of contextual bias. Each group was given a set of six side-by-side comparisons of an unknown fingerprint and a known fingerprint and asked to provide their conclusions. The control groups were given no contextual information, the low-bias groups were provided with the conclusions of a "latent print examiner trained to competency," and the high-bias groups were provided with the conclusions of a "latent print examiner trained to competency" but were also told, in person, by an internationally known latent print expert, that the conclusions were his or hers. The results showed that the effect of contextual bias was stronger for the novice groups than for the experts. In fact, the results of the low- and high-bias groups showed that the experts were more susceptible to contextual bias toward an inconclusive result than toward identification results; that they were more likely to provide definitive (identification or exclusion) conclusions and thus make fewer errors; and that the high-bias group was no more swayed by the opinion of an internationally known expert than an anonymous examiner trained to competency.

The 2009 article "A Performance Study of the ACE-V Process: A Pilot Study to Measure the Accuracy, Precision, Reproducibility, Repeatability, and Biasability of Conclusions Resulting from the ACE-V Process" written by Glenn Langenburg and published in the *Journal of Forensic Identification* reports the results of testing of the ACE and ACE-V processes. For this experiment, six fingerprint experts participated in three phases of testing: Phase 1, which tested ACE; Phase 2, which tested ACE-V; and Phase 3, which involved re-presenting errors. In Phase 1, each expert was given 60 latent prints and 8 known exemplars and asked to compare the prints using the ACE. Allowable conclusions were identification, exclusion, inconclusive, and no value. The experts reached 100% consensus on 43 of the 60 latent prints (72%). One of the latent prints resulted in four experts correctly making an identification and two experts making erroneous exclusions—this is explained by the author as being due to the mistaken inclusion of an image reversal (none of the participants were aware that an image reversal could be in the pool of latents). The remaining latents had mixed results in which some experts reached the correct definitive conclusion (identification or exclusion) and some experts felt that there was a lack of sufficiency in information (leading to an inconclusive determination) or that the latent was of no value for comparison.

In Phase 2, each of the six experts performed 30 ACE examinations and then passed his or her conclusions on to a second expert for verification, resulting in a total of 60 trials each. Before passing his or her conclusions on, the initial examiner was asked to change at least one of his or her responses to an erroneous identification (a close nonmatch). A total of nine erroneous identifications were passed on to verifiers and the verifiers detected all nine. In addition, a total of six false negatives were passed on to the verifiers and the verifiers detected none of them.

Phase 3 tested the repeatability of the comparison conclusions by re-presenting the errors made by the experts in phases 1 and 2 to those who made them to determine whether the individual would maintain the error. In the ten re-presentations of errors, all three of the false positives were corrected by the examiner and four of the seven false negatives were also corrected.

Forensic Disciplines That Have Not Adopted ACE-V

While ACE-V is outlined as a comparison process in publications for several different forensic disciplines, these disciplines have not necessarily adopted the acronym ACE-V or the terms analysis, comparison, evaluation, and verification as a whole.

According to members of SWGGUN (the Scientific Working Group for Firearms and Toolmarks), the traditional comparison method in firearms and toolmarks identification is pattern matching. The four-step process involves (1) evaluation—in which evidence is examined to determine if class characteristics between the two specimens are the same; (2) comparison—in which a side-by-side comparison is conducted; (3) conclusion—a conclusion is reached; and (4) verification—an independent evaluation of the conclusion by another qualified examiner. These steps, while using different terminology, are essentially the same process as ACE-V.

SWGTREAD (the Scientific Working Group for Shoeprint and Tiretread Evidence) at a recent meeting voted not to use the term "ACE-V" in a footwear/tiretread comparison methodology document currently under development. While the group does not formally support ACE-V, they have developed a "Guide for the Examination of Footwear and Tire Impression Evidence," which is published on their Web site. In the guide examination procedures include evaluating the impression evidence for quality, clarity, comparative, and enhancement potential, and the presence or absence of class characteristics and comparison with known footwear or tires. In addition, the Web site offers acceptable conclusions for the examinations. These procedures are very similar to ACE-V.

Conclusion

There are many different types of evidence that require examination, but for almost every type, a comparison must be conducted in order to relate the evidence to a specific source. For many disciplines of forensic science, this comparison is conducted using the analysis, comparison, evaluation, and verification or ACE-V process. As Huber states in his 1972 article "Thus we find that various fields of identification work do have a common denominator, which is the reasoning process by which identifications are made." ACE-V acts as a framework to maintain a maximum amount of objectivity and guide the forensic examiner through the comparison process in a thorough and orderly manner so that all available information can be taken into account and weighed before reaching a conclusion.

See also: **Anthropology/Odontology:** Odontology; **Documents:** Handwriting; **Foundations:** Overview and Meaning of Identification/Individualization; Interpretation/The Comparative Method; **Pattern Evidence:** Bare Footprint Marks; Footwear Marks; Palm Prints; Vehicle Tire Marks and Tire Track Measurement; **Pattern Evidence/History:** Fingerprint Sciences.

Further Reading

Ashbaugh, D.R., 1994. The premises of friction ridge identification, clarity, and the identification process. Journal of Forensic Identification 44, 499–516.

Ashbaugh, D.R., 1999. Quantitative-Qualitative Friction Ridge Analysis. CRC Press, Boca Raton, FL (Chapters I and IV).

Budowle, B., Buscaglia, J., Schwartz, P.R., 2006. Review of the scientific basis for friction ridge comparisons as a means of identification: committee findings and recommendations. Forensic Science Communications 8.

Cassidy, M.J., 1980. Footwear Identification. RCMP GRC, Ottawa (Chapter 5).

Champod, C., 2008. Fingerprint examination: towards more transparency. Law, Probability, and Risk 7, 111–118.

Champod, C., Lennard, C., Margot, P., Stoilovic, M., 2004. Fingerprints and Other Ridge Skin Impressions. CRC Press, Boca Raton, FL (Chapter 2).

DiMaggio, J.A., Vernon, W., 2011. Forensic Podiatry: Principles and Methods. Springer Science+Business Media, New York (Chapter 2).

Haber, L., Haber, R.N., 2006. Letter to the editor. Re: a report of latent print examiner accuracy during comparison training exercises. Journal of Forensic Identification 56, 493–499.

Haber, L., Haber, R.N., 2008. Scientific validation of fingerprint evidence under Daubert. Law, Probability, and Risk 7, 89–109.

Huber, R.A., 1959. Expert witnesses: in defence of expert witnesses in general and of document examiners in particular. The Criminal Law Quarterly 2, 276–295.

Huber, R.A., 1962. I.A.I. document seminar – St. Louis, Missouri. Identification News 12 (11), 5–8.

Huber, R.A., Headrick, A.M., 1999. Handwriting Identification: Facts and Fundamentals. CRC Press, Boca Raton, FL (Chapter 3).

Langenburg, G., 2004. Pilot study: a statistical analysis of the ACE-V methodology – analysis stage. Journal of Forensic Identification 54, 64–79.

Langenburg, G., 2009. A performance study of the ACE-V process: a pilot study to measure the accuracy, precision, reproducibility, repeatability, and bias ability of conclusions resulting from the ACE-V process. Journal of Forensic Identification 59, 219–257.

Langenburg, G., Champod, C., Wertheim, P., 2009. Testing for potential contextual bias effects during the verification stage of the ACE-V methodology when conducting fingerprint comparisons. Journal of Forensic Sciences 54, 571–582.

Nause, L., 2001. Forensic Tire Impression Identification. Canadian Police Research Centre, Ottawa (Chapter 13).

Rudin, N., Inman, K., 2005. Fingerprints in Print, the Sequel. CAC News, 2nd Quarter, pp. 6–8.

Schiffer, B., Champod, C., 2007. The potential (negative) influence of observational biases at the analysis stage of fingermark identification. Forensic Science International 167, 116–120.

Speckles, C., 2011. Can ACE-V be validated? Journal of Forensic Identification 61, 201–209.

SWGFAST, 2011. Standards for Examining Friction Ridge Impressions and Resulting Conclusions – Revised Draft for Comment (accessed 31.05.11.). http://www.swgfast.org/Documents.html.

SWGGUN. Elimination Factors Related to FA/TM Identification. www.swggun.org.

SWGGUN. SWGGUN Quality Assurance Guidelines. www.swggun.org/swg/index.php?option=com_content&view=section&id=3&Itemid=6.

SWGIT, 2007. Best Practices for Forensic Image Analysis. www.theiai.org/guidelines/swgit/guidelines/section_12_v1-6.pdf.

SWGIT, 2009. Best Practices for Forensic Photographic Comparison. www.theiai.org/guidelines/swgit/guidelines/section_16_v1-0.pdf.

SWGTREAD, 2006. Guide for the Examination of Footwear and Tire Impression Evidence. www.swggun.org/swg/index.php?option=com_content&view=section&id=3& Itemid=6.

SWGTREAD, 2006. Standard Terminology for Expressing Conclusions of Forensic Footwear and Tire Impression Examinations. www.swgtread.org/standards/published.html.

Tuthill, H., George, G., 2004. Individualization: Principles and Procedures in Criminalistics, second ed. Lightning Powder Company, Jacksonville.

Vanderkolk, J.R., 2001. Levels of quality and quantity in detail. Journal of Forensic Identification 51, 461–468.

Vanderkolk, J.R., 2004. ACE-V: a model. Journal of Forensic Identification 54, 45–52.

Vanderkolk, J.R., 2009. Forensic Comparative Science. Elsevier Academic Press, Amsterdam (Chapter 5).

Vanderkolk, J.R., 2011. Examination Process. The Fingerprint Sourcebook. National Institute of Justice, Washington, DC.

Wertheim, K., Langenburg, G., Moenssens, A., 2006a. A report of latent print examiner accuracy during comparison training exercises. Journal of Forensic Identification 56, 55–93.

Wertheim, K., Langenburg, G., Moenssens, A., 2006b. Authors' response to letter (of Haber and Haber). Journal of Forensic Identification 56, 500–510.

Identification and Classification

LA Hutchins, US Government, Washington, DC, USA

2013 Published by Elsevier Ltd.
This article is a revision of the previous edition article by B. Dalrymple, volume 2, pp. 869–877, © 2000, Elsevier Ltd.

Glossary

Algorithm A step-by-step procedure for solving a problem or accomplishing some end, especially by a computer.

Anthropometry Distinct measurements of the human body.

Arch A pattern type in which the friction ridges enter on one side of the impression and flow, or tend to flow, out the other side with a rise or wave in the center. Arches are subdivided into plain and tented arches.

Automated Fingerprint Identification System (AFIS) A generic term for a fingerprint matching, storage, and retrieval system.

Bifurcation The point at which one friction ridge divides into two friction ridges.

Classification system Alphanumeric formula of finger and palm print patterns used as a guide for filing and searching.

Dermal papillae Peg-like formations on the surface of the dermis.

Dermis The layer of skin beneath the epidermis.

Differentiation Becoming different, that is, the cells of an embryo differentiate into organs and parts as it grows; specific friction ridge patterns become unique.

Embryology A branch of biology that deals with the formation and development of embryos.

Enclosure A single friction ridge that bifurcates and rejoins after a short course and continues as a single friction ridge.

Ending ridge A single friction ridge that terminates within the friction ridge structure.

Epidermis The outer layer of the skin.

Friction ridge A raised portion of the epidermis on the palmar or plantar skin consisting of one or more connected ridge units.

Friction ridge skin Corrugated skin on the volar areas that enhances friction of the surface.

Furrows Valleys or depressions between friction ridges.

Henry classification An alphanumeric system of fingerprint classification named after Sir Edward Richard Henry used for filing, searching, and retrieving 10-print records.

Identification The determination by an examiner that there is neither sufficient agreement to individualize nor sufficient disagreement to exclude.

Impression Friction ridge detail deposited on a surface.

Incipient ridge An incipient ridge is an immature friction ridge.

Known fingerprints The fingerprints of an individual, associated with a known or claimed identity, and deliberately recorded electronically, by ink or another medium. Also known as exemplars.

Latent print Transferred impression of friction ridge detail not readily visible. Generic term used for unintentionally deposited friction ridge detail.

Loop A type of pattern in which one or more friction ridges enter upon either side, recurve, touch, or pass an imaginary line between delta and core and flow out, or tend to flow out, on the same side the friction ridges entered. Loops are subdivided into radial and ulnar loops.

Minutiae Events along a ridge path, including bifurcations, ending ridges, and dots (also known as Galton details).

Mugshot Police photograph of a suspect's face or profile.

Papillary ridges Orderly rows of eccrine glands positioned along the path of the friction ridge.

Pattern type Fundamental pattern of the ridge flow: arch, loop, whorl.

Persistence Having lasting qualities; remaining the same; nonchanging.

Primary ridge Ridge on the bottom of the epidermis under the surface friction ridges.

Recidivist A habitual criminal.

Secondary ridges Ridges on the bottom of the epidermis under the surface furrows.

Short ridge A single friction ridge beginning, traveling a short distance, and then ending.

Spur A bifurcation with one short friction ridge branching off a longer friction ridge.

Volar pad Palmar and plantar fetal tissue growth that affects friction ridge skin development and patterns.

Whorl A fingerprint pattern type that consists of one or more friction ridges that make, or tend to make, a complete circuit, with two deltas, between which, when an imaginary line is drawn, at least one recurving friction ridge within the inner pattern area is cut or touched. Whorls are subdivided into plain whorls, double loops, pocket loops, and accidental whorls.

Introduction

The classification and identification of friction ridge impressions rests on the two principal foundations of friction ridge skin: uniqueness and persistence. These two premises are rooted in the scientific research conducted on the development and structure of friction ridge skin coupled with empirical studies. It was this marriage of research and application that led to the establishment of friction ridge impressions as the primary method of personal and criminal identification.

Development of Friction Ridge Skin

The embryology of fetal growth is well researched and documented in the scientific literature. At 5 days postfertilization, embryonic cells are differentiating into nerve cells, blood cells, skin cells, and so on. At approximately 6 weeks gestational age, the hands have developed into flat-like scalloped paddles representing the five digits. At the same time, the volar pads begin to appear. Volar pads are areas of swollen undifferentiated connective tissue, known as mesenchymal tissue. The placements of the volar pads are predetermined in all normal and healthy human fetuses. Any deviations are due to genetic deformation or disease. While the initial placement of the volar pad is predetermined, the specific location, shape, and size of the volar pad influence the friction ridge pattern.

The volar pads stop growing at about 10 weeks, and by 12 weeks the pads are being reabsorbed back into the hand. As the volar pads shrink, the friction ridges of the fetus start to develop on the bottom of the epidermis, projecting down into the dermis. These ridges, known as primary ridges, continue to proliferate and within 3–4 weeks, the entire underside of the epidermis contains primary ridges that are anchored in the dermis. The proliferation of the primary ridges and the resulting paths and path deviations are random and dependent upon localized stresses and growth factors due to genetics and environment factors. It is this randomness both in the growth of the fingers and the proliferation of the ridges that contributes to the formation of a unique arrangement of friction ridge skin.

Each ridge consists of ridge units that have formed together, with each unit containing a sweat gland (14th week). The number of ridge units that then form into a ridge is random and dependent on genetic and physical variances that constitute growth. By the 15th–17th week, primary ridge proliferation ceases. At this point, secondary ridges start growing between the rows of primary ridges and down into the dermis. Although the proliferation of primary ridges has ceased, growth continues and the ridges push up through the surface. Beginning at approximately 17 weeks, the epidermal ridges can be viewed on the epidermis. Unlike primary ridges, secondary ridges do not contain sweat glands. Secondary ridge proliferation continues until 24 weeks. At this point, there is a one-to-one correspondence between the primary and secondary ridge. The path of the primary ridge corresponds to the epidermal surface friction ridge, whereas the path of the secondary ridge corresponds to surface furrows that exist between friction ridges (**Figure 1**). By the fifth month of fetal development, all friction ridge growth and proliferation has taken place and is established in its permanent form. This permanent formation can be viewed as the template that is maintained throughout one's life. Once friction ridges and their paths are established, the only factor that may cause a change in the template is damage down into the dermis.

Structure of Friction Ridge Skin

There are two types of skin: thin and thick skin. Thin skin covers most of the body and contains hair follicles, pigment, smooth muscles, and sebaceous glands (glands that secrete a waxy matter called sebum that lubricates the skin and the hair). Friction ridge skin is considered thick skin and is hairless, has no pigment, and contains sweat glands. Friction ridge skin covers the palmar area of the hands and the plantar area of the feet. It is considered specialized skin that serves to aid in grasping and holding. Like all skin, friction ridge skin is composed of two layers: epidermis, the outermost layer, and dermis, the underlying vascular support for the epidermis.

Thick skin epidermis contains five layers (**Figure 1**), starting from the bottommost layer to the topmost: (1) stratum basale, (2) stratum spinosum, (3) stratum granulosum, (4) stratum lucidum, and (5) stratum corneum. The stratum basale is also known as the generating layer because this is the layer that generates new skin cells through mitosis that then migrate up through the remaining layers. Cells in this layer are columnar in shape and flatten out as they progress to the surface where they eventually die. Cells that move into the stratum spinosum layer start to synthesize keratin, the structural protein that makes up skin, and begin to take the shape of a polygon. In the stratum

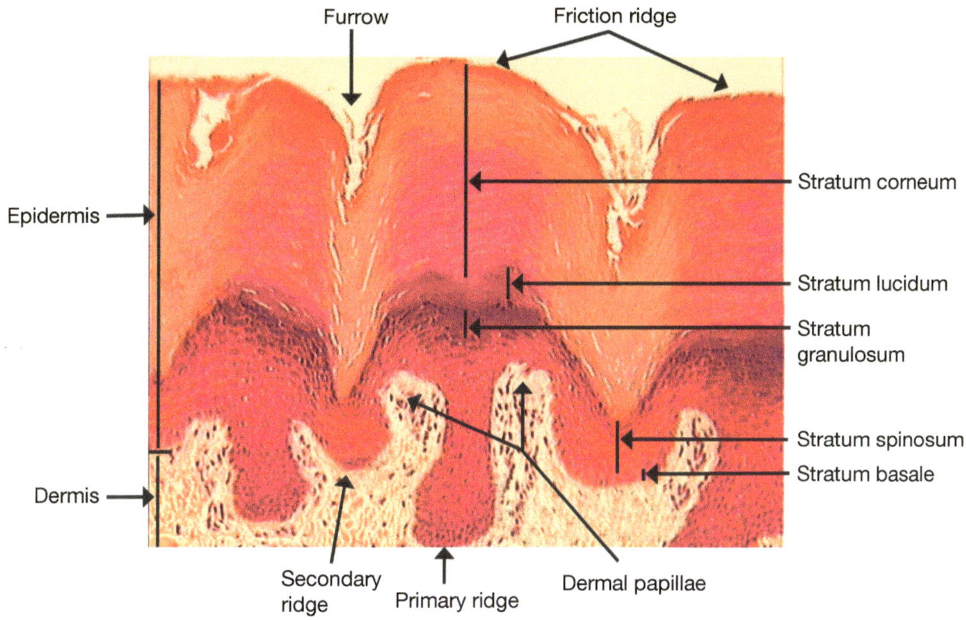

Figure 1

granulosum, cells are increasingly flattened and filled with keratin proteins and waterproofing lipids. This is the last layer of skin that is considered alive. The next layer of skin, the stratum lucidum, is only present in thick skin and is considered as a barrier layer of skin because of its waterproofing properties. The outermost layer, the stratum corneum, contains flat cells composed mainly of keratin protein in order to absorb water, provide strength, and serve as a protective layer. The progression of a cell from the stratum spinosum layer to the stratum corneum takes approximately 60 days. The structural integrity of the migrating skin cells is maintained by desmosomes, cell-adhesion proteins that tightly link adjacent cells together.

Connecting the epidermis to the dermis is the basement membrane. This connective tissue is strongly attached to the epidermis through fine fibers known as hemidesmosomes. The dermis is divided into two areas: (1) the papillary region and (2) the reticular region. The papillary region contains dermal papillae (**Figure 1**). Dermal papillae are fingerlike projections arranged into double rows, increasing the surface area between the epidermis and dermis, thereby strengthening the juncture with the epidermis and increasing the amount exchange of oxygen, nutrients, and waste. With regard to thick skin, the dermal papillae are extremely prominent. As a result, the epidermis follows the contour of the prominent double rows of dermal papillae. Each double row of dermal papillae corresponds to a surface friction ridge. The reticular region is composed of thick connective tissue that supports larger blood vessels and nerves.

Historical Scientific Research into Friction Ridge Skin

The use of fingerprints as a means of identification has existed for thousands of years. While early applications of fingerprint impressions specifically associated an impression left by a person with that person's identity, scientific research into the study of friction ridges did not start until the mid-to-late 1600s. This early research documented the anatomical and morphological structure of friction ridge skin.

In 1684, Nehemiah Grew studied the anatomy of the friction ridge skin and described the ridges, their arrangements, furrows, and sweat pores. His work contained accurate drawings of the palms, to include fingerprint patterns. A year later, Govard Bidloo (1649–1713) illustrated papillary ridges on the underside of the fingers. His book also contained a drawing of the friction ridges on a thumb. Marcello Malpighi (1628–1694) was the first to use the microscope to detail the different layers of skin and the form, structure, and function of friction ridge skin in his 1686 treatise *Concerning the External Tactile Organs*.

Continuing scientific research led anatomist J.C.A. Mayer to conclude in his book *Anatomical Copper-Plates with Appropriate Explanations* (1788) that while friction ridge patterns may bear a certain likeness, the formation of the individual ridges is random and they are thus never duplicated. This was the first observation that friction ridge patterns can be classified while the specific arrangement of the ridges and deviations therein are unique.

The first detailing of the different types of fingerprint patterns was by Johannes Evangelista Purkinje in his 1823 thesis *Commentary on the Physiological Examination of the Organs of Vision and the Cutaneous System*. Purkinje classified and illustrated nine different patterns, which served as the historical basis for future systems of fingerprint classification.

In 1883, Dr Arthur Kollmann researched the fetal development of friction ridges in his book *The Tactile Apparatus of the Hand of the Human Races and Apes in Its Development and Structure*. Kollmann was the first scientist to determine that friction ridges are formed by the sixth month. Kollmann identified embryological volar pads, the swelling of loose connective tissue, present on the hands and feet. He also formulated the theory that differential growth, caused by random stresses on the forming friction ridge skin, influenced friction ridge development.

One of the most prolific researches into friction ridge skin was by Harris Hawthorne Wilder. Over a 30-year period, Wilder researched the evolution, genetics, formation, structure, and differential growth of friction ridge skin. In conjunction with Bert Wentworth, a Police Commissioner in Dover, New Hampshire, Wilder authored the influential book *Personal Identification* in 1918. In this book, Wilder and Wentworth formulated the premise that, due to differential growth, all friction ridge skin is unique.

Modern scientific research into the embryological growth and development of friction ridges continued to support the premise that friction ridges are unique due to differential growth. Dr Harold Cummins known as the "Father of Dermatoglyphics" conducted the most extensive research into the study of friction ridges. He researched volar pad formation, development during key stages of fetal growth, to include growth during times of disease and genetic abnormality, and uniqueness of friction ridge skin. With Charles Midlo, Cummins authored the book *Fingerprints, Palms, and Soles – An Introduction to Dermatoglyphics* in 1943.

Like Cummins, Dr Alfred Hale conducted extensive research into the development and differential growth of friction ridges. Hale analyzed thin cross sections of fetal skin to document friction ridge growth and development at various stages. This significant research was published in his paper "Morphogenesis of the Volar Skin in the Human Fetus." Building on the foundations established by Cummins and Hale, Michio Okajima, researched immature friction ridges, known as incipient ridges, and established their uniqueness and permanence.

Research by Dr William Babler into the prenatal development of friction ridge skin has solidified the theory that volar pad shape and the timing of primary ridge formation determine pattern type and the width of the volar pad is a factor in ridge configuration. In addition, Babler also established that the bone width of the distal phalanx, the last digit in each finger or toe, influences the friction ridge pattern.

Uniqueness and Permanence—The Foundations of Friction Ridge Identification

The previous sections discussed the development and structure of friction ridge skin. The scientific research into both areas has established that friction ridge skin is both persistent and unique. The fact that epidermal cells are cemented together by desmosomes, coupled with the fact that the stratum spinosum is firmly attached to the dermis via the basement membrane, is the structural basis for the permanence of friction ridge detail. This structuring of the epidermis and the dermis allows for the renewal of skin cells while maintaining the friction ridge arrangements. As previously mentioned, the friction ridge template established in the developing fetus does not change throughout one's life except for the occurrence of damage to the dermis. However, while the damage may alter the friction ridges in a specific location, the resulting scar is both permanent and unique.

The principle of uniqueness of friction ridge configurations has been strongly supported by the research conducted in the fetal development of friction ridges. This research has demonstrated that primary ridge proliferation and the resulting ridge paths are mostly random and dependent upon random, localized stresses. Ridge units that make up each ridge populate randomly yet are influenced by the randomness of the units within the same vicinity. As a result, developing ridges are influenced by the random paths of other ridges that surround them. This random proliferation creates ridges that continue, stop, split, or develop spurs or islands. This random proliferation is also believed to be influenced by the environment of the growing fetus. While a fetus may be predisposed to a certain pattern type (arch, loop, or whorl) due to genetics (genotype), the specific path and its deviations are individual (phenotype) and not genetically controlled (although they may be highly influenced by pattern type or disease conditions). The prevailing theory of random ridge development is that the environmental experience of every fetus will never be duplicated. The exact pressures that a fetus experiences will always be unique to each fetus, including that of a twin growing in the same womb.

Early Applications of Friction Ridge Identification

In the mid-to-late 1800s numerous scientific studies proposed that friction ridges are both unique and persistent. However, these two premises of friction ridge identification had not been applied outside the scientific arena. It was not until Sir William Herschel, Dr Henry Faulds, and Sir Francis Galton articulated these premises that the groundwork was laid establishing that fingerprints could be used to identify recidivists, used in forensic science applications, and accepted as evidence in courts of law.

As a magistrate in India, Sir William James Herschel realized the utility of using friction ridge impressions for identification purposes on a large scale. He instituted the use of leaving one's fingerprints or palm prints as a signature for pension payments, authenticating transactions, and the fingerprinting of criminals to ensure that jail sentences were not carried out by a paid imposter. Herschel also researched fingerprint impressions obtained from friends and family members that he collected over the years and observed that friction ridges were both unique and persistent. While Herschel was instrumental in the institutionalization of fingerprints as a means of personal identification, his work did not extend to the realm of catching criminals.

In Japan, Dr Henry Faulds, a Scottish missionary, began research into the use of friction ridge impressions as a method of identification. After developing a method of recording inked impressions of each finger on a card, Faulds began to amass a large collection of fingerprint cards. Faulds analyzed this collection and determined that each impression in his sampling was unique. In addition to researching the individualizing power of friction ridges, Faulds explored the persistence of friction ridges by observing friction ridges growing back exactly the same after minor destruction. Faulds also observed persistence with relation to human growth by analyzing the friction ridges of children over a 2-year time period. The concept of uniqueness was first utilized in a criminal investigation when a member of Dr Henry Faulds' staff was accused of burglary. Faulds compared the latent print left by the perpetrator with the known prints of the accused staff member and concluded that the prints were not the same. This is considered the first latent print comparison used in relation to a criminal matter. In 1880, *Nature* magazine published an article written by Faulds in which he described the comparison of latent prints to known prints as evidence in criminal proceedings. Although Faulds specifically referenced the use of fingerprints left at crime scenes, the use of latent prints in criminal proceedings did not occur for a number of years and was not associated with the work of Faulds.

In 1888, Francis Galton, the cousin of Charles Darwin, began investigating fingerprints in preparation for a lecture on personal identification. In his investigations, Galton reviewed the work of Herschel and Faulds. Realizing the value of friction ridge impressions, Galton began his own scientific research. Galton collected over 8000 fingerprint impressions in order to study the fingerprint as a whole and the minutiae contained within each fingerprint. Four years of empirical studies resulted in Galton publishing his seminal work on friction ridges in 1892. In his book, *Finger Prints*, Galton detailed why and how fingerprints are unique and persistent. He also was the first to define and name the friction ridge deviations, known as minutiae, in a fingerprint. He described a bifurcation, ending ridge, short ridge, and enclosure. Galton's detailing of the uniqueness and persistence of friction ridges and its minutiae provided the foundation for the use of friction ridge identification in criminal proceedings (administrative and forensic).

After proposing the principles of uniqueness and persistence of friction ridges, the ability to associate a latent print left at a crime scene with a record print became a reality. In the years following the publication of Galton's book, police agencies determined that accidental recordings of fingerprints left at crime scenes could be compared to the prints of known individuals in order to solve criminal cases. As a result, the use of latent print impressions as evidence in criminal proceedings has been institutionalized in both the criminal justice and forensic science arenas since the late 1800s.

Criminal Identification Prior to the Use of Fingerprints

The impetus for the development of a reliable and accurate means of criminal identification came with the technological revolution, also known as the Second Industrial Revolution. This era ushered in technological advances (transportation, electricity, modern manufacturing, and food processing) that brought more people into cities, thereby creating an atmosphere that nurtured the criminal element. As crime rates grew, police agencies recognized the need to document criminals and their record in order to identify recidivists. The first method of documentation came with the development of photography. Photography allowed for the creation of rogues galleries, posters for the police to reference, and mug shots. While the use of photography was an improvement, it certainly was not the solution to the problem of certain identity. A criminal could easily change their appearance by changing their hairstyle or shaving off facial hair. Additionally, police departments did not have standard procedures for photographing criminals. It was common to see men wearing hats and women wearing veils in mug shots.

Seeing the need for a new method of criminal identification, Alphonse Bertillon, a police clerk in Paris, developed a system of body measurements for personal identification, known as anthropometry. The thought was that specific body measurements of an individual would not change over time. As such, once a person's measurements were recorded, that individual would be identified with his or her record. Bertillon's method of anthropometry was put into use in 1882. At that time, anthropometry was viewed as a truly scientific method of criminal identification and the technique spread worldwide. However, as more agencies came to use the system and as files grew, it became obvious that anthropometry was failing. It was realized that different technicians took dissimilar measurements of the same person, thereby either determining that an individual was not in the record or that they were the wrong person.

In 1888, Sir Francis Galton was asked to deliver a lecture on the methods of personal identification for the Royal Institution of Great Britain. Galton's research led him to conclude that anthropometry was a failing system that would not survive the test of time. Anthropometry did not account for natural variability due to growth or aging, interdependence of body parts, and suffered from the inability of technicians to take the exact measurement. All these reasons could potentially cause missed or erroneous identifications. As a result, Galton set out to develop a method of personal identification based on fingerprints. Having determined the uniqueness and persistence of friction ridges, Galton knew that fingerprints could be used as an accurate and reliable means of personal identification. As a result, Galton devised a 10-print classification system based on three classes of fingerprint patterns, the arch, loop, and whorl. While Galton's classification system was too rudimentary for large collections of fingerprint cards, his establishment of the three classes of fingerprint patterns laid the foundation for superior methods to be developed.

Development of Friction Ridge Classification Systems

In order to achieve a workable 10-print classification system, fingerprint cards had to be classified into a formula that could differentiate large amounts of fingerprint cards. Each card could then be systematically filed according to its classification formula. A classified incoming 10-print card could be searched in the filing system according to its formula. If the same formula was located, the incoming 10-print card was compared to each card assigned the same classification formula. If a match was not made, the incoming card would be filed with the same classification formula. If the comparison of the two cards resulted in the identification of a recidivist, then the police agency could add the applicable criminal charges to that person's rap sheet.

In addition to training police officers on the process of fingerprint comparison and identification, Juan Vucetich also developed his own 10-print fingerprint classification system. Vucetich's system divided the loop into two patterns (internal and external), added subcategories to further distinguish the patterns, incorporated ridge counts, and was expressed in the form of a ratio. In 1891, Vucetich successfully lobbied to have fingerprints replace anthropometry as a means of personal identification. Owing to the publication of his book, *Comparative Dactyloscopy*, in 1904, Vucitech's method of fingerprint classification received worldwide recognition.

Sir Richard Henry was also influenced by Galton's book. Realizing the need for a classification system that handles large amounts of data, Henry tasked two of his police officers in the Bengal District of India to create a workable 10-print fingerprint classification system. The two officers created a mathematical method that involved a pattern determination, ridge counts, and pattern tracings. In 1900, the Henry Classification System became the sole method of personal identification at Scotland Yard. Like Vucetich's classification system, the Henry system came to be used worldwide.

Numerous other 10-print classification systems were developed that were considered offshoots or extensions of the Henry or the Vucetich classification systems. For example, the Federal Bureau of Investigation (FBI) modified the Henry system to account for its large volume of fingerprint cards. In addition to 10-print classification systems, palm print classification systems, sole print, and single fingerprint classification systems were also developed.

Incorporation of Computers into the Science of Friction Ridge Identification

With technological advances in computer systems, friction ridge records were automated, thereby revolutionizing criminal identification. The establishment of Automated Fingerprint Identification System (AFIS) was based on the incorporation of the premises of friction ridge identification into the theoretical development of mathematical algorithms. Building on the science of uniqueness and persistence, software developers created computer algorithms that could extract the friction ridge paths and deviations and record this information as binary (zeros and ones) and then create mathematical maps of the extracted information. When a fingerprint or palm print card is entered into an AFIS, the resulting map is a series of numbers that have a direct relationship to the unique friction ridges contained therein. When a card is searched in an AFIS, the system compares the mathematical maps of the incoming card with the maps of the cards in the system and generates a list of potential candidates. AFIS also provide an invaluable service to forensic science and latent print examinations. The technology developed for the extraction of minutiae of known cards allows for the encoding of minutiae in a latent print. The minutia within a latent print is encoded and, like a known print card, a mathematical map of the latent print is created. This mathematical map is searched in the database of known print cards, resulting in a list of potential candidates that a competently trained latent print examiner can manually compare and potentially make identifications to persons previously unknown.

Conclusion

Friction ridge impressions remain the primary method of reliable identification due to the principles that friction ridges are unique and persistent. Friction ridge identification and classification has a long history rooted in scientific research and empirical observations. From the 1600s to the present day, the study and use of friction ridge information has served to modernize the criminal justice system and forensic science. The use of friction ridge classification systems as a method of personal identification revolutionized the criminal justice system by creating a reliable and usable method of identification.

While classification systems were the workhorse of criminal identification for over 100 years, modern computing technologies have eliminated its use. Friction ridge impressions are now digitized. Current computer technologies allow for the application of mathematical algorithms to digitized friction ridge impressions in order to automatically recognize patterns, establish mathematical maps for every friction ridge impression based upon the type, location, and direction of minutiae, and the generation of a list of potential candidates as a match for a questioned print. This technology is not limited to known impressions taken under controlled conditions but also allows for the searching of latent prints from crime scenes in the digitized databases of known prints to establish previously unknown suspects.

See also: **Management/Quality in Forensic Science:** *Sequential Unmasking*: Minimizing Observer Effects in Forensic Science; **Pattern Evidence:** Analysis, Comparison, Evaluation, and Verification (ACE-V); Bare Footprint Marks; Palm Prints; Physical Match; The Friction Ridge Skin of the Feet; **Pattern Evidence/Fingerprints (Dactyloscopy):** Automated Fingerprint Identification Systems (AFIS); Automated Methods, Including Criminal Records Administration; Friction Ridge Skin Impression Evidence – Standards of Proof; **Pattern Evidence/Firearms:** Laboratory Analysis; **Pattern Evidence/History:** Fingerprint Sciences.

Further Reading

Ashbaugh, D.R., 1999. Quantitative-Qualitative Friction Ridge Analysis: An Introduction to Basic and Advanced Ridgeology. CRC Press, Boca Raton, FL.

Babler, W.J., 1991. Embryologic development of epidermal ridges and their configurations. In: Plato, C., Garruto, R.M., Schaumann, B.A. (Eds.), Birth Defects: Original Article Series; Dermatoglyphics: Science in Transition. March of Dimes, New York.

Barnes, J.G., 2010. History. Fingerprint Sourcebook. National Institute of Justice/NCJRS, Rockville, MD (Chapter 1). http://www.ncjrs.gov/pdffiles1/nij/225321.pdf.

Cowger, J.F., 1983. Friction Ridge Skin: Comparison and Identification of Fingerprints. Elsevier Science Publishing Co., Inc, New York.

Cummins, H., Midlo, C., 1943. Finger Prints, Palms and Soles: An Introduction to Dermatoglyphics. Dover Publications, Inc, New York.

Faulds, H., 1880. On the skin furrows of the hand. Nature 22, 605.

Federal Bureau of Investigation, 1984. The Science of Fingerprints. U.S. Department of Justice. U.S. Government Printing Office, Washington, DC.

Galton, F., 1892. Finger Prints. MacMillan, New York.

Hale, A., 1952. Morphogenesis of volar skin in the human fetus. The American Journal of Anatomy 91 (1), 147–173.

Henry, E.R., 1934. Classification and Uses of Fingerprints, seventh ed. H. M. Stationery Office, London.

Hepburn, D., 1895. The papillary ridges on the hands and feet of monkeys and men. The Scientific Transactions of the Royal Dublin Society 5 (2), 525–537.

Herschel, W.J., 1916. The Origin of Finger-Printing. Oxford University Press, London.

Holt, S.B., 1968. The Genetics of Dermal Ridges. Charles C. Thomas, Springfield, IL.

New Scotland Yard, 1990. Fingerprint History: A Synopsis of the Development of the System of Fingerprint Identification with Particular Reference to New Scotland Yard. Metropolitan Police, New Scotland Yard, London.

Wertheim, K., 2011. Embryology and Morphology of Friction Ridge Skin. Fingerprint Sourcebook. National Institute of Justice/NCJRS, Rockville, MD (Chapter 1). http://www.ncjrs.gov/pdffiles1/nij/225321.pdf.

Wilder, H.H., Wentworth, B., 1918. Personal Identification. The Gorham Press, Boston.

Key Terms

ACE-V, Analysis, Anthropometry, Arthur Kollmann, Automated fingerprint identification system (AFIS), Basement membrane, Blind verification, Classification, Comparative sciences, Comparison, Conflict resolution, Consultation, Dermal papillae, Dermatoglyphics, Dermis, Desmosomes, Differential growth, Dr Alfred Hale, Dr Harold Cummins, Dr Henry Faulds, Dr William Babler, Embryology, Epidermis, Evaluation, Examination documentation, Fingerprint, Forensic science, Francis Galton, Friction ridge patterns, Friction ridge print examinations, Friction ridge skin, Friction ridge unit, Friction ridges, Genetics, Harris Hawthorne Wilder, Henry Faulds, Identification, International Association for Identification (IAI), J.C.A. Mayer, Johannes Evangelista Purkinje, Juan Vucetich, Latent fingerprint development, Latent print, Lights out, Marcello Malpighi, Minutiae, Nehemiah Grew, Palmar, Permanence, Persistence, Personal identification, Plantar, Primary ridge, Quality/quantity, Recidivist, Reproducible, Secondary ridge, Sir Edward Henry, Sir Francis Galton, Sir Richard Henry, Sir William Herschel, Suitability, Tolerance, Transparency, Uniqueness, Verification, Volar pads.

Review Questions

1. Who was the first scientist to recognize friction ridge formations? When were these observations made?
2. Who was Malpighi? Who was Purkinje? What were their contributions to fingerprinting?

3. How did Herschel first use fingerprints?
4. Who first used fingerprints left at a crime scene to identify criminals?
5. How did Galton become involved in the study of fingerprints?
6. When did the FBI establish its Identification Division?
7. When was one of the first fabrications of fingerprint evidence? What were the circumstances?
8. Why was the 2010 IAI resolution (2010–18) significant for fingerprinting?
9. Why are exclusions stronger than inclusions?
10. What was the role of the RCMP in the development of ACE-V?
11. Name each step in ACE-V and describe it.
12. One criticism of ACE-V is that it is too generic to be a "method" but rather is a process. Do you agree? Why or why not?
13. What goes into the basis for deciding a comparison is "inconclusive"? Is this a repeatable process or is subjectivity involved?
14. What is blind verification? Why is it important for forensic fingerprinting?
15. What should go into the documentation of a fingerprint examination and comparison? Why? Who is this documentation for?
16. When do primary ridges begin to form?
17. What are the five layers of the thick skin?
18. In what year did Kollmann publish on the development of friction ridge skin?
19. What is the current system of fingerprint classification used by the FBI?
20. Why was anthropometry considered to be "defunct" by Galton?

Discussion Questions

1. Consider the case of the wrongful prosecution of Alfred de Marigny. What are the implications for this kind of malfeasance at the crime scene by police? How could this kind of misconduct be prevented?
2. What is the basis for saying that friction ridge patterns are unique and permanent? Are these supportable claims? Why or why not?
3. If friction ridge patterns in the skin are considered to be unique, what are the implications for transferring those patterns to a substrate? Is the resulting transferred print also unique? Why or why not? If they are unique, how could you prove this scientifically?
4. Should an examiner testify solely to what is in their report or can they go beyond that information to assist the trier of fact? If they do, what is the basis for their statements?
5. What is the error rate for fingerprints? How is it determined? Is this a reasonable assessment?

Additional Readings

Champod, C., 2015. Fingerprint identification: advances since the 2009 National Research Council report. Philosophical Transactions of the Royal Society B 370 (1674), 20140259.

Kukucka, J., 2014. The journey or the destination? Disentangling process and outcome in forensic identification. Forensic Science Policy & Management: An International Journal 5 (3–4), 112–114.

Mustonen, V., Hakkarainen, K., Tuunainen, J., Pohjola, P., 2015. Discrepancies in expert decision-making in forensic fingerprint examination. Forensic Science International 254, 215–226.

Ulery, B.T., Hicklin, R.A., Roberts, M.A., Buscaglia, J., 2014. Measuring what latent fingerprint examiners consider sufficient information for individualization determinations. PLoS One 9 (11).

Section 4. Automation

If fingerprints did not realize their full potential for identification until they could be organized and searched, computerization is then the pinnacle of their utility. Computerized searching not only sped up the identification of a suspect or victim in one jurisdiction, but held the potential to communicate the search and identification across the globe. Ironically, the communication part was left to the open market and multiple automation vendors devised incompatible proprietary methods for cataloging and searching print records. At one time, it was not possible for New York City and New Jersey to share a computerized fingerprint search; the print or a copy had to be physically sent to be manually entered into the computing system. This lack of interoperability is being solved, if slowly, through support from governments and the professional community. The old adage remains, however; "garbage in, garbage out" is still the cautionary mantra because a search is only as good as the print that is entered.

Automated Methods, Including Criminal Records Administration

LA Hutchins, US Government, Washington, DC, USA

Glossary

Algorithm A step-by-step procedure for solving a problem or accomplishing some end especially by a computer.

Alias Otherwise known as.

Anthropometry Distinct measurements of the human body.

Arch A pattern type in which the friction ridges enter on one side of the impression and flow, or tend to flow, out the other side with a rise or wave in the center. Arches are subdivided into plain and tented arches.

Automated Fingerprint Identification System (AFIS) A generic term for a fingerprint matching, storage, and retrieval system.

Classification system Alphanumeric formula of finger and palm print patterns used as a guide for filing and searching.

Friction ridge A raised portion of the epidermis on the palmar or plantar skin, consisting of one or more connected ridge units.

Henry classification An alphanumeric system of fingerprint classification named after Sir Edward Richard Henry used for filing, searching, and retrieving 10-print records.

Identification The determination by an examiner that there is neither sufficient agreement to individualize nor sufficient disagreement to exclude.

Impression Friction ridge detail deposited on a surface.

Integrated Automated Fingerprint Identification System (IAFIS) The acronym for Integrated Automated Fingerprint Identification System, the FBI's national AFIS.

Interoperable The ability of computer hardware and software to be interchanged between manufacturers.

Joint Automated Booking System (JABS) An information sharing system and a conduit for sending standard booking data directly to the Federal Bureau of Investigation's (FBI's) IAFIS.

Known fingerprints The fingerprints of an individual, associated with a known or claimed identity, and deliberately recorded electronically, by ink, or another medium. Also known as exemplars.

Latent print Transferred impression of friction ridge detail not readily visible. Generic term used for unintentionally deposited friction ridge detail.

Live-scan Technology used to capture fingerprints, palm prints, and descriptive information electronically.

Loop A type of pattern in which one or more friction ridges enter on either side, recurve, touch, or pass an imaginary line between delta and core and flow out, or tend to flow out on the same side the friction ridges entered. Loops are subdivided into radial and ulnar loops.

 http://dx.doi.org/10.1016/B978-0-12-800573-6.00012-4

Minutiae Events along a ridge path, including bifurcations, ending ridges, and dots (also known as Galton details).
Mug shot Police photograph of a suspect's face or profile.
Next-generation identification (NGI) FBI's incremental replacement for IAFIS that will offer state-of-the-art biometric identification services.
Pattern type Fundamental pattern of the ridge flow: arch, loop, and whorl.
Persistence Having lasting qualities; remaining the same; nonchanging.
Proprietary Something that is used, produced, or marketed under exclusive legal right of the inventor or maker.
Recidivist A habitual criminal.
Scotland Yard Metropolitan Police Service of London, United Kingdom.
Uniqueness Very uncommon, unusual, atypical, or remarkable; a degree of distinguishing distinctiveness.
Verification The act or process of confirming.
Whorl A fingerprint pattern type that consists of one or more friction ridges that make or tends to make, a complete circuit, with two deltas, between which, when an imaginary line is drawn, at least one recurving friction ridge within the inner pattern area is cut or touched. Whorls are subdivided into plain whorls, double loops, pocket loops, and accidental whorls.

Introduction

The root of fingerprint automation began with the concept of uniqueness and persistence of friction ridges and the ability of known fingerprints to be classified into a system in which fingerprint cards can be filed and retrieved. The invention of a classification system that was fairly easy to use and could accommodate fairly large amounts of data was a pivotal moment in the history of fingerprint automation. However, as classified fingerprint files became larger and larger, the time it took a fingerprint technician to find a specific fingerprint card became longer and longer. The solution to this time delay rested with the invention of the computer and the eventual automation of fingerprint and palm print files. The fingerprint files were associated with the valuable information regarding those individuals. Not only did the file hold one's fingerprint impressions but also contained the descriptive information of the individual and the previous criminal activity. As one can see, the act of automating fingerprint files was a major milestone in the advancement of modern forensic science.

Brief History of Fingerprint Classification

The first instance of the scientific recognition of friction ridges dates back to the early 1800s when Professor Johannes Evanglista Purkinje (1787–1869) wrote his thesis entitled "A Commentary on the Physiological Examination of the Organs of Vision and the Cutaneous System" (1823). In this, Purkinje illustrated nine different types of fingerprint patterns: transverse curves, central longitudinal stria, oblique stria, oblique sinus, almond, spiral, elliptical whorl, circular whorl, and double whorl. Although Purkinje's work was purely of the anatomical nature, the delineation of classifiable patterns as the basis of a method of personal identification was born.

It was not for another 50 years that the topic of fingerprint classification was broached. In 1880, Dr Henry Faulds, a Scottish missionary working in Japan, began his own research into fingerprint identification and classification. Faulds was crucial to the science of fingerprints in that he conducted experiments to prove that fingerprints were both unique and persistent. With this basis, he proposed that friction ridge impressions could be classified into a system and used to identify criminals. Faulds also was the first to develop a 10-digit fingerprint card to record all 10 fingerprint impressions using ink. Faulds began collecting fingerprints and soon had thousands of known fingerprint cards. With these cards in hand, Faulds attempted to create a system of fingerprint classification. His system was based on assigning syllables that he constructed to each finger of the hand and then syllables to the pattern characteristics within each finger. Faulds offered to bring his classification system to Scotland Yard, but it was declined because of the fact that Scotland Yard was currently using a method of personal identification known as anthropometry (officially named Bertillonage after its inventor, Alphonse Bertillon).

Sir Francis Galton (1822–1911) became interested in the use of fingerprints when he was asked to give a lecture on personal identification. In researching the current method of the time, Bertillonage, Galton realized its inadequacy and thus initiated his research into fingerprints. Galton amassed a large collection of fingerprints (approximately 8000 sets) and began formal studies into human friction ridges. In 1892, Galton published his seminal work, *Finger Prints*, in which he established the two tenets of fingerprint identification, uniqueness, and persistence. In this groundbreaking work, Galton described how friction ridges did not flow uninterrupted but may end, split into more ridges, split and then reconnect, or connect to other ridges. These deviations are commonly referred to as minutiae or Galton details. In this book, Galton also developed a classification method. Like Purkinje, 69 years earlier, Galton described distinct types of fingerprint patterns. While Purkinje detailed nine pattern types, Galton described only three, the arch, loop, and whorl. To this day, fingerprints are still divided into these three major classes of patterns. Galton's classification was based on analyzing the pattern of each finger impression, assigning the impression letter, and then grouping the fingers of the right hand and left hand into predetermined groups. This classification would create a string of 10 letters, representing each finger of the hand in a certain order. Although this classification system was the first system to be incorporated into criminal files within an organization (Scotland Yard), it was too general of a system to handle large numbers of files and proved useless.

In Argentina, Juan Vucetich (1858–1925), the head of the Office of Identification in the Buenos Aires Police Department, read a scientific review of Galton's work with fingerprints. Like Galton, Vucetich realized the value of fingerprint identification and began to collect the fingerprints of all those arrested by his police department. In 1891, Vucetich also realized that in order for fingerprints to be truly recognized as the foremost means of personal identification, it had to have a successful classification system. Using Galton's three-pattern classification system, Vucetich devised an alphanumeric system that added an additional pattern for a total of four (arch, internal loop, external loop, and whorl) and incorporated a secondary classification and ridge counts. His classification was expressed in the form of a ratio, with the right hand as the numerator and the left hand as the denominator. The incorporation of this additional discriminatory sorting allowed fingerprint cards to be categorized into small groups, which were easily searched. Having now created a successful classification system, in 1894, he successfully campaigned for the use of fingerprints to be the sole means of personal identification within his agency, thereby completely eliminating the use of anthropometry.

During the same time that Vucetich was creating his classification, Sir Edward Henry (1850–1931) had also realized the need for a robust method of personal identification as a district Inspector General in India. After reading Galton's *Finger Prints*, Henry instituted that the fingerprints of all prisoners in his district be recorded. He also obtained all of Galton's research materials with the intent to create a formidable classification system. Henry assigned this task to two police officers from the Calcutta Anthropometric Bureau. By 1897, the two officers, Azizul Haque and Hem Chandra Bose, using Galton's three patterns, devised a classification system that involved three separate alphanumerical classifications, the primary, secondary, and subsecondary, and was expressed as a ratio, with the even fingers calculation as the numerator and the odd fingers calculation as the denominator. The primary classification was based on the presence of whorls on the fingers, the secondary was determined by the pattern types on the right and left index fingers, and the subsecondary represented the ridge counts or ridge tracings for the remaining fingers. In 1900, the Belper Committee in England, established to determine the best method of criminal identification, recommended that the Henry classification system be the sole means of criminal identification. With this recommendation, the Henry classification system was adopted by the Scotland Yard as its official means of personal identification in 1901.

The classification systems discussed above could only be used for cataloging and comparing fingerprint cards containing 10 fingerprint impressions. The systems were instituted to identify individuals for whom 10 fingerprint images could be recorded. This certainly worked for recidivists and other known individuals. However, these systems fell short with regard to the searching of single fingerprints obtained from crime scenes, commonly known as latent prints. In these cases, investigations could only go as far as the development of potential suspects and then obtaining a full set of fingerprint impressions in order to compare with the latent print. It was this obvious limitation that led to the development of single-fingerprint classification systems.

Single-fingerprint classification systems were based on either the existing 10-print classification systems or the original. Establishing single-fingerprint files involved creating entirely new cards for each fingerprint of an individual. Each card contained descriptive information, the written classification, and either the fingerprint image itself or a verbal description of the classification. If a latent fingerprint could be classified, it could then be searched in the single-fingerprint files. The most popular single-fingerprint system was developed at New Scotland Yard and was known as the Battley single-fingerprint system. While these files served a function that the 10 print files could not offer, they added another layer of time-consuming labor and volume.

History of Criminal Identification

An individual's criminal history record associates personal identifiers to arrest and disposition data. Until the mid-1850s, this information was haphazardly recorded as notes and associated with a name, of which could easily have been an alias. As populations and the criminal element grew, it became increasingly difficult to accurately document a person's criminal record and associate descriptive data with a record in order to accurately identify recidivists. The advent of photography was a pivotal moment in the criminal justice community. Officials could now attach a photograph (the mug shot) to a criminal history record. While the use of photographs greatly advanced the criminal justice system, it was not the be-all and end-all of criminal identification because of the fact that a criminal could easily change his/her appearance. In addition, many police departments did not institute standard operating procedures for mug shots. Historic mug shots often contained people wearing hats, women with veils, and heads tilted.

The next milestone in criminal identification was initially viewed as the first truly scientific method of criminal identification. In 1882, Alphonse Bertillon, a police clerk in Paris, France, developed a system of body measurements to be used for identification. Known as anthropometry, the system involved distinct measurements of the human body. These measurements, a total of 11, were recorded with descriptive data such as height and eye color, body deformities or marks such as scars, mug shots, and the 11 measurements. In 1894, Galton's fingerprint classification was added to the Bertillonage record of criminal identification. Not long after Bertillonage was instituted as a means of identification, the problem with anthropometry was becoming apparent in three ways. First, different officers could record different measurements of the same body parts. The difference was enough that false identifications could be made or recidivists could be missed. Second, the system did not account for growth or aging of the body. Measurements taken from an individual throughout growth and the aging processing could be different enough to preclude an identification. Third, the system was proving unable to handle large amounts of data. As files grew, the time it took for the officers to search and locate a file became debilitating. As the problems with anthropometry intensified the use of a fingerprint classification system to accurately identify individuals emerged as the premier method of identification.

History of Fingerprint Automation

As agency files of classified fingerprint cards became larger and larger, the time it took to conduct a search became longer and longer, oftentimes taking months to report back that a 10-print card did or did not match an existing card in the files. In addition, departments that added single-fingerprint files compounded the man-hours it took to conduct an investigation. Obviously, the timeliness and high personnel costs of 10-print card searches coupled with the inefficient and inadequate single-print systems became a paramount concern for the criminal justice and forensic community.

The first attempt to automate was conducted by the Federal Bureau of Investigation (FBI) in 1934. A mere 10 years after the United States Congress created the FBI and established it as the national fingerprint repository, whereby it took possession of over 800 000 fingerprint records from the Leavenworth prison, the FBI was feeling the pains of a large repository that was time-consuming to search. Even with modifications to the Henry classification system in order to create additional subclassification groupings, the FBI's files were bourgeoning and the bureau recognized the need for some type of automation. This automation came in the form of the data punch card and card-sorting machines. A data punch card is a stiff card that contains rows and columns of holes, each hole representing a piece of data. The data punch card would be encoded with descriptive information for individuals along with their fingerprint classification. Cards could later be searched with a card-sorting machine. If the machine detected a card with the same data (i.e., the desired Henry classification) then the fingerprint examiner could then manually pull that card and compare it to the submitted card from the contributor. Even though this process reduced the amount of time it took a fingerprint technician to search for a card, the FBI determined that the continued use of this automated punch card system was still not feasible for the collection of its size and abandoned the project. However, the use of the punch card systems for cataloging fingerprint files was adequate for smaller and more manageable fingerprint files, thus it was used by state and local agencies.

It was not until the 1960s that the advancement in computer technology opened the door for viable method of fingerprint automation. Computer technology had advanced to the point where the ability of computers to read and match fingerprints automatically was certainly within the realm of reality. With this in mind, agencies across the map began to initiate fingerprint automation projects.

In the late 1960s, the FBI's Identification Division initiated its Automated Identification Division System (AIDS) program and in conjunction with the National Bureau of Standards (NBS) (NBS; currently known as the National Institute of Standards and Technology (NIST)) looked into the technological requirements needed to develop special purpose computers to automate fingerprint records. The FBI and the NBS determined that in order to build an Automated Fingerprint Identification System (AFIS), new technologies would have to be developed. This involved a scanner that would be able to detect fingerprint impressions on a 10-print card, software to accurately read the fingerprint impression and detect minutiae, and computer algorithms that could accurately compare the information (pattern type and minutiae location) from the scanned print with a database of known prints. With these requirements, the FBI issued a request for proposal (RFP) to the community to build the AFIS demonstration models that would address the first two milestones. The third technology was addressed by the NBS. In the early 1970s, two additional RFPs were issued, which incorporated speed and accuracy requirements. By the mid-1970s, the FBI's AIDS program possessed five AFIS machines that were used for the digital conversion of the FBI's criminal fingerprint file. In 1979, the FBI was testing the search function of the new AFIS, and by 1983, automatic searches were routine.

While the FBI was experimenting and developing their AFIS system, numerous other agencies, national and international, started down the same path of fingerprint automation. Some agencies successfully worked on in-house computer systems (United Kingdom's Home Office), while others either experienced budgetary constraints that caused them to shut the program down or developed systems with technology that was not as applicable as that developed by the FBI. Other agencies, such as the FBI, contracted with firms to develop their own AFIS. In France, the French National Police contracted with a subsidiary of Morpho Systems (Currently Safran Morpho, Inc.) to develop an AFIS. In Japan, the National Police Agency contracted with NEC Corporation to develop their AFIS. With the success of the AFIS technology, companies began marketing their own AFISs that were based on proprietary software. As a result, many agencies were purchasing systems that were not interoperable with each other. Some agencies developed funding strategies that allowed regions to combine resources in order to purchase a single-source AFIS, thereby creating a shared network of AFIS. For example, the Western Identification Network (WIN) in the United States combines the fingerprint records of Alaska, California, Idaho, Montana, Nevada, Oregon, Utah, Washington, and Wyoming.

Key to the success of AFIS was the fact that it was based on the AFIS pattern classifications, minutiae extraction, and matching algorithms. With this new technology, the fingerprint classification systems that were previously discussed became outdated, at least for those agencies utilizing the new AFIS technology. The new AFISs had no use for the traditional classification systems. Each fingerprint on a 10-print card was automatically classified by a computer algorithm into 8 possible patterns: arch, whorl, right-slant loop, left-slant loop, complete scar, amputation, unable to classify, and unable to print. AFIS fingerprint classification was now based strictly on the location of extracted minutiae (bifurcations and ending ridges only) and the spatial relationships between the minutiae. As a result, the minutiae extraction algorithms created mathematical maps of each fingerprint on the card. New cards entering the system would be automatically classified into AFIS pattern classifications, and the minutiae in each fingerprint would be automatically encoded.

AFISs are composed of two subsystems: (1) known print subsystem and (2) latent subsystem. The known print subsystem achieves what the manual classification systems of the past did, identity verification. It is through this subsystem that identification queries take place. This subsystem is used for criminal identification and employment application processes. The latent subsystem incorporates additional software that facilitates the searching and matching of latent prints against a designated database. This latent aspect involves the encoding of the minutiae from the latent print in order to create a mathematical map. The mathematical map of the latent print can then be compared to the mathematical maps in the queried database. This comparison results in a list of potential candidates, which a latent print examiner trained to competency can compare and render a conclusion.

In an effort to institute some form of standardization across multiple AFIS vendors, in the early to the mid-1990s, the NIST established standards for the transmission of fingerprint information. These standards include types of records that are sent through the live-scan technology and AFISs. Record types include information on the sending and receiving agency; descriptive and arrest information; signatures; image resolution; latent and known images; marked minutiae; and facial, scars, marks, and tattoo image transmission. Additional standards exist regarding the image quality of equipment and the image compression for transmission.

Criminal History Information Systems

The integration of computer technologies into the criminal justice community also afforded agencies the ability to automate and then eventually centralize criminal history records. Up until the 1960s, criminal record histories were paper-based and in manual files. Obviously, paper-based files were only valuable for the area covered by that particular agency. Even if the files were automated, if it was not possible for the criminal history files to be shared between agencies, then they were no better than paper-based files. If the criminal justice community was going to address multijurisdictional offenders, then a centralized system was in order. Beyond traditional criminal justice purposes, a centralized database would assist in background checks for licensing, employment suitability, and national security clearances. The push for agencies in the United States to automate their criminal records began with the passage of the Omnibus Crime Control and Safe Streets Act of 1968. The establishment of the Law Enforcement Assistance Administration provided grant money to states to develop computerized criminal history record systems. As of December 31, 2008, there were 85 836 300 automated criminal history files in the United States (Survey of State Criminal History Information Systems, 2008. SEARCH National Consortium for Justice Information and Statistics. US Department of Justice, Bureau of Justice Statistics, Published October, 2009.).

The National Crime Information Center (NCIC) was established in 1965 as the United State's centralized electronic criminal database of wanted and missing persons and stolen property. While the NCIC is maintained by and housed at the FBI's Criminal Justice Information Services (CJIS) Division of the FBI, since inception, it has operated under a shared management structure with the FBI and local, state, and other federal agencies. States, districts, and territories can access the NCIC through dedicated lines of telecommunication. The purpose of the NCIC was to create a database that could be constantly and immediately updated and searched by local, state, and federal agencies. The obvious advantages being that the agencies can conduct instant checks regarding people and property. This computerized database consists of personal records (fugitives, missing persons, and wanted individuals, etc.) and stolen property records that can be searched 24 h a day, 7 days a week.

Associated with the personal records database is the NCIC fingerprint classification. Like the Henry fingerprint classification system, the NCIC fingerprint classification was established to assist users in tentatively identifying wanted criminals. For example, police officers can query the system with a suspect's NCIC fingerprint classification to establish if that person may be in the NCIC personal records file as a wanted person. Unlike the Henry system, the NCIC fingerprint classification system is simpler to use and understand and could be transmitted with far less error than the Henry classification. The system is alphanumeric, consists of a 20-character code in a single row, where each finger is represented by two characters, and can be converted into the Henry classification. The code starts with the right thumb and ends with left little finger. For example, a person possessing plain arches on all fingers, with the exception that both index fingers have tented arches, would have an NCIC fingerprint classification of AA TT AA AA AA AA TT AA AA AA.

The FBI created the nation's automated criminal history record information, the Interstate Identification Index (III), in 1978. The III is an index of a person's federal or state arrest record and is accessed through the NCIC. Participation in the III is voluntary. In order to participate in the III, the state, district, or territory must be authorized by the FBI, possess an automated system that is compatible with the III system, be capable of providing electronic criminal history updates and responses to inquiries, and meet certain standards in order to ensure accuracy, completeness, integrity, and security of the information. Currently, all 50 states participate in the III. Agencies can query an individual's descriptive information (name, social security number, date of birth) or identification numbers (state identification or FBI number) in the III to determine if an existing record is in the system. If a record is located, the system automatically retrieves the information from the agency holding the record and forwards it to the requestor.

The National Fingerprint File (NFF) is a separate component of the III. The NFF contains fingerprint and palm print images of all federal offenders and participating states, districts, and territories. States, districts, and territories can participate in the III alone or in the III and the NFF. Like the III, the NFF is voluntary. Participating states submit the descriptive information, arrest information, state identification number, and the fingerprint and palm print images of an individual's first arrest and the FBI assigns an FBI number. Subsequent arrests are maintained at the local level. As of June 2010, 14 states participate in the NFF (Colorado, Florida, Georgia, Hawaii, Idaho, Kansas, Maryland, Montana, North Carolina, New Jersey, Oklahoma, Oregon, Tennessee, and Wyoming) (http://www.search.org/about/news/2010/nff.asp; accessed 21.05.11.).

Current Practice and Future Improvement

The modernization of fingerprint and palm print information and criminal history records has resulted in the combination of both types of information through the use of a live-scan machine. Live-scan technology allows for the digital recording of physical descriptive information, arrest data, capturing of fingerprint and palm print images, mug shots, scars, marks, tattoos, and other information associated with the individual under arrest (i.e., aliases, known associates, addresses, and employment). A key aspect of the live-scan technology is the ability to conduct immediate searches to verify the identity of an individual while still in custody. Live-scan systems can be integrated into AFIS and criminal history systems, whereby the live-scan feeds information into the agency's other automated systems. A key element to the live-scan technology is the automated quality control function. This ensures that minimum quality standards of the recorded fingerprints and palm prints are met, thus ensuring that quality prints are entering the database. This quality control mechanism also guarantees that the 10 rolled fingerprints, the plane impressions, and the palm prints are validated (i.e., the rolled fingerprints of the right hand, the plain impressions of the right hand, and the right palm all correspond).

In the 1990s, the FBI initiated the next stage of fingerprint automation. The new AFIS technology that was developed achieved higher performance standards regarding all aspects of its operations. In July 1999, the FBI implemented this Integrated AFIS (IAFIS). IAFIS combined the new AFIS and the III into one system. A third system, the Identification Tasking and Networking (ITN) was established to manage the workflow information in IAFIS. This workflow involves the computer applications used for processing 10-print fingerprint submissions, latent print processing, and record search requests. Through IAFIS, the FBI provides the following services to its customers: criminal and civil 10-print submission service, providing electronic images (fingerprints and photographs), latent fingerprint matching, enrollment of unsolved latent prints into a database that is searched by all incoming criminal fingerprint cards, III access, and remote access to IAFIS. Access to IAFIS for latent print processing by external non-FBI-authorized users is achieved through the use of free software product provided by the FBI. This software can be installed on desktop personal computers, which are in compliance with the FBI's quality specifications.

Federal agencies in the United States use the Joint Automated Booking System (JABS) as the interface between the live-scan system, the agency's AFIS and IAFIS. With regards to IAFIS, JABS sends the data to IAFIS to determine if the individual has a record in the system, and IAFIS responds back to JABS with the result. Not only does JABS securely and efficiently manage transactions to and from IAFIS but also the system stores the booking data from all the federal agencies. This allows federal agencies to search for arrests conducted by other federal agencies.

In 2001, the United Kingdom established an integrated identification service known as IDENT1. IDENT1 integrated friction ridge (fingerprints and palm prints) and criminal history information from Scotland, England, and Wales through the use of desktop workstations and live-scan machines. Features of IDENT1 include known 10-print and palm print services, latent fingerprint and palm print searching capabilities, enrollment of latent prints into a database that is searched by all incoming 10-print cards, the storage and searching of known prints and latent prints related to specific policing events, and the ability to interface with the United Kingdom's Immigration and Asylum Fingerprint System. Recent improvements include enhanced search accuracy and performance, incorporation of hand-held mobile fingerprint readers, and the development of an open architecture that will allow for the integration of additional biometrics.

The FBI is currently developing their next-generation identification (NGI). NGI will address the growing needs of international and national partners. NGI will incrementally replace the existing IAFIS with technical improvements and additional functionalities. Ten-print and latent fingerprint services have already been expanded to enable faster and more accurate searching capabilities. Additional capabilities will include the National Palm Print System, whereby agencies can submit known palm prints and can search latent palm prints against the database. An added Repository of Individuals of Special Concern (RISC) will enable agencies to rapidly identify wanted persons, sex offender registry subjects, known or suspected terrorists, and other individuals of special interest. A new "Rap Back" service will alert participating agencies of criminal activity by employees in positions of trust. The system will also include an interstate photo system to facilitate the submission and searching of mug shots, scars, marks, and tattoos. The FBI is moving from a single mode of biometrics (fingerprints) to multimodal. As a result, the NGI will eventually incorporate other biometrics such as iris scans, voice, and facial recognition. This flexible system design will allow for the incorporation of additional biometrics as they emerge.

Conclusion

As technological advances occur, the criminal justice and forensic science communities will continue to take advantage of emerging technologies. Within a 100-year time frame, the science of criminal identification has grown from rudimentary and manual means to automated and highly advanced technologies. With emerging threats to global security, innovation is the key to overcoming the never-ending challenge of an equally innovative criminal element. New technologies will enable international partnerships to be established whereby biometric and criminal history information can be exchanged on a global scale.

See also: **Pattern Evidence:** Analysis, Comparison, Evaluation, and Verification (ACE-V); Palm Prints; **Pattern Evidence/Fingerprints (Dactyloscopy):** Automated Fingerprint Identification Systems (AFIS); Friction Ridge Skin Impression Evidence – Standards of Proof; Identification and Classification; **Pattern Evidence/Firearms:** Laboratory Analysis; **Pattern Evidence/History:** Fingerprint Sciences.

Further Reading

Allen, R., Sankar, P., Prabhakar, S., 2005. Fingerprint identification technology. In: Wayman, J., Jain, A., Maltoni, D., Maio, D. (Eds.), Biometric Systems: Technology, Design and Performance Evaluation, first ed. Springer-Verlag, London.

Cole, S.A., 2004. History of fingerprint pattern recognition. In: Ratha, N.K., Bolle, R. (Eds.), Automatic Fingerprint Recognition Systems, first ed. Springer-Verlag, New York, pp. 1–26.

Galton, F., 1892. Finger Prints. MacMillan, New York.

Hutchins, L.A., 2009. What the future can hold: a look at the connectivity of automated fingerprint identification systems. Journal of Forensic Identification 59 (3), 275–284.

Komarinski, P., Higgins, P.T., Higgins, K.M., Fox, L.K., 2005. Automated Fingerprint Identification Systems, first ed. Elsevier Press, New York.

Maltoni, D., Maio, D., Jain, A.K., Prabhakar, S., 2009. Handbook of Fingerprint Recognition, second ed. Springer-Verlag, London.

Moses, K.R., Higgins, P., McCabe, M., Probhakar, S., Swann, S., 2010. Automated fingerprint identification system (AFIS). In: Fingerprint Sourcebook. National Institute of Justice (NIJ), Washington (Chapter 6). http://www.nij.gov/pubs-sum/225320.htm.

U.S. Congress, Office of Technology Assessment, 1991. The FBI Fingerprint Identification Automation Program: Issues and Options – Background Paper. U.S. Government Printing Office, Washington, DC.

U.S. Department of Justice Office of the Attorney General, 2006. The Attorney General's Report on Criminal History Background Checks. U.S. Government Printing Office, Washington, DC.

Automated Fingerprint Identification Systems (AFIS)

A Loll, Phoenix Police Crime Laboratory, Phoenix, AZ, USA

Glossary

AFIS Automated Fingerprint Identification System.

Biometric system Any system that serves to identify an individual based on anatomical or behavioral traits.

Exemplar A controlled recording of the friction ridge skin used for the purpose of identification; may be taken using black printers ink or Live Scan.

Friction ridge skin The skin on the hands and feet that has both ridges (raised skin) and furrows (depressed skin).

Hit An AFIS designation to indicate that the print that was entered into the system is from the same source as a candidate; some AFIS call this an Ident.

Identification A conclusion that may be reached by a latent print examiner after comparing the ridge flow, spatial relationships of minutiae, and, if possible, pore and ridge shapes between a latent print and a known print and finding sufficient agreement to conclude that the prints were made by the same individual.

Latent print An impression of friction ridge skin that has been recovered from the scene of a crime through the use of powder, photography, and/or chemical development.

Live Scan An inkless fingerprinting technology that electronically records friction ridge skin by rolling the skin over a specially coated glass platform and recording the information on a charged coupled device.

Minutiae Locations in the ridge flow on friction ridge skin where a ridge ends or bifurcates.

No Hit An AFIS designation to indicate that the print that was entered into the system is not from the same source as a candidate; some AFIS call this a non-Ident.

Pixel A single unit of a digital image.

Specificity A measure of how often an arrangement of minutiae occurs on the friction ridge skin.

Introduction

Automated fingerprint identification system (AFIS) is a biometric system that is used to identify individuals using fingerprints and palm prints. AFIS was developed in the early 1960s as a means to classify, search, and consolidate 10-print records in an automated manner rather than manually. The need for such a system was great, considering that the Federal Bureau of Investigations (FBI) fingerprint database around this time consisted of over 15 million criminal files. In the United States, the FBI collaborated with engineer Joe Wegstein from the National Institute of Standards and Technology (NIST) in order to develop an algorithm capable of matching fingerprints. Fifteen years later, the FBI was using this technology and shortly thereafter, Minneapolis–St. Paul became the first United States city to install an AFIS. Other nations were creating similar systems as well. Around the same time, France was focusing on creating automated latent print searches. These efforts led to the formation of Sagem Morpho Inc., which recently merged with Motorola's company, Printrak, to establish Morpho Trak in the United States. Together, Morpho and Morpho Trak are very prominent worldwide AFIS vendors. In the United Kingdom, research led to the first AFIS vendor that included ridge counts in latent print searches. NEC in Japan visited various AFIS sites before they began developing their AFIS. They began by working on the issue of matching inked records, and within a year of developing software to do that successfully (1982), they also began conducting latent print searches. In 2003, NEC AFIS software was rated the top performing system in a fingerprint vendor technology evaluation conducted by the NIST that included 18 AFIS vendors.

In the 1980s, there was an experiment conducted in San Francisco, CA, that conducted a test of competing fingerprint systems latent print matching capabilities. The competitors included Rockwell, NEC, Printrak, and Logica (developed for New Scotland Yard). NEC won the contract for the San Francisco Police Department AFIS. The system was installed in late 1983 and as a result, there were 10 times as many latent print identifications in 1984 and between 1984 and 1986, the city saw a 26% reduction in burglaries. Following this huge success, AFIS were rapidly purchased by police agencies; by 1999, the International Association for Identification recognized 500 AFIS sites in the world. The major vendors during this time were Printrak, NEC, Morpho, and Cogent; owing to

 http://dx.doi.org/10.1016/B978-0-12-800573-6.00013-6

competition and proprietary rights to the software of each AFIS vendor, interoperability of AFIS among different vendors remains a significant problem.

Exemplar Database

AFIS contain a digital database of exemplars that is populated with a combination of inked print records that were scanned into the database using a flat-bed scanner and electronic recordings of the friction ridge skin taken using Live Scan technology. It is common for an AFIS database to contain millions of records including both criminal and civil files. Each AFIS record contains a rolled and plain impression of the first finger joint of all 10 fingers and, if obtained, both palms. Demographic data such as the individual's name, date of birth, sex, and any relevant identification numbers are linked to each record.

Before fingerprint and palm print records are added to the database, locations and orientations of bifurcations and ridge endings (collectively called minutiae) are coded, automatically by either the AFIS or a fingerprint technician. Exemplars typically have minimal background noise; therefore, the system can accurately determine where a ridge ends or bifurcates, as well as the direction of ridge flow, by measuring changes in the intensity value (zero being black (ridges) and white being a high pixel value (furrows)) of surrounding pixels. On the screen, the locations and orientations of minutiae are shown by a marker with a circle (and sometimes a square for bifurcations, depending on vendor) over the minutiae itself and a tail that points in the direction of the ridge flow. Collectively, the markers make a map of the Cartesian (x, y, θ) coordinates of minutiae (with (0, 0) being the lower left corner of the image and θ measuring the angle of rotation from the horizontal). Exemplars of palms generally have hundreds to thousands of minutiae mapped out in this manner, and fingers can have approximately 50–100 features. On the basis of the arrangements of the minutiae, the system defines a pattern type for fingers with the option to cross-refer more than one pattern.

After the minutiae of a new record have been coded, the AFIS will search the record against all other records in the database to determine if an exemplar for the individual already exists. This can be done in a matter of minutes and it is particularly useful when linking fingerprint records that bear different names/aliases. These types of searches are called *exemplar to exemplar searches* and they are almost 100% accurate in systems where 10-print operators check the candidate before consolidating records. When duplicate records do exist, the system may keep only the highest quality record, the most recent record, or several records for an individual depending on site location and the database capacity.

The number of records contained in AFIS databases worldwide is growing everyday as more records are constantly being added. The FBI maintains the largest digital database of 10-print records, which contains over 60 million records (both civil and criminal). Besides obtaining their own records, more than 18 000 agencies contribute daily to the database by electronically sending the FBI any felony records they collect. Consequently, the size of the FBI's database increases by up to 10 000 subjects each day, and 96% of those submissions are electronic. INTERPOL, the world's largest police organization, has a database of 104 000 fingerprint records.

Searching Latent Prints in AFIS

The major advantage of having AFIS technology in the field of forensics is the ability to search latent prints recovered from crime scenes against millions of records in a very short period of time. Many times latent prints are recovered at the scene of a crime where there is no suspect. Ideally, a forensic scientist will search recovered latent print evidence through an AFIS and then be able to provide a person of interest to law enforcement. Not all latent prints can be searched, however. The quality of the latent print must be fairly high; therefore, extreme care must be used when processing latent prints so as to provide the best possible evidence. The latent print must come from a part of the hand that is searchable in AFIS, and the forensic scientist should be confident in the orientation. One must also consider the specificity of the ridge detail and the number of high-quality minutiae; six minutiae in a delta (low specificity) are not considered an equal weight of evidence to six minutiae near the core of a tightly wound whorl (high specificity). **Figure 1** shows an example of a latent print with a low count of minutiae that would be searched by most latent print examiners, and another latent print with a similar number of minutiae which may be deemed of no value for AFIS entry.

Latent prints that are suitable for entry into the AFIS are uploaded from a digital capture device or other digital storage media. **Figure 2** shows a representative screen shot using a Morpho system where two latent prints have been selected to be searched in AFIS. Each of the latent prints will be coded and searched independently using only the area within the selected boxed regions. The double bar in the box represents "up" in terms of latent print orientation.

If possible, the forensic scientist will try to limit the search parameters in order to increase the speed of the search and provide the best list of the candidates. This can be done in a variety of ways. The most common way is to designate the pattern type for a finger so that only fingers with those pattern type(s) are searched. The user may choose to limit which fingers or the specific area of the palm to search. If the fingerprint evidence is part of a simultaneous touch with two or more fingers, the user may designate the pattern types of adjacent fingers. If any of these parameters are unknown, the search may

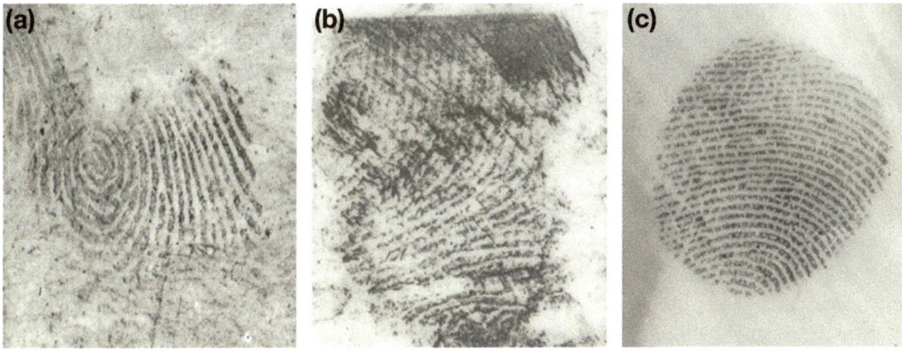

Figure 1 Three latent prints that have a similar number of minutiae but different levels of specificity. The latent print labeled (a) is whorl pattern with high specificity and high quality; latent print (a) would be searched in Automated Fingerprint Identification System (AFIS) by most latent print examiners. Latent print (b) shows smearing and is of an unknown pattern type. Owing to the quality and low specificity, latent print (b) may not be searched in AFIS by some examiners. Latent print (c) shows a very high-quality latent print, however, it originates from the extreme distal finger tip, a region of the finger where minutiae are not recorded in AFIS, making latent print (c) unsearchable.

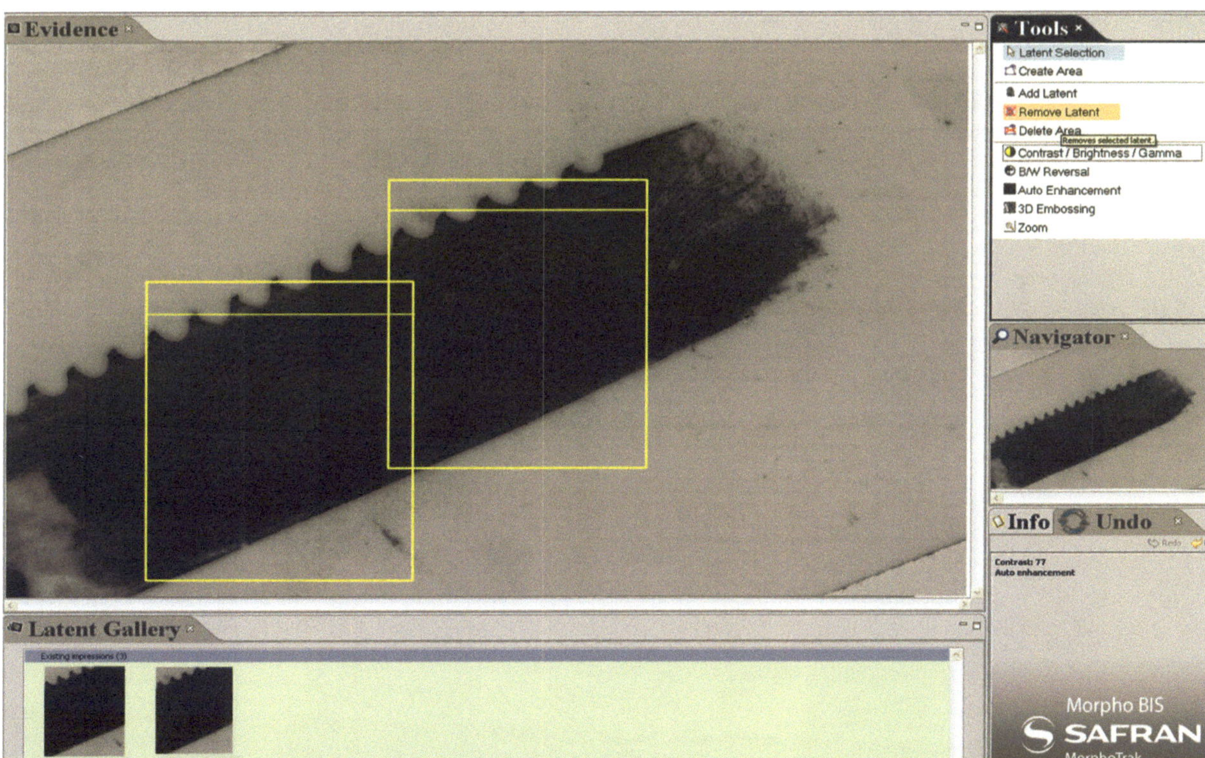

Figure 2 A screenshot of a Morpho system which shows two latent prints that have been selected for Automated Fingerprint Identification System (AFIS) entry. The double bar at the top of the yellow boxes represents the upward direction. Note the enhancement tools on the right sidebar. Courtesy of Morpho, Inc.

be completed with all possibilities of either/both the fingers and/or the palms. AFIS also has the option of marking the cores of the fingerprint and deltas on fingers and palms. There is a tool that allows the user to map the ridge flow if, for example, a palm has a large loop in the hypothenar area. It is recommended that the latent print be entered with the correct orientation; although some AFIS have the option of searching a latent print in all orientations, according to NIST Interagency/Internal Report 7775, this can decrease the efficiency of the system by up to 18%. All of these tools and several others aid the forensic scientist in narrowing the number of records that will be searched, thereby decreasing the time it takes to receive results.

Next, the forensic scientist must code the minutiae in the latent print. Typically, latent prints contain significant "noise" that can potentially obscure the latent print because of a large variety of reasons (see **Figure 1**, right and **Figure 3**, left). This introduces many more shades of gray (or a wider range of pixel values) in latent print images compared to exemplars. This makes it more difficult for the AFIS to accurately autocode minutiae based on the pixel intensity. Most often, the forensic scientist will code the minutiae in latent prints manually to increase the accuracy of minutiae placement. There are several enhancement tools that allow the user to change the contrast, brightness, and magnification of the image to aid in this process.

When all of the coding is complete, the latent print is searched by the system against all of the exemplar records that meet the specifications provided by the user. In most cases, the image is deleted and the only searchable information that remains are the (x, y, θ) positions created by the forensic scientist, although a recent study by NIST indicates that performance increases when both the image and minutiae maps are kept. The arrangement of those coordinates is then compared by the system to every record in the database that fits within the parameters that the user specified to be searched. The thresholds on how different the minutiae can be from any given exemplar vary from vendor to vendor, and because of the proprietary nature of the computer algorithms of these vendors, the exact thresholds are not known. However, each system allows for a given amount of rotation from vertical and x, y positional shifts when searching for a corresponding candidate to account for distortions and the flexibility of the skin.

AFIS Results

The forensic scientist specifies how many of the closest matching candidates they would like returned, and the number chosen varies widely between users, agencies, and crime types. There may also be a default option to have the system designate the number of candidates. When the search is complete, typically in a matter of minutes to just a few hours, the list of candidates will be numerically ranked based on the amount of agreement between the (x, y, θ) coordinates of the minutia between the latent print and the known record. The images of the latent print and the known record are displayed side-by-side and the forensic scientist can begin comparing them to determine if they are from the same source (see **Figure 3**). The forensic scientist may use the enhancement tools on both the latent print and exemplar if necessary. Some systems also have

Figure 3 A screenshot of a Morpho, Inc. results screen. The latent print is on the left and the known print is on the right. Circle markers represent ridge endings and square markers represent bifurcations. Courtesy of Morpho, Inc.

tools that allow the forensic scientist to place markers on both prints in order to more easily note the features they are comparing. The system can also display which minutiae were correlated during the search and also which minutiae were not correlated. Demographic information, such as the candidate's name, ethnic background, or criminal history, is typically not available. If a latent print and a candidate are determined to be from the same source, the forensic scientist will declare a "Hit" or "Ident" and will proceed to use the information contained in the AFIS to locate the original record. If the latent prints are not of the same source, the forensic scientist declares a "no Hit" or "non-Ident" and then continues to compare the next candidate until either a Hit is declared or all of the candidates have been cleared.

If an entire AFIS search is conducted and no candidates result in a Hit, the latent print may be maintained in the unsolved latent print database. The latent prints in this database are searched against every incoming AFIS record on a daily basis and will continually be searched until the latent print is taken out of the system by either deletion or a future Hit. Reasons for deleting a latent print may be based on quality factors, crime type, or statute of limitations; the retention policies are determined by the administration of each agency.

The success rate of AFIS returning the proper candidate, provided that candidate exists in the database, is completely dependent on the correlation between the minutiae map of the exemplar and the minutiae map of the latent print. Differences in the coding processes and also the image quality between exemplars and latent prints will inevitably cause slight differences in the exact locations and orientations of the minutiae. Still, care in the coding process is crucial to the success of the system; if there are minutiae incorrectly marked in the latent print, the rank associated with the correct candidate will decrease proportionately, possibly below other (incorrect) candidates. The same is true if the latent print is significantly distorted but accurately mapped, which may cause the relationships of the minutiae to be outside of the system-defined tolerances and then the corresponding candidate would not make the candidate list. Often an unsolved latent print may Hit to an individual that has a new record added to the database but who also had a record in the system at the time of the original search; this demonstrates that the correct candidate may be missed based on minutiae maps being coded by two different sources. Studies by NIST of various vendors showed that success of AFIS is very dependent on the number of minutiae present and the quality of the latent print. It is intuitive that a high-quality latent print with 20 minutiae is more likely to Hit than a low-quality latent print with a low minutiae count. Orientation can also significantly affect the matching capability of the system by up to 18%. If the AFIS being used differentiates between bifurcations and ridge endings, there is the added possibility that bifurcations were marked as ridge endings and vice versa. AFIS with ridge counts may introduce additional error of differing ridge counts in regions where the latent print quality is low. Another factor is having large gaps between coded minutiae—coded clusters of minutiae in latent prints are more effectively searched than latent prints that cover a large surface area but which have minutiae sporadically coded throughout. Creases, especially in the thenar area of the palms, also complicate the agreement between the minutiae coded by the forensic scientist and the autocoded records. Personal communiqué and unpublished studies by Ron Huston (OH, USA) have shown that 50% of palm Hits come from the hypothenar region, the area with the fewest number of creases. The interdigital and lower thenar region each make up about 23–25% of palm Hits, and only about 2% of palm Hits come from the upper thenar area. Note that these statistics may be influenced by the number of latent prints that come from each area of the palm and are not necessarily due to AFIS matching capabilities.

There is growing concern that the use of AFIS could result in more erroneous identifications. It is argued that proper testing has not been conducted dealing with the likelihood of an AFIS search producing candidates who have incidental similarities, but are not from the same source. The latent print community uses the term "close nonmatch" for latent prints that have candidates with similar but not completely corresponding prints. Some researchers believe that latent print examiners must be more cautious when identifying a print as a result of an AFIS search verses identifying a latent print to a requested comparison subject. This reasoning is based on the premise that the probability of coincidental correspondence between a latent print and an exemplar print is less likely for a single specific individual (often provided as a result of intelligence during a police investigation) versus the same latent print compared to 60 million individuals. The idea is similar to the well-known statistical birthday problem which estimates the probability that a group of any given size will contain two people with the same birthday. Caution should be used when comparing and identifying AFIS candidates, especially for latent prints of low quality, low minutiae count, and low specificity. These factors should be weighed heavily during the analysis phase when a latent print examiner is determining AFIS suitability. Very high quality and specificity is recommended in regions of converging ridge systems (i.e., deltas) which are common in almost all pattern types and in the palm. It is also important that an agency has an effective quality control system that includes verification by a second latent print examiner in order to reduce the chances of an erroneous identification being reported. Current statistical and probabilistic research in the field of latent print identifications are underway and may be used in the future to provide a quantitative way to describe the likelihood that two prints came from the same source, which could be proved to be very useful in the case of low minutiae count AFIS cases.

Interoperability

The existence of several AFIS vendors, each of which have developed proprietary algorithms, has led to a problem of interoperability between agencies who may have a reason to search a given latent print through a different database. In 1985, NIST developed standards for how fingerprint records could be shared between various agencies; however, these standards were not mandatory to specific vendors. The FBI developed the Universal Latent Workstation (ULW), which is a free software that provides access to the Integrated Automated Fingerprint Identification System (IAFIS) to non-FBI authorized users around the world, as an attempt to make their database available to those who need it. The INTERPOL fingerprint database is accessible to 188 member countries. Unfortunately, private vendors have not made the same efforts and interoperability between neighboring cities, counties, and states remains a serious problem in many areas.

The Future of AFIS

Latent prints and DNA are the only two forensic sciences that have the ability to link a specific individual to a crime scene, and with the speed of the AFIS searches and the low cost of developing latent prints compared to DNA analysis, latent prints remain a crucial part of forensic evidence that is used in the criminal justice system. As such an important identifying tool, there is a significant amount of research being conducted that will improve the system in the future. Research is highly focused on the possibility of including additional features such as pores, creases, and ridge edge shapes, incipient ridges, and dots in AFIS searches. Reproducibility of these features is dependent on the development methods, whether the evidence is porous or nonporous, and the condition of the donor's skin. In the case of pores, research studies showed that the improvement in matching accuracy was considerably dependent on the quality of both the latent print and the exemplar. The quality and clarity of a latent print must be very high for pore detail to be seen, and the resolution of both the latent print and exemplar should have a minimum of 1000 ppi (pixels per inch) to be useful for this purpose. The implementation of searches that include the abovementioned details may be conducted after a search using only minutiae did not result in a Hit. Still, the quality must be present in the latent print to include information such as creases and pores, therefore, and the extra time it will take to perform all of the extra coding of the latent print must also be considered. NIST research suggests that the improvement to latent print searches using more than just minutiae is only significant in latent prints with very low numbers of minutiae. Significantly, this means that AFIS usually work very well using only the minutiae (second-level information) to locate candidates. There are also plans for some vendors to begin including the second and third finger joints in AFIS searches. Like the thenar area of the palm, though, large amounts of creases complicate the ability to accurately code the minutiae in these regions. Currently, the research indicates that third-level details improve the matching capability of AFIS only for high-quality latent prints that have a low minutiae count.

The FBI is planning a major upgrade to IAFIS to include more accurate results, upgraded ULW software, and a searchable palm database, called Next Generation Identification and built by Lockheed Martin with the algorithms provided by Morpho Trak. Additionally, it is intended to further increase the interoperability of the FBI's fingerprint database to other federal, state, local, and international AFIS. The first increment of this upgrade was implemented in February 2011, and replaced AFIS with Advanced Fingerprint Identification Technology to provide significantly improved matching algorithms. The full system upgrade is planned for 2014.

With the speed, accuracy, and many aspects of functionality, the AFIS has become a critical component to the law enforcement system. The amount of information searched in a few hours using an AFIS system could not be completed in a human lifetime. AFIS is arguably the most significant addition to the forensic science discipline in the last 25 years with respect to the cost, speed, and number of investigative leads that have come from these algorithm-based searches. It is an ever evolving system that will continue to be researched and improved upon for years to come.

See also: **Investigations:** Fingerprints; **Pattern Evidence:** Palm Prints; **Pattern Evidence/Fingerprints (Dactyloscopy):** Automated Methods, Including Criminal Records Administration; Identification and Classification; **Pattern Evidence/History:** Fingerprint Sciences.

Further Reading

Anthonioz, A., Champod, C., 2010. Integration of pore characteristics into the evaluation of fingerprint evidence. Impression and Pattern Evidence Symposium.

Anthonioz, A., Egli, N., Champod, C., Neumann, C., Puch-Solis, R., Bromage-Griffiths, A., 2011. Investigation of the reproducibility of third-level characteristics. Journal of Forensic Identification 61 (2), 171–178.

Champod, C., 1995. Edmond Locard – numerical standards and 'probable' identifications. Journal of Forensic Identification 45 (2), 136–163.

Dror, I.E., Mnookin, J.L., 2010. The use of technology in human expert domains: challenges and risks arising front the use of automated fingerprint identification systems in forensic science. Law, Probability and Risk 9 (1), 47–67.

Hutchins, L.A., 2009. What the future can hold: a look at the connectivity of automated fingerprint identification systems. Journal of Forensic Identification 59 (3), 275–283.

Indovina, M., Hicklin, R.A., Kiebuzinski, G.I., 2011. ELFT-EFS Evaluation of Latent Fingerprint Technologies: Extended Feature Sets [Evaluation #1]. NIST Interagency/Internal Report 7775.

Neumann, C., Champod, C., Puch-Solis, R., Egli, N., Anthonioz, A., Bromage-Griffiths, A., 2007. Computation of likelihood ratios in fingerprint identification for configurations of any number of minutiae. Journal of Forensic Sciences 52 (1), 54–64.

Scientific Working Group on Friction Ridge Analysis, Study and Technology, Moses, K.R., Higgins, P., McCabe, M., Probhakar, S., Swann, S., 2011. The Fingerprint Sourcebook (Chapter 6). http://www.nij.gov/pubs-sum/225320.htm.
U.S. Department of Justice, Office of the Inspector General, 2006. A Review of the FBI's Handling of the Brandon Mayfield Case. http://www.justice.gov/oig/.
Ulery, B.T., Hicklin, R.A., Buscaglia, J., Roberts, M.A., 2011. Accuracy and reliability of forensic latent fingerprint decisions. Proceedings of the National Academy of Sciences of the United States of America 19, 7733–7738.
Zhao, Q., Feng, J., Jain, A.K., 2010. Latent Fingerprint Matching: Utility of Level 3 Features. MSU Technical Report, MCU-CSE-10–14.

Relevant Websites

http://www.nist.gov—ANSI/NIST-ITL Standard.
http://www.fbi.gov—FBI IAFIS.
http://www.interpol.int/—INTERPOL.
http://www.nist.gov—NIST.
http://www.nij.gov/pubs-sum—The Fingerprint Sourcebook.

Key Terms

Automated Fingerprint Identification System (AFIS), Biometric, Candidate, Classification, Criminal record history, Fingerprint, Fingerprint patterns, Friction ridges, IDENT1, Integrated Automated Fingerprint Identification System (IAFIS), INTERPOL, Interstate Identification Index (III), Latent fingerprint, Latent print, Minutiae, National crime information center (NCIC), National fingerprint file (NFF), Next generation identification (NGI), Palm print, Personal identification, Rap sheet.

Review Questions

1. What does AFIS stand for? What about IAFIS?
2. Who was the first to develop a ten-digit fingerprint card? Why wasn't it adopted?
3. Who is Juan Vucetich?
4. When was the Henry System adopted by Scotland Yard?
5. Although mug shots were useful for criminal identification, what were some of the early problems with them?
6. What were the main problems with finding a file using the Bertillon System?
7. The FBI was the first national fingerprint repository, inheriting 800 000 fingerprint records from Leavenworth Prison. What were some of the problems in searching that collection of records? How were they initially addressed?
8. What agency assisted the FBI in the development of AFIS? What was its role?
9. What are the subsystems of AFIS?
10. What law helped to push for automation of criminal records, including fingerprints?
11. What is the NFF?
12. What is "live-scan"?
13. What is a "rap back" service and what does it do?
14. What is contained in an AFIS file?
15. How many minutiae can each exemplar finger have plotted in a file?
16. How many records are currently in the FBI database?
17. What is the most common way to limit search parameters for faster searching in AFIS?
18. Why would a latent be deleted a fingerprint from the database?
19. How much of a factor is orientation in the matching capability of a AFIS search?
20. When is Level three detail important in an AFIS search?

Discussion Questions

1. What does an AFIS "hit" mean? Is it an identification? What role does—and should—the human expert play in this process?
2. Read Dror's article on cognitive neurosciences in forensic science. Could a person bias an AFIS search? How? Could the results of an AFIS search bias an expert? How? What could be done to prevent this from happening?
3. Standardization is essential to the success of large-scale database searches. Why haven't standards been established and enforced for AFIS systems? What role do the vendors who make the systems play in this?
4. NIST (then NBS) had the first forensic laboratory in the US, with Wilmer Souder being a key scientist (he assisted in the Lindberg Kidnapping). What role did NIST play in the development of AFIS? Why that agency?
5. Why is interoperability of AFIS systems so important? With 18 000 law enforcement agencies in the US alone, how do jurisdictional borders affect AFIS searches that cross them?

Additional Readings

Alberink, I., Jongh, A., Rodriguez, C.M., 2014. Fingermark evidence evaluation based on AFIS matching scores: sensitivity of likelihood ratios to different types of conditioning. Journal of Forensic Sciences 59 (1), 70–81.

Dror, I.E., 2015. Cognitive neuroscience in forensic science: understanding and utilizing the human element. Philosophical Transactions of the Royal Society B 370 (1674), 20140255.

Krish, R.P., Fierrez, J., Ramos, D., Veldhuis, R., Wang, R., 2014. Evaluation of AFIS-ranked latent fingerprint matched templates. In: Image and Video Technology. Springer, Berlin, pp. 230–241.

Langenburg, G., Hall, C., Rosemarie, Q., 2015. Utilizing AFIS searching tools to reduce errors in fingerprint casework. Forensic Science International 257, 123–133.

Persinger, M., Ericson, L., Greene, M., 2014. Latent Fingerprint Interoperability Survey: A National Study of Automated Fingerprint Information Systems (AFIS) Maintained by Law Enforcement Agencies: Summary Reporting of Data Provided by Responding Agencies. U.S. Department of Justice, National Institute of Justice, Washington, DC.

Souder, W., 1936. Crime laboratory science clears up mysteries. The Science News-Letter 29 (793), 394–395.

Section 5. Interpretation

Whether Saks and Koehler's paper in *Science* about the coming paradigm shift in individualization in forensic science heralded the change or caused it is immaterial—the article was a watershed moment, regardless. No longer could any forensic science hide behind the claim of infallibility or a century of pairwise comparisons that purported to represent uniqueness throughout all time and space. That it took two nonforensic scientists to publish that article in one of the most prestigious science journals in the world says a great deal about the nonscientific culture of the forensic profession. The interpretation of all evidence, including forensic, must be probabilistic in nature:

> One attribute of human inference common across different situations is that *conclusive* evidence is either in very short supply or is quite impossible to obtain... Such evidence, if it existed, would make *necessary* a particular hypothesis or possible conclusion being entertained. In lieu of such perfection we often make use of *masses* of *inconclusive* evidence having additional properties: the evidence is *incomplete* on matters relevant to our conclusions, and it comes to us from sources that are, for various reasons, *not completely credible*. Thus inferences from such evidence can only be probabilistic in nature, and our conclusions have to be hedged in some way.[1]

DNA forced forensic science to confront the probabilistic nature of evidence, but the profession has been slow to adopt it. Change should come from within a discipline for it to be mature and valid. For too long, forensic science has waited for others to push it in the directions it needs to go. Maybe the issues surrounding fingerprints over the last several years will provide impetus for the profession to take the lead on its future.

Friction Ridge Skin Impression Evidence—Standards of Proof

C Champod, University of Lausanne, Lausanne, Switzerland

Introduction

Papillary surfaces are covered in fine lines, or "ridges" arranged generally in patterns such as loops, whorls, and arches. The ridges form characteristics called minutiae, such as bifurcations, ridge endings (or combined minutiae), and also smaller features (pores, ridge edges, and structures). These detailed features are the consequence of a morphogenesis, so sensitive to outside influence that they are difficult to predict, unlike general patterns, in their position and their form. The variability is such that even monozygotic twins have distinguishable friction ridge skin in this respect.

Following a comparison between a mark (recovered, for example, in association with a crime) and a print (controlled impression associated with a suspect), suppose that the examiner observes agreement—within allowed tolerances given the flexibility of the skin, the distortion during the deposition process, etc.—between the mark and the print without any significant discrepancy. The question is then often expressed as follows: "how many similarities are required to identify?" or "what is the required sufficient agreement to conclude an individualization?" Both terms "identification" and "individualization" are used here and hereinafter as synonymous.

The aim of this article is to try to address these questions of the "standard of proof," by reviewing international views and practices. The perspective adopted here is essentially the one of the forensic practitioners dealing with friction ridge skin and not the perspective of the court or judiciary.

[1] David A. Schum, 1994. Evidential Foundations of Probabilistic Reasoning. John Wiley & Sons, New York, pp. 1–2.

 http://dx.doi.org/10.1016/B978-0-12-800573-6.00014-8

Historical Milestone

The first rule establishing the minimum number requirements for fingerprint identification can be attributed to the French Edmond Locard, in 1911–1912 and officially published in 1914. He suggested a tripartite rule, which followed from the discovery of the use of pores when visible to help in the identification process (often referred to as *poroscopy*). Locard's rule can be summarized as follows:

1. If more than 12 concurring points are present and the fingerprint is sharp, then the certainty of identity is beyond debate. (The imperative requirement for the absence of significant differences is implicit.)
2. If there are 8–12 concurring points, then the case is borderline and the certainty of identity will depend on (1) the sharpness of the fingerprint; (2) the rarity of its type; (3) the presence of the center of the figure (core) and the triangle (delta) in the exploitable part of the print; (4) the presence of pores; and (5) the perfect and obvious identity regarding the width of the papillary ridges and valleys, the direction of the lines, and the angular value of the bifurcations. In these instances, certainty can only be established after discussion of the case by at least two competent and experienced specialists.
3. If a limited number of characteristic points are present, the fingermark cannot provide certainty for an identification, but only a presumption proportional to the number of points available and their clarity.

Locard based his tripartite rule on various sources of information: the discovery of poroscopy, the practice gathered by the identification bureaux around the world, and the early statistical models by Galton and Balthazard. This approach persists throughout the extensive writings of Locard. His considerations (principally the first two) were largely taken up by the most eminent dactyloscopists or criminalists of the first half of this century.

Current Views and Practice

On the fringe of the pragmatic view expressed above, the practice has led to various positions. The different positions that currently exist were not established without controversy after the views expressed by Locard.

Approach Based on a Predetermined Minimum Number of Minutiae

The majority of European examiners (and examiners from South America) have favored a purely quantitative approach, leaving qualitative aspects in the background, by fixing a numerical standard: a minimum number of minutiae necessary to establish identification. It is also referred to as the "numerical standard" approach or the "empirical" approach.

The numerical standard approach represents a lower limit; above this value, the identification is considered as beyond doubt, regardless of the type of minutiae that is found. The interpretation of the concept of numerical standard may vary from agency to agency; some positions are summarized in **Table 1**.

Despite the systematic use of a numerical standard, various countries (e.g., Greece, Holland, Israel, and Portugal) have developed methods to bypass the rigid number when certain features (visibility of pores, ridge structures, or rare combinations of minutiae) are observed in the comparison. The adoption of a range from 8 (or 10) to 12 points is a way to relax a rigid threshold. It is also reported in numerous countries that in some cases, an expert with more experience and a high standing in the profession can make an identification that does not meet the usual standard.

Approach Based on a Nonnumerical Standard

Before the 1970s, American examiners followed Locard's view. As a result, the 12-point rule was generally respected, and below this threshold, qualitative factors in the comparison were taken into consideration. In 1970, a commission of experts from the IAI was established to study the question of the relevance of a fixed numerical standard for decision-making in this area. The work of this committee (for "standardization") resulted in a number of articles and reports tracing the state of empirical and scientific knowledge. Apart from the fact that the justification of any number could not be based on statistical research pertaining to fingerprints, another powerful argument against any numerical standard derives from knowledge of the morphogenesis of the papillary lines. The development of papillary lines on corresponding surfaces is initiated (for the fingers) after 7 weeks of fetal life with the growth of volar pads on a papillary area. After 10 weeks, as the volar pads regress, primary ridges begin to grow in the dermis followed by secondary ridges. The various stresses involved in this process (regression of the volar pads, development of size, meeting of multiple development fronts) induce a highly variable formation of minutiae (in terms of type and positioning). Around week 25, the development of papillary lines is completed on the dermis and is projected onto the epidermis of the skin. The fact that the complete pattern is secured on the dermis explains the durability of the fingerprints. From that moment, a final differentiation occurs on the papillae, which dictates the form of pores and ridge edges. This final stage also produces a highly variable pattern (however, less reproducible from mark to mark). Hence, it is clearly not legitimate to reduce the fingerprint discriminative power to the minutiae as is suggested with any numerical standards. The number of specific features is much broader than minutiae alone. The nature of the papillary

Table 1 Principal positions regarding numerical standards adopted in some countries

Country(ies)	*Numerical standard*	*Origin (when known) and specificity*
Italy	16–17	Probabilistic calculation by Balthazard dating back to 1911. The minimum standard is expressly mentioned from a jurisprudence referring to Balthazard's work. The jurisprudence dated back to 1954 but has been confirmed in 1959 and 1989
England and Wales (1924–2000), Scotland (before 2006), Australia (prior to 1941)	16	The origins of this standard (adopted by New Scotland Yard in 1924) dated back to an erroneous interpretation of a document published by Bertillon in 1912. The work by Balthazard had probably also played a role, as it was taken at face value in fingerprint training manuals. The numerical standard was virtually impossible to circumvent
Bosnia, Germany, Romania, Switzerland (before 2007)	8–12	In agreement with Locard, even though in practice, there is a clear tendency to respect a "12-point" rule
Albania, Australia (from 1942 to 1999), Belgium, England, and Wales (before 1924), Finland, France, Hong Kong, Israel, Greece, Poland, Portugal, Romania, Slovenia, Spain, the Netherlands, Turkey, the USA (before 1973), South American countries	12	Number probably derived from the first rule of Locard (although Locard's writing stated "more than 12"). Note that in numerous countries, mechanisms to bypass the rigid threshold are in place. For example, in the Netherlands, a case of identification can be submitted with 10 minutiae if a committee of three examiners concurred to that conclusion
Czech Republic, Denmark	10	In Czech Republic, based in part on a statistical model developed by Jozefek in 1972 along with a survey of the relative occurrences of different types of minutiae
Russia, South Africa	7	According to a recent survey carried out by the IAI Standardization II Committee

variability prevents the adoption of any predefined number of ridge characteristics necessary (without significant differences) for identification. Following such arguments, the following resolution was adopted by the IAI in 1973: "The International Association for Identification, based upon a 3-year study by its Standardisation Committee, hereby state that no valid basis exists for requiring a predetermined minimum number of friction ridge characteristics that must be present in two impressions in order to establish positive identification."

This resolution is also endorsed by practical observations as follows:

- Some minutiae are rare than others (for example, a double bifurcation in the periphery of the pattern is six times less frequent than two separate bifurcations). Hence, counting minutiae up to a predefined number without taking into account their relative and distinct values is not adequate.
- The absence of any minutiae, from a papillary surface is as relevant as their presence. It would be very exceptional to observe a core area or a delta area where the ridges do not display any minutiae.
- The pore structure and ridge edge structure can be used to discriminate and, when visible, contribute to the identification decision.

It is hence accepted that the concept of identification cannot be reduced to counting minutiae; each identification represents a specific set of circumstances and the identification value of concurring points between a mark and a print on a variety of conditions that automatically excludes any minimum standard. This approach is then also known as the "holistic" approach or the "nonnumerical" approach.

In 1995, a conference meeting on fingerprint detection techniques and identification in Ne'Urim (Israel) unanimously approved a slight variation of the IAI 1973 resolution. The 1973 resolution was reassessed and reaffirmed by the Standardization II committee in 2011 which now reads: "There currently exists no scientific basis for requiring a minimum amount of corresponding friction ridge detail information between two impressions to arrive at an opinion of single source attribution."

When an expert concludes an identification, he reaches a decision threshold (refer to Entry 197). This threshold may be a number of concurring points and, in addition to this quantitative element, consideration of other factors such as the rarity of the general pattern, the type of minutiae observed, the relative frequencies of these minutiae, or the visibility of ridge edges or pores. In this way, the identification process is a global assessment that balances both quantitative and qualitative aspects. The term *ridgeology* refers to this global assessment.

Various countries follow the IAI position, as indicated in **Table 2**.

Table 2 Main positions and dates regarding the abandon of a numerical standard

Country(ies)	*Origin (when known) and specificity*
USA and Canada	Since 1973, following the IAI resolution
Norway	Other Scandinavian countries (Sweden, Finland) have now moved toward the abandonment of any numerical standard
England and Wales (from 2001), Scotland (from 2006)	In 1988, a committee was named by ACPO (Association of Chief Police Officers) and the Home Office to undertake a review of the origin and relevancy of the 16-point standard. Following this report, the abandonment of the numerical standard was recommended. It took more than 10 years to implement in England and Wales, longer in Scotland because of the McKie/Asbury case
Australia, New Zealand	In Australia, the move toward the abandonment started in some states and territories in 1992. The "12-point rule" was nationally abandoned in favor of the IAI resolution in 1999
Switzerland (from 2007)	Taking advantage of the debate in the UK and Australia and following the Ne'Urim declaration, a committee was created in 1998 to manage the change toward a nonnumerical practice. The change was approved by the heads of fingerprint bureaux in 2007. The previous standard was 12 and has been kept as a Q/A filter to distinguish between simple and complex cases

It must be noted that the work done by the English committee has been a determinant in the various moves toward the late adoption of the IAI resolution in countries that applied a numerical standard. In 1989, a collaborative study among 130 fingerprint examiners in England and Wales was conducted by Evett and Williams. Each participant was sent 10 mark/print comparisons (nine associations and one exclusion) and was asked to mark the number of concordant minutiae and to express an opinion with respect to the identification. No erroneous identifications were reported. But, when examining genuine pairs of prints, examiners varied widely in the number of points of comparison they found. In the case of one print, it varied from 11 to 40 minutiae reported by examiners. In other words, some examiners would not have gone to court with this pair of impression, although most would have done so. An identical survey in Switzerland in 1997 led to analogous results.

These studies led to the following conclusions:

- The dogma adopted by some examiners that fingerprint identification is an "exact" science is a misconception. The essence of science is inductive inference. Inference is a mental process that cannot be exact (or deductive). Fingerprint identification is scientific in that sense.
- The precision implied by any number (12, 16, etc.) is also a lure because of the high variability in feature selection between examiners. The determination of individual minutiae or features is highly dependent on training and experience but over all the quality of the mark itself.

As a means of achieving quality, adopting only a numerical standard is rather a poor instrument. The way forward is to concentrate on professional standards rather than on rules about numbers of minutiae. A scheme of quality management should be instituted, including training, certification testing, performance testing, file audits, and blind trials. This is part of the mandate of the FBI-sponsored *Scientific Working Group on Friction Ridge Analysis, Study and Technology* (SWGFAST) that proposes standards covering the above-mentioned quality components.

In relation to the standard of proof, the latest SWGFAST document: *Standards for Examining Friction Ridge Impressions and Resulting Conclusions* stresses three aspects:

- It is aligned with the 1973 IAI resolution through a statement saying that: "The use of a fixed number of friction ridge features as a threshold for the establishment of an individualization is not scientifically supported."
- It is acknowledged that a conclusion is a decision (REFER TO ENTRY 197), for example, it states that "Individualization is the decision by an examiner that there are sufficient features in agreement to conclude that two areas of friction ridge impressions originated from the same source. Individualization of an impression to one source is the decision that the likelihood the impression was made by another (different) source is so remote that it is considered as a practical impossibility."
- It proposed a sufficiency graph (**Figure 1**) that reflects the interplay between quality of the mark and quantity of minutiae observed during the analysis of the mark and its relation to the decision thresholds and levels of complexity based on a consensus of collective experience. The sufficiency graph is intended to illustrate the intellectual process involved with the examination of friction ridge detail and the ensuing decisions. It illustrates thresholds wherein examiners should recognize the need for, and provide, enhanced documentation supporting their conclusions.

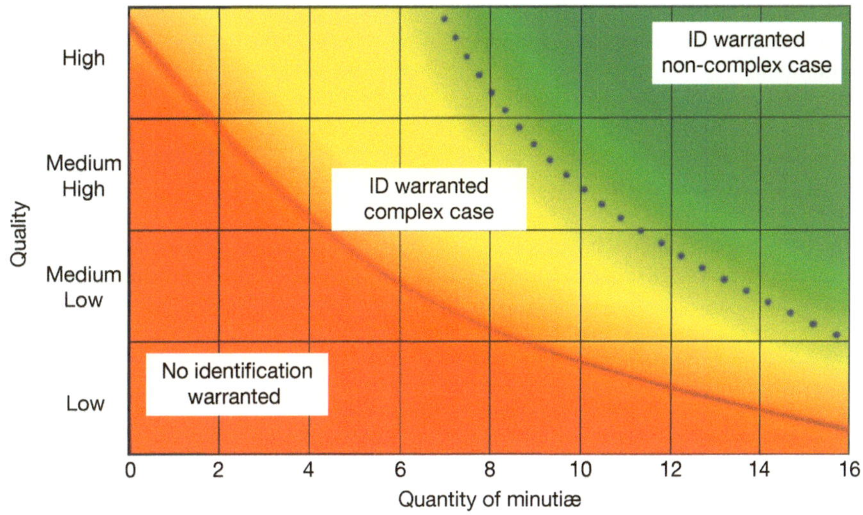

Figure 1 Sufficiency graph showing the interplay between quality and quantity of minutiae observed during the analysis of the mark and its relation to the decision thresholds and levels of complexity. Adapted from Scientific Working Group on Friction Ridge Analysis Study and Technology (SWGFAST), Standards for Examining Friction Ridge Impressions and Resulting Conclusions, Ver. 1.0, http://www.swgfast.org/documents/examinations-conclusions/111026_Examinations-Conclusions_1.0.pdf.

Hence, it is important not to view the IAI 1973 resolution and its progeny as the promotion of a "laissez-faire" approach. It has to be deployed within explicit guidelines defining quality and quantity.

Range of Possible Conclusions in the Field

Most contemporary experts refuse to give qualified opinions on friction ridge skin comparisons that do not meet the minimum requirements for an identification. From this standpoint, it is not encouraged to speak of association of strengths weaker than an individualization. It means that the last part of Locard's tripartite rule is not used in most countries. Only a few other countries are using such evidence as corroborative evidence. For example, in Belgium where there are between 8 and 12 points of agreement between a questioned fingermark and a fingerprint (without discrepancies), it is stated that "the fingerprint could be the same as the fingermark being examined." Therefore, apart from a few exceptions, Locard's third directive was totally forgotten as the use of dactyloscopy became widespread, thus giving this form of evidence its very distinctive character compared to other forms of impression evidence. In widespread practice, nowadays, the comparison between a mark and a print can be proof of identification or exclusion or it is declared as "inconclusive," without conveying any assessment of its evidential value. This is sometimes described as the "positivity" of the field. In 1979, during the annual IAI conference, a resolution was approved prohibiting members from giving testimony on qualified identifications. This resolution was widely debated before being revised and accepted in 1980. The IAI experts then rejected the idea of using friction ridge skin evidence as corroborative evidence in the following terms (Resolution 1980-5, Amending Resolution 1979-7): "THEREFORE BE IT RESOLVED that any member, officer or certified latent print examiner who initiates or volunteers oral or written reports, or testimony of possible, probable or likely friction ridge identification, or who, when required in a judicial proceeding to provide such reports or testimony, does not qualify it with a statement that the print in question could be that of someone else, shall be deemed to be engaged in conduct unbecoming such member,…".

Adopting such a policy means that in countries using numerical standards, for instance Italy, a fingerprint comparison with 16 concordant minutiae is an identification, whereas a comparison presenting only 15 points is not a probative evidence and should not be presented in court. Such a rule can easily result in difficult situations when, for example, a suspect is arrested and identified in one country on the basis of an identification with 12 points is to be judged in a neighboring country where 16 points are explicitly required.

Some authors and sources consider that the resolution voted by the IAI in 1980—rejecting any testimony providing support in favor of identification or exclusion—is opposed to the scientific principles governing the interpretation of evidence in forensic science. They propose that it is erroneous to consider that evidence from friction ridge skin comparison is only a dichotomic form of proof, uniquely applicable to identifications or nonidentifications. The interpretation cannot be so drastic, so clear-cut; there is an increasing scale of strength from exclusion to identification.

In fact, there is no logical reason to suppress these levels between exclusion and identification. Each piece of evidence is relevant if it tends to make the matter at issue more or less probable than otherwise. The refusal of qualified opinions is only a policy decision.

Often, probabilities have been excluded from the field arguing that each portion of a friction ridge skin impression, no matter how small, can only have come from one finger. It is the individuality of the papillary impression that is at question and not the individuality of the skin surface that produced it. The transfer of material in criminalistics, as defined by Locard, logically implies, by definition, a loss of information. For friction ridge skin, this loss may be of two types: quantitative (due to the limited size of the trace) and qualitative (blurring, bad definition, loss of pore details, etc.). The concept encapsulates a continuum of values in that a feature may have a discriminative value ranging from very low to very high.

Locard's third directive is fundamental and permits evidence from friction ridge skin to be on the same level as other types of impression evidence (or more generally forensic evidence). Some will no doubt argue that judges expect such evidence to be univocal and without compromise. This idea is false. It is obvious that any judge will prefer indisputable forms of proof but would also wish to be informed of any evidence that can lead closer to the truth. Much useful evidence should not be kept out of the courts on decision of technicians; it is up to the court to decide whether the evidence adduced is relevant.

The perceived absence of extensive statistical data on fingerprint individuality can be viewed as the main reason to prevent giving qualified opinions. Statistical data could make experts feel more comfortable in this area and make statements based on sound data obtained from significant samples. The Standardization II committee indeed recognized "the potential value that a validated probability model would have when expressing what is currently viewed as an 'inconclusive' conclusion." Following its committee report, the IAI 1979/1980 resolutions have been recently rescinded (Resolution 2010-18).

Recently, Neumann et al. have shown that very high weights of evidence (appropriately measured using a likelihood ratio) could be obtained from comparisons between marks and prints possessing a limited number of corresponding minutiae. When mark and prints are originating from the same source, an average likelihood ratio of 10^5 is obtained for comparison involving only four minutiae. This strongly shows the feasibility of evaluating evidence from friction ridge skin in a probabilistic way. It is possible to obtain, with some specific minutiae on a surface (or in the absence of minutiae on a large papillary surface), probability figures that exceed the value proposed in other forensic fields (e.g., DNA), even with fewer than 12 minutiae.

The Move toward Quality

Occurrences of Errors

Analysis of results from proficiency testing or from casework clearly indicates that error is possible and that some examiners do not reach adequate quality standards. The publications of S. Cole and J. Koehler are important here. The two most notorious cases of misattribution are the case against Brandon Mayfield (USA) and the case against Shirley McKie and David Asbury (Scotland). The largest controlled study by Ulery et al. involved 17 121 presentations to a pool of examiners ($N = 169$). It led to six cases of false identifications—a false positive rate of 0.2%.

But the evaluation of the standard of proof (or the quality of the evidence) cannot be limited to the examination of proficiency testing programs. Indeed, the corrective actions taken in an agency, following an erroneous identification, are far better indicators of quality than the report of errors (or successes). A global assessment of quality is then needed. The inquiry reports associated with the Mayfield case and the McKie/Asbury show the importance of a quality management system.

Total Quality Management

A total quality management system, based for example on the European Foundation for Quality Management (EFQM) model, can be recommended and is the basis of the most recent changes in the fingerprint practice. The various aspects of such a system are illustrated in **Figure 2**; the program is divided here into three parts: examiners, processes, and products. For each category, the quality management scheme must specify the needs and objectives, along with the quality indicators used to monitor the system and the corrective actions available. Audits (internal and independent) permit the claims to be checked regularly.

In such a general context, proficiency testing must be regarded as only one block of the building. The value of identifications based on the examination of friction ridge skin will be better assessed on the basis of a strict quality assurance program. A large number of laboratories have now implemented quality assurance programs. A convergence is currently seen toward the adoption of the EN ISO/IEC 17020 or 17025 standards. In 2009, the European Council issued a decision (EU Council Framework Decision 2009/905/JHA) requiring all forensic laboratories dealing with friction ridge skin impressions to gain accreditation under EN ISO/IEC 17025 by 2018.

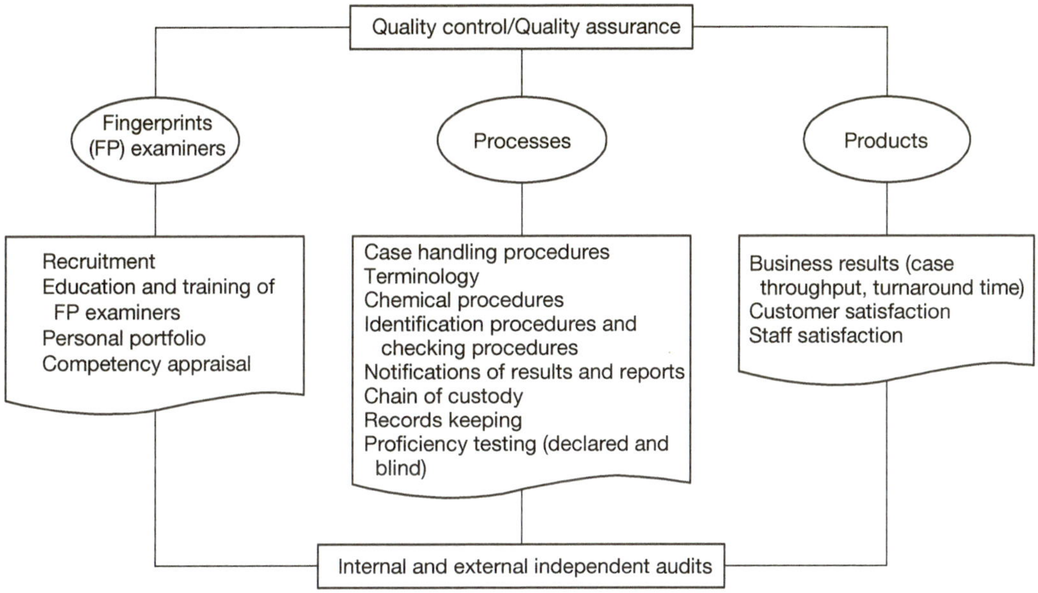

Figure 2 Outline of a total quality management system for a service dealing with friction ridge skin examinations.

Conclusion

Locard proposed the basic concepts determining the value of fingerprint evidence. Locard's opinions were enlightening and, above all, the most topical. From this early perspective, a large number of countries adopted a fixed (sometimes negotiable) standard in the form of a minimum number of matching minutiae required in order to conclude to an identification. This is now known as the numerical (or empirical) approach. Even if some practitioners rely on minimum numbers, they do not escape, thanks to the arbitrary limit, from the quality issues because, depending on the examiners, the interpretation of the number of minutiae in a comparison may vary to a large extent.

However, the detailed analysis of the factors contributing to the discriminating power of friction ridge skin shows that there is no scientific argument in favor of any predefined number of minutiae (in the absence of discordance) in order to pronounce an identification. Every comparison bears its own specificity, which refrains from defining a priori the amount or volume of information needed for the identification. The decision is then taken on a case-by-case basis by the expert. The approach is called holistic (or nonnumeric). It forces the field to rely on experience, professionalism, and integrity of the examiners.

Finally, following this description of fingerprint practices, what is the standard of proof? Definitely, the standard is not a predefined number of minutiae. Indeed, insisting dogmatically on any particular minimum number of points is not an effective way of insuring quality. But the holistic approach should not promote a culture of "laissez-faire" without boundaries. The recent document by SWGFAST provides essential limits to the practitioner. The way forward goes also hand in hand with the adoption of a scheme of quality management dealing with the various aspects of education and training, laboratory procedures, and audits.

Concerning the possibility of giving corroborative opinions based on such evidence (in favor or otherwise of an individualization), it seems that from a scientific point of view, there is no argument to justify the so-called "positivity" of the field. Nothing opposes the use of such evidence as corroborative evidence in the same way as other forensic evidence.

See also: **Foundations:** Overview and Meaning of Identification/Individualization.

Sequential Unmasking: Minimizing Observer Effects in Forensic Science

K Inman, California State University, Hayward, CA, USA
N Rudin, Forensic DNA Consultant, Mountain View, CA, USA

Glossary

Blind testing Blind testing is a method of testing in which an examiner records the results of any test or procedure without knowing the identity of the samples or what result might be expected. In forensic science most blind testing is done in a situation where the examiner knows he/she is being tested, but does not know what the answer is or should be. Double-blind testing is a procedure in which neither the analyst performing the testing nor the persons administering or assigning the testing (case) know the expected results of the examination. A double-blind procedure is used to guard against both confirmation bias and observer effects.

Confirmation bias The tendency to test a hypothesis by looking for instances that confirm it rather than by searching for potentially falsifying instances. In a less scientific setting, the tendency to seek and interpret information that confirms existing beliefs.

Context effects The influence of environmental factors on one's perception of a stimulus using top-down cognitive processing of sensory information to construct a completed perception of the observation or phenomenon.

Domain-relevant The domain of a model that necessitates a restriction on the values that can be used in the task at hand. In forensic science, this comprises only that information necessary and sufficient (domain-relevant) for an analysis, comparison, or interpretation of an item or items of evidence. It is information without which the most basic physical evidence examination, analysis, and comparison cannot be correctly accomplished.

Observer bias Errors that occur when the observers (or researcher team) know the goals of the study or the hypotheses and allow this knowledge to influence their observations during the study. Error is introduced into measurement and judgment when observers overemphasize results that they expect to find and fail to notice results that they do not expect.

Observer effects The tendency for the desires and expectations that a person possesses to influence his/her perception and interpretation of what he/she observes. In other words, the results of an observation depend upon the state of the observer as well as the thing observed.

Sequential unmasking A process of testing whereby relevant information about the evidence is revealed (unmasked) in an orderly fashion, providing the appropriate level of domain-relevant information necessary and sufficient to perform an analysis, comparison, or interpretation on a piece of physical evidence.

The Concept of Sequential Unmasking

In 2008, a letter to the editor of *Journal of Forensic Science*, entitled Sequential Unmasking: A Means of Minimizing Observer Effects in Forensic DNA Interpretation, was published. Although this certainly was not the first time the concept of blinding a forensic examiner to extraneous information had been suggested, it was the first publication in the knowledge of the authors that included forensic practitioners among the authors. Other disciplines represented among the diverse group included law, psychology, economics, and statistics.

The initiative used forensic DNA typing as a model system, in part because both the existing procedures and the data itself are relatively well defined. The main contribution of the piece was to reimagine conventional blind testing in a way that would be more pertinent to the way forensic science is practiced. Hence the authors proffered the term "sequential unmasking" to highlight the idea that forensic scientists would receive all relevant information in an orderly fashion. The idea was to minimize the opportunities for inadvertent bias, while still providing the examiner with all the information needed for a complete and relevant analysis.

Several key points attempted to address the practical implementation of sequential unmasking procedures. In addition to the idea of sequentially unmasking of (rather than withholding) information, the authors suggested using a case

 http://dx.doi.org/10.1016/B978-0-12-800573-6.00015-X

manager (not a new idea in and of itself) to manage the flow of information. Another concept discussed was the idea of domain-relevant and domain-irrelevant information. The abbreviated nature of a letter to the editor did not allow for expansion of this idea, and it will be explored further in this article. Finally, the authors proposed that, although it undoubtedly would be more challenging, sequential unmasking procedures should certainly be applied to forensic disciplines other than DNA.

The Foundational Basis for Cognitive Effects

The previous edition of this Encyclopedia included an article by William C. Thompson on observer effects, context effects, and confirmation bias in forensic science. So as not to be repetitive, the reader is referred to that article for more extensive background information that is only briefly summarized here. An extensive list of references is also provided at the end of this article.

Although many different terms are used to describe different aspects of effects that may induce cognitive bias, the reader is cautioned to avoid being distracted by the different terms of art such as observer effects, context effects, confirmation bias; the important point is that no human being, and forensic practitioners are human beings, operates in a vacuum. Human beings live in the real world and are constantly bombarded by external stimuli. The way in which humans process those stimuli allows them to function at a high level. However, the filters (schemata in the language of psychology) that higher brain functions use to organize information prioritize and emphasize some information over other information. While this is useful and necessary for survival, it can affect, indeed bias, the way we make decisions. Judgment and decision making lie at the heart of interpreting forensic data.

The underlying idea of context and observer effects derives from a rich and well-documented cognitive psychology literature. Certainly, the idea that human beings do not always recognize all of the factors that influence their judgments and decisions is widely accepted in the field of psychology. Additionally, an extensive knowledge base documenting the existence of cognitive effects exists in the history of science itself, as well as current systematic empirical studies, and syntheses and meta-analyses of experimental data, and case reports. It is simply impossible to disassociate the inherent characteristics of an object or event from the state of the observer and the context in which the observation takes place; the very act of human observation alters the ultimate perception. The tendency of observers to perceive and interpret data in a manner consistent with their preconceptions is exhibited most strongly in the face of ambiguous data, and either strong emotions or clear expectations.

Cognitive Effects Occur at a Subconscious Level

It is worthwhile emphasizing two key concepts that seem to be perpetually misunderstood. First, the type of potential bias exerted by context, observer, and other related effects occurs without humans being aware of it; it works at a level that cannot be accessed by the conscious mind. Therefore, no matter how well meaning, well educated, and well trained the analyst, he/she is incapable of simply willing away such influences; expertise does not insulate one from the influence of expectation and situation. This means that the most effective way to minimize opportunities for potential bias is procedural.

Susceptibility to Cognitive Effects is Not a Flaw

Second, susceptibility to context effects is not a weakness or failing in the expert; it derives from the way the human brain processes and organizes information, a capability essential to the functioning and survival of humans in the natural world. However, in the situations previously described, including the examination of physical evidence in a forensic context, it can work against individuals.

The Most Effective Antidote to Cognitive Effects is Procedural

In order to combat the potential biasing effects inherent in the observer and ubiquitous in context, blind testing protocols have become standard operating procedure in many scientific disciplines, including clinical "evidence-based" medicine, research science, and other applied sciences; the idea is culturally embedded to the point that it is simply taken for granted as "good practice." It is even exemplified in scholarly publications as the well-known anonymous peer-review process. Blind and double-blind testing protocols further pervade such diverse arenas as consumer product testing, music auditions, and grading student exams.

Support for Blind Testing in Forensic Science

Given that physical evidence items associated with crime events can, by their very nature, present extremely ambiguous data, and that, unquestionably, the criminal arena, and even the civil arena, represent some of the most emotionally heightened contexts imaginable, the forensic examination of physical evidence provides a strong confluence of factors provoking cognitive effects. Additionally, subjective judgment by the human observer pervades the interpretation of forensic evidence. Although no discipline is immune, including DNA typing, it is pattern evidence (e.g., fingerprints, shoe prints, toolmarks, and firearms) that appears most vulnerable to biasing influences. The random pattern nature of this type of evidence is both strength and weakness. The randomness of the patterns generates the diversity; however, that same characteristic also creates challenges in defining objective interpretation criteria. Additionally, as currently practiced, the comparisons rely almost entirely on human judgment to form conclusions about whether a particular evidence item could derive from a specific source. Lest the reader infer that DNA and other types of instrumental evidence are immune to observer effects, it is important to point out that any physical evidence loses clarity and gains ambiguity as it increases in complexity and decreases in quantity and quality. Interestingly, while research has been performed to investigate the consequence of context effects on fingerprints, proposals to investigate whether the same phenomenon occurs with ambiguous DNA profiles have been dismissed as unnecessary research (personal knowledge, authors).

Nevertheless, no one, not even the most vocal critics, has suggested that most, or even many, conclusions derived from the comparison of pattern evidence are patently erroneous due to the subtle influence of observer effects. However, psychology predicts and a growing body of research confirms that in a demonstrable number of cases in which ambiguous evidence is analyzed by an examiner who is presented with information that is unnecessary to perform the initial comparison, his/her conclusion may change substantively and directionally with the extraneous information. Sufficient evidence exists, both from research and from casework examples, that the potential for observer bias can no longer be refuted or ignored.

Psychological and social studies of science inform us that context information, such as expectations about what one is supposed to see or conclude, has been found to exert a small but relentless impact on human perception, judgment, and decision-making. Given the potentially momentous consequences of an erroneous conclusion made in the forensic setting, it seems surprising to many observers that safeguards to minimize the chance of analyst bias are not instituted as a matter of course. Even if a frank error resulting from one of several types of cognitive bias occurs only rarely, is not the cost (whether monetary or in human resources) worth the potential benefit (life or liberty of a human being)? And if the cost is relatively small, would it not be easier for forensic scientists to be able preemptively to dismiss any accusation of possible bias affecting their examination? In the next section, some of the objections voiced from within the forensic community to implementing sequential unmasking protocols are discussed.

Arguments against Blind Testing in Forensic Science

Although isolated pockets of support exist, the forensic science profession as a whole has yet to embrace the idea of instituting infrastructural and procedural solutions that minimize the opportunity for analyst bias. Although the profession appears to be slowly accepting the idea that potential for inadvertent bias exists, there remains a general resistance to embrace procedural solutions to minimize the opportunity for context and observer effects. Why is this?

Perhaps because forensic scientists operate in an adversarial situation imposed by the legal system, they tend to be sensitive to perceived accusations implying a lack of integrity. Some, whether through mishearing or misunderstanding, confuse observer effects with deliberate fraud or base incompetence. They point to the fact that examples of patent fraud are relatively rare (true, but irrelevant) and that competence should be addressed through training and education (also true, and also irrelevant). Although some instances of these other problems may be detected using procedures to minimize bias, the directed goal of sequential unmasking is to address the unintentional and unintended influences of observer and context effects on forensic examinations. They should be welcomed as protective measures to insulate the expert from both the actuality and the perception of bias.

Another argument is that the potential cost in both monetary and human resources to institute sequential unmasking protocols outweighs the benefit of reducing the relatively small number of frank errors resulting from observer effects. Some argue that it would be very difficult to make the changes in an institutionalized system, and that efficiency would be so severely affected as to render implementation of sequential unmasking procedures unworkable. Certainly, some of this depends on the extent of the changes, as well as how they are implemented. Supporters argue that relatively simple measures can be put in place immediately, and more complex institutional changes could be introduced over time. One way to actually measure impact and efficiency might be first to implement variations of sequential unmasking procedures on a limited basis, perhaps using a model system. This would be particularly useful for disciplines in which the information flow is less obvious than for forensic DNA typing. On the other hand, several laboratories are known which have already implemented at least first level type sequential unmasking procedures (analyzing and documenting evidence items before comparison with reference items) in their DNA sections virtually seamlessly.

Yet another objection to implement sequential unmasking procedures via a case-manager approach decries a waste of expertise among laboratory personnel. Those who make this argument have apparently misunderstood the intention of a case-manager system in the context of sequential unmasking. The case manager would be a high-level scientist within the laboratory (not a law enforcement officer external to the laboratory, as has been suggested by at least one critic), and no reason exists why the duty should not rotate among qualified examiners. The assumption of a static case-manager role that would relegate all other analysts in the laboratory to mere technicians is an artificial and insubstantial roadblock. Said another way, it is the proverbial straw man.

A more substantial complaint about sequential unmasking is that it would somehow deprive the examiner of information required to competently and fully interpret forensic evidence in the context of the case. Again, the fear appears to embody the image of a laboratory full of mere technicians, supervised by detectives and attorneys, who would direct the flow of information and interpret the evidence in the context of the case. This could not be further from the intention of the architects of sequential unmasking. Assuming the forensic scientist has received the appropriate education and training, and acquired some reasonable amount of experience, that expert can and should assist the justice system in understanding the evidence in the context of the case; in fact it would be incompetent and irresponsible not to provide this expertise. However, it is not necessary for the practitioner to receive all the information at the beginning of the examination to accomplish this goal. The examiner can be protected from context and observer effects by sequentially revealing information to him/her in a sequential fashion, on an as-needed basis. This might begin with the minimal information required to properly and adequately sample and analyze a piece of evidence. At each subsequent step of analysis and interpretation, additional information required to proceed would be revealed. At the end of any particular procedure, the analyst would be privy to all domain-relevant information; when the technical analysis has been completed and documented, information that might only be questionably domain-relevant can be unveiled as well. This allows for the documentation of results in an orderly fashion, including any modifications resulting from the new information. This will generate a complete record of how conclusions may have been updated with the acquisition of new knowledge about the case.

Some have acknowledged that the potential for cognitive bias exists, but that those concerns are completely addressed by quality assurance measures already in place. Specifically they offer that "peer review" and "blind verification" offer protection equivalent to or better than sequential unmasking procedures. First, the term "peer review" properly applies to a specific process through which a manuscript submitted for publication in a professional journal is anonymously reviewed by several individuals in the same field to determine its suitability for publication. Co-opting this term as a synonym for the internal technical review performed in a forensic laboratory is inappropriate and misleading. It implies greater weight and authority to an internal technical review than is merited, conferring upon it a false sense of autonomy and independence.

Use of the term "verification" to describe an independent examination of an item or data is also problematic. The term strongly implies that the conclusion of the primary analyst will in fact be verified and would seem to leave little room for refutation. As thought follows language, it has been suggested that more neutral terms, such as independent examination, analysis, or interpretation, are more appropriate than verification. Most importantly though, there is no knowledge of any published data that indicate that the implementation of these types of quality assurance measures, as used by forensic laboratories today, minimizes observer bias. These procedures, while useful and necessary for other reasons, do not substitute for sequential unmasking.

One highly debated parallel is the experience of clinical medicine, in particular, radiology. Some advocates of blinding procedures in forensic science point to the interpretation of body scans as an analogy for interpreting forensic evidence. They offer that radiologic films are always interpreted by technicians who are expert in reading the data, but who are never provided with information about other symptoms. The physician, then, is the expert who puts the blind conclusion of the radiologist into context with the rest of the symptoms and diagnoses the disease. Many in the forensic community are offended by this analogy, arguing that (1) the forensic practitioner is more analogous to the physician than to the radiologic technician and (2) many radiologists are provided with patient histories, and in fact are not blinded to extraneous information. A paucity of information, published or otherwise, makes it difficult to determine whether strong support exists for either point of view.

Finally, critics have complained that advocates of sequential unmasking intend that it should be imposed only upon prosecution laboratories, while independent experts working mostly for the defense remain privy to all case information from the beginning of their review. While implementation is certainly more challenging in the private sector for a variety of reasons, independent experts should not be immune from implementing sequential unmasking procedures. The most critical aspect, that of analyzing evidence items, as well as documenting the characteristics of the evidence before comparison to any reference items, can be readily accomplished even by the sole practitioner. Any laboratory, government or independent, would require additional infrastructure to completely implement sequential unmasking protocols.

Sequential Unmasking in Forensic Science

Because so many forensic practitioners interpret blind testing procedures to mean that they will be forever and enduringly blind to any and all case information, and will be restricted to performing a simple technician-type comparison as an endpoint, it is important to clarify the basic sequential unmasking protocol. Both descriptors, sequential and unmasking, are meaningful and critical. Together, they describe a linear flow of information, beginning with only the most essential pieces, and then in an orderly stepwise fashion, revealing additional information that may expand to include the entire case circumstance, if appropriate. The idea is that observations, results, and conclusions will be documented at each step. The practitioner is not locked into any particular statement made at some point in the analysis; rather, if his/her conclusions change, the reasoning supporting that change is documented such that it may be subject to future review. While, at first, this may seem restrictive, even burdensome, such a stepwise procedure not only minimizes opportunities for potentially biasing context and observer effects but also protects the analyst from gratuitous accusations of bias. If the analyst has documented the initial characterization of the evidence and the subsequent comparison, he/she may then properly consider additional information, and eventually, interpret the evidence in the context of the case, secure in the knowledge that he/she has protected herself from undue influences during the initial evaluation, examination, analysis, and comparison. Such a process patently precludes any notion that the analyst would ultimately lack information relevant to a complete and informed conclusion.

The responsible forensic professional not only may, but must, eventually consider the evidence in the context of the case. Both the initial blinding and the subsequent revelation are critical to the competent practice of forensic science. Interpreting the evidence in context with other physical evidence analyses, case facts, or other information should not be left to law enforcement or legal players, who may lack critical expertise in the examination or interpretation of physical evidence. In the perennial words of Robert Rosenthal, the practitioner should be kept "as blind as possible for as long as possible." The requisite addition to that statement is that the practitioner should receive information in an orderly, documented fashion so as to fully assist the judicial system in understanding the import of the physical evidence.

Domain-Relevant (and Domain-Irrelevant) Information

The idea of domain-relevant (and conversely domain-irrelevant) information may have been introduced in the seminal paper by Saks et al. It is a fundamental concept in applying sequential unmasking and is mentioned in the JFS letter, but because it has not been subject to subsequent discussion or expansion, the concept has remained unnecessarily mysterious. Consequently, a fair amount of consternation has ensued about this concept. This concern is exacerbated by the fact that no detailed discussion has followed, nor has any guidance been provided as to how to incorporate it into an evidence examination protocol.

The idea of domain relevance is probably better defined dynamically rather than statically. In other words, although examples and general guidelines can be proffered, determining the relevancy of various pieces of information on a case-by-case basis is, in fact, one of the roles of the case manager. In a larger sense, determining what information is necessary and sufficient (domain-relevant) for a technical comparison and at what stage it should be provided is likely a discipline-specific exercise. It cannot and should not be imposed from above or from outside the discipline. That would be a recipe for disaster. Only those intimately involved in the examination and analysis of a particular type of evidence know what information is intrinsic and essential to an initial analysis or comparison, and which information can be revealed at later stages in the process to optimize the sequential unmasking procedure for the best analysis with the least opportunity for bias.

Generally, domain-relevant information can be understood as that without which the most basic physical evidence examination, analysis, and comparison cannot be accomplished. The primary items obviously include the evidence sample and, after the evidence examination is complete and fully documented, the reference or exemplar sample. However, the comparison of the two might require additional information that is not intrinsic to the items being compared. For example, the presence of a scale is required for both the evidence and exemplar prints in a shoeprint comparison; otherwise an insufficient basis exists on which to base a comparison. In DNA analysis, information that the evidence derives from an intimate sample would be revealed early in the process so that the analyst could proceed with mixture deconvolution, but only after the evidence sample was analyzed and a commitment made (in the form of documentation) to the types present. It would certainly be appropriate to reveal the profile of the intimate reference source so as to deconvolve a mixture before comparison with a suspect reference sample. Some examiners have argued that knowledge about the substrate on which a fingerprint was deposited is critical domain-relevant information required for a competent analysis; other observers, however, have argued that the pattern inherent in the print can and should be interpreted first absent this knowledge, or even that this information would and should not change determination of characteristics in the evidence print. Another point of current discussion in the fingerprint community is when an examiner should be informed that a set of exemplars is the result of an Automated Fingerprint Identification System (AFIS) database search.

One might ask whether an examiner should consider the results of a related analysis from another discipline in the interpretation of his/her results. For example, assume that a usable fingerprint is located on a gun, and a small portion of the ridge detail is also tested for DNA. Assume that they implicate different individuals. One would not want to take the chance that either analyst would be influenced by the conclusions of the other, especially if the evidence is ambiguous. However, clearly, someone eventually has to think about an explanation for the apparently discrepant results. Was there an error in collection or analysis? Was another fluid present on the weapon underneath the fingerprint? Was an adjacent area sampled that would inform the examiner about background material? Does another possible case-related explanation exist that could reconcile the results? Again, this is the value of the case manager. But ultimately, after each discipline-specific examiner has completed his/her analysis, and documented his/her results and conclusions, no reason exists to withhold this information, or not to solicit his/her input as to explanations for the apparent discrepancy. The solution lies in the orderly sequence of unmasking information, and careful and complete documentation of data, interpretations and conclusions at each step.

Finally, examples of information that are clearly domain-irrelevant are considered. For example, the physical evidence examiner does not need to know that the suspect has a rap sheet 12 miles long, or that he/she has confessed to the crime, or that eyewitness reports place him/her at the scene. He/she does not need to know that this is a high-profile case commanding media attention. Yet this type of information is regularly included in sensational fashion on requests for evidence examination. A generalization of such a request is to name the suspect as the factual perpetrator of the crime, and to emphasize that positive results are required to arrest and charge a suspect, or to apprehend him/her because he/she is a flight risk. Every examiner has seen specific variations of this transmittal. While the back story certainly serves to put a human face on what might otherwise be a mundane, even boring, occupation, providing this information up front jeopardizes the objective analysis that can, in the end, provide the most reliable and useful results to the judicial system. No one is suggesting that the analyst never learn the case story; in fact by the conclusion of a case, often after a conversation with the detective, and certainly if a case proceeds to trial, the examiner will be fully informed, fully aware, perhaps even immersed, in the case details. However, if the order of information revelation is controlled, both the practitioner and the analysis are protected and the information offered to the criminal justice system is more secure.

It is neither an easy nor a trivial exercise to formulate standards for domain-relevant information or to determine a dividing point between that and domain-irrelevant information. Nevertheless, such difficulties do not justify the complete absence of standards of practice that now exist. A useful and practical plan would be for the various disciplines that comprise forensic science to meet and begin discussing this matter. The forensic community would do well to take ownership of this issue before it is imposed upon them from the outside.

Exemplar Line-Ups

A procedure that is different from conventional blind testing, and which could be very useful to incorporate into a sequential unmasking protocol, is exemplar line-ups. This procedure has in the past been referred to as "evidence line-ups." This is a misnomer, hence confusing. The line-up consists of several known reference samples that might be considered as the source of the evidence; no additional evidence samples are introduced.

Everyone is familiar with photo line-ups presented to eyewitnesses. It is standard practice for the photo pack to be presented as a line-up (a group of images at the same time), and officers are instructed to avoid either verbal or physical cues to the eyewitness that might prejudice them toward a particular photo. How well this is accomplished in practice can be debated, but the intent is correct.

A physical evidence line-up would proceed in a similar fashion. For example, the fingerprint examiner would receive a group of ten-print exemplars, one of which is from the suspect; the others would be prints exhibiting similar patterns, but unrelated to the crime event. In this way, the examiner avoids the inherent bias that the suspect is the source of the evidence print simply because his/her 10-print card was submitted as the only exemplar for comparison to the evidence print. This procedure is readily extended to just about any discipline in which comparisons are required to determine source. Certainly, detractors will argue that the extra time and work to perform multiple comparisons is not worth the cost in human and monetary resources to achieve the potential benefit. These questions could be addressed by simple experiments using model systems.

Conclusion

While the existence of cognitive effects leading to observer bias is well documented in the cognitive psychology literature, and the idea of blind testing is widely accepted across various scientific and medical disciplines, these ideas have historically been dismissed by the forensic profession. Although the potential for bias is beginning to be more widely accepted by forensic practitioners, resistance to procedural solutions remains significant. The reader is referred to the extensive bibliography offered below for additional information and education on these current and critical issues.

See also: **Biology/DNA:** Forensic DNA Advisory Groups: DAB, SWGDAM, ENFSI, and BSAG; Low-Template DNA Testing; Mixture Interpretation (Interpretation of Mixed DNA Profiles with STRs Only); **Chemistry/Trace/Fibers:** Fiber: Protocols for Examination; Identification and Comparison; Interpretation of Fiber Evidence; **Chemistry/Trace/Glass:** Interpretation of Glass Evidence; **Chemistry/Trace/Miscellaneous Unknowns:** The Forensic Analysis of Chemical Unknowns; **Chemistry/Trace/Paint and Coating:** Interpretation of Paint Evidence; **Foundations:** Evidence/Classification; Forensic Intelligence;

History of Forensic Sciences; Overview and Meaning of Identification/Individualization; Principles of Forensic Science; Semiotics, Heuristics, and Inferences Used by Forensic Scientists; Statistical Interpretation of Evidence: Bayesian Analysis; The Frequentist Approach to Forensic Evidence Interpretation; **Foundations/Fundamentals:** Measurement Uncertainty; **Legal:** DNA Exonerations; Expert Witness Qualifications and Testimony; Forensic Laboratory Reports; History of the Law's Reception of Forensic Science; International Courts and Forensic Science; Legal Aspects of Forensic Science; Legal Systems: Adversarial and Inquisitorial; The Innocence Project; When Science Changes, How Does Law Respond; **Management/Quality in Forensic Science:** Accreditation; Certification; Effectiveness; Risk Management; Standard Methods; **Pattern Evidence:** Analysis, Comparison, Evaluation, and Verification (ACE-V); Bare Footprint Marks; Footwear Marks; Palm Prints; Physical Match; Plastic Bag Striations; The Friction Ridge Skin of the Feet; Tools; Vehicle Tire Marks and Tire Track Measurement; **Pattern Evidence/ Fingerprints (Dactyloscopy):** Friction Ridge Print Examination – Interpretation and the Comparative Method; Friction Ridge Skin Impression Evidence – Standards of Proof; **Pattern Evidence/ History:** Fingerprint Sciences; **Professional:** Continuing Professional Development; Education and Accreditation in Forensic Science; Ethics; National Academy of Sciences (NAS); Research and Publishing; Training to Competence.

Further Reading

Asimov, E., May 7, 2008. Wine's Pleasures: Are They All in Your Head? New York Times.

Balcetis, E., Dale, R., 2007. Conceptual set as a top-down constraint on visual object identification. Perception 36, 581–595.

Balcetis, E., Dunning, D., 2006. See what you want to see: motivational influences on visual perception. Journal of Personality and Social Psychology 91 (4), 612–625.

Berkson, J., Magath, T.B., Hurn, M., 1940. The error of estimate of the blood cell count as made with the hemocytometer. American Journal of Physiology 128, 309–323.

Bolton, J., 1995. Medical practice and anthropological bias. Social Science and Medicine 40 (12), 1655–1661.

Boring, E.G., 1950. A History of Experimental Psychology, second ed. Appleton-Century-Crofts, New York.

Budowle, B., August 2010. Public Commentary at the NIJ Impression and Pattern Evidence Symposium. Clearwater, FL.

Budowle, B., Bottrell, M.C., Bunch, S.G., et al., 2009. A perspective on errors, bias, and interpretation in the forensic sciences and direction for continuing advancement. Journal of Forensic Sciences 54 (4), 798–809.

Buss, D.M. (Ed.), 2005. The Handbook of Evolutionary Psychology. John Wiley & Sons, Hoboken, NJ.

Byrne, A., Eysenck, M.V., 1993. Individual differences in positive and negative interpretative biases. Personality and Individual Differences 14, 849–851.

Cahen, L.S., 1965. An Experimental Manipulation of the 'Halo Effect': A Study of Teacher Bias. Unpublished manuscript, Stanford University (Cited In: Rosenthal, R., 1976. Experimenter Effects in Behavioral Research, enlarged ed. Appleton-Century-Crofts, New York).

Campbell, D.T., 1993. Systematic errors to be expected of the social scientist on the basis of a general psychology of cognitive bias. In: Blanck, P.D. (Ed.), Interpersonal Expectations: Theory, Research, and Applications. Cambridge University Press, New York.

Caverni, J.P., Peris, J.L., 1990. The anchoring-adjustment heuristic in an "information rich, real world setting": knowledge assessment by experts. In: Caverni, J.P., Fabre, M., Gonzalez, M. (Eds.), Advances in Psychology, vol. 68. Elsevier Science Publishers B.V, Amsterdam, pp. 35–46.

Charlton, D., Fraser-Mackenzie, P., Dror, I.E., 2010. Emotional experiences and motivating factors associated with fingerprint analysis. Journal of Forensic Science 55, 385–393.

Cordaro, L., Ison, J.R., 1963. Observer bias classical conditioning of the planarian. Psychological Reports 13, 787–789.

Das-Smaal, E.A., 1990. Biases in categorization. In: Caverni, J.P., Fabre, M., Gonzalez, M. (Eds.), Advances in Psychology, vol. 68. Elsevier Science Publishers B.V, Amsterdam, pp. 349–386.

Daston, L.J., 2005. Scientific error and the ethos of belief. Social Research 72 (18), 1–18.

Ditto, P.H., Lopez, D.F., 1992. Motivated skepticism: use of differential decision criteria for preferred and non preferred conclusions. Journal of Personality and Social Psychology 63, 568–584.

Dror, I.E. Friction Ridge Sourcebook, SWGFAST, NIJ. http://www.ojp.usdoj.gov/nij/pubs-sum/225320.htm.

Dror, I.E. How can Francis Bacon help forensic science? the four idols of human biases. Jurimetrics: The Journal of Law, Science, and Technology.

Dror, I.E. Paradoxical functional degradation in human expertise. In: Kapur, N., Pascual-Leone, Ramachandran, V.S. (Eds.), The Paradoxical Brain. Cambridge University Press, Cambridge, UK.

Dror, I.E., Charlton, D., 2006. Why experts make errors. Journal of Forensic Identification 56 (4), 600–616.

Dror, I.E., Charlton, D., Peron, A., 2006. Contextual information renders experts vulnerable to making erroneous identification. Forensic Science International 156, 74–78.

Dror, I.E., Cole, S.A. The vision in 'blind' justice: expert perception, judgment and visual cognition in forensic pattern recognition. Psychonomic Bulletin and Review.

Dror, I.E., Fraser-Mackenzie, P.A.F., 2008. Cognitive biases in human perception, judgment, and decision making: bridging theory and the real world. In: Rossmo, K. (Ed.), Criminal Investigative Failures. Taylor & Francis, Oxford, UK.

Dror, I.E.,Mnookin, J. The use of technology in human expert domains: challenges and risks arising from the use of automated fingerprint identification systems in forensics. Law, Probability and Risk.

Dror, I.E., Peron, A.E., Hind, S.-L., Charlton, D., 2005. When emotions get the better of us: the effect of contextual top-down processing on matching fingerprints. Applied Cognitive Psychology 19, 799–809.

Dror, I.E., Rosenthal, R., 2008. Meta-analytically quantifying the reliability and biasability of forensic experts. Journal of Forensic Sciences 53 (4), 900–903.

Edwards, K., Smith, E.E., 1996. A disconfirmation bias in the evaluation of arguments. Journal of Personality and Social Psychology 71, 5–24.

Feinstein, A.R., 1960. The stethoscope. A source of diagnostic and conceptual errors in rheumatic heart disease. Journal of Chronic Diseases 11, 91–101.

Fisher, R.A., 1936. Has Mendel's work been rediscovered? Annals of Science 1, 115–137.

Gilovich, T., 1991. How We Know What Isn't So: The Fallibility of Human Reason in Everyday Life. The Free Press, New York, NY.

Girotto, V., Politzer, G., 1990. Conversational and world knowledge constraints on deductive reasoning. In: Caverni, J.P., Fabre, M., Gonzalez, M. (Eds.), Advances in Psychology, vol. 68. Elsevier Science Publishers B.V, Amsterdam, pp. 87–108.

Goldin, C., Rouse, C., 2000. Orchestrating impartiality: the impact of "blind" auditions on female musicians. The American Economic Review 90 (4), 715–741.

Goldstein, R., Almenberg, J., Dreber, A., Emerson, J.W., Herschkowitsch, A., Katz, J., 2008. Do More Expensive Wines Taste Better? Evidence from a Large Sample of Blind Tastings. AAWE Working Paper No. 16. American Association of Wine Economists.

Guerin, B., 1994. What do people think about the risks of driving? Implications for traffic safety interventions. Journal of Applied Social Psychology 24, 994–1021.

Harris, M.J., Rosenthal, R., 1985. The mediation of interpersonal expectancy effects: 31 meta-analyses. Psychological Bulletin 97, 363–386.

Hartl, D.L., Fairbanks, D.J., 2007. Mud sticks: on the alleged falsification of Mendel's data in perspectives. In: Crow, J.F., Dove, W.F. (Eds.), Anecdotal, Historical and Critical Commentaries on Genetics. Genetics Society of America, Bethesda, MD.

Haselton, M.G., Nettle, D., Andrews, P.W., 2005. The evolution of cognitive bias. In: Buss, D.M. (Ed.), Handbook of Evolutionary Psychology. Wiley, Hoboken, pp. 724–746.

Heuer Jr., R.J., 1999. Psychology of Intelligence Analysis. Center for the Study of Intelligence. Central Intelligence Agency, Washington, DC.

Hodge, E., 1988. Guarding against error. Journal of the Association of Firearms and Toolmark Examiners 20, 290–292.

JStBT, E., 1989. Bias in Human Reasoning: Causes and Consequences. Erlbaum, Hillsdale, NJ.

JStBT, E., Barston, J.L., Pollard, P., 1983. On the logic and belief in syllogistic reasoning. Memory and Cognition 11 (3), 295–306.

JStBT, E., Pollard, P., 1990. Belief bias and problem complexity in deductive reasoning. In: Caverni, J.P., Fabre, M., Gonzalez, M. (Eds.), Advances in Psychology, vol. 68. Elsevier Science Publishers, Amsterdam, pp. 131–154.

Kennedy, J.L., Uphoff, H.F., 1939. Experiments on the nature of extra-sensory perception: III. The recording error criticism of extra-chance scores. Journal of Parapsychology 3, 226–245.

Kerstholt, J.H., Paashuis, R., Sjerps, M., 2006. Shoe print examinations: effects of expectation, complexity and experience. Forensic Science International 165, 30–34.

Kety, S., 1959. Biochemical theories of schizophrenia. Science 129, 1528–1532; 1590–1596.

Krane, D.E., Ford, F., Gilder, J.R., et al., 2008. Sequential unmasking: a means of minimizing observer effects in forensic DNA interpretation. Journal of Forensic Sciences 53 (4), 1006–1007.

Kunda, Z., 1990. The case for motivated reasoning. Psychological Bulletin 108 (3), 480–498.

Langenburg, G., Champod, C., Wertheim, P., 2009. Testing for potential contextual bias effects during the verification stage of the ACE-V methodology when conducting fingerprint comparisons. Journal of Forensic Sciences 54 (3), 571–582.

Lee, L., Frederick, S., Ariely, D., 2006. Try it, you'll like it. Psychological Science 17 (12), 1054–1058.

Lord, C.G., Lee, R., Lepper, M.R., 1979. Biased assimilation and attitude polarization: the effects of prior theories on subsequently considered evidence. Journal of Personality and Social Psychology 37 (11), 2098–2109.

Miller, L.S., 1984. Bias among professional document examiners: a need for procedural change. Journal of Police Science and Administration 12, 407.

Miller, L.S., 1987. Procedural bias in forensic examination of hair. Law and Human Behavior 11 (2), 157–163.

Nickerson, R.S., 1998. Confirmation bias: a ubiquitous phenomenon in many guises. Review of General Psychology 2, 175–220.

Nisbett, R., Ross, L., 1980. Human Inference. Prentice Hall, Englewood Cliffs, NJ.

Office of the Inspector General, U.S. Department of Justice, 2006. A Review of the FBI's Handling of the Brandon Mayfield Case. Office of the Inspector General, U.S. Department of Justice, Washington, DC, pp. 1–330.

Paine, R.R., Harpending, H.C., 1998. Effect of sample bias on paleodemographic fertility estimates. American Journal of Physical Anthropology 105 (2), 231–240.

Parducci, A., 1990. Response bias and contextual effects: when biased. In: Caverni, J.P., Fabre, M., Gonzalez, M. (Eds.), Advances in Psychology, vol. 68. Elsevier Science Publishers B.V, Amsterdam, pp. 207–220.

Perrow, C., 1984. Normal Accidents: Living with High-Risk Technologies. Princeton University Press, Princeton, NJ.

Plous, S., 1993. The Psychology of Judgment and Decision Making. McGraw-Hill, New York, NY.

Potchen, E.J., Gard, J.W., Lazar, P., Lahaie, P., Andary, M., 1979. The effect of clinical history data on chest film interpretation: direction or distraction? Investigative Radiology 14, 404–405.

Risinger, D.M., Saks, M.J., Thompson, W.C., Rosenthal, R., 2002. The Daubert/Kumho implications of observer effects in forensic science: hidden problems of expectation and suggestion. California Law Review 90 (1), 1–56.

Roethlisberger, F.J., Dickson, W.J., 1939. Management and the Worker. Harvard University Press, Cambridge, MA.

Rosenthal, R., 1966. Experimenter Effects in Behavioral Research, enlarged ed. Appleton-Century-Crofts, New York. 1976.

Rosenthal, R., 1978. How often are our numbers wrong? American Psychologist 33, 1005–1008.

Rosenthal, R., Jacobson, L., 1992. Pygmalion in the Classroom, expanded ed. Holt, Rinehart & Winston, New York.

Saks, M.J., Risinger, D.M., Rosenthal, R., Thompson, W.C., 2003. Context effects in forensic science: a review and application of the science of science to crime laboratory practice in the United States. Science and Justice 43 (2), 77–90.

Schiffer, B., Champod, C., 2007. The potential (negative) influence of observational biases at the analysis stage of fingermark individualization. Forensic Science International 167, 116–120.

Schneider, D.J., Hastorf, A.H., Ellsworth, P.C., 1979. Person Perception, second ed. Addison-Wesley, Reading, MA.

Sebeok, T.A., Rosenthal, R. (Eds.), 1981. The Clever Hans Phenomenon: Communication with Horses, Whales, Apes, and People. New York Academy of Sciences, New York.

Stacey, R.M., 2004. A report on the erroneous fingerprint individualization in the Madrid train bombing case. Journal of Forensic Identification 54.

Steblay, N., Dysart, J., Fulero, S., Lindsay, R.C.L., 2001. Eyewitness accuracy rates in sequential and simultaneous line-up presentations: a meta-analytic comparison. Law and Human Behavior 25, 459–473.

Tetlock, P.W., 1983. Accountability and the perseverance of first impressions. Social Psychology Quarterly 46 (4), 285–292.

Thomson, M.A., 1974. Bias and quality control in forensic science; a cause for concern. Journal of Forensic Sciences 10 (3), 504–517.

Thompson, W.C., 1995. Subjective interpretation, laboratory error and the value of DNA evidence: three case studies. Genetica 96, 153–168.

Thompson, W.C., 2009a. Observer effects, context effects and confirmation bias in forensic science. In: Jamieson, A., Moenssens, A. (Eds.), Wiley Encyclopedia of Forensic Science. John Wiley & Sons, Chichester, UK.

Thompson, W.C., 2009b. Painting the target around the matching profile: the Texas sharpshooter fallacy in forensic DNA interpretation. Law Probability and Risk 8 (3), 257–276.

Tversky, A., Kahneman, D., 1974. Judgment under uncertainty: heuristics and biases. Science, New Series 85, 1124–1131.

Ubelaker, D., Scammell, H., 1992. Bones: A Forensic Detective's Casebook. Edward Burlingame Books, New York.

Wertheim, K., Langenburg, G., Moenssens, A., 2006. Report of latent print examiner accuracy during comparison training exercises. Journal of Forensic Identifier 56 (1), 55–127.

Whiting, P., Rutjes, A.W., Reitsma, J.B., Glas, A.S., Bossuyt, P.M., Kleijnen, J., 2004. Sources of variation and bias in studies of diagnostic accuracy. Annals of Internal Medicine 140, 189–203.

Wilson, E.B., 1952. An Introduction to Scientific Research. McGraw-Hill, New York.

Winkel, F.W., Koppelaar, L., 1992. Perceived credibility of the communicator: studies of perceptual bias in police officers conducting rape interviews. In: Losel, F., Bender, D., Bliesener, T. (Eds.), Psychology and Law: International Perspectives. Walter de Gruyter, Berlin & New York, pp. 223–228.

Wood, F.G., 1962. Pitfall. Science 135, 261.

Yule, G.U., 1927. On reading a scale. Journal of the Royal Statistical Society 90 (3), 570–587.

Zeppa, J., 1999. The primary analyst. In: 94th Semi-Annual Seminar of the California Association of Criminalists, Ontario, CA, 14–16 October.

Zhaoping, L., Guyader, N., 2007. Interference with bottom-up feature detection by higher-level object recognition. Current Biology 17, 26–31.

Overview and Meaning of Identification/Individualization

C Champod, University of Lausanne, Lausanne, Switzerland

The Identification Process: A Reduction Process to a Single Source

The definition of identification in forensic science may differ largely from the one accepted in science, where the term "identification" is simply used to describe the attribution of an object to a definite class. In criminalistics, the identification process seeks, ultimately, individualization. For forensic scientists, identifying an object means it is possible to distinguish this object from all the objects considered. In the forensic literature, the problem of identity of source is often and unfortunately treated by reference to "class" and "individual" characteristics (**Table 1**).

Comparisons that lead to agreement, only in terms of class characteristics (without significant differences), will end up with "group identification" conclusions. Only when corresponding individual characteristics are present in conjunction with class characteristics, positive identification or individualization conclusions can be drawn. The definitions of "class" and "individual" characteristics are only conventional ways of describing selectivity.

However, the problem of inferring identity of source is more complex than a simple dichotomy between class and individual characteristics. As illustrated in **Table 2**, practitioners have traditionally distinguished the forensic fields that can lead to individualization and those leading rarely (in the present state of the art) to individualization, but more commonly to corroborative information of various strengths.

The arguments developed in this article should bring the reader to realize that these contrasts (class vs individual; corroborative vs individualization) have no foundation. All identification disciplines constitute corroborative information of strengths that change from one discipline to the other as a function of the discriminative ability of the features revealed by the unknown mark under consideration.

In most forensic scenarios, the pool of potential sources is not entirely forensically investigated, but the inquiry will focus on a limited set of suspected sources. Had all the other sources but the suspect been excluded by forensic examination, then identity of source would be declared applying a trivial deductive argument (regardless of the features considered). But in typical casework, such a deductive process is not feasible, and therefore, identity of source must be inferred and the process is probabilistic in nature. We had to wait for Kwan in 1977 to provide a reasoned account of how criminalists infer identity of source. The identification process can be seen as a reduction process, from an initial population to a restricted class or, ultimately, to unity. The initial population constitutes control objects or persons, depending on the type of evidence. The process combines two factors:

- A relevant population of control persons or objects defined by its size (and/or other particularities). Put in another way, each member of this population of sources can be seen as a possible source.
- A reduction factor resulting from the combination of concordant characteristics of determined selectivity. In fact, the reduction is proportional to the rarity or relative occurrence of these observed characteristics in that relevant population. We will call it at times, the match probability. As Kwan indicates: "this is the sheer rarity of a feature that is important as rarity of that feature with respect to the set of suspected sources being considered. It is important to stress that rarity is relative to the situation at hand."

With respect to the size of the relevant population, an "open set" framework will be distinguished from a "closed set" framework.

- The open set framework implies that the population at large is considered; meaning, for example, that all living persons on Earth or all produced objects on Earth are taken into consideration as potential sources. Given the population considered here, the term "Earth population paradigm" is sometimes used synonymously to describe this framework.
- The closed set framework corresponds to a situation in which the number of control objects or persons is restricted to a specified set of suspected sources (e.g., by taking into account other evidence available from the inquiry describing the putative sources).

To illustrate the identification process graphically, we will assume the following generic case leading to an association. A mark is found in association with a crime. Following inquiry, a potential source is submitted to the laboratory for examination. The comparison shows that the recovered and the control materials share some common features (named hereinafter forensic findings or results). Moreover, there is no significant difference to be accounted for. It is worth noting that the

 http://dx.doi.org/10.1016/B978-0-12-800573-6.00016-1

Table 1 Distinction between "class" and "individual" characteristics in some identification fields

Field	*"Class" characteristics*	*"Individual" characteristics*
Fingermark identification	General pattern, ridge count, ridge tracing	Minutiae, pore structure, ridge structure
Shoemark identification	General patterns, size, manufacturing characteristics	Cuts, accidentally acquired characteristics, transient wear features
Bullet identification	Caliber, number of grooves/lands impressions, angles of grooves/lands impressions, width of lands/grooves	Striations on grooves/ lands impressions

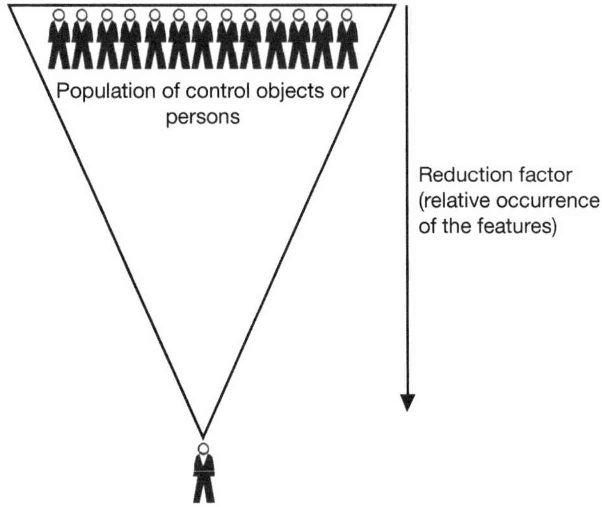

Figure 1 Schematic description of the identification process (here focused individuals, but will apply by analogy to objects as well).

Table 2 Classification of forensic evidence types with respect to their identification capabilities

Individualization	*Corroborative*
Fingermarks (more generally marks left by friction ridge skin)	Microtraces (glass, paint, hairs, fibers)
Footwear marks	Biological fluids (now mostly DNA)
Earmarks	Drugs and toxicology
Toolmarks and firearms	Explosives and fire residue analysis
Handwriting and signature examination	Soils

Table 3 Features used to identify in some forensic fields

Field	*Features used to characterize or (ultimately to individualize)*
Fingerprints	General pattern, minutiae, pores, and ridge structures
Shoesoles	Manufacturing characteristics (pattern, size, peculiarities of the manufacturing process) and acquired characteristics (wear features, cuts)
DNA	Various polymorphic loci on the DNA molecule
Microtraces	Optical (color, microscopic features, refractive index), physical (size, length, diameter), and chemical characteristics (FTIR, elemental composition, pyrolysis coupled with gas chromatography, etc.)

arguments will hold, without loss of generality, when the features would guide toward exclusion. Given this scenario, the identification process may be illustrated as shown in **Figure 1**. The identification process (in an open set or a closed set framework) is a narrowing-down process, reducing the number of possible sources or hypotheses.

The hypothesis that a designated suspect or object is the source is considered "proven" by showing that all alternative hypotheses that could explain the phenomenon at hand are excluded. The term "proven" is used loosely here as the decision process itself will be covered in the next section.

The importance of selecting features judiciously cannot be overemphasized. The criteria for selecting features fall into five areas (without taking cost into account): distinguishability, high intersource-to-intrasource variance, known variance in time, normalization (standardization), and independence. Of course, each field is focused on different features, and it is worth giving a few examples of adequately chosen features in some forensic areas (**Table 3**).

The Inferential Schemes

In practice, for obscure reasons, the identification process leading to individualization is generally operated in an open set framework. The Earth population paradigm prevails. This leads to two types of inferential schemes: toward an individualization decision, complemented, and, when allowed to the practitioners, by the provision of corroborative information.

Individualization Decision

For Tuthill and George:

> The individualization of an impression is established by finding agreement of corresponding individual characteristics of such number and significance as to preclude the possibility (or probability) of their having occurred by mere coincidence, and establishing that there are no differences that cannot be accounted for.

Following this definition, the size of the control population is indeed systematically set to its maximum (the open set framework). This practice is generally used and implicitly required in fields like those of fingerprints, footwear marks, toolmarks, or firearms. For example, for footwear/tire marks, SWGTREAD (Scientific Working Group for Shoeprint and Tire Tread Evidence) indicated in 1996 that the individualization opinion means that "the particular shoe or tire made the impression to the exclusion of all other shoes or tires."

The conclusion of individualization is then an opinion, a statement expressing the view that the chance of observing on Earth another object or person presenting the same characteristics is considered as negligible. For the expert, at this stage, he/she cannot conceive that any contrary evidence (e.g., an alibi) will ever shake his/her certainty. As to the mechanism used by examiners to reach this belief of certainty, Stoney describes a decision analogous to a "leap of faith."

The move from a given probability of association to a decision of individualization is fully described by Biedermann, Bozza, and Taroni in the context of formal Bayesian decision theory. Formally, the decision requires, after the establishment of a probability of association, the use of a gain/loss function amounting to weighing of the benefits and costs associated to the possible decisions. The schematic description of the identification process can now include this decision step toward individualization (**Figure 2**).

Overall, the decision scheme calls for the following comments:

- It is odd to set the size of the relevant population at its maximum a priori in all cases. Indeed, the number of potential sources from which the mark could originate may be restricted by other evidence available (witness testimonies, other forensic evidence, etc.). Presenting the forensic findings in an open set framework is too conservative, adopting systematically the extreme defense attorney's position in trying to make the court believe that all persons or objects on Earth could be the origin of the marks of interest. The forensic scientists or the courts rarely question this systematic reliance on the Earth population paradigm.
- The decision threshold, the leap of faith, is in essence a qualification of the acceptable level of reasonable doubt (weighted by a gain/loss function) adopted by the expert. Jurists may interpret this threshold as an expression of the criminal standard "beyond reasonable doubt" regarding the issue of the identification. However, courts have generally accepted delegating that burden. The recent calls for caution were addressed to the perceived 100% factual certainty that the term "individualization" may convey, but not on the fact that the scientist decides on the source issue. As long as the scientist is not claiming to 100% certainty or an establishment of an uncontroversial fact, courts will generally not object to him/her expressing an opinion of individualization. This leads to the development of phraseology of the kind: "he is the bitter to a reasonable degree of dental certainty" or "the bullet is identified to that barrel to a reasonable degree of ballistic certainty."

The fact that individualization is a decision that accounts for a probabilistic assessment starts to be recognized by practitioners. For friction ridge skin, SWGFAST in 2011 defines individualization as the "decision by an examiner that there are sufficient features in agreement to conclude that two areas of friction ridge impressions originated from the same source. Individualization of an impression to one source is the decision that the likelihood the impression was made by another (different) source is so remote that it is considered as a practical impossibility." However, the framework ("open set" or "closed set") and the gain/loss function (admission of a cost/benefit analysis before taking the decision) remain completely

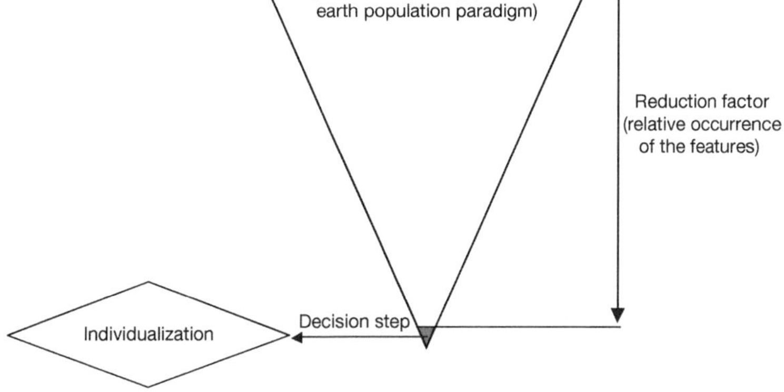

Figure 2 Schematic description of the identification process completed with a decision of individualization.

implicit. As soon as it is made explicit, the author will argue that such a decision scheme is no longer tenable in forensic science.

Provision of Corroborative Information

In some forensic fields (typically fingerprints), practitioners have voluntarily excluded corroborative statements—other than exclusion and individualization—from their conclusions. All results between these extremes are classified as "inconclusive." There is no logical reason for avoiding such corroborative statements, and the author would support any move to bring corroborative information in these fields. Each piece of information is relevant if it tends to make the matter that requires proof more or less probable than otherwise. Hence, a piece of information that only approaches the extremes constitutes relevant information that should not be ignored, and it is necessary for the expert to express a probability statement, verbally or numerically, which attempts to assess the weight of the forensic findings.

Examiners have expressed the meanings of corroborative conclusion terms pragmatically. Their respective meaning relates somewhat to their power of reduction of the initial population. An agreement on the terms has been achieved in some disciplines. For example, in the area of footwear marks, the range of recommended corroborative terms are *probably made, could have made, inconclusive (could not be determined)*, and *probably did not make*. Another example is the ASTM standard E 1658–04 for document examination that enforces the terms: *strong probability (highly probable, very probable), probable, indications (evidence to suggest), no conclusion (totally inconclusive, indeterminable), indications did not, probably did not*, and *strong probability did not*.

This identification process scheme leading to the provision of corroborative information is illustrated in **Figure 3**. Note that there is no decision required here, the conclusion being only a verbal translation of the position reached down the funnel (combination of the population of controls with the reduction factor).

This inferential scheme calls for two comments:

- Conversion between the end position in the reduction process and the verbal statement is never declared or explained. This naturally leads to obvious variations between examiners when assessing the same case.
- Allegiance to the Earth population paradigm is either not questioned or the logic of the terminology is justified using a highly debatable 0.5 prior probability as discussed by Biedermann, Taroni, and Garbolino. Adopting a prior probability of 50% is akin to consider that, outside any consideration of the case circumstances, only two potential sources are considered initially, the source under investigation being one of them. The adoption, by the forensic scientist, of such a default starting position is highly prejudicial to the source under investigation.

Relationship with Probabilities

Individualization

From a probabilistic point of view, to conclude individualization would mean that the probability (Pr) of the event, here the event is "identification," after examining the forensic material at hand, is equal to 1. Because of the probabilistic nature of the identification process, such a probability of 1 is an absolute that cannot ever be reached. Hence, the examiner expresses an opinion of individualization when this probability is so near 1

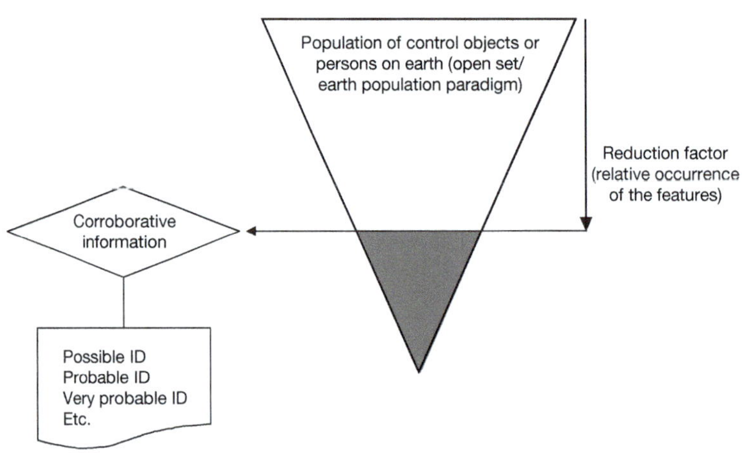

Figure 3 Schematic description of the identification process leading to the provision of corroborative information.

that it maximizes his/her implicit expected utility. It is worth asking ourselves the order of magnitude of that probability (and that of the relative occurrence of the features) in the mind of an examiner at the moment of its decision.

This probability of individualization, given the forensic findings, can be represented in the form Pr(ID|E), where ID denotes the event individualization, which is uncertain, and E denotes the information available, the results of the forensic examination, which has been taken into account. In this way, the vertical line can be seen as shorthand for the word "given."

We have seen, at this stage, that the identification process is related to the specificity of the mark under examination—its relative occurrence in the relevant population—and the size (N) of the relevant population being considered. The probability that we are interested in is then conditioned on both E and N and becomes Pr(ID|E, N).

We can derive the probabilities of interest by simply using the odds form of the Bayes' theorem.

$$\frac{\Pr(\mathrm{ID}|\mathrm{E},N)}{\Pr(\overline{\mathrm{ID}}|\mathrm{E},N)} = \frac{\Pr(\mathrm{E}|\mathrm{ID},N)}{\Pr(\mathrm{E}|\overline{\mathrm{ID}},N)}\frac{\Pr(\mathrm{ID}|N)}{\Pr(\overline{\mathrm{ID}}|N)} \quad [1]$$

Let us denote $\Pr(\mathrm{E}|\overline{\mathrm{ID}},N)$, the relative occurrence of the features, by γ, note that $\Pr(\mathrm{ID}|N) = 1 - \Pr(\mathrm{ID}|N)$ and $\Pr(\overline{\mathrm{ID}}|\mathrm{E},N) = 1 - \Pr(\mathrm{ID}|\mathrm{E},N)$, and finally assume for the sake of the example that $\Pr(\mathrm{E}|\mathrm{ID},N) = 1$ and $\Pr(\mathrm{ID}|N) = 1/N$, we obtain by rearranging eqn [1]:

$$\Pr(\mathrm{ID}|\mathrm{E},N) = \frac{1}{[1+(N-1)\gamma]} \quad [2]$$

$$\gamma = \frac{1-\Pr(\mathrm{ID}|\mathrm{E},N)}{\Pr(\mathrm{ID}|\mathrm{E},N)(N-1)} \quad [3]$$

At this stage, a note on the assumption of a prior probability Pr(ID|N) equals to $1/N$ is necessary. The Earth population paradigm invites to assign to each member of that population a prior probability higher than 0. Indeed, by definition, to be considered in the pool of possible sources requires the prior probability for each source to be higher than 0. The form of the probability distribution that should be adopted is not a trivial matter. However, if a forensic scientist operates within an open set framework, in the absence of any information, and in order to maintain fairness between all potential sources, he/she will have no choice than to adopt a uniform prior between all members, hence the suggestion for $1/N$. In any case, that constraint will be relaxed later in this article.

We turn back to the question of the orders of magnitude of Pr(ID|E, N) and γ in the mind of an examiner at the moment of its decision. If the population is set to $N = 7$ billion (including the control) as suggested by the Earth population paradigm, and $\gamma = 1$ in 7 billion, then, using eqn [1], Pr(ID|E, N) is very close to 0.5. This means that if you have a control object or person at hand with such a rare relative occurrence, the probability that you have the wrong one is about 0.5! It means that in order to have probabilities on the individualization higher than 0.5, we need match probabilities γ that are much lower than the inverse of N, the size of the considered population. This is counterintuitive, but correct in the context of the present Earth population paradigm.

If we accept that Pr(ID|E, N) must be above a certain threshold value in order to declare an individualization (hence maximizing the expected utility function), then it is possible to calculate the match probability (γ) that must be considered to achieve such a preset value. If Pr(ID|E, N) is fixed at 0.9998—meaning "I want to be sure at 99.98% of the individualization"—with $N = 7$ billion, using eqn [3], we see that γ must be equal to 2.9E-14, which represents 1 in about 5000 times the size of the initial population of 7 billion.

If a conclusion of individualization (according to this threshold and in an open set framework) must be at least the expression of such a small match probability in order to maximize the gain function, then we face the prospect of articulating probabilities out of reach from today's systematic research. Taking fingerprints as an example, the recent published statistical research would allow us to quote confidently match probabilities in the order of one in a billion. Articulating any smaller number (down to the probability of zero) is difficult if not impossible to support.

The above treatment tends to demonstrate that decisions of individualization taken by practitioners cannot be made in the open set framework, but they certainly operate implicitly in an undefined closed set. The probabilistic analysis of corroborative information will reinforce that point.

Corroborative Information

What is the probabilistic meaning, in the open set framework, of conclusions such as "it is possible (or probable or highly likely) that this print/mark has been made by this particular item"? Such verbal scales can be translated into numbers expressing Pr(ID|E, N). These terms are understood quite uniformly (in a numerical conversion) by forensic scientists or jurists. The numerical conversion is given in **Table 4** (columns 1 and 2). From these probabilities, their corresponding match probabilities (γ) can be derived, using eqn [3], considering an open set framework ($N = 7$ billion) as shown in **Table 4** (column 3).

The analysis of **Table 4** leads to a paradox. In the open set framework (as claimed to be adopted mostly all forensic fields), the rarity of the shared features, which corresponds to the most negative verbal statement *(likelihood bordering certainty for the exclusion)*, is quite small (1.4E-7). For the court, every piece of information that would lead to such small match probability will be considered as highly indicative (by analogy with DNA findings, for example). Hence, the verbal statement proposed here does not make this evidential value very clear. To escape this paradox, forensic scientists could be tempted to

Table 4 Relationship between verbal statements in qualified opinions and the probability of identification along with the corresponding match probabilities γ (assuming a relevant population of 7 billion, including the control)

Verbal statement	*Pr(ID|E, N) (%)*	*Match probability (γ)*
Terms in favor of individualization		
Likelihood bordering to certainty for the individualization	99.98	2.9×10^{-14}
Highly (very) likely	98	2.19×10^{-12}
Likely	85	2.5×10^{-11}
Very well possible (plausible)	75	4.8×10^{-11}
Possible	60	9.5×10^{-11}
Terms in favor of exclusion		
Possible not	40	2.1×10^{-10}
Very well possible (plausible) not	25	4.3×10^{-10}
Not likely/unlikely	15	8.1×10^{-10}
Highly (very) unlikely	2	7.0×10^{-9}
Likelihood bordering certainty for the exclusion	0.1	1.4×10^{-7}

adjust the size of the relevant population, hence to pass from an open set framework to a closed set framework. As aforementioned, some have even suggested to adopt a default prior probability $\Pr(\mathrm{ID}|N)$ of 0.5—qualified as fair and neutral—in every case!

The analysis of these two inferential schemes with their counterintuitive and paradoxical consequences shows that there is an urgent need to find a common, coherent, and harmonized framework to assess such information. The proposal below advocates the use of a Bayesian model to properly position and convey the value of identification information.

The Bayesian Framework for Evaluating Identification Findings

In the Bayesian framework, both closed set and open set situations can be handled; the open set constitutes a specific situation. From information gathered through normal investigation or through the use of a database, a limited number of people or objects, or a single person or object, can be pinpointed in a general or limited population. There is no way to go back along the time axis and deduce the identification. The only way to evaluate the strength of the forensic findings is to consider them from two perspectives: that the designated person or object is, or is not, the source. The Bayesian approach permits the revision of a measure of uncertainty about the truth or otherwise of an issue (here the individualization ID) based on new information. It shows how data can be combined with prior or background information to give posterior probabilities for particular issues. The following events can be defined from the previous example:

I	Some background information has been collected before the forensic examination. For example, data from police investigation, eyewitness statements, or data from the criminal historical record of the suspect will contribute to I. Typically this information will reduce the number of potential suspects or objects that could be at the origin of the mark
E	The features agreement (without significant differences) reported as the forensic results between the mark left at a scene and a person or object under examination
ID	The mark has been produced by this person or object in examination
$\overline{\mathrm{ID}}$	The mark has not been produced by this object or person, and another unknown person or object is at the origin of the mark. The definition of the two exclusive hypotheses (ID and $\overline{\mathrm{ID}}$) requires consideration of the context of the case (the defense's strategy, for example); they are not always as straightforward or exhaustive as could be deduced from our example

The Bayes' formula (eqn [4]—similar to eqn [1]) shows how prior odds on ID are modified by the results E to obtain posterior odds on the issue:

$$\mathrm{O}(\mathrm{ID}|\mathrm{E},\mathrm{I}) = \frac{\Pr(\mathrm{E}|\mathrm{ID},\mathrm{I})}{\Pr(\mathrm{E}|\overline{\mathrm{ID}},\mathrm{I})}\mathrm{O}(\mathrm{ID}|\mathrm{I}) \qquad [4]$$

where $\mathrm{O}(\mathrm{ID}|\mathrm{I})$ = the odds on the individualization before forensic examination, the prior odds on ID equal to the ratio $\Pr(\mathrm{ID}|\mathrm{I})/\Pr(\overline{\mathrm{ID}}|\mathrm{I})$; $\mathrm{O}(\mathrm{ID}|\mathrm{E},\mathrm{I})$ = the odds on the individualization given the results E, the posterior odds on ID equal to the ratio $\Pr(\mathrm{ID}|\mathrm{E},\mathrm{I})/\Pr(\overline{\mathrm{ID}}|\mathrm{E},\mathrm{I})$; $\Pr(\mathrm{E}|\mathrm{ID},\mathrm{I})$ = the probability of the shared features between the mark and the control, given that the mark has been left by the suspect or object in examination (ID is true)—generally, this value is close to 1, but this is not a requirement; $\Pr(\mathrm{E}|\overline{\mathrm{ID}},\mathrm{I})$ = the probability of the shared features between the mark and the control, given that the mark has not been left by this person or object ($\overline{\mathrm{ID}}$ is true); γ has been used throughout to refer to this probability.

In this Bayesian perspective, the open set framework covers the situation where the prior odds are estimated in reference to the total population possible (I represents no prior knowledge at all); any other situation with an estimate of the prior odds can be viewed as a closed set framework.

Compared to eqn [1], the only difference is that I is used instead of *N*. It was previously suggested (eqn [2]) that the prior probability was strictly in relation to *N*. Here, *N* is omitted and replaced by I to stress upon the fact that the prior probability will depend on more factors than only on *N*, that is, investigation, eyewitness statements, or data from the criminal

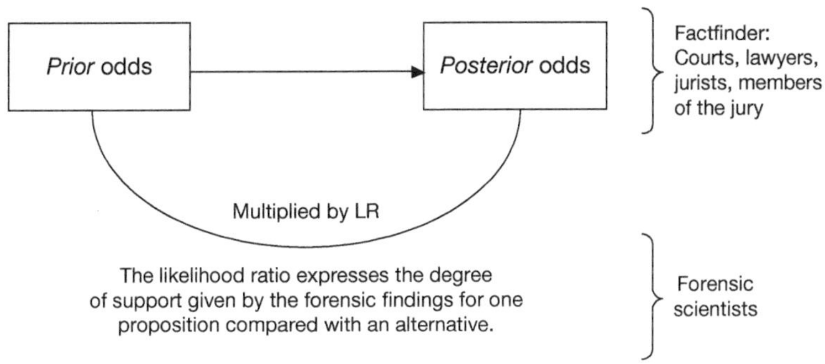

Figure 4 Schematic representation of the Bayesian framework positioning the actors of the judicial system.

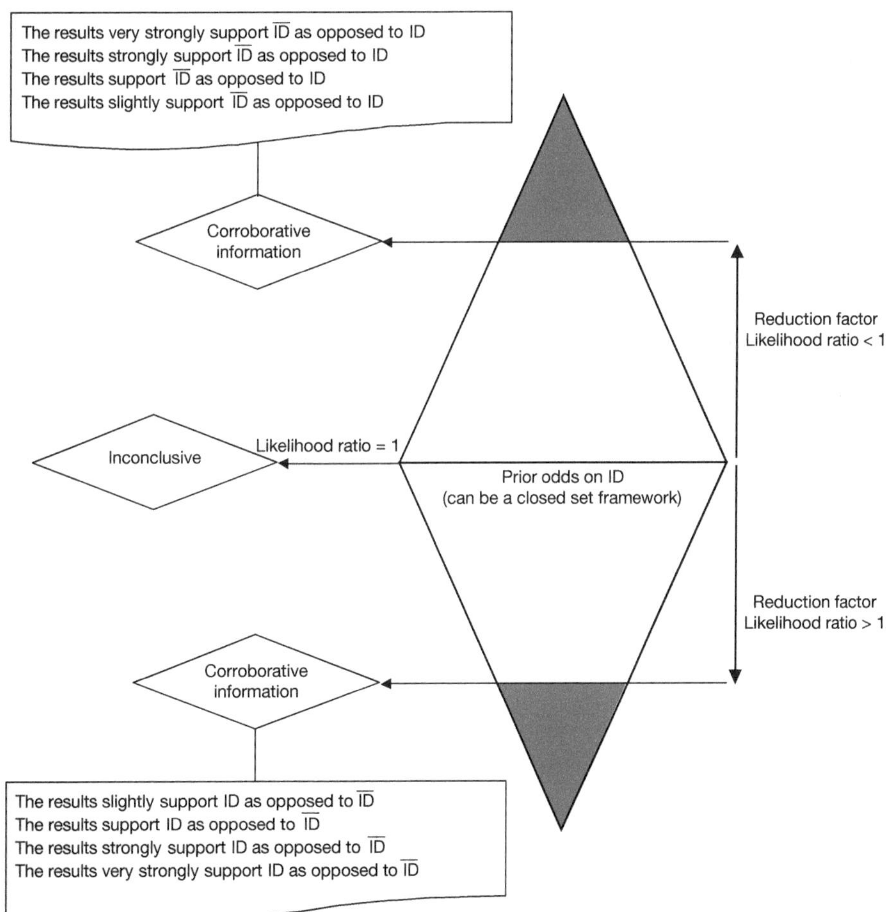

Figure 5 Schematic representation of the value of forensic findings (or results) in the identification process.

historical record of the suspect, etc. In fact, each case bears its own specificity in this regard. But, generally, these data are not known to the forensic examiner and are outside his or her province. Hence, the assessment of the prior odds remains the confines of the fact finder (judges, members of the jury, etc.). As a consequence, before the presentation of the expert results, it will be up to the fact finder and not the forensic scientist to assess the prior odds on the individualization. By the way of consequence, it is up to the fact finder to take the final decision (and applying their own gain/loss function).

The framework itself, here, does not belong anymore to the forensic scientist but belongs to the fact finder. The statement (numerical or subjective) made to the court by the forensic scientist should then only be the expression of the reduction factor to be applied to the prior odds (opinion of the court without the knowledge derived from the scientific results). Without the information about the prior odds, it is not possible for the scientist to state the fact itself (the probability that this particular person or object has produced this mark): he can only state the degree of support given to this hypothesis (or version) versus the alternative. The strength of the forensic findings is then given by the probability of observing them under two chosen propositions. This ratio is called the "likelihood ratio."

The statement given by the scientist alone is not sufficient to decide on the issue. The scientist's statement is then completely different from assessing the fact itself. The concept of the weight to be assigned to forensic results is therefore relative: it shows how observations should be interpreted as support for ID versus its counterpart, but it makes no mention of how those observations should be interpreted as evidence in relation to ID alone. Therefore, the same piece of information may be an insufficient proof for a fact finder in one context, but may be the factor essential in clinching the case in another. The odds, in favor of the individualization itself, that the person or object in examination has produced the mark given the circumstances of the case (background I) and the observations made by the forensic scientist (the results E) is a judgment based on posterior odds combined with the results. The essence of the decision on the individualization remains the province of the fact finder. This logical tool permits an understanding of how events interact mathematically. It clarifies the position of the scientist as well as that of the judge and defines their relationship. The scientist is concerned solely with the likelihood ratio, whereas the fact finder deals with the odds on the individualization (**Figure 4**) and ultimately the associated decisions.

The Bayesian model helps us to understand the respective duties of the fact finder and of the forensic scientists (**Figure 4**). Our schematic representation of the identification process can then be refined, taking into account the Bayesian perspective (**Figure 5**).

Conclusion

The traditional inferential schemes for the question of identification of source have been presented. They lead either to decisions of individualization/exclusion or to the provision of corroborative opinions (possible, probable, very probable, etc.). Both of these schemes are operated with reference to a relevant population size set to its maximum in what has been called an open set framework (or the Earth population paradigm).

These schemes perpetuate the vision that forensic scientists can deal—sometimes without being aware of—with prior or posterior probabilities on the issue and with gain/loss function when making decisions. Moreover, the probabilistic relationship between verbal opinions and probability of occurrence of the shared features has shown counterintuitive and paradoxical consequences.

It appears legitimate to question if these practices are reasonable for forensic cases. Another scheme, the Bayesian interpretation framework, overcomes most of these difficulties, in particular, by relaxing the necessity of adopting an open set framework and avoiding the final decision step. It provides a coherent way of assessing and presenting identification evidence. From a logical point of view, the strength to be attached to forensic findings is essentially relative to the case and its value is best expressed using a likelihood ratio. The question of the size of the relevant population—which impacts on prior probabilities—and decision thresholds are finally outside the province of forensic scientists but rightly belong to the fact finder.

See also: **Behavioral:** Interpretation; **Foundations:** Statistical Interpretation of Evidence: Bayesian Analysis; **Pattern Evidence/Fingerprints (Dactyloscopy):** Friction Ridge Skin Impression Evidence – Standards of Proof.

Further Reading

Biedermann, A., Bozza, S., Taroni, F., 2008. Decision theoretic properties of forensic identification: underlying logic and argumentative implications. Forensic Science International 177 (2–3), 120–132.

Biedermann, A., Taroni, F., Garbolino, P., 2007. Equal prior probabilities: can one do any better? Forensic Science International 172 (2–3), 85–93.

Champod, C., 2008. Fingerprint examination: towards more transparency. Law, Probability and Risk 7 (2), 111–118.

Champod, C., Evett, I.W., 2001. A probabilistic approach to fingerprint evidence. Journal of Forensic Identification 51 (2), 101–122.

Cole, S.A., 2009. Forensics without uniqueness, conclusions without individualization: the new epistemology of forensic identification. Law, Probability and Risk 8 (3), 233–255.

Kaye, D.H., 2011. Probability, individualization, and uniqueness in forensic science evidence: listening to the academies. Brooklyn Law Review 75 (4), 1163–1185.

Kaye, D.H., Bernstein, D.E., Mnookin, J.L. (Eds.), 2011. The New Wigmore, A Treatise on Evidence: Expert Evidence, second ed. Aspen Publishers Inc, New York, pp. 665–697 (Chapter 15).

Kirk, P.L., 1963. The ontogeny of criminalistics. Journal of Criminal Law, Criminology and Police Science 54, 235–238.

Kwan, Q.Y., 1977. Inference of Identity of Source (Ph.D. thesis). University of California, Berkeley.

Stoney, D.A., 1991. What made us ever think we could individualize using statistics? Journal of the Forensic Science Society 31 (2), 197–199.

Tuthill, H., George, G., 2002. Individualization: Principles and Procedures in Criminalistics. Lightning Powder Co, Jacksonville.

Key Terms

Bayesian framework, Bias, Blind testing, Cognitive bias, Confirmation bias, Context effects, Corroborative evidence, Domain-relevant, Fingerprint identification, Forensic science, Friction ridge skin, Identification, Individualization, Inference of source, Line-up, Numerical standard, Observer bias, Psychology, Sequential unmasking.

Review Questions

1. What were Locard's rules for the minimum requirements for a fingerprint identification?
2. What are the two main objections to a numerical approach to fingerprint identifications?
3. Are all minutiae equally rare? Why or why not?
4. Is it feasible to evaluate fingerprint evidence in a probabilistic way?
5. What is the false error rate for fingerprint identifications? What is the best evidence for this value?
6. Is there any scientific support for a fixed number of points to be required for an identification?
7. What are observer effects?
8. What is sequential unmasking? Does it relate to fingerprint examinations?
9. Are cognitive effects conscious?
10. If an examiner is susceptible to cognitive effects, does that make them a "bad" examiner? Why or why not?
11. What is the best way to overcome cognitive effects?
12. How does sequential unmasking supposedly avoid cognitive effects?
13. What is the difference between domain relevant and domain irrelevant information? Why does this matter?
14. If a submitting officer tells an examiner, "We need to have this guy match the prints at the crime scene because he's a flight risk," is that information relevant to the fingerprint comparison process? What could be the problem with this kind of statement made to an examiner?
15. What is an exemplar line-up? How could it assist the forensic fingerprint examiner?
16. According to Champod, the identification process is reductive and combines two factors. What are they?
17. What is the difference between an open set and a closed set framework?
18. The criteria for selecting features for a fingerprint identification fall into what five areas?
19. What is Tuthill and George's definition of individualizing an impression? Which framework does this definition use?
20. Why are two hypotheses or propositions required for an examiner to reach an opinion?

Discussion Questions

1. Is fingerprint identification an exact science? Defend your answer.
2. What are the arguments against the IAI's 1980-5 Resolution (Amending Resolution 1979-7): "...any member, officer or certified latent print examiner who initiates or volunteers oral or written reports, or testimony of possible, probable or likely friction ridge identification, or who, when required in a judicial proceeding to provide such reports or testimony, does not qualify it with a statement that the print in question could be that of someone else, shall be deemed to be engaged in conduct unbecoming such member,..."? Why is this Resolution problematic?
3. When Champod says, "All identification disciplines constitute corroborative information of strengths that change from one discipline to the other as a function of the discriminative ability of the features revealed by the unknown mark under consideration," what do you think that means? What are the practical implications of this statement for casework?
4. Is individualization of a fingerprint a fact or an opinion? Defend your answer.
5. How does the Bayesian interpretation approach overcome the difficulties of the other two methods (name them)? Is it practical to use in reporting and court? Why or why not?

Additional Readings

Anthonioz, N.E., Champod, C., 2014. Evidence evaluation in fingerprint comparison and automated fingerprint identification systems—modeling between finger variability. Forensic Science International 235, 86–101.

Edmond, G., Cole, S.A., 2014. Identification technologies in policing and proof. In: Encyclopedia of Criminology and Criminal Justice. Springer, New York, pp. 2407–2419.

Pacheco, I., Cerchiai, B., Stoiloff, S., 2014. Miami-Dade Research Study for the Reliability of the ACE-V Process: Accuracy & Precision in Latent Fingerprint Examinations. U.S. Department of Justice, National Institute of Justice, Washington, D.C.

Saks, M.J., 2010. Forensic identification: from a faith-based "science" to a scientific science. Forensic Science International 201 (1), 14–17.

Saks, M.J., Koehler, J.J., 2008. The individualization fallacy in forensic science evidence. Vanderbilt Law Review 61 (1), 199–219.

Servick, K., 2015. Forensic labs explore blind testing to prevent errors. Science 349 (6247), 462–463.

Section 6. Other Methods

Barefoot Print Marks

SL Massey, Campbell River, BC, Canada
RB Kennedy, Orleans, ON, Canada

This article is a revision of the previous edition article by R.B. Kennedy, volume 3, pp. 1189–1195, © 2000, Elsevier Ltd.

Glossary

Barefoot morphology comparison A comparison conducted of the shapes of the weight-bearing impression of the foot, barefoot, socked foot, or three-dimensional, in the case where a friction ridge comparison cannot be conducted.

Barefoot print mark The weight-bearing impression of the human foot, either barefoot, socked foot, or left inside of footwear. The impression can be two- or three-dimensional and created in a single step or through multiple steps of the foot in one location, such as inside of footwear.

Multistep impression The impression of the foot left inside footwear created overtime through repeated steps of the foot, creating indentations, and darkened sweat stains of the wearer's foot.

Single step impression The impression of the foot left by a single step of the foot either two- or three-dimensional.

Sock foot impression The impression of a foot clad in a sock.

Weight-bearing impression The impression the foot left on a surface when weight is borne on the foot.

History

Barefoot evidence was introduced in courts as early as 1888 in France, when a criminal by the name of LeDru was identified through the analysis of footprints. Early cases were based simply on the assumption of the uniqueness of barefoot impressions; however, it is only in the past few decades that research has been conducted, published, and peer-reviewed, which supports this earlier assumption.

In 1909, G.W. Gayer commented that the footprint features have as much character as the features of the face and that it was obvious that every individual footprint must have a distinct individuality.

Some of the earliest research that sought to determine if the human footprint is highly individual was conducted in India. One such study, in 1980, involved a collection of 725 individuals' footprints and found that a comparison of the foot impressions indicated that combined probabilities could prove reasonably reliable circumstantial evidence to link a criminal with crime.

Research is often case inspired; for instance, in 1981 in New Jersey, USA, a case involved a partial bloody socked foot impression at a homicide scene, which was compared to the foot impressions of two suspects. One suspect's foot impressions were eliminated as having created the impression at the crime scene while the other suspect's foot impressions were found to be such that the expert declared a high probability that the impression was hers. Researchers, in this case, collected 100 persons' footprints and compared them to the suspect's known foot impressions. They compared the suspect's impressions with the 100 research subjects' foot impressions and concluded that the more unique the individual features of a particular print, the smaller will be the probability that another individual could have left a sufficiently similar print to allow nonexclusion of that person. In addition, they conducted an independent test of this theory where a series of partial prints taken from research volunteers were selected for testing. Identifiers were removed and compared to a random sample of 50 barefoot. The results demonstrated the accuracy of non-exclusion method applied to partial prints and complete prints.

 http://dx.doi.org/10.1016/B978-0-12-800573-6.00017-3

Another research project conducted by the FBI started in 1986 included 500 adults' footprints in order to provide more information about the degree of individuality expressed in the impression left by the human foot. This study too found that basic size and shape features varied considerably among the footprints collected reflecting a highly significant degree of individuality. Blind searches of impressions that were either in or not in the database were made as a measure of determining how these factors could be used to discriminate footprint impressions from one another, and it was determined that only five or fewer of the more general characteristics were necessary to either identify or discriminate these footprints from all others in the study.

In 1989, the largest scale research project to date was initiated by the Royal Canadian Mounted Police, which sought to build on the earlier research conducted, taking into account intraindividual differences of persons' footprints contrasted against interpersonal differences between individuals encompassing a cross section of male/female and Caucasian/ non-Caucasian (self-declared) sampling.

The initial pilot project included 960 people, with a repetitive sample of 20 persons who provided footprint impressions three times a day, over 3 days during a week period to provide the intrapersonal differences. Subsequently, a larger study was undertaken, involving 5755 people with a repetition sample of 134 people.

In this study, foot impressions of monozygotic twins (**Figure 1**) and numerous contributors who donated their foot impressions to the research database multiple times over the span of 5–15 years demonstrated both the high degree of variability and the persistency of the weight-bearing impressions of the foot. The friction ridge skin of the plantar surface of the foot has the same individualizing ability based on its uniqueness even in a small area, as well as its persistence over the life span of the individual, as the friction ridges on the palmar surfaces. In the case of foot morphology, however, the morphological weight-bearing impressions left by the foot are examined, where the friction ridges are not visible or do not display sufficient clarity to conduct a friction ridge comparison. The repeated donors of weight-bearing impressions over the span of a number of years have shown that the morphological shape of the weight-bearing impressions of the foot are persistent over time and unique to the individual (**Figure 2**).

Foot impressions were measured and scanned, and the foot impressions were searched against all other impressions in the database. At first, exact measurements were used to search the database to see whether any two barefoot impressions matched, and it quickly became apparent that after only three to five measurements, every foot was found to be new to the database, even those from repeat donors. This demonstrated that barefoot impressions from the same donor could not be repeated exactly. As in any impression-making process, it is highly unlikely that two impressions of the same items will be identical; therefore, even barefoot impressions from the same donor show small, but measurable, differences. As new foot impressions were entered into the database, they were automatically measured by the program and searched against the existing database as it was being entered, initially using a 5-mm window on each measurement to increase the chances of finding two feet that were similar. This was successful in finding apparent matches by the computer search; however, every pair selected was examined and confirmed to be two impressions from the same volunteer. Only when the search window was widened to 15 mm, impressions from two different individuals come up as a match based on the measurements. In each case, when an examination by a trained forensic specialist was conducted, it was confirmed that the impressions were in fact easily distinguishable as being from different people.

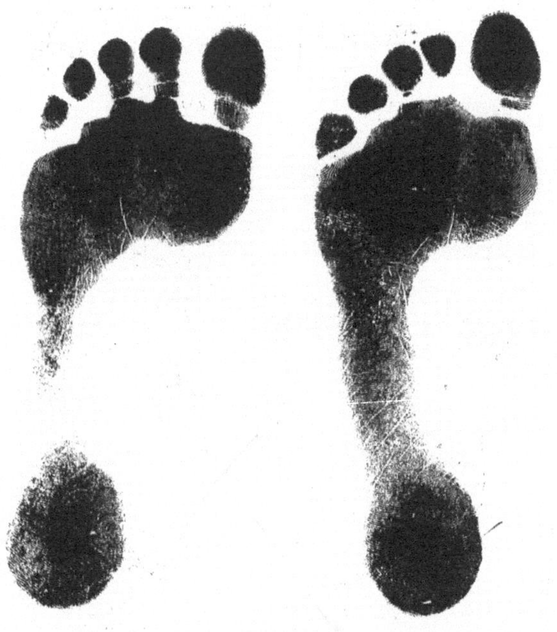

Figure 1 Inked barefoot impressions of the left feet of a pair of monozygotic twins. This shows the differences between the placement of the toes, the presence of toe stems, and differences in the arches between the two persons' foot impressions, demonstrating the high degree of variability.

A statistical analysis has been carried out using only 19 of the possible 119 measurements of 5755 pairs of inked barefoot impressions, which resulted in the probability of a random match of 1 in 1.27 billion, indicating the high degree of variability of barefoot impressions. It is recognized, however, by forensic specialists conducting examinations, that the research completed utilized ideal footprint impressions, which are whole, clear, distinct barefoot walking impressions on paper by a cooperative donor. Poor-quality samples, or ones that were

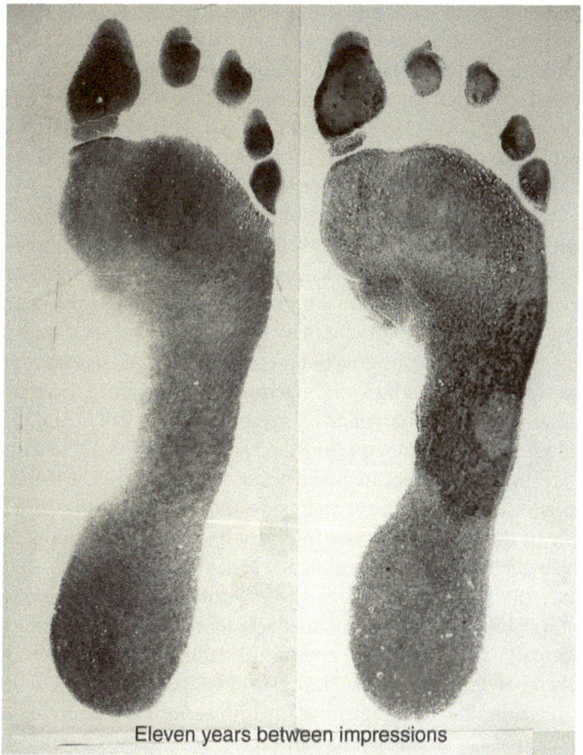

Figure 2 Inked right barefoot impressions of the same person taken 11 years apart. Demonstrates persistence of the foot morphology of the weight-bearing impression over time.

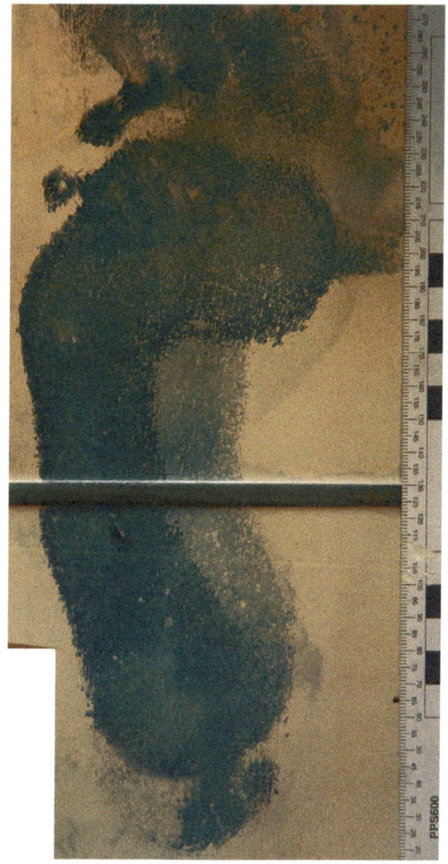

Figure 3 Examination quality photograph of a barefoot crime scene impression enhanced chemically with Amido Black. Photo taken by Cst J. Jackson.

smeared or unclear, were not utilized in the research. In actual case work, the impressions collected at a crime scene will likely not meet these specific criteria, and the crime scene examiner does not have the option of choosing only the pristine impressions. Consequently, barefoot morphology examiners use a much more conservative approach in expressing the level of certainty of their conclusions and do not use a numerical statistical probability.

Crime Scene Evidence Collection

The forensic investigator who attends the scene of a crime is the first person who will determine whether there is barefoot impression evidence present and collect it for later examination by a barefoot morphology examiner. It is recommended that all impressions visible be photographed before enhancement and post enhancement using proper forensic photography principles and protocols. Examination of quality photographs of the barefoot impression evidence must be taken using a scale in the photographs with the film plane or charge-coupled device of the camera parallel to the impression being photographed (**Figure 3**).

Enhancement techniques may be necessary, including but not limited to the use of forensic lighting techniques and chemical enhancement techniques. Impressions may need to be lifted using electrostatic lifting devices, gelatin lifting if dust impressions are present, or regular footwear impression lifting techniques may be necessary depending on the development technique utilized. Whenever possible, if the case warrants it, cutouts of the impressions should be considered as well. Items are marked as exhibits, and continuity should be strictly maintained.

Collection of Exemplars from a Person of Interest

The collection of known impressions from individuals is the next step in the process.

Every effort should be taken by the investigators collecting the exemplars to adhere to the standard operating procedures or guidelines available, and appropriate care is taken to ensure that the necessary and best possible exemplars are collected. The list of specific types of exemplars will be based on the crime scene impressions, and whether they are two- or three-dimensional.

When footwear is the questioned/unknown exhibit requiring foot morphology analysis and comparison, in addition to the other exemplars previously described, the footwear worn by the suspect should be seized as well, either pursuant to arrest or by judicial warrant. If possible, other footwear known to be worn by the suspect should be seized.

Photographs should be taken of the subject's feet with scale, including the soles, tops of the toes, sides of the feet, and heels. Photography is normally followed by the taking of three-dimensional weight-bearing impressions of the soles of the feet, using a foam material such as Biofoam or Foam Art, which is used by chiropodists (podiatrists). The impressions are taken by having the subject place weight on the foot into the foam material. An actual-sized representation of the bottom of the subject's feet will later be prepared by pouring dental stone into the foam impressions, making a positive cast of the individual's foot (**Figure 4**).

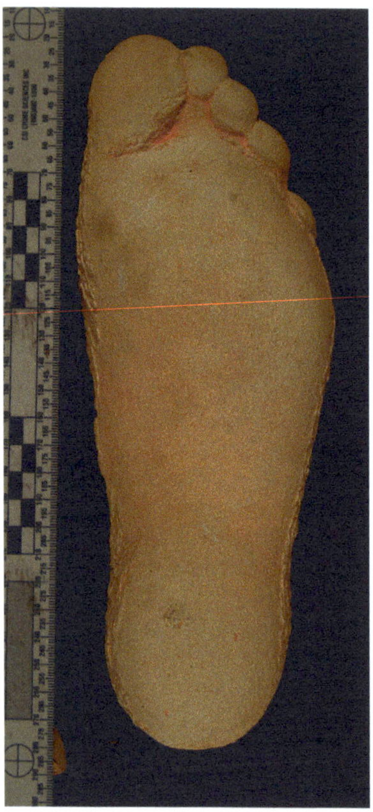

Figure 4 Photograph of a three-dimensional dental stone cast created from an impression of a subject's foot in Biofoam.

Actual-sized casts are made of the tops of the toes using a silicone-casting material such as Ruthinium Labor Mass, a silicone material commonly used by dentists. The material is mixed with catalyst, which is placed over the subject's toes, and allowed to harden before being removed. This too will later be cast with dental stone by the foot morphology examiner, making a positive cast of the subject's toes (**Figure 5**).

Next, inked impressions should be taken of the subject's feet. It is important that both standing and walking impressions, with and without socks, are taken. The inked impressions are taken from an individual on a piece of paper approximately 5–6 m long and approximately 1 m wide. An inking pad is made using an acetate-covered piece of cardboard large enough for a person to stand on. Fingerprint ink is spread over the acetate using an ink roller to smooth out the ink. The individual stands barefoot on the inked pad, rocking back and forth to ensure that the feet are inked properly. He/she then walks the length of the paper to the right side and walks back on the left side of the paper. Sufficient ink must be applied to ensure that the subject deposits a diminishing series of foot impressions of each foot (8–12 impressions of each foot). Attention should be paid to the individual's feet to ensure that the person is walking normally. Ink is reapplied and static (standing) impressions are taken barefoot. Next close fitting, thin socks are supplied to the subject and the walking and static impressions are taken in the same manner as the barefoot impressions described previously (**Figure 6**).

If the specifics of the creation of the crime scene impression are known, for example, through surveillance video footage, it is a possible attempt to take additional exemplars recreating

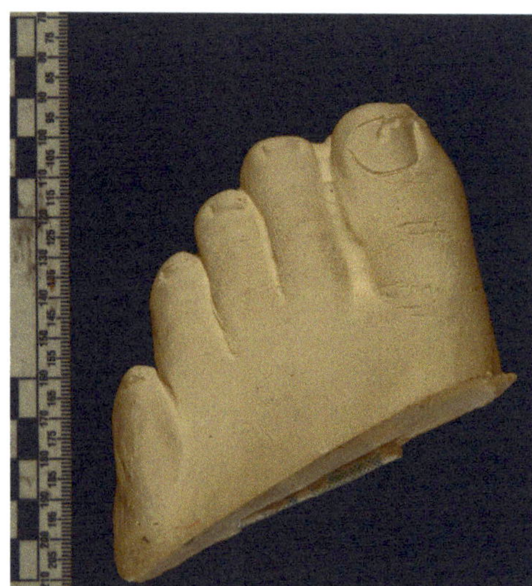

Figure 5 A three-dimensional dental stone cast created from a Ruthinium Labor Mass Silicone cast of the top of a subject's toes.

Figure 6 Inked barefoot walking impressions and inked socked foot walking impressions taken for foot morphology comparison purposes.

unusual barefoot impressions. An example of this would be if there existed evidence that the crime scene impression was produced while running, or traveling up or down a set of stairs. Any additional exemplars that might be considered should only be done after consultation with the barefoot morphology examiner, with the authority of the court, and after taking the standard format exemplars already described.

Methodology for Examination of Foot Morphology Cases

When a forensic specialist receives a case for examination, strict evidence continuity must be maintained for court purposes. When exhibits are received, they should be initialed and dated by the examiner to maintain the continuity. The examination is conducted, following accepted forensic methodology, known as ACE-V. The acronym ACE-V is commonly used to describe the process involving analysis, comparison, evaluation, and verification. The crime scene impressions or unknowns are analyzed first, before analyzing the known exemplars, and the comparison is conducted from unknown to known. An evaluation of the similarities and differences is undertaken, after which the examiner reaches a conclusion of elimination, inclusion as the possible source of the crime scene impressions, or, in rare circumstances, individualization.

Analysis of Crime Scene Impressions

Crime scene impressions are invariably not pristine impressions. They may be partial impressions, multitap, distorted impressions, or stepped on by other feet/footwear. During the analysis phase, the examiner must attempt to determine what variables existed in the depositing of the crime scene impressions so that they can be taken into consideration. For example, the impression could be wet or dry in origin. A wet-origin blood impression on a tile surface floor has different inherent traits than a dry-origin dust impression on a fabric surface. An impression may have been deposited in a normal walking stride, or it may have been deposited with significant movement during a quick turn during a running stride. All factors concerning the deposition of the impression must be analyzed by the examiner.

Factors that affect the impression-making process are analyzed by the examiner. Areas to consider, when possible to determine, are the surface on which the impression is deposited, the medium of which it is made, deposition pressure, movement and pressure distortion, the development medium, and any inherent signatures of that process. Although all these factors are analyzed and considered, the primary limiting factor of the weight-bearing foot impression is the clarity of detail visible.

All crime scene impressions supplied to the examiner are enlarged to actual size and analyzed. If necessary, digital enhancements will be used, adhering to established protocols and making a record of all adjustments made, on a copy of the original image. The actual-sized photograph is overlaid with acetate and the examiner will trace all visible detail and make other bench notes concerning their analysis of each crime scene impression.

When the unknown crime scene impression is inside footwear, the shoes will be photographed, paying close attention to the location of general and specific wear on the outsole of the footwear. The wear on the outsole of shoes and the weight-bearing impressions inside footwear are multistep impressions, created by stepping thousands of times per day, leaving wear on the outsole and sweat stains, wear marks, holes, and indentations on the insoles. The degree of wear and visibility of the damage is dependent on multiple factors of the footwear itself and the wearer of the shoes. The top portion will be cut from the shoe and any foreign material present (hair, fibers, soil, dirt, etc.) will be collected from inside the footwear and provided to the investigator who can then submit this trace evidence for analysis to the appropriate section of a forensic laboratory. An examination of the inside upper and insole of the shoe will be conducted, and all visible damage, wear marks, and stains that may have been caused by the feet will be photographed (**Figures 7 and 8**).

To date, the best enhancement techniques have been found to be in the use of specialized forensic light sources. The light source that provides optimum results will be used to photographically record the impressions within the footwear. The photographs taken with the scale of damage and weight-bearing impressions inside the footwear are enhanced, enlarged to actual size, and analyzed similar to the process used for two-dimensional impressions described above. Analyses of the impressions inside footwear are also limited by the clarity of the weight-bearing impressions and stains and damage visible within them.

Analysis of the Known Exemplars

Persons of interest to the investigation may have a vested interest and may attempt to provide inaccurate representations of their weight-bearing foot impressions. The subject may deliberately attempt to disguise their impressions by scrunching their feet, walking in a manner that is not normal for them, or twisting their feet while walking. It is important to visually observe, and if possible, have video recording of the person of interest walking before being advised of the reason of the collection of the exemplars, as well as during the impression taking procedure. This assists the barefoot morphology examiner by allowing them to view the video and determine if attempts were made to deliberately change their weight-bearing impressions. The examiner will view and enlarge if necessary the photographs taken of the subject's feet for visualization and recording of any peculiarities or damage to the feet that may have been caused by the footwear.

The three-dimensional molds that were made of the subjects' feet will be cast with dental stone, to create life-sized molds of the subject's feet. The inked impressions are examined to discern if there are any discrepancies that might be present between the standing and walking impressions. When examining the walking impressions, all left-foot impressions should have similar shapes and size, as should all right-foot impressions. Representative samples are cut out from the roll

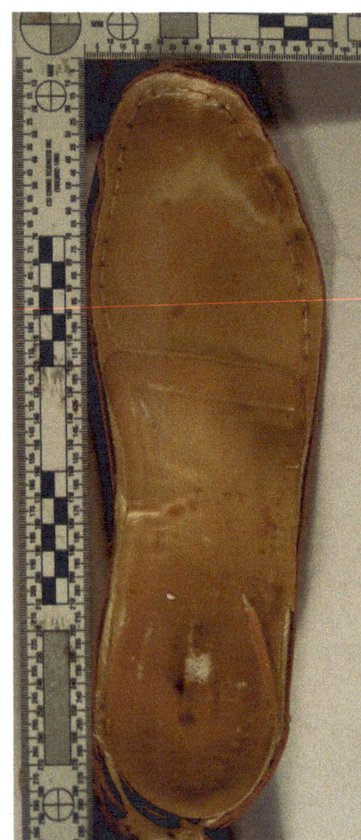

Figure 7 The weight-bearing impression visible on the insole of a shoe cut apart for foot morphology comparison.

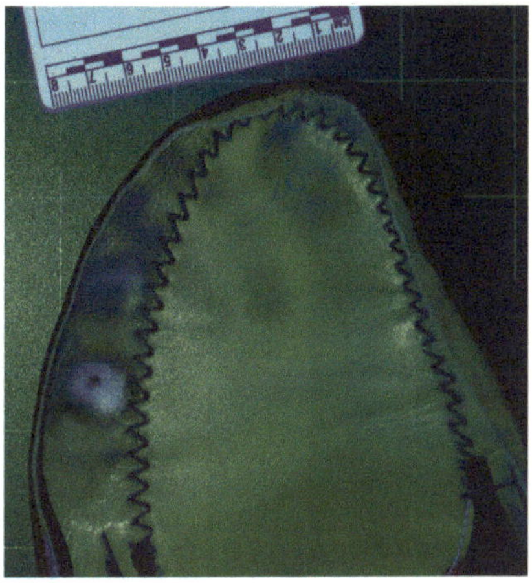

Figure 8 The inside upper portion of a shoe that has been cut apart, showing the marks and damage left by the tops and ends of the toes inside the shoe.

of walking impressions. All material such as other footwear, molded impressions, and photographs obtained of the feet of the subject should be examined.

Comparison

It is preferable, but not absolutely necessary, to compare the like impressions, that is, comparing two-dimensional impressions with two-dimensional impressions and three-dimensional impressions with three-dimensional impressions. Actual-sized photographs that had been prepared along with traced overlays created by the examiner of both the known and the exemplar impressions are used. Traced overlays are an invaluable investigative tool when comparing the location and shape of various characteristics or areas of the foot.

The comparison of barefoot impressions is treated as any other physical match and incorporates the same methodologies and scientific approaches. Clarity is one of the most important elements. All characteristics in a physical match must be analyzed, compared, and evaluated before a conclusion is reached.

Examiners work from unknown to known, with the first goal being to attempt to eliminate the person as the source of the impression if possible. If elimination of the person is not possible, then the comparison process continues.

The first step in the comparison process is to examine what may be described as class characteristics. Class characteristics are those that are common to more than one foot; for example, the overall size of the foot, the fact that the correct number of toes are present, and the width of the ball and heel of the foot. The finer details of the foot impressions are then compared. For example, the examiner should look at the shape and placement of each toe, the spatial relationship of the toes to one another, the distance from the ridge that separates the ball of the foot from the toe pads, the contour of that ridge, the contour of the ball of the foot, and the shape and length of the arch, shape and size of the heel area.

While each feature individually may not be unique, the features in combination can make the impressions of different persons distinguishable. An examiner must also evaluate any temporary changes in characteristics that may have been caused by injury to the foot and that are not part of the permanent foot morphology. Accidental characteristics such as a nail through the sole of the shoe, which has damaged the foot, or visible permanent features such as creases can be used in conjunction with foot morphology to individualize the barefoot.

When comparing impressions inside a shoe, the same process is used. All details present in the shoe are examined in a similar manner, and all known exemplars available are used in the comparison process. If no shoes known to be worn by the subject are available for comparison purposes, comparisons can be conducted with the use of inked barefoot impressions to the weight-bearing impressions inside of unknown shoes. One researcher who specifically explored this type of comparison found that inked impressions as known exemplars can be used though caution should be employed.

Evaluation

The examiner reaches a conclusion based on the evaluation of the comparison process and the similarities and differences noted during comparison. For example, there may be differences noted, which are explainable from the factors or distortions observed during the analysis of the unknown impressions or known impressions. The examiner articulates the process used and, ultimately, expresses an opinion. Once their opinion has been reached, the examiner prepares a written report and submits this with all of the materials used to a second qualified examiner for independent analysis, and if they agree with the conclusion stated, verify the original examiner's opinion.

The opinion or conclusion reached can range from the following:

1. A lack of sufficient detail for a meaningful comparison, whereby in the opinion of the examiner, there is insufficient detail in the unknown impression to conduct a meaningful comparison/evaluation.
2. Elimination/exclusion, whereby in the opinion of the examiner, there are sufficient differences, without explanation, such that the examiner would eliminate the suspect as a source of the unknown impressions.

3. Inclusion of the source of the known exemplars as being the possible donor of the unknown foot impressions, whereby in the examiner's opinion, there is an agreement of morphology of the weight-bearing impression, such that they could have made the unknown impressions.
4. Individualization of the unknown impression as having originating from the subject who provided the known exemplars, whereby in the examiner's opinion, there is an agreement of the morphology of the weight-bearing impression and the presence of additional accidental characteristics (e.g., flexion creases, scars) that are visible and also found to be in agreement between the unknown and known impressions.

Verification

Once the examiner has conducted a full examination, involving analysis, comparison, and evaluation, a full report is prepared, and the case file and all materials used are submitted to a second qualified examiner for a peer review of the process and conclusions reached. The second examiner's role is to repeat the process used, verify the methodology that was followed, and reach their own opinion, which if in agreement, verifies the opinion of the first examiner.

Barefoot morphology comparison should only be undertaken by properly trained forensic specialists, using established comparison methodologies of forensic physical evidence comparison, which may provide circumstantial evidence to assist in the exclusion or inclusion of a person as the potential source of the crime scene barefoot impression, providing additional information to the courts if required.

See also: **Pattern Evidence:** Footwear Marks; Palm Prints; The Friction Ridge Skin of the Feet.

Further Reading

Bodziak, W.J., 2000. Footwear Impression Evidence: Detection, Recovery and Examination, second ed. CRC Press LLC, Boca Raton, pp. 381–411.
Cassidy, M.J., 1980. Footwear Identification. Government Printing Center, Quebec, Canada.
Gupta, S.R., 1967. Footprint and shoeprint identification. International Criminal Police Review 205, 55–61.
Kennedy, R.B., 1996a. Preliminary study on the uniqueness of barefoot impressions. Canadian Society of Forensic Science Journal 29 (4), 233–238.
Kennedy, R.B., 1996b. Uniqueness of bare feet and its use as a possible means of identification. Forensic Science International 82 (1), 81–87.
Kennedy, R.B., 2000. Bare Footprint Marks. In: Siegel, J.A., Saukko, P.J., Knupfer, G.C. (Eds.), Encyclopedia of Forensic Sciences, vol. 3. Academic Press, London, pp. 1189–1195.
Kennedy, R.B., 2005. Ongoing research into barefoot impression evidence. In: Rich, J., Dean, D.E., Powers, R.H. (Eds.), Forensic Medicine of the Lower Extremity. Humana Press, Totowa, NJ, pp. 401–413.
Kennedy, R.B., Gel, S., Massey, S., Saunders, G., 2002. Use of barefoot morphology in criminal investigations. Identification Canada 25 (4), 4–6.
Laskowski, G.E., Kyle, V.L., 1988. Barefoot impressions: a preliminary study of identification characteristics and population frequency of their morphological features. Journal of Forest Science 33 (2), 378–388.
Lemieux, M., 2002. Histoire de pied/a foot story. Identification Canada 25 (4), 16–17.
Massey, S.L., 2004. Persistence of creases of the foot and their value for forensic identification purposes. Journal of Forensic Identification 54 (3), 296–315.
Nayar, P.S., Das Gupta, S.K., 1976. Personal identification based on footprints found on footwear. International Criminal Police Review 236, 83–87.
Puri, D.K.S., 1965. Footprints. International Criminal Police Review 187, 106–111.
Qamra, S.R., Sharma, B.R., Kaila, P., 1980. Naked foot marks: a preliminary study of identification factors. Forensic Science International 16 (2), 145–152.
Smerecki, C.J., Lovejoy, C.O., 1985. Identification via pedal morphology. Identification News 35 (12), 5–12.

The Friction Ridge Skin of the Feet

D Johnson, Las Vegas Metropolitan Police Department, Las Vegas, NV, USA

Introduction

Friction ridge skin has been used for over a hundred years for personal identification and for the identification of latent prints left at crime scenes. A majority of the focus of the study of friction ridge skin has been on the fingers and palms. The same type of friction ridge skin that covers the surface of the hand also covers the soles of the feet. It is both persistent and unique through the same mechanisms as that of the friction ridge skin of the hands. However, the general ridge flow and pattern types found on the feet can be very different. The notable differences in physiology and embryology of the foot and volar pad size, shape, and placement on the foot lead to some stark differences in the ridge flow and crease patterns on the plantar surface.

History

The use of friction ridge footprint evidence in US courts dates back to 1938 with the case of the Commonwealth versus Bartolini. Bartolini had been identified as the person who left a barefoot print on the floor of a homicide scene. The defense challenged the use of footprints citing that the expert in the case may have been familiar with fingerprints but was not qualified to give testimony on footprints. The court affirmed the conviction of Bartolini stating that the expert in the case had sufficient knowledge of footprints and that there was "ample evidence that footprints, like fingerprints, remain constant throughout life and furnish and adequate and reliable means of identification."

The first use of toe prints in the United Kingdom dates back to 1952. In HMA versus William Gourley, a bakery was broken into and several footwear impressions and two impressions of the left foot were recovered. The lock on the safe had been blown and a pry bar was used to open the safe. The two impressions recovered from the safe contained sufficient detail of what appeared to be the left big toe. Gourley was arrested, exemplars of his feet and toe prints were taken, and he was identified to the toe print that was recovered from the safe. The defense challenged the identification saying that the witness did not have enough experience to testify on toe prints. This was the first case in the United Kingdom where a toe print was the sole evidence against the suspect. The jury found Gourley guilty within 15 min and he was sentenced to 3 years in prison.

Later that year, in December 1952, in the United Kingdom, there was a break-in at an Aberdeen warehouse. The scene was processed for fingerprints, but only glove marks and the impressions of stockinged feet were recovered. The suspect had taken care not to leave footwear impressions and fingerprints by removing his shoes and wearing gloves. The stockings appeared to have holes in them allowing the transfer of some of the friction ridge detail from the feet to be recovered. James Walker Adams was identified as a suspect because he had used a similar Modus Operandi in previous break-ins and had been identified through the use of fingerprint and footwear on previous occasions. Adams was identified as having left three impressions. The same defense counsel that represented Gourley was used in HMA versus James Walker Adams, and the defense questioning of the expert witness followed much the same line. The jury found Adams guilty in only 5 min and he was sentenced to a year of jail time.

Recent court challenges using the Daubert or Frye standard in the United States have focused their attacks on the friction ridges of the fingers and the palm. Subsequently, research conducted to answer those Daubert and Frye challenges has only been on the fingers and the palms. While the courts currently recognize the acceptance of friction ridge identification in general, research could be conducted to strengthen this area of the science.

Embryology and Development of the Friction Ridges of the Foot

The development of the foot, the friction ridges, and the creases takes place over an estimated gestational age of 6–18 weeks. The sequence of events in the foot is very similar to that of the palms and fingers; however, the timing of events in the feet is delayed by about a week to 2 weeks. Several different factors help determine the overall ridge flow and pattern types present in the toes and feet. The shape and growth stresses of the foot and the genetic, environmental, and random factors cause the individual ridge and crease paths to be random. To understand this critical time in

 http://dx.doi.org/10.1016/B978-0-12-800573-6.00018-5

friction ridge development is to understand the resulting friction ridge patterns that can be seen on the skin.

Between 6 and 13 weeks of gestation, the feet will develop from flat paddlelike structures to something that resembles an infant's foot. Although at 6 weeks there are interdigital notches in the hands, they do not form in the feet till about 7 weeks. At about 8 weeks, the toe rays have formed and the heel is raised. At 9 weeks of gestation, the thenar, hypothenar, and interdigital pads are formed and one of the primary creases, the metatarsophalangeal creases, is visible. At 11 weeks of gestation, the pads have begun to regress, and by 13 weeks, the pad regression is all but complete on both the hands and the feet. Most of the primary creases have formed, but there is still some development of creases up until 20 weeks of gestation. While all fetuses will undergo the sequence of events described above, there will be variation between the size, shape, and timing of the regression of the volar pads. All these factors help contribute to the unique friction ridge pattern that is formed on the feet (**Figure 1**).

Development of the Arch

Children are born with flat feet and, the foot will continue to grow and develop as they age. It is not until 2–3 years of age that the arch begins to develop. The development of the arch can cause the formation of many new secondary creases in the tibial thenar. These creases are the result of the new concave shape of the foot in this area. In cases of flat-footedness, these creases are absent.

Recording Known Impressions of the Foot

One method that is used to obtain inked prints of the feet is to apply ink to the soles of the feet and have the individual walk across a large sheet of paper. This will typically record the weight-bearing areas of the foot as well as the friction ridge detail. This can make these types of known prints useful for not only latent print comparison but also for the comparison of the shape of barefoot impressions. The disadvantage of this method is that it will not give the friction ridge examiner a complete recording of the friction ridge detail of the feet. Most of the surface of the toes, the arch, and the outer portions of the hypothenar and the heel will not be recorded.

Similar to the method used for rolling palm prints, a large cylinder ~5″ in diameter and a legal size piece of paper (8.5″ by 14″) can be used to roll an impression of the feet. Just as in the procedure for palm prints, the foot should be rolled across the surface of the cylinder in one continuous motion, from the heel to the toes.

Alternatively, a light coating of powder can be applied to the surface of the feet and a white adhesive lifter

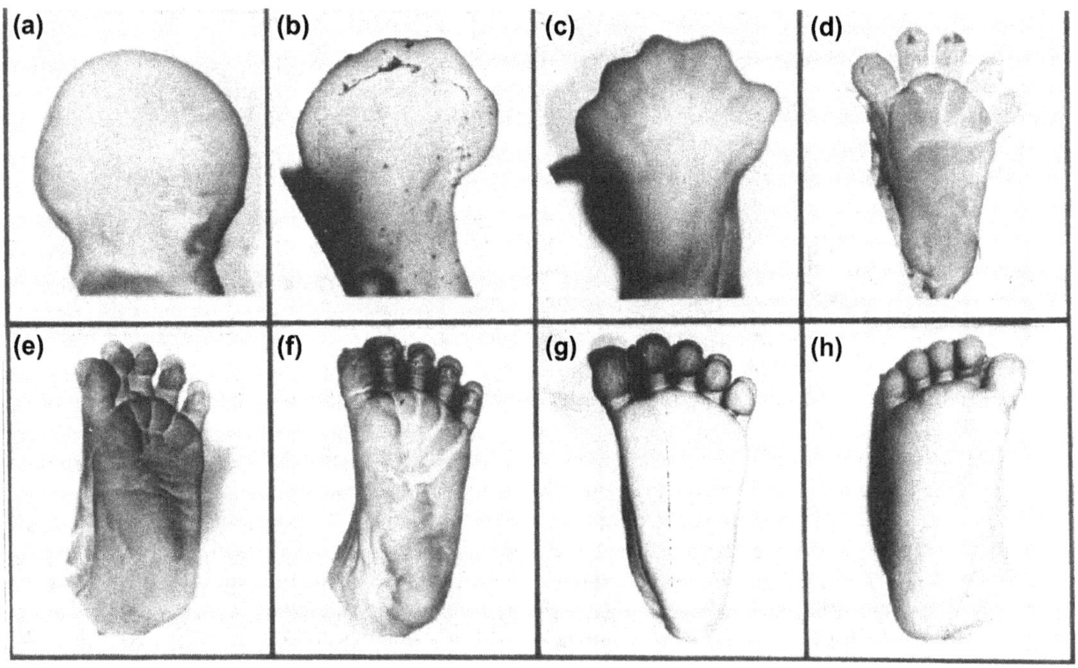

Figure 1 Kimura, et al., 1988.

(e.g., Quikprint, Handiprint). This technique has the advantage of being able to wrap the lifter around the surface of the foot, thereby recovering a more complete recording of the friction ridge detail.

When taking exemplars of infants, it is suggested that a ceramic inkpad and a rigid surface such as a clipboard will produce the most reliable images. Several steps are necessary to capture infant footprints. The foot should be washed to remove any biological fluid and thoroughly dried. Using an inkpad, a light coating of ink should be applied and using very light pressure pressed against a rigid surface.

Ridge Flow of the Feet

Latent prints from the feet are occasionally recovered from the crime scene. When the impression is of sufficient quality and size, it is very easy to determine the source as having come from a foot. However, when the latent print is of a reduced size and quality, it can be difficult to determine that the source is a foot. These impressions can often be confused as having come from a palm (**Figure 2**).

The same principles of identification that are employed in fingerprint and palm print identification should be used in footprint identification. As footprints and toe prints are not routinely compared by latent print examiners, care should be employed. The question of how much is enough, still an unanswered question in the areas of fingerprint and palm print identification, has received even less attention in the footprint identifications.

The foot can be divided into eight areas that can aid in classification. Distal and proximal retain their meaning; however, the terms ulnar and radial should be replaced with tibular and fibular, respectively, to reflect the bones of the calf rather than the bones of the forearm (**Figure 3**).

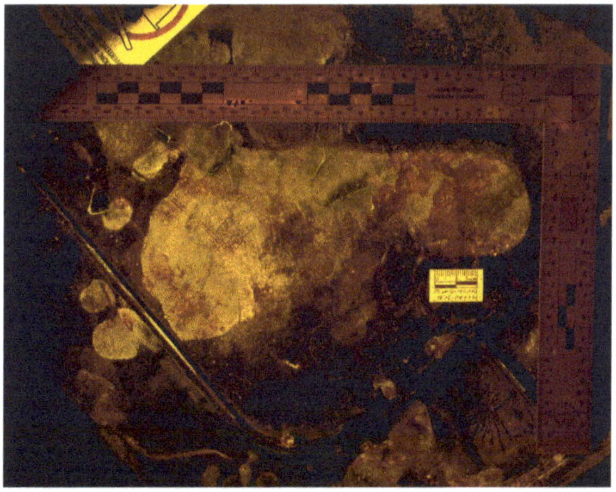

Figure 2 Footprint developed with rhodamine 6G.

Hallucal (Distal Thenar and First Interdigital Area)

This is the major pattern area of the foot. This is the combination of the first interdigital area and the distal thenar. This is the most patterned area of the foot and can contain a wide variation of loops, whorls, and arches. Understanding the types and shapes in this area can greatly aid in identifying latent prints, as having come from the foot as the hallucal is one of the more common areas that will leave a latent print (**Figure 4**).

In a small collection of 84 feet, there were only two distal arches.

II, III, and IV Interdigital Areas

The remaining interdigital area can be divided into three separate pattern areas. The five triradii that are typically found in the interdigital area can be used to delineate the different pattern areas as shown in **Figure 5**. These triradii bear the same designation as they would in the palm, with the exception of "E" under the great toe, which has no corresponding delta in the palm.

Interdigital area	*Whorl (%)*	*Loop, distal (%)*	*Loop, proximal (%)*	*Open (%)*
II	0.15	6.6	2.05	91.2
III	0.65	57.7	0.2	41.55
IV	0.0[a]	8.05	0.1	91.9

[a]There were no occurrences of a whorl in the IV interdigital area.
Based on data from Takeya 1933, 1000 right and 1000 left feet.

Distal/Proximal Hypothenar

When examining the weight-bearing portion of the distal and proximal hypothenar, it was found that most feet exhibited horizontal flowing ridges. When the fully rolled impression was recorded, a loop in the distal portion was found with increasing frequency. While different variants of pattern types are possible in this area, they were fairly uncommon with the distal loop near the IV interdigital being the most common pattern.

	Open field (%)	*Vestige (%)*	*Loop (%)*
Distal hypothenar	27.0	37.1	35.9
Proximal hypothenar	81.7	15.3	3.1

Based on data from Takeya 1933, 1000 right and 1000 left feet.

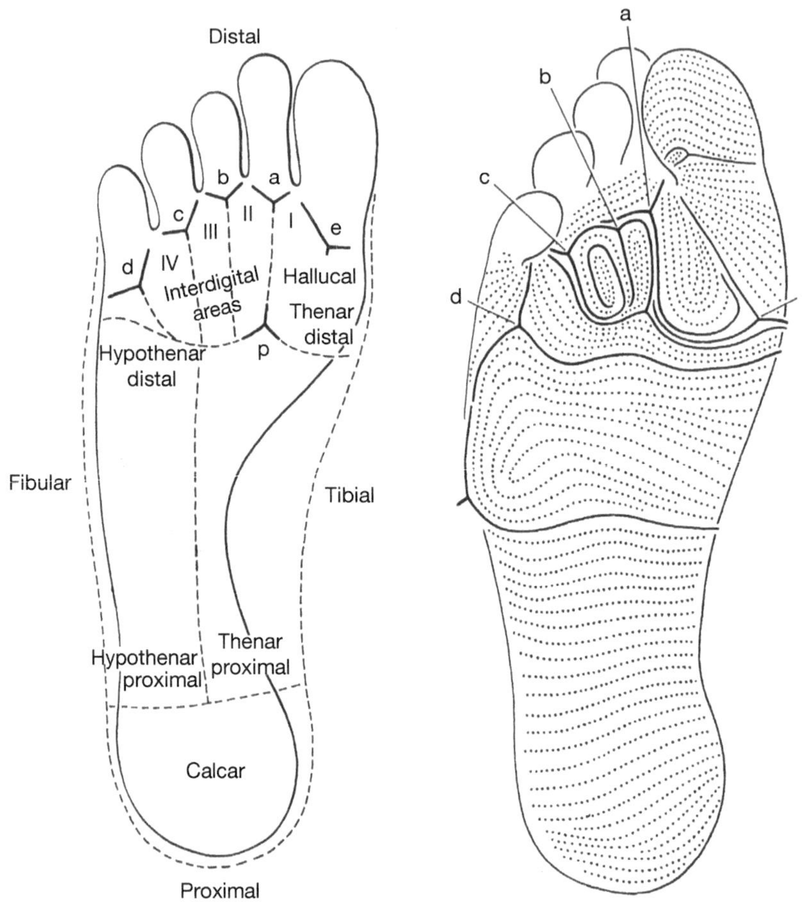

Figure 3 Holt, Genetics of Dermal Ridges. Areas of the foot: hallucal (I interdigital and thenar distal); II, III, and IV interdigital; hypothenar distal; hypothenar proximal; thenar proximal; and calcar.

Tibial Thenar

The tibial thenar area is most typically highly creased and the ridge flow is very similar to the weight-bearing portion of the hypothenar. The most common feature of this area is the straight horizontally flowing ridges with little to no patterning. In the proximal portion of the tibial thenar lies the thenar rudiment. The thenar rudiment is a wedge-shaped ridge flow pattern that is commonly found where the arch of the foot ends and the heel begins. As this area is not often fully recorded, additional variants of the ridge flow are possible.

Calcar

The calcar or heel area of the foot is predominantly an open field. The calcar area bears patterns in approximately 1.0% of the cases. Some of the subsets of populations surveyed had percentages ranging from 0.7% to 2.2%. It is still fairly clear that any type of pattern in the calcar region is a rare event. There is some evidence to suggest that patterning in the calcar region is genetic and can be shared among siblings and passed down from generation to generation. However, as most recording of the heels are incomplete, the calcar loop may be more common than is currently thought.

Toes

The distribution of pattern types on the fingers is fairly well known and studied. Again, this is an area that has received little attention in the feet. There is very little information that has been published on the toes. The toes provide some difficulties

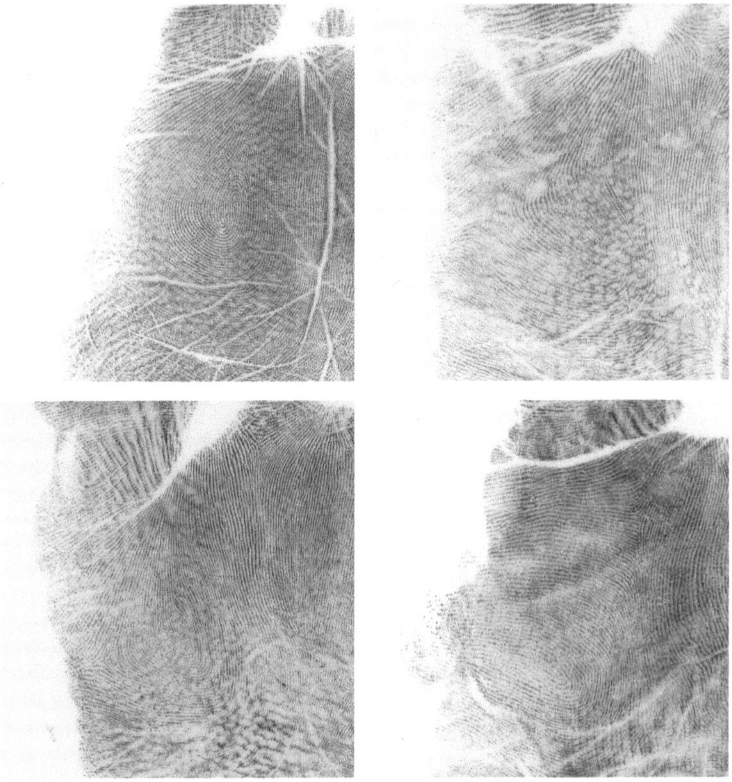

Figure 4 Picture of whorl, loop, open, and arch. Whorls, 30.7%; distal loops, 48.5%; tibial loops, 7.3%; and open, 12.2%. Based on data from Takeya 1933, 1000 right and 1000 left feet.

Figure 5 Interdigital area of the left foot.

to researchers, and the pattern area is not recorded on typical plain impressions. The big toe is typically flat, but the remaining toes curl under so that only the tips are recorded (**Figure 6**).

The distribution of pattern types on the toes is very different than that of the fingers. Arches are far more common and whorls are less common. The loops, however, only occur about 5% less than they do in the fingers.

	Arches (%)	*Loops (%)*	*Whorls (%)*
European Americans (Neman)	13	64.4	22.6
Germans (Steffens)	19	59.3	21.7
Chinese (Takeya)	21.8	59.9	20.7
Japanese (Hasebe)	21.8	61	17.2

Toe patterns tend to have smaller ridge counts than the fingers. In a study of twins, it was found that the average ridge count for the fingers was ~14.3 and for the toes 10.6 (**Figure 7**).

Without knowledge of the ridge flow of the feet, this impression may be interpreted as being from the thumb and part of a palm. If the latent print had been identified as having come from the thumb or part of the palm, it would have resulted in the exclusion of the subject in the case.

Figure 6 Different pattern types of the toes.

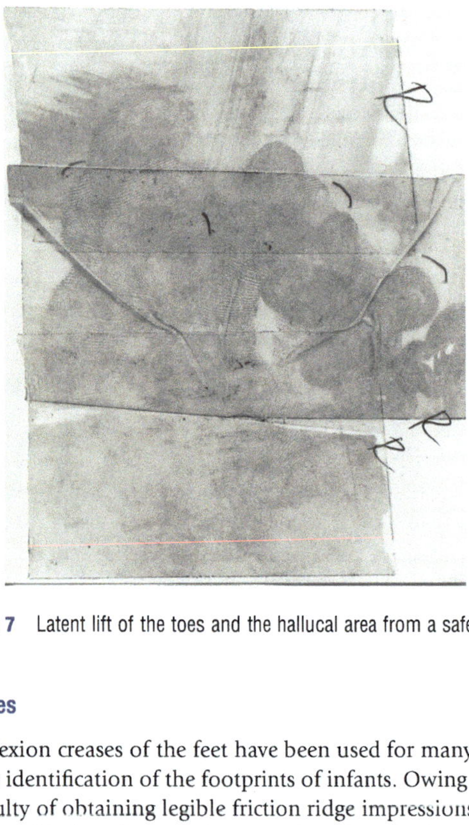

Figure 7 Latent lift of the toes and the hallucal area from a safe.

Creases

The flexion creases of the feet have been used for many years in the identification of the footprints of infants. Owing to the difficulty of obtaining legible friction ridge impressions from the feet of infants, latent prints examiners have had to rely on the flexion creases to identify the subjects. As early as 1959, the use of flexion creases to identify infants was being used and accepted by the courts. In the case of the People versus Iavaroni—County Court, Brooklyn, NY—an infant found in the possession of Mrs Iavaroni was identified as Lisa Rose Chioncho. She had been kidnapped from the nursery of St. Peter's Hospital. The hospital had taken impressions of Lisa Rose's footprints at birth, but due to the lack of training of the hospital staff, the impressions did not contain any legible ridge detail. When Lisa Rose was found 9 days after the kidnapping, the examiners in the case, Detectives Mandella and Fusci, were able to identify the girl based on the flexion creases alone.

Formation of the Creases

The formation of most of the primary creases is independent of the movement of the hands and feet. Spontaneous movement does not occur in the hands and feet until 11.5 weeks and some of the major primary creases have already formed by this time. Additionally, there are cases in which the primary creases are absent, but the individual still has normal movement. Primary crease formation is more closely related to the volar pads than to the movement of the hand and foot. Secondary creases form after the friction ridge skin, and many continue to form in the feet as a person ages.

Creases in the feet are highly variable. Unlike the consistent pattern of the major primary creases in the palm, the feet show a wide variety of crease patterns both in number and configuration. There are anywhere from 0 to 90 creases in the weight-bearing area of the feet, with an average of 15 creases per foot. If the tibular thenar area (arch) were to be included, the number of creases would be much higher.

It is the combination of the differences in physiology, embryology of the foot and volar pad size, shape, and placement on the foot that leads to some stark differences between the ridge flow and crease patterns on the plantar surface and that of the fingers and palms. Familiarity with the different ridge flow and crease patterns of the feet will help friction ridge examiners identify possible foot impressions and avoid erroneous exclusions.

See also: **Anthropology/Odontology:** Personal Identification in Forensic Anthropology; **Investigations:** Fingerprints; **Pattern Evidence:** Analysis, Comparison, Evaluation, and Verification (ACE-V); Bare Footprint Marks; Palm Prints; **Pattern Evidence/History:** Fingerprint Sciences.

Further Reading

Blake, J.W., 1959. Identification of the new-born by flexure creases. Identification News 9 (9), 3–5.

Cummins, H., 1929. The topographic history of the volar pads (walking pads; tastballen) in the human embryo. Contributions to Embryology 113, 103–126.

Cummins, H., Midlo, C., 1943. Finger Prints, Palms, and Soles: An Introduction to Dermatoglyphics. The Blakiston Company, Philadelphia.

Fox, K.M., Plato, C.C., 1987. Toe and plantar dermatoglyphics in adult American Caucasians. American Journal of Physical Anthropology 74 (1), 55–64.

Holt, S.B., 1968. The Genetics of Dermal Ridges. Charles C. Thomas, Springfield.

Kimura, S., Schaumann, B.A., Plato, C.C., Kitagawa, T., 1988. Developmental aspects of human palmar, plantar, and digital flexion creases. In: Durham, N.M., Plato, C.C. (Eds.), Trends in Dermatoglyphic Research: Proceedings of a Symposium from the 12th International Congress of Anthropological and Ethnological Sciences. Kluwer Academic Publishers, Dordrecht, pp. 84–98.

Lohnes, R.C., 1986. Infant footprint identification by flexure creases. Identification News 36 (8), 10–13.

Massey, S.L., 2004. Persistence of creases of the foot and their value for forensic identification purposes. Journal of Forensic Identification 54 (3), 296–315.

Montgomery, R.B., 1926a. Sole patterns of twins. The Biological Bulletin 50 (4), 293–300.

Montgomery, R.B., 1926b. Sole patterns. A study of the footprints of two thousand individuals. The Anatomical Record 33 (2), 107–114.

Montgomery, R.B., 1927. Classification of foot-prints. Journal of the American Institute of Criminal Law and Criminology 18 (1), 105–110.

Taylor, R.A., 1979. Flexure creases: alternative method for infant footprint identification. Identification News 29 (9), 12–14.

Wilder, H.H., 1916. Palm and sole studies. The Biological Bulletin 30 (2–3), 135–252.

Palm Prints

A Maceo, M Carter, and B Stromback, Las Vegas Metropolitan Police Department Forensic Laboratory, Las Vegas, NV, USA

The friction ridges on the palmar surface of the hands develop in utero during the first and second trimester. Like fingerprints, the ridge flows and patterns that emerge on the palms are the product of the growth stresses and strains on the surface of the skin at the time of friction ridge development. These growth stresses, and the size and shape of any volar pads (VPs) present, influence the resulting patterns displayed on the palms (Wertheim and Maceo).

The friction ridge skin on the palmar surfaces has been studied for more than a century. In the late 1890s through the early 1900s, Inez Whipple researched the ventral surfaces of various species of monkeys' feet, focusing on the apical pads, ridge patterns, deltas, and other "epidermal markings," comparing them to human hands and feet. Harris Wilder, in his Palm and Sole Studies, created a system for recording the configurations of various features on the palms and soles into a formula, easily understood and visualized by someone knowing the system. Cummins and Midlo researched pattern frequencies and intensities (number of deltas) in both right and left palms and soles of chimpanzees. Penrose also studied the pattern frequencies of palms and soles, and he and Loesch classified palmar dermatoglyphics, both normal and abnormal. Malhotra et al. researched the methodology for palmar pattern ridge counts, specifically in Indian genetics. Most recently, in 2001, Tietze and Witthuhn published their work on palm patterns, flows, and deltas, including statistical data in left and right palms. Given that the book is written in German, translation and interpretation is limited; however, the charts and graphs and numerous images are most useful.

To further study the distribution of the various patterns on the palms, the authors devised a classification scheme and recorded the various pattern types present in 800 pairs of inked palm prints (left and right). The palm prints were randomly selected from male arrestees in Clark County, Nevada, from the 1990s. The palms were divided into three regions: interdigital, hypothenar, and thenar. **Figure 1** illustrates the different regions of the palm.

Interdigital Region

Deltas

The interdigital region is the most complex area of the palm. In this study, the interdigital region contained anywhere from three to seven deltas. These deltas often existed in various combinations with tented arches (TAs), loops, columns, or whorls in the interdigital region. Seven possible delta positions were documented. Four of the delta positions were situated at or near the base of each finger (finger deltas) and were labeled index (I), middle (M), ring (R), and little (L). The remaining three delta positions occurred between the fingers and were labeled index/middle (I/M), middle/ring (M/R), and ring/little (R/L). Occasionally, more than one delta was located in a position (e.g., two deltas under the ring finger). **Table 1** shows the number of palms with the corresponding number of deltas from the 800 left and right palms. The most common number of interdigital deltas in the left and right hands was four.

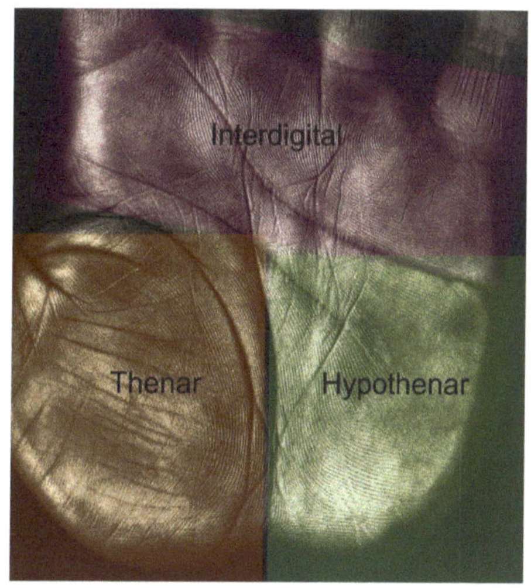

Figure 1 Three palmar regions: interdigital, hypothenar, and thenar.

Table 1 Number of deltas in the interdigital region ($n = 800$ for left and right palms each)

Number of deltas	*Left palm*	*Right palm*
3	32 (4.0%)	19 (2.4%)
4	586 (73%)	605 (76%)
5	154 (19%)	137 (17%)
6	28 (3.5%)	37 (4.6%)
7	0	2 (0.25%)

 http://dx.doi.org/10.1016/B978-0-12-800573-6.00019-7

Table 2 The number of palms containing 0, 1, or 2 deltas in each interdigital delta position ($n = 800$ for left and right palms each)

	Left palm			*Right palm*		
	Number of deltas present			*Number of deltas present*		
Delta position	*0 Delta*	*1 Delta*	*2 Deltas*	*0 Delta*	*1 Delta*	*2 Deltas*
Index (I)	0	800 (100%)	0	0	800 (100%)	0
I/M	773 (97%)	27 (3.4%)	0	732 (92%)	68 (8.5%)	0
Middle (M)	1 (0.12%)	799 (99.9%)	0	0	800 (100%)	0
M/R	797 (99.6%)	3 (0.38%)	0	782 (98%)	18 (2.2%)	0
Ring (R)	69 (8.6%)	726 (91%)	5 (0.62%)	39 (4.9%)	755 (94%)	6 (0.75%)
R/L	696 (87%)	94 (12%)	10 (1.2%)	661 (83%)	132 (16%)	7 (0.88%)
Little (L)	1 (0.12%)	799 (100%)	0	3 (0.38%)	797 (100%)	0

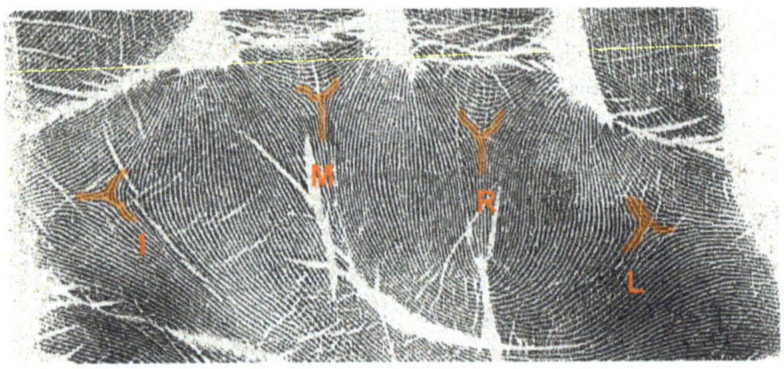

Figure 2 Right palm interdigital region displaying the index (I), middle (M), ring (R), and little (L) deltas.

Figure 3 Interdigital region below the right ring finger. The ring finger delta is absent.

The position of each delta and the number of deltas in each position were also recorded. **Table 2** shows the number of palms that contained 0, 1, or 2 deltas in each delta position in the interdigital region. As shown in **Table 2**, the overwhelming majority of palms had a delta associated with each finger.

It was very common for the palms to have only the four finger deltas: 553 of the 586 left palms and 591 of the 605 right palms with four interdigital deltas had only the four finger deltas (I, M, R, and L). **Figure 2** is a right palm interdigital region displaying the four finger deltas.

In palms containing only three interdigital deltas, the most common configuration was a delta under the index, middle, and little finger each (the ring finger delta was absent): 31 of 32 left palms and 19 of 19 right palms with three interdigital deltas were missing the ring finger delta. **Figure 3** shows the interdigital region below the right ring finger. In this palm, the ring finger delta is absent.

Interdigital regions with four or more deltas often contained at least one pattern area in the interdigital region. The more patterns present in the interdigital region, generally the higher the number of deltas present. **Figure 4** is a right palm interdigital region displaying six deltas associated with three interdigital loop patterns. In this study, 13 left palms (1.6%) and 18 right palms (2.2%) presented this configuration of six deltas and three loops.

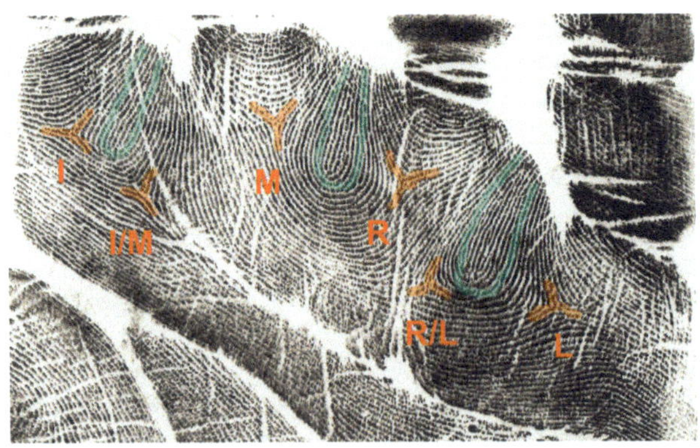

Figure 4 Right palm interdigital region with six deltas (I, I/M, M, R, R/L, and L) and three loop patterns (highlighted in blue).

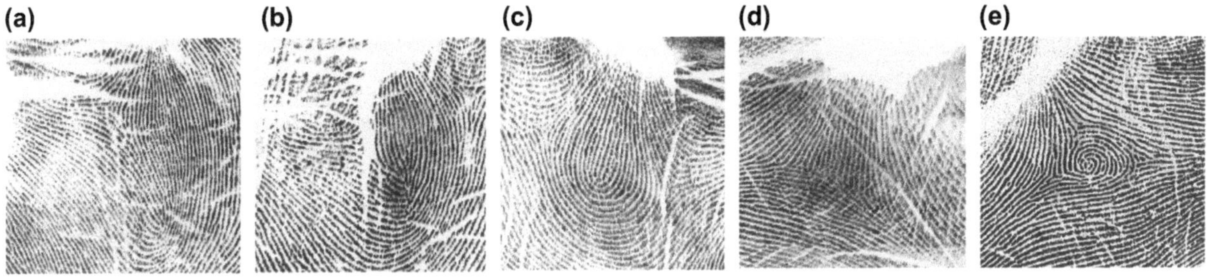

Figure 5 Patterns of the interdigital region. (a and b) Tented arch, (c) loop, (d) column, and (e) whorl.

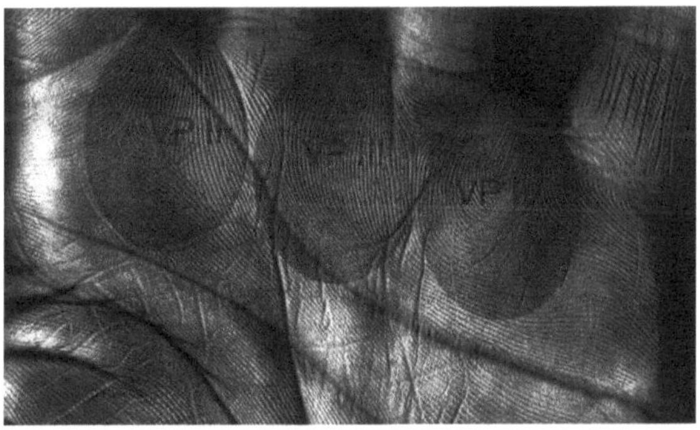

Figure 6 Volar pad (VP) regions of the right palm interdigital region.

Patterns

The position and types of patterns in the interdigital region were also documented. These patterns included TAs, loops, columns, and whorls. **Figure 5** illustrates the different patterns. Designation as TAs, loops, and whorls followed basic fingerprint classification rules. In the interdigital region, however, a TA was a ridge flow over an interdigital delta that formed a looplike pattern (**Figure 5(a) and (b)**). Columns are a series of three or more ending ridges flanked on one or both sides by a delta (**Figure 5(d)**).

The interdigital region was divided into VP regions II, III, and IV as depicted in **Figure 6**. The VP II region is between the index and middle fingers. The VP III region is between the middle and ring fingers. The VP IV region is between the ring and little fingers.

The patterns present in each VP position were recorded for the 800 left and right palms. Only 40 of the 800 (5%) left palms and 29 of the 800 (3.6%) right palms displayed no patterns in the interdigital region. **Table 3** indicates the number of palms with the various patterns in the VP II position, including the number of palms with TAs over the middle finger delta. **Table 4** indicates the number of palms with the various patterns in the VP III position, including the number of palms with TAs over the ring finger delta. **Table 5** indicates the number of palms with the various patterns in the VP IV position, including the number of palms with TAs over the little finger delta. In the VP IV position, there could be a single loop or two loops, which is the reason **Table 5** has "1 Loop" and "2 Loops" indicated.

Loops and columns were more prevalent on the right hand (versus the left hand) in the VP II position. This naturally

Table 3 Number of palms with the designated patterns present in the volar pad (VP) II position ($n = 800$ left and right palms each)

VP II	*Loop*	*Column*	*Tented arch middle delta*
Left palm	25 (3.1%)	3 (0.38%)	0
Right palm	53 (6.6%)	16 (2.0%)	1 (0.12%)

Table 4 Number of palms with the designated patterns present in the volar pad (VP) III position ($n = 800$ left and right palms each)

VP III	*Loop*	*Column*	*Whorl*	*Tented arch ring delta*
Left palm	185 (23%)	2 (0.25%)	0	192 (24%)
Right palm	373 (47%)	3 (0.38%)	2 (0.25%)	111 (14%)

Table 5 Number of palms with the designated patterns present in the volar pad (VP) IV position ($n = 800$ left and right palms each). The VP IV position was the only VP position in this study where two loops occurred in the same VP position

VP IV	*1 Loop*	*2 Loops*	*Column*	*Whorl*	*Tented arch little delta*
Left palm	438 (55%)	31 (3.9%)	58 (7.2%)	4 (0.50%)	1 (0.12%)
Right palm	374 (47%)	9 (1.1%)	36 (4.5%)	2 (0.25%)	0

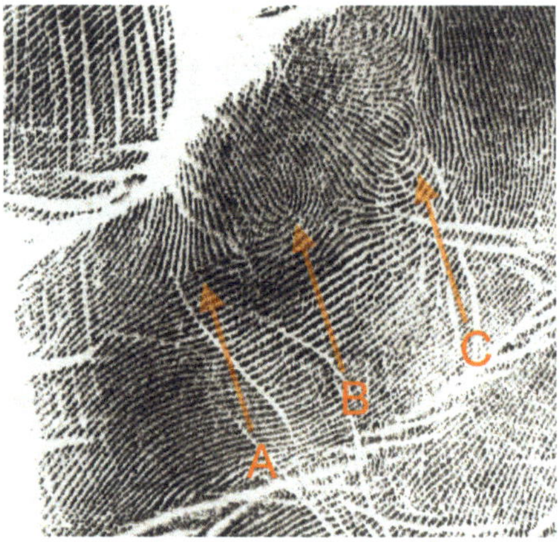

Figure 7 Left palm volar pad (VP) IV region containing a column (A) and two loops (B and C).

Table 6 The number of left palms with different configurations of loops in the three volar pad (VP) positions ($n = 800$)

Left palm			
No. of palms	*VP II loop*	*VP III loop*	*VP IV loop*
1 (0.12%)	1		
111 (14%)		1	
363 (45%)			1
13 (1.6%)	1	1	1
5 (0.62%)	1	1	
56 (7.0%)		1	1
6 (0.75%)	1		1
31 (3.9%)			2
0	1	1	2
0		1	2
0	1		2

correlates with the higher occurrence of I/M deltas in right palms. The right palms had an equal occurrence of loops in the VP III and IV positions, while left palms had the highest occurrence of loops in the VP IV position. **Figure 7** illustrates a rare and complex VP IV position in a left palm. This palm has a column (a) and two loops (b and c) in the VP IV position.

Loops are the most common pattern in the interdigital region of palms. **Tables 6 and 7** demonstrate the number of left and right palms containing specific configurations of loops in the various VP positions. For example, there were 111 left palms (14%) with a loop in the VP III position only. There were 13 left palms (1.6%) with a loop in all three VP positions. These tables only refer to loops; other patterns may be present in the VP regions.

Table 7 The number of right palms with different configurations of loops in the three volar pad (VP) positions ($n = 800$)

Right palm			
No. of palms	*VP II loop*	*VP III loop*	*VP IV loop*
7 (0.88%)	1		
255 (32%)		1	
276 (34%)			1
18 (2.2%)	1	1	1
23 (2.9%)	1	1	
75 (9.4%)		1	1
5 (0.62%)	1		1
7 (0.88%)			2
0	1	1	2
2 (0.25%)		1	2
0	1		2

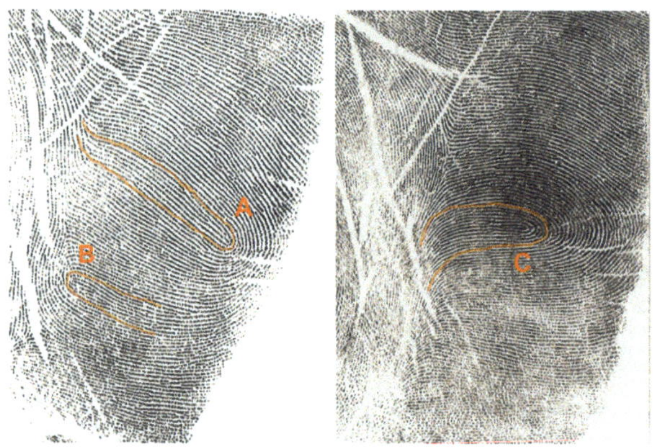

Figure 8 Right palm hypothenars displaying an "ulnar loop—top" (A), a radial loop (B), and an "ulnar loop—base" (C).

Hypothenar

The hypothenar region also contained a variety of patterns. Like fingers, the loops found in the palms flow in a certain direction. For the purposes of this study, the direction the top of the loop was pointing to is indicated (this is reverse from fingerprint classification). For instance, a loop pointing toward the outer edge of the palm is called an "ulnar loop." A loop pointing toward the center of the palm is called a "radial loop," and a loop pointing toward the base of the palm is called a "proximal loop." The ulnar loops are further described by the origin of the ridge flow. If the ridges flow into an ulnar loop pattern from the top of the palm, it is called an "ulnar loop—top." If the ridges flow into an ulnar loop pattern from the bottom of the palm, it is called an "ulnar loop—base." **Figure 8** illustrates two right hand hypothenars. One hypothenar has an "ulnar

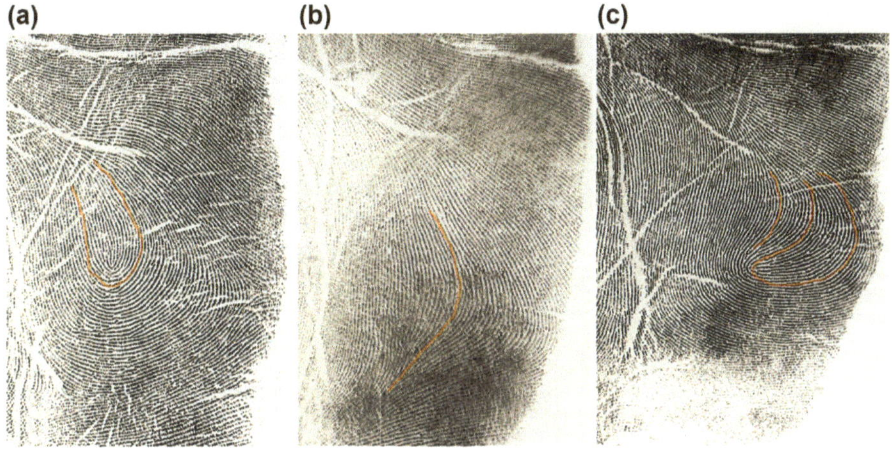

Figure 9 Right palm hypothenars classified as proximal loop (a), arch (b), and proximal loop/arch (c).

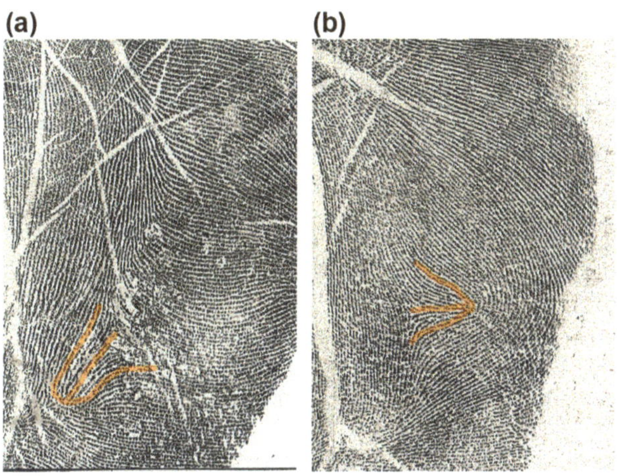

Figure 10 Right palm hypothenars classified as a proximal tented arch (a) and an ulnar tented arch (b).

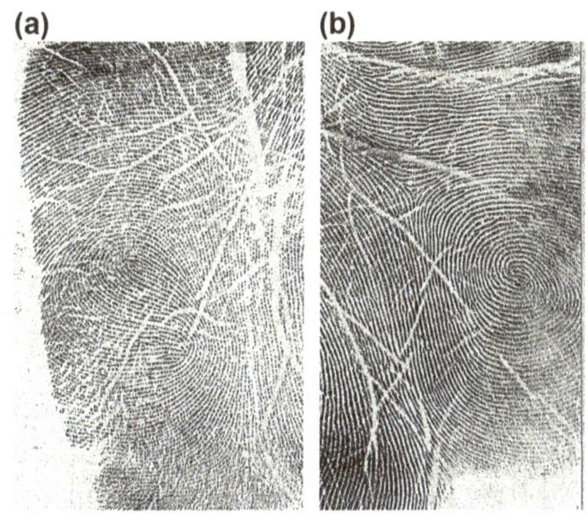

Figure 11 Left palm hypothenar classified as a double-loop whorl (a) and a right palm hypothenar classified as a plain whorl (b).

loop—top" (a) and a radial loop (b). The other hypothenar has an "ulnar loop—base" (c). The pattern counts for ulnar loops may be artificially low due to the manner in which the palms were recorded. Sometimes ulnar loops are located far out on the edge of the palm and are not displayed during the recording process; for this reason, the data should be viewed with caution.

Figure 9 illustrates the patterns classified as proximal loop, arch, and proximal loop/arch combination. The proximal loop in the proximal loop/arch classification approaches the radial loop classification; however, it is distinguished by the distinct arch pattern.

Figure 10 illustrates the TA patterns noted in the hypothenar region. The TAs can point in the proximal direction (a) or the ulnar direction (b).

Whorl patterns can also be found in the hypothenar region. **Figure 11** illustrates a double-loop whorl (a) and a plain whorl (b) in the hypothenar.

Columns of ridges can also be present in the hypothenar. These columns can manifest vertically near the carpal delta (delta typically found at the base of the palm that separates the hypothenar and thenar regions) or horizontally throughout the hypothenar. **Figure 12** illustrates a right palm hypothenar with a vertical column (a) and a right palm hypothenar with a horizontal column (b) and an ulnar loop (c).

There was no pattern present in 547 of the 800 (68%) left palm hypothenars and 514 of the 800 (64%) right palm hypothenars. The most common pattern found in the hypothenar was an ulnar loop—top: 156 (20%) left palms and 146 (18%) right palms. The most common pattern combination in

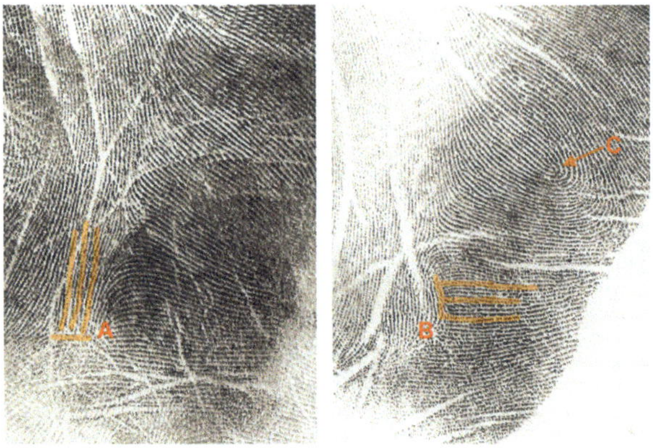

Figure 12 Right palm hypothenars displaying a vertical column (A), a horizontal column (B), and an ulnar loop (C).

Table 8 Hypothenar patterns ($n = 800$ for left and right palms each)

Patterns	No. of left palms	No. of right palms
No pattern	547 (68%)	514 (64%)
Ulnar loop—top (1)	156 (20%)	146 (18%)
Ulnar loop—top (2)	1 (0.12%)	0
Ulnar loop—base (1)	6 (0.75%)	15 (1.9%)
Ulnar loop—base (2)	1 (0.12%)	0
Radial loop (1)	71 (8.9%)	69 (8.6%)
Radial loop (2)	1 (0.12%)	1 (0.12%)
Proximal loop	7 (0.88%)	12 (1.5%)
Proximal loop/arch	1 (0.12%)	9 (1.1%)
Arch	2 (0.25%)	8 (1.0%)
Proximal tented arch	1 (0.12%)	5 (0.62%)
Ulnar tented arch	0	2 (0.25%)
Plain whorl	2 (0.25%)	9 (1.1%)
Double-loop whorl	6 (0.75%)	10 (1.2%)
Horizontal column (1)	10 (1.2%)	21 (2.6%)
Horizontal column (2)	0	1 (0.12%)
Vertical column	3 (0.38%)	12 (1.5%)

the hypothenar was an ulnar loop—top and a radial loop: 9 (1.1%) left palms and 11 (1.4%) right palms. **Figure 8(a) and (b)** illustrates this combination.

Table 8 shows the number of palms containing the various hypothenar patterns. Occasionally, two ulnar loops, two radial loops, or two horizontal columns appeared in the hypothenar. A single pattern is designated "(1)" and a double pattern is designated "(2)." One palm could have multiple patterns (e.g., a loop and a horizontal column).

Thenar

The thenar region displays fewer overall patterns than the other regions of the palm. There is, however, one pattern unique to the thenar—the vestige. A vestige is a ridge flow that runs opposite to the main flow of the ridges. A vestige can be small and independent, or it may be quite large and accompanied by loops, columns, or whorls.

The loops and columns were counted together; hence the combined classification of "loop/column." A loop/column above the vestige was termed "proximal loop/column" because the nose of the loop or ending ridges of the column point toward the base of the palm. Occasionally, both a loop and a column appeared above the vestige. The loop/column below the vestige was termed a "distal loop/column" because the nose of the loop or the ending ridges of the column generally pointed toward the top of the palm.

Figure 13 illustrates right palm thenars with an independent vestige (a and b), a vestige with a narrow proximal loop/column and narrow distal loop/column (c), and a vestige with a wide proximal loop/column and wide distal loop/column (d).

Figure 14 illustrates the whorl (a) and double-loop whorl (b) that can be found accompanying vestiges in the thenar region. The whorl and vestige are also associated with proximal loops/columns above the vestige. Occasionally, a proximal

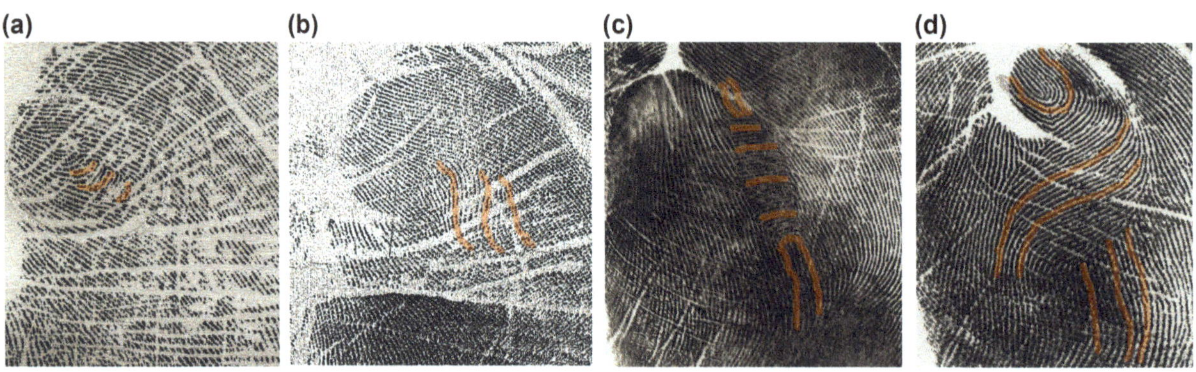

Figure 13 Right palm thenars displaying vestiges.

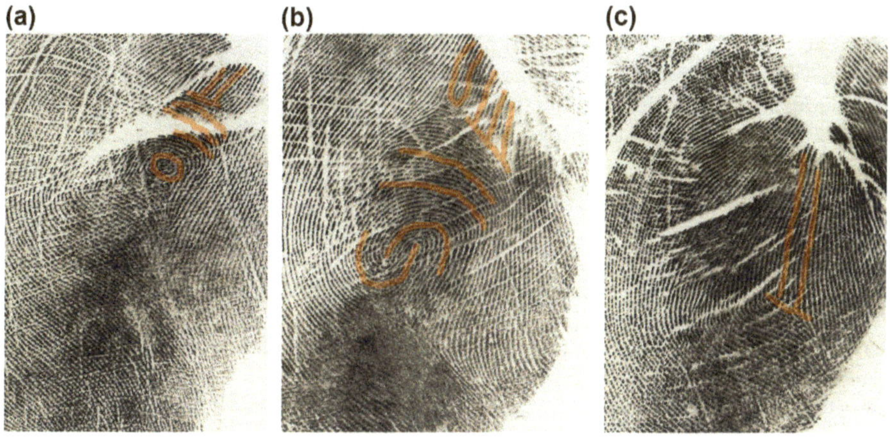

Figure 14 Left palm thenars displaying vestiges associated with a plain whorl (a) and a double-loop whorl (b). Also shown is an independent proximal loop/column in the thenar (c).

Table 9 The number of palms containing the various patterns (and combinations of patterns) in the thenar region ($n = 800$ for left and right palms each)

Pattern	*No. of left palms*	*No. of right palms*
No pattern	659 (82%)	745 (93%)
Vestige (in any configuration)	119 (15%)	49 (6.1%)
Vestige only	12 (1.5%)	9 (1.1%)
Vestige, proximal loop/column, and distal loop/column	72 (9%)	27 (3.4%)
Vestige and proximal loop/column only	16 (2.0%)	7 (0.88%)
Vestige and distal loop/column only	10 (1.2%)	2 (0.25%)
Vestige, proximal loop/column, and plain whorl	7 (0.88%)	3 (0.38%)
Vestige, proximal loop/column, and double-loop whorl	2 (0.25%)	1 (0.12%)
Proximal loop/column only (no vestige)	20 (2.5%)	5 (0.62%)
Distal loop/column only (no vestige)	1 (0.12%)	1 (0.12%)

loop/column (c) or a distal loop/column can occur in the thenar independently (no vestige).

Table 9 contains the number of palms displaying a different pattern and combinations of patterns, found in the thenar region.

Palm prints display four different basic patterns: arches, loops, whorls, and columns. These patterns can occur, independently or in combination, in the interdigital, hypothenar, or thenar regions. The interdigital region displayed the highest frequency of patterns—more than 95% of palms displayed at least one pattern in the interdigital region. Less than 15% of the thenar regions contained a pattern, while ~34% of hypothenar regions displayed a pattern.

Latent palm prints are routinely encountered in forensic casework. Through training and experience, analysts develop a sense of the rarity of features, including patterns, in the various regions of the palm. Using data such as these, analysts can better inform their judgments regarding the rarity of these features.

See also: **Pattern Evidence:** Bare Footprint Marks; Footwear Marks; The Friction Ridge Skin of the Feet.

Further Reading

Cummins, H., Midlo, C., 1943. Fingerprints, Palms and Soles. Blakiston Co, Philadelphia.

Cummins, H., Spragg, S.D.S., 1938. Dermatoglyphics in the chimpanzee: description and comparison with man. Human Biology 10, 457–510.

Durhan, N.M., Plato, C.C. (Eds.), 1990. Trends in Dermatoglyphic Research. Studies in Human Biology, vol. 1. Kluwer Academic, The Netherlands.

Loesch, D., 1971. Genetics of dermatoglyphic patterns on palms. Annals of Human Genetics 34, 277–293.

Malhotra, K.C., Karmaker, B., Vijayakumar, M., 1981. Genetics of Palmar Pattern Research. Technology Report No. Anthropology 1. Indian Statistical Institute, Calcutta.

Midlo, C., Cummins, H., 1942. Palmar and Plantar Dermatoglyphics in Primates. American Anatomical Memoris No. 20. Wistar Institute of Anatomy and Biology, Philadelphia, pp. 1–198.

Penrose, L.S., Loesch, D., 1970. Topological classification of palmar dermatoglyphics. Journal of Mental Deficiency Research 14, 111–128.

Tietze, S., Witthuhn, K., 2001. Papillarleistenstruktur der Menschlichen Handinnenfl-ache. Luchterhand, Germany.

Wertheim, K., Maceo, A., 2002. The critical stage of friction ridge and pattern formation. Journal of Forensic Identification 52 (1), 35–85.

Whipple, I.L., 1904. The ventral surface of the mammalian chiridium. Zeitschrift für Morphologie und Anthropologie 7, 261–268.

Wilder, H.H., 1916. Palm and sole studies. Biology Bulletin 30, 135–172.

Key Terms

Arch, Ball, Bare footprint, Barefoot impression, Barefoot morphology, Carpal delta, Column, Creases, Delta, Feet, Fingerprint, Foot, Friction ridge skin, Hallucal, Hypothenar, Insole impression, Interdigital, Latent print, Loop, Multistep impression, Palm, Palm print, Plantar, Single-step impression, Socked-foot impression, Sole, Tented arch, Thenar, Vestige, Volar pad, Weight-bearing impression, Whorl.

Review Questions

1. Does the friction ridge skin on the plantar surfaces have the same significance for identification as friction ridges on the palmar surfaces? What is your answer based on?
2. What studies have been conducted on bare footmarks? List them with their year of publication and their relevant findings.
3. How should bare footmarks be dealt with at a crime scene?
4. How are exemplar footmarks taken?
5. How does the examination of footmarks differ from that of fingerprint examination? How are they the same?
6. What conclusions can be drawn from a footmark examination?
7. Identify the areas of friction ridge skin. Which can be used for identification purposes?
8. When was the first case of a bare footprint in a criminal case?
9. Compare and contrast the development of the friction ridge skin on the hands and the feet.
10. How does the development of the foot effect the development and use of friction ridge skin for identification?
11. What is the major pattern area of the foot called?
12. What flow patterns do most feet exhibit in the weight-bearing region of the foot?
13. How often does the heel present patterns?
14. Are creases useful for identification purposes? Why or why not?
15. How long has friction ridge skin on the palms been studied?
16. Which region of the palm is the most complex?
17. How does the friction ridge skin of the fingers compare to that of the palm area? Why would this be?
18. What is the value of the study of Maceo et al. to palm print examinations?
19. List the regions of the palm.
20. Why should the terms fibular and tibular be used instead of radial and ulnar?

Discussion Questions

1. In what kinds of cases can footmarks be useful? Why is this?
2. Can footmarks provide identification to the same level as fingerprints? Why or why not?
3. Consider the circumstances of the Iavaroni case from Brooklyn in 1959. How would that case likely be resolved now? What differences would there be in timeliness and accuracy given the methods used?
4. Given fingerprints, footmarks, and palm prints at a crime scene, which would be most probative? Why?
5. If fingerprints are a valid form of identification, does that validity transfer or translate to palm and footprints? Why or why not?

Additional Readings

Burrow, J.G., 2015. Ghosting of images in barefoot exemplar prints collection: issues for analyses. Journal of Forensic Identification 65 (5), 884.

Section 7. Professional Issues

Like any other forensic science, fingerprints require a high level of professionalism. Identifying or excluding individuals, whether suspects or victims, in criminal cases is an awesome responsibility and will effect the lives of many for decades. The various chemicals and materials used to visualize latent prints require health and safety awareness and expertise. Fingerprint examiners enjoy the luxury of working with an evidence type that is readily understood and appreciated; this does not change the examiner's responsibility to write reports and provide testimonies that are intelligible and accurate.

Crime Scene to Court

K Ramsey and E Burton, Greater Manchester Police Forensic Services Branch, Manchester, UK

Glossary

CBRN Chemical, biological, radiation, and nuclear incidents.
CCTV Closed circuit television (cameras or evidence from).
CPD Continuous professional development.
CPS Crown Prosecution Service (UK).
HTCU Hi-tech crime unit (examination of hardware/software/data/images from any system or device).
L2 Level 2 investigations, specific skills required for, e.g., covert operations, deployment and substitution of items, forensic markers.
LCH Local Clearing House (firearms).
NABIS National Ballistics Intelligence Service (UK).
NCA National Crime Agency (UK).
NOS National Occupational Standards.
T1/2/3 CSI Skill tiers defined for crime scene investigation officers, with 1 being the most basic level of training (usually volume crime offenses only); 2 being the range of volume, serious, and major crime investigations; and 3 being trained in crime scene management/the coordination of complex investigations.
VSC/ESDA Video spectral comparison—the analysis of inks, primarily in fraudulent documents; electrostatic detection analysis—the examination of (writing) indentations on paper.

Introduction

A multitude of disciplines evolved within forensic science during the twentieth century, resulting in highly specialized fields of evidential opportunities to support criminal investigations. Many of the more traditional disciplines, for example, footwear analysis and blood pattern interpretation, now have well-established principles and methodologies that have been proven in a criminal justice context; developments in these areas are largely confined to technical support systems and information sharing through databases. The very rapid rate of development of DNA profiling techniques during the 1980s and 1990s led to the emergence of national and international DNA databases; however, the pace of change has now significantly reduced. Conversely, the end of the twentieth century and the early part of the twenty-first century have seen an explosion of new forensic evidence types that are less established in court—disciplines such as CCTV, mobile phone, computer analysis, and the use of digital images and social media are collectively referred to as e-forensics.

Owing to the highly specialized nature of each forensic discipline and the varied rate of evolution, forensic science

 http://dx.doi.org/10.1016/B978-0-12-800573-6.00020-3

effectively represents a composite of interrelated, and often distinct, opportunities to support criminal investigations.

Most current models of forensic service delivery, especially where part of a wider organization, for example, police forces and enforcement agencies, have arisen over time by bolting on additional elements and clustering together within related fields. If the current capability of forensic science were to be designed from scratch as an effective entity, it is certain that a more integrated, and hence effective, structure would be proposed.

In addition, there has been a professionalization of forensic science in the workplace and increasing requirements for regulation; as recently as the 1980s, crime scene investigation, for example, was widely undertaken by police officers and was largely restricted to recording/recovering visible evidence; this was used in a limited capacity to support that particular investigation without scope for wider intelligence development. Now, crime scene investigation is predominantly undertaken by specialist staff employed to exclusively undertake these duties.

To practice in a forensic discipline, specialized training, qualifications, and competency levels are required. The range of evidence types that have potential to support investigations has widened considerably. Some disciplines lend themselves to cross-skilling.

Public expectations of what forensic science can deliver have been heightened by highly popular mainstream television programs, both documentary and fictional. Often, the expectation of what can be delivered exceeds what is either possible or financially sensible. This leads to a requirement on service providers and users to make informed (evidential and financial) decisions regarding the best use of forensic evidence in support of investigations.

This article considers options to optimize the use of forensic evidence types recovered from crime scenes in the context of the different models available to criminal justice systems; the concept of integrated case management is outlined and discussed.

Task

To bring together all potential forensic evidential opportunities, holistically review their significance to the investigation, prioritize the progression of work, deliver the best evidence to the court for testing (complying with all continuity, integrity, and quality requirements), and ensure the best value for money when determining spend on forensic evidence.

Internationally, there are variable constraints and opportunities due both to the different criminal justice models and the commercial market situation at state/regional and country levels.

Models

1. All forensic evidence sourced within a law enforcement agency, for example, a police laboratory.
2. All forensic evidence provided by external specialists contracted to a law enforcement agency.
3. Composite of (1) and (2).

Forensic Strategies

The recovery of evidence from the crime scene is only the start of the forensic process. Once the evidence has been collected, packaged, and preserved, it needs to be analyzed in order to provide meaningful information to the investigation and subsequently to the courts.

Forensic examinations are carried out in order to implicate or eliminate individuals and also in order to establish what has occurred during the commission of an offense or incident.

Deciding what analysis is required can be a complex process. Some of the issues for consideration include the following:

- Is it necessary to examine all the evidence that is recovered?
- Should every possible test be carried out?

In an ideal world, it would be preferable to carry out every possible analysis; however, in reality, it is likely that this will be neither practicable nor financially viable. In addition, carrying out every possible analysis would overload forensic laboratories.

When making decisions about what forensic analysis should be carried out, it is vitally important that consideration is given to both the potential prosecution and defense cases. An impartial approach must be taken to assessing examination requirements. It is often not necessary to carry out an examination of every item of evidence recovered, but examinations should be directed to where value could potentially be added to an investigation.

A forensic strategy should be developed around every case where forensic evidence plays a part and may relate to an overall case or to an individual item of evidence. A forensic strategy should be developed in a holistic manner taking into account all potential evidence types and should direct and coordinate the forensic examinations/analyses that are required.

Forensic strategies can be developed in different ways by one or more of the following:

- Investigating officer
- Crime scene investigator (CSI) or crime scene manager
- Forensic scientist/forensic specialist
- Forensic submissions officer (forensic submissions officer is a role that can be variably named; this role relates to an

informed individual within a police force or law enforcement agency who uses knowledge and expertise to advise on forensic analysis and who has decision-making authority and control of the budgetary spend. He/she may also be known as forensic advisor, scientific support manager, etc.)
- Legal representative
- Pathologist

Forensic strategies are generally initially developed and applied by individuals involved in the prosecution aspects of a crime. Although this is the case, it is vitally important that a balanced and unbiased approach is taken to the development of a strategy and consideration is given to information that may support the defense case as well as the prosecution case. Examinations that are likely to add value or provide information to an investigation (irrespective of whether it will support or weaken the prosecution case) should be carried out and all results must be disclosed to the defense team. Defense should also be given the opportunity to carry out any review of strategies, examination processes, and/or results that they require and be provided with access to any items of evidence that they want to examine themselves in order to build the defense case.

In order to develop the forensic strategy and make appropriate decisions about which forensic examinations will be of value to the investigation, the following are necessary:

- To be able to gather as much information as possible about the circumstances of the case
  - circumstances of evidence recovery
  - accounts given by victim(s), witnesses, suspect(s), etc.
- To have an understanding and knowledge of forensic science and its application to investigations

A forensic strategy meeting is a useful way of ensuring that all relevant parties are aware of the full circumstances of the case and enables a "multiagency" discussion about the processing of all exhibits to optimize evidential potential in a comprehensive and coordinated manner.

It can often be the case that police officers do not have a full understanding or knowledge of forensic science, likewise forensic scientists historically have had a relatively poor understanding of police and investigative processes; this can lead to miscommunication and confusion in relation to the application of forensic science to meet investigative needs. A joint approach to the development of forensic strategies helps to improve the communication and understanding on a case-by-case basis.

A formal forensic strategy meeting is often required only in more serious cases; however, the general approach can be applied to any investigation. Even in the most simple of cases, it is often beneficial for discussions to take place between the investigating officer, the CSI, the forensic advisor/budget holder/decision maker, and the prosecutor. Alternatively, generic strategies can be implemented; for example, for a particular crime type or modus operandi.

When making an assessment regarding the potential examination of a particular item and the development of a forensic strategy, the requirements of the investigation are the primary concern and consideration should be given to the following issues:

- The type and nature of the item/exhibit
- The context of the item
  - Exactly where and when it was recovered
  - Condition of the item, that is, wet, damaged, etc.
- The integrity of the item
  - Has it been appropriately recovered, handled, packaged, and preserved?
  - Is the security and continuity of the item intact?
- The potential evidence that may be obtained from the item; for example, DNA, fingerprints, fibers, footwear marks
- The information these evidence types may provide to the investigation
- Whether this potential information is likely to add value to the investigation
  - Is it possible that new information will be provided?
  - Is it possible that an account given by a witness, victim, or suspect will be supported or refuted?
  - Will the information help to establish what has occurred?
- Whether there is a conflict between potential evidence types, and if so, which evidence type will be of most value under the circumstances?
  - For example, swabbing/taping for DNA may damage fingerprints, but where the DNA is likely to be at low levels and requires specialized low-template DNA analysis, the presence of DNA may not necessarily prove contact with an item, whereas fingerprints will always prove that contact has occurred
- The chances of success, that is, obtaining a result/information of value to the investigation (this may be inclusive or exclusive)

Much work has historically been completed in relation to developing and understanding the success rates relating to DNA profiling; however, relatively little work has been undertaken to fully understand the success rates associated with other forensic evidence. This is largely due to the fact that other evidence types, such as fibers, gunshot residue, footwear marks, etc., are generally more complex to interpret than DNA. In relation to DNA profiling, success rates are generally based on the chances of obtaining a DNA profile; however, with the other evidence types, the value of the outcome is very much dependent on the circumstances of the investigation. For example, when searching an item of clothing taken from a suspect for glass, the absence of glass or the presence of glass could both be of value to the investigation depending on the circumstances. The presence of glass on the clothing that matches control sample(s) from the crime scene is only of value if its presence cannot be accounted for in any legitimate way; conversely, the absence of glass on the item of clothing may lead to a conclusion that the suspect was not involved in the offense, depending on the circumstances of the offense and arrest.

In addition to being able to understand and evaluate the chances of being able to obtain a meaningful result, it is also vital that the value of the overall contribution to the entire case is understood. This involves being able to understand the value and contribution of the forensic examination to the detection of the offense as well as the outcome of the court process. This is an even more difficult issue to evaluate and understand than the chances of being able to obtain a forensic test result.

Because the value of forensic evidence is so dependent on the individual case circumstances, decisions about examinations must be made on an individual case basis. There have been recent developments in some agencies/forces to better understand the chances of success of different types of forensic evidence and the value to investigations; this will help to better inform decisions about evidential potential and examination viability as well as assisting to achieve value for money. This approach is best described as *forensic effectiveness.*

The forensic strategy should also take into account the timescales associated with the investigative process and the criminal justice system, and it should be ensured that forensic analysis can meet the requirements of the criminal justice process, including court dates and any requirements to disclose appropriate information to the defense team(s).

Each police force/law enforcement agency will have its own approach to the submission of exhibits for forensic

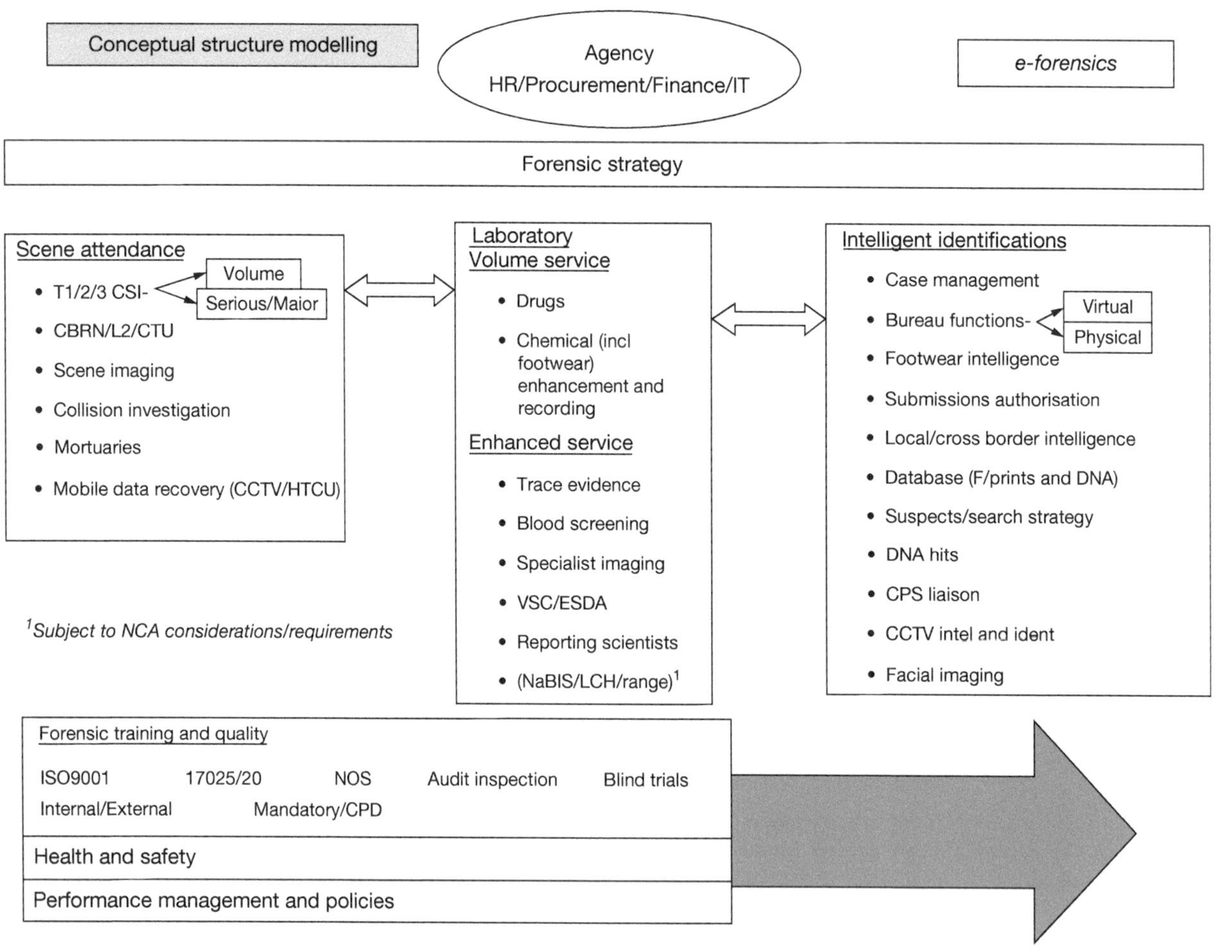

Figure 1 Conceptual structure modeling.

examination/analysis; irrespective of whether the analysis is carried out in an internal police laboratory, external commercial company, or government-owned laboratory, these approaches can be applied to all examinations and all evidence types.

These approaches help to ensure that decisions are made based on scientific knowledge, viability, and evidential value taking into account all aspects of the investigation. They will help to ensure that the best evidence is obtained while considering value for money and that it can be applied to any investigation irrespective of the seriousness of the offense or the scale of the investigation.

Integrated Case Management

The concept and use of forensic strategies in directing investigations is not new, but is often limited by the evolved structure of forensic disciplines within investigative agencies. Classically, DNA and fingerprint evidence from volume crimes will be independently submitted at the same time by different routes and this often results in wasted effort/spends and duplicated results. The development and use of forensic intelligence has been variable. Emerging thinking includes organizational redesign of forensics to better integrate with related functions such as intelligence collection, targeted deployment of resources, and prioritized forensic submissions.

The concept of integrated case management draws together informed operational deployment (e.g., of crime scene investigators) followed by a more holistic approach to submissions for testing. The strategy takes greater account of supporting intelligence and desired outcomes. Regular reviews and trigger points are included for the staged submission of potential evidence, and communication with investigators is enhanced so allowing for a more responsive and directed investigation.

Ultimately, the production of *intelligent identifications* can be better achieved by having an integrated process that links the enforcement priorities, available resources, potential forensic evidence, intelligence, and prosecutor requirements; this model provides flexibility to respond to changing demands and gives an increased likelihood of efficient and effective spend on forensic support to investigations. There is no single way to achieve this, but an illustration of how to rethink some of the traditional silo-based forensic disciplines is provided in **Figure 1**.

Summary

The single biggest challenge to the forensic science community during the twenty-first century is to modernize delivery of integrated services in support of investigations. This must:

- build on the previous development of each discipline;
- accommodate the new and emerging technological disciplines;
- meet the regulatory requirements;
- reflect the changing workforce and skills;
- deliver the best evidence to courts in support of investigations.

See also: **Foundations:** Forensic Intelligence; History of Forensic Sciences; Principles of Forensic Science.

Further Reading

Faigman, et al., 2006. Modern Scientific Evidence: The Law and Science of Expert Testimony.

Fisher, B.A.J., Fisher, D.R., 2012. Techniques of Crime Scene Investigation, eighth ed. CRC, Boca Raton, FL.

Houck, M., Crispino, F., McAdam, T., 2013. The Science of Crime Scenes. Elsevier.

Innocence Project, 2011. http://www.innocenceproject.org/Content/Facts_on_PostConviction_DNA_Exonerations.php (accessed 10.03.11.).

Kirk, P.L., 1974. In: Thornton, J.L. (Ed.), Crime Investigation, second ed. Wiley, New York. (1985 reprint edn. Malabar, FL: Krieger Publishing Company).

NAS, 2009. Strengthening Forensic Science in the United States: A Path Forward. NAS Report: Committee on Identifying the Needs of the Forensic Sciences Community. National Academies Press, Washington, DC.

White, P., 2010. Crime Scene to Court: The Essentials of Forensic Science. Royal Society of Chemistry, Cambridge, ISBN 978-1-84755-882-4.

Forensic Laboratory Reports

J Epstein, Widener University School of Law, Wilmington, DE, USA

There is no precise formula, dictated by law or science, as to what a forensic laboratory report must contain when it reports test results or analysis outcomes. Its content may be determined by the individual examiner's predilections, internal laboratory policy, the law of the jurisdiction, accreditation organization standards, or the reason(s) for its production. What can be said with certainty is that by understanding the current criticism of the practice of producing forensic laboratory reports and trends in standards for reports, and by considering the use to which the report may be put in the court process and the legal and ethical commands regarding reporting and, more generally, the duties of the forensic scientist, a model for forensic laboratory reports can be identified.

Before discussing these factors, it bears mention that the term "report" itself lacks clarity, as it may refer to the complete case file documenting the examination or just to the compilation of results. For this article, the term "report" denotes the latter—the document prepared for the consumer (the investigator, counsel, or court official who directed that the examination and testing be conducted). Even this report may vary in degree of detail, as there can be the summary report advising the requesting party of the outcome; a more formal report prepared for disclosure to the court or opposing counsel as part of pretrial discovery; an amplification of the initial discovery-generated report when it is determined that the expert will in fact testify; and a report that will be presented in lieu of actual testimony. Additional documentation may include an administrative or dispositional report detailing the receipt or return of the item(s) sent for analysis.

What must also be acknowledged is that the expert's role in the adjudicative process is in some ways defined by whether the system is adversarial, with the expert being called by the party seeking to establish a point, as in the United States; or "inquisitorial/common law," where the expert is a court witness, presumed to be neutral, and without allegiance to a particular party, as in France, Belgium, and Germany. These demarcations are not always adhered to, as American law permits a trial judge to appoint and take testimony from a "court" expert under Federal Rule of Evidence 706, and in some cases involving offenses of fraud and falsification, as France permits competing experts. These differing roles, however, do not alter the necessary components of a forensic laboratory report (and, as is detailed below); both ethical and legal considerations as well as a commitment to the role of science may require the report to be neutral and to acknowledge any limitations and/or weaknesses.

Contents of a Report—A "Science" Standard

At least in the United States, there has been substantial criticism of forensic laboratory reporting. This is found in *Strengthening Forensic Science: A Path Forward*, the 2009 report of the National Research Council of the National Academy of Sciences. After reporting that forensic laboratory reports lack precise terminology, it concluded that most laboratory reports do not meet the standard it proposed:

> As a general matter, laboratory reports generated as the result of a scientific analysis should be complete and thorough. They should describe, at a minimum, methods and materials, procedures, results, and conclusions, and they should identify, as appropriate, the sources of uncertainty in the procedures and conclusions along with estimates of their scale (to indicate the level of confidence in the results). Although it is not appropriate and practicable to provide as much detail as might be expected in a research paper, sufficient content should be provided to allow the nonscientist reader to understand what has been done and permit informed and unbiased scrutiny of the conclusion.

This criticism does not stand in isolation. A 2011 British court decision also expressed concern over the sufficiency of detail and documentation in a forensic (latent print) prosecution. After noting the failure of the examiner to contemporaneously record "detailed notes of his examination and the reasons for his conclusions[,]" the court added that "[t]he quality of the reports provided by the Nottinghamshire Fingerprint Bureau for the trial reflected standards that existed in other areas of forensic science some years ago, and not the vastly improved standards expected in contemporary forensic science."

The Nuclear Regulatory Commission (NRC) standard is more detailed than that of various forensic organizations. ASCLD/LAB, for example, requires that only written reports be generated for "all analytical work" and must contain conclusions and opinions and a clear communication of "the significance of associations made…."

 http://dx.doi.org/10.1016/B978-0-12-800573-6.00021-5

Other standards address the need for full documentation, but do not distinguish between a laboratory's bench notes and the final product. For example, International Organization for Standardization's ISO/IEC Standard 5.10.5 requires that "the laboratory shall document the basis upon which the opinions and interpretations have been made" without specifying where that information is to be recorded. Similar language is used for ballistics reports, as recommended by the Scientific Working Group on firearms (SWGGUN) requiring that "[w]hen opinions and interpretations are included, the laboratory shall document the basis upon which the opinions and interpretations have been made. Opinions and interpretations shall be clearly marked as such in the test report."

Yet, the more detailed mandate urged by the NRC report is not unique. Scholars and agencies have articulated similar or at least substantial standards. A publication of *The Royal Society of Chemistry* (RSC) in 2004 suggested the following information as appropriate for inclusion in an expert report:

- A summary of the event to contextualize the scientific test(s);
- An outline of the scientific work conducted;
- A listing of items examined;
- Description of the work performed;
- A statement interpreting the findings; and
- An overall conclusion.

The RSC text also urges that the report identifies the assistants in the testing and the role each played and includes appendices with tables or similar displays of test results.

For DNA analysis, the Federal Bureau of Investigation's standards for DNA laboratories require reports to include a description of the evidence examined and the technology, results and/or conclusions, and a "quantitative or qualitative interpretative statement."

One final scientific issue regarding the contents of a report is the concern over bias. Research has shown that information received by the analyst might affect his/her judgment, as when the examiner receives domain-irrelevant information such as the fact that the suspect whose fingerprints are being examined "confessed to the crime" or when the verification is not "blind." Documentation of such information in a laboratory report (or the bench notes) is one responsive action, as is an internal laboratory policy to reduce analyst or verifier exposure to potentially biasing information.

Contents of Report: Legal Standards

That which science requires is to some extent mirrored in legal requirements for expert reports. These vary from nation to nation and within nations when states or regions have their own authority to legislate criminal practice.

In the United Kingdom, Rule 33.3, Criminal Procedure Rules 2010, mandates contents of a full report, that is, one for submission in court, as follows:

1. The findings on which they have relied in making the report or statement;
2. Details of which of the findings stated in the report or statement are within their own knowledge, which were obtained as a result of examinations, measurements, tests, etc., carried out by another person and whether or not those examinations, measurements, tests, etc., were carried out under the expert's supervision;
3. The identity, qualifications, relevant experience, and any certification of the person who carried out the examination, measurement, test, etc.;
4. Details of any statements of fact, literature, or other information upon which they have relied, either to identify the examination or test requirements, or which are material to the opinions expressed in the report or statement or upon which those opinions are based;
5. A summary of the conclusions and opinions reached and a rationale for these;
6. A statement that if any of the information on which their conclusions or opinions are based changes then the conclusions or opinions will have to be reviewed;
7. Where there is a range of opinion on the matters dealt with in the report or statement, a summary of the range of opinion, and reasons for the expert's own opinion;
8. Any information that may cast doubt on their interpretation or opinion; and
9. If the expert is not able to give an opinion without qualification, what the qualification is.

Much less specific is the legislated mandate for federal criminal prosecutions in the United States. Under Federal Rule of Criminal Procedure 16, the Government must permit the defense to inspect and to copy or photograph the results or reports of any scientific test or experiment and must produce before trial a written summary of any proposed expert testimony that describes the witness's opinions, the bases and reasons for those opinions, and the witness's qualifications. Defense counsel in criminal cases has a reciprocal disclosure requirement. Despite the seeming generality of these terms, American courts have at times interpreted them to require some greater detail in the reports, such as underlying documentation.

In the United States, an additional requirement derived from the Constitution's guarantee of Due Process of Law may affect what must be included in a laboratory report issued by a police or other government agency. The prosecution must disclose information that is "favorable to the accused" and "material either to guilt or to punishment" as well as "evidence that the defense might have used to impeach the Government's witnesses by showing bias or interest." This extends to "evidence affecting credibility[.]" This information is generally denominated "Brady material."

The applicability of these rules to official (police or state) laboratories is settled. The US Supreme Court has held that the disclosure obligation extends to police agencies working with the prosecution, and this has been extended to forensic examiners. Hence, in a report or some other communication, a forensic examiner in government employ must ensure that "Brady material" is disclosed.

What remains to be defined are the terms "exculpatory" or "impeachment" information. The core of each is easily described. Evidence is "exculpatory" if it tends to reduce the degree of guilt or question proof of culpability; "impeachment" information is proof of a bias or interest, or otherwise information that could be used to contradict or attack the credibility of the analyst or report. This type of disclosure parallels that of forensic laboratory reports imposed by the United Kingdom's evidence code. The code requires inclusion in the report of "a summary of the range of opinion and reasons for the expert's own opinion; [] any information that may cast doubt on their interpretation or opinion; and if the expert is not able to give an opinion without qualification, what the qualification is."

Reports: Stand-Alone Evidence or Support for a Testifying Expert

Whether a laboratory report may stand on its own as evidence in a trial, or instead must be accompanied by testimony of the forensic analyst, is a function of the law of the jurisdiction in which the case is tried. In the United States, a prosecution expert's report may not be admitted on its own, as this is deemed to violate the defendant's right to confront adverse witnesses. The Supreme Court in Melendez-Diaz versus Massachusetts held that a certificate of analysis fell within the core class of testimonial statements because it was a solemn "declaration or affirmation made for the purpose of establishing or proving some fact." In the 2011 follow-up of the Melendez-Diaz decision, the Court further held that another lab analyst may not come in to testify to the report's contents, at least where the other analyst neither supervised nor observed the initial testing. (This applies only to prosecution expert reports, as in the United States only the defendant has a guarantee of the right to confront witnesses. Admissibility of a defense forensic report without examiner testimony would be determined by the state's rules of evidence, but is generally unheard of.)

At the same time, the confrontation right does not mean that the analyst must testify. A state may create a notice and demand statute under which the prosecution notifies the defendant of its intent to use an analyst's report as evidence at trial, after which the defendant has a specified period of time in which to demand the expert's live testimony. A defendant's failure to "demand" waives the need for the analyst's presence and allows use of the report. As well, an accused may always agree to stipulate to the report's content, eliminating the need for any live testimony.

The Melendez-Diaz approach is not followed uniformly on an international basis. Canada permits proof by means of an expert report, without live testimony, where the proponent of the report has provided it to the opposing party and the trial court recognizes the author as a legitimate expert. The court retains discretion to mandate the expert's appearance for cross-examination. Australia's Evidence Act of 1995 similarly authorizes expert proof by certificate, but the opposing party may require the offering side to "call the person who signed the certificate to give evidence." In the United Kingdom, expert reports are themselves admissible as evidence, subject to the judge's discretion in requiring the analyst or examiner to appear.

Ethical Considerations and Forensic Reports

The decision of what to include in a forensic laboratory report, beyond that required by law or by science, may be informed by ethical considerations. Forensics organizations often have ethical codes, but they may be silent as to the particulars of report writing. Illustrative is the Code of the American Board of Criminalistics, which only asserts general obligations such as "[e]nsure that a full and complete disclosure of the findings is made to the submitting agency[.]" Other codes may not mention reporting at all but instead address only the delivery of information without distinguishing between the written report and a courtroom presentation of evidence. An exception is that of the Australian and New Zealand Forensic Science Society, Inc., which requires that a report be nonpartisan when results are ambiguous. "Where test results or conclusions are capable of being interpreted to the advantage of either side in a legal proceeding, each result or conclusion should be given weight according to its merit."

Ethical considerations may also be imposed by law. In the United Kingdom, the expert is deemed to hold only one allegiance, that to the court, regardless of the party who retained the individual. Specific ethical obligations are imposed for written reports. First, where there is a range of opinion, the expert must summarize the various positions. Second, if the opinion rendered cannot be given without qualification, the expert must disclose that and state the qualifying aspects or concerns.

Conclusion

Within and across nations, there is no clear standard for forensic reports intended for court use, except where prescribed by law. What should be manifest is that the more detailed the report, and thus the more it is capable of rigorous assessment by an independent expert evaluator, the more credibility will be attributed to both the results and the examiner.

See also: **Legal:** History of the Law's Reception of Forensic Science; Legal Aspects of Forensic Science; Legal Systems: Adversarial and Inquisitorial; **Management/Quality in Forensic Science:** *Sequential Unmasking*: Minimizing Observer Effects in Forensic Science; **Professional:** Ethics.

Further Reading

Codes of Practice and Conduct for Forensic Science Providers and Practitioners in the Criminal Justice System 44–45 (United Kingdom). http://www.homeoffice.gov.uk/publications/police/forensic-science-regulator1/quality-standards-codes-practice?view=Binary.

Dror, I.E., Cole, S., 2010. The vision in 'blind' justice: expert perception, judgment and visual cognition in forensic pattern recognition. Psychonomic Bulletin and Review 17 (2), 161–167.

Dror, I.E., Rosenthal, R., 2008. Meta-analytically quantifying the reliability and biasability of forensic experts. Journal of Forensic Sciences 53 (4), 900–903.

National Research Council, 2009. Strengthening Forensic Science in the United States: A Path Forward. National Academies Press, Washington, DC. http://www.ncjrs.gov/pdffiles1/nij/grants/228091.pdf.

Quality Assurance Standards for Forensic DNA Testing Laboratories, Standard 11.2. http://www.cstl.nist.gov/strbase/QAS/Final-FBI-Director-Forensic-Standards.pdf.

Reviewing Historical Practices of Forensic Science Laboratories, September 29, 2010. http://www.ascld.org/.

Rothwell, T., 2004. Presentation of expert forensic evidence. In: White, P. (Ed.), Crime Scene to Court: The Essentials of Forensic Science, second ed. RSC, Cambridge, pp. 430–432 (Chapter 15).

Spencer, J.R., 2002. Evidence. European Criminal Procedures. Cambridge University Press, New York, pp. 632–635 (Chapter 15).

Relevant Websites

http://www.criminalistics.com/ethics.cfm—American Board of Criminalistics, Rules of Professional Conduct.

http://www.forensicdna.com/Media/Bias_FS.htm—An Extended List of Articles on the Issue of Bias in Forensic Examinations.

http://www.afte.org/AssociationInfo/a_codeofethics.htm—Association of Firearms and Toolmarks Examiners, AFTE Code of Ethics.

http://www.anzfss.org.au/code_of_ethics.htm—Australian and New Zealand Forensic Science Society.

http://www.iso.org/iso/home.html—International Organization for Standardization.

http://www.swggun.org/swg/index.php?option=com_content&view=article&id=25:transition-from-ascldlab-legacy-to-isoiec-17025&catid=10:guidelines-adopted&Itemid=6—SWGGUN, Transition from ASCLD/LAB Legacy to ISO/IEC 17025.

http://www.ascld.org/—The American Society of Crime Laboratory Directors.

http://www.ascld-lab.org/—The American Society of Crime Laboratory Directors Laboratory Accreditation Board.

http://webarchive.nationalarchives.gov.uk/+/http://www.justice.gov.uk/criminal/procrules_fin/contents/rules/part_33.htm—United Kingdom, Criminal Procedure Rules 2010.

Health and Safety

N Scudder and B Saw, Australian Federal Police, Canberra, ACT, Australia

Glossary

Clandestine laboratory ("Clan Labs") Setting up of equipment or supplies for the manufacture of illegal compounds such as drugs or explosives.

Confined space An enclosed or partially enclosed space that is not intended or designed primarily for human occupancy, within which there is a risk of one or more of the following: (1) an oxygen concentration outside the safe oxygen range. (2) A concentration of airborne contaminant that may cause impairment, loss of consciousness, or asphyxiation. (3) A concentration of flammable airborne contaminant that may cause injury from fire or explosion. (4) Engulfment in a stored free-flowing solid or a rising level of liquid that may cause suffocation or drowning.

Dynamic risk management The continuous assessment of risk in the rapidly changing circumstances of an operational incident, in order to implement the control measures necessary to ensure an acceptable level of safety.

Hazard The potential for a substance to cause adverse effects.

Hierarchy of control measures Ranking of measures taken to prevent or reduce hazard exposure according to effectiveness, from the most effective measures that eliminate hazards to the least effective, that achieve only limited protection.

OHS policy A policy document indicating an organization's commitment to OHS, its intentions, objectives, and priorities and identifying roles and responsibilities.

Risk The likelihood of injury or illness arising from exposure to any hazard(s) and the magnitude of the adverse effect.

Occupational Health and Safety Policy

The legislation in many countries places the onus of responsibility on employers to provide a healthy and safe working environment under occupational health and safety (OHS) legislation and common law. Employers should ensure that all managers, supervisors, and staff are aware of their OHS responsibilities. Management leadership can positively influence OHS outcomes for an organization.

Workplace health and safety is an ongoing process. Subject to the legislative requirements of each jurisdiction, in most instances a documented OHS policy is required. The development of such a policy requires the commitment of both staff and management. Once commitment has been achieved, the OHS policy should be developed with involvement from all stakeholders, and promulgated.

The OHS policy should:

- articulate the organization's commitment to OHS;
- indicate that sufficient resources (both financial and personnel) will be provided to promote and maintain OHS standards and meet OHS requirements;
- outline the organization's intentions, objectives, and priorities OHS;
- describe in broad terms the means by which the objectives will be met;
- identify the roles and responsibilities of management, supervisors, and staff in meeting OHS requirements; and
- be signed off by the most senior manager of the organization, reflecting the importance of the policy.

The OHS policy should be reviewed periodically to ensure its currency.

The OHS policy is, however, only one part of an appropriate OHS strategy for a forensic organization. The OHS policy must be underpinned by risk assessments and incident/accident reports that enable the organization to assess its OHS exposure, to meet legislative requirements such as reporting obligations, and to respond to risks appropriately.

An organization can develop a list of the main hazards that its staff are likely to be exposed to in the course of their duties, utilizing OHS reports, incident/accident reports, and previous risk assessments. Prioritizing the main health and safety issues allows the organization to develop appropriate action plans to meet the objectives of its OHS policy.

Forensic organizations may consider integration of some OHS requirements with their quality assurance system. Many laboratories effectively use their quality system to embed OHS

 http://dx.doi.org/10.1016/B978-0-12-800573-6.00022-7

requirements in their documented procedures, to review OHS hazards as part of a periodic audit program, or to manage elements of their OHS action plans through their corrective action system. OHS, like quality, can then be viewed as an important yet integrated component of an effective management system.

Risk Assessments

Once potential OHS hazards have been identified, forensic organizations should evaluate the likelihood of injury from the interaction to the hazard and the magnitude of the adverse effect. The process of risk assessment will be very useful for managing potential OHS hazards within the facility and the expected external work environment. The purpose of the risk assessment process is to ensure that all workplace hazards have been identified, recorded, assessed, controlled, and reviewed. The desired outcome of this process is to eliminate, as far as practicable, the risk of injury or illness to personnel, damage to property, and damage to the environment. The process of developing risk assessment is often better suited to the known work environment. An OHS assessment of an office or laboratory can quickly identify specific hazards that may require attention. Obviously, this works well for the office and laboratory environment within one's control; however, each external scene will be different.

It is important that the range of potential hazards in external crime scenes and work environments is considered. While some risks can be grouped and managed collectively, the specific hazard and risk mitigation and control will vary from scene to scene given the circumstances. Given this, forensic practitioners should have an ability to undertake dynamic risk assessments, or "risk on the run" as it is known in some jurisdictions.

Dynamic Risk Management

Dynamic risk assessments are conducted by a forensic practitioner as part of the attendance and examination process. In some instances, such as attendance at a clan lab, a person may be designated as the Site Safety Officer and have carriage of this as well as health and safety for all personnel at the site. Practitioners should be trained to assess the risk given the circumstances at the time, considering the actual hazards present at a crime scene.

A designated forensic practitioner or Site Safety Officer should undertake a quick reconnaissance of the crime scene to ensure the safety of forensic practitioners and others working at the scene. A review of the scene should be repeated whenever the situation at the scene changes. This could involve a visual inspection without entering the crime scene and asking a number of questions. For example:

- Does the crime scene involve structures that are now unstable?
- Has confirmation been obtained from the Fire Brigade or other emergency responders that power, gas, and water to the site have been turned off?
- Is there adequate shelter so that practitioners can rest without succumbing to environmental stressors such as heat, cold, wind, or rain?

It is important to close the loop and incorporate any strategic elements of each dynamic risk assessment in OHS policy and planning. After each incident, any relevant information obtained during the dynamic risk assessment should be recorded and collated for strategic analysis.

Hierarchy of Control Measures

Within OHS, there is a "hierarchy of control" designed to mitigate or resolve a risk deemed unacceptably high.

The hierarchy of control is a sequence of options which offer a number of ways to approach the hazard control process. Various control options may be available. It is important to choose the control that most effectively eliminates the hazard or minimizes the risk in the circumstances. This may involve a single control measure or a combination of different controls that together provide the highest level of protection that is reasonably practicable.

1. Eliminate the hazard. If this is not practical, then:
2. Substitute the hazard with a lesser risk. If this is not practical, then:
3. Isolate the hazard. If this is not practical, then:
4. Use engineering controls. If this is not practical, then:
5. Use administrative controls, such as safe work practices, instruction, and training. If this is not practical, then:
6. Use personal protective equipment (PPE), such as gloves, eye protection, boots, and respirators.

It is important that management and staff discuss and consult, where possible, during all phases of the hazard identification, risk assessment and risk control process.

Examples

1. If an organization is considering purchasing a piece of analytical equipment, and two products have the same capabilities but substantially different noise levels during operation, the organization may consider the noise level of the equipment during procurement and opt for the quieter system. This example demonstrates the principle of

eliminating the hazard at source, which is the most effective control measure, when compared to training and provision of PPE such as hearing protection.

2. In the case of a fire scene of a building, applying a hierarchy of control approach, it is first necessary to consider the elimination or substitution of hazards. In a fire scene, this is not possible. It is, however, possible to isolate the scene to prevent danger to the public and to maintain the integrity of the scene. Power, water, and gas to a building should be disconnected prior to entering the site. A structural engineer's opinion may be necessary prior to entry to the building. Safe entry and exit to the site can be established. Other administrative controls, such as briefing practitioners and maintaining records of the entry and exit of personnel, may be applied. Finally, practitioners can be prevented from entering the fire scene unless utilizing the appropriate PPE.

Specific Laboratory Hazards

The likely hazards within a laboratory environment include the following.

Chemicals

Chemical exposure may occur through inhalation, skin absorption, or direct ingestion and, once absorbed, are either stored in a particular organ or tissue, metabolized, or excreted. The effect of a chemical on a person is dependent on a number of factors such as duration and frequency of exposure, concentration of the chemical, and an individual's metabolism. A synergistic effect may occur when the undesirable effects of one substance are intensified if exposure has occurred to another substance.

Some nanomaterials exhibit different chemical properties compared to what they exhibit on a macroscale. As this is a relatively new field, there is insufficient knowledge regarding the hazards posed by nanomaterials. The potential hazards associated with nanomaterials may include increased reactivity because of their increased surface-area-to-volume ratio, the ability to cross some of the body's protective mechanism, and the lack of the body's immunity against such small particles. Because of this lack of knowledge, the suggested control strategy to be used when working with nanomaterials should be "as low as reasonably achievable" (ALARA) approach to reduce exposure.

The effects of chemicals on the body may be categorized:

- poisonous or toxic chemicals are absorbed into the body and exert either an acute or short-term effect, such as headache, nausea, or loss of consciousness, or a long-term effect such as liver or kidney damage, cancer, or chronic lung disease;
- corrosive chemicals burn the skin, eyes, or respiratory tract;
- irritants can inflame the skin or lungs, causing conditions such as dermatitis or bronchitis;
- sensitizers may exert long-term effects, especially to the skin (such as contact dermatitis) and to the respiratory tract (such as occupational asthma) by inducing an allergic reaction; and
- explosive or flammable substances pose immediate danger of fire and explosion, causing damage to the body through direct burning, or through inhalation of toxic fumes emitted during combustion.

Safety Data Sheets (SDS), also known as Material Safety Data Sheets (MSDS), are designed to provide relevant information regarding the identity, physical characteristics, safe storage, use, disposal, first aid treatment, and spill management of substances that are handled in the workplace. The information includes whether the substance is deemed to be a hazardous and/or a dangerous goods item. At a minimum, the SDS should be consulted before the first use of a chemical or other substance within a laboratory, or if practitioners are unfamiliar with the product. Copies of SDS should be retained according to legislative requirements. In some jurisdictions, electronic SDS management systems can allow an efficient way of accessing up-to-date SDS information.

Sharps

Sharps are objects that have sharp edges or points that have the potential to cut, scratch, or puncture the skin. Sharps can cause physical injury and have the potential to introduce infectious and toxic agents through the wounds created in the skin. Examples include hypodermic syringes and needles, knives, or broken glassware.

All forensic practitioners have a responsibility to handle and package sharps safely. Particular care should be given to ensuring that sharps are appropriately labeled when packaged. Sharps such as knives could, for example, be packaged in clear plastic tubes, making it easier for a person opening the item to identify the contents and the direction the sharp items are facing. Forensic labs should be encouraged to develop policies that encourage forensic practitioners and others that submit items to develop safe-packaging procedures.

Biological Material

Examples of "biological material" commonly encountered in forensic examinations include body tissue, blood, and body fluids (urine, saliva, vomit, pus, seminal fluid, vaginal fluid, and feces). Biological material is potentially hazardous as it may contain infectious agents such as viruses, bacteria, fungi, and parasites that cause a variety of communicable diseases.

Hair, fur, and items of clothing that have been in close contact with humans or animals may also harbor parasites such as fleas or nits.

When examining plant material such as cannabis, consideration should be given to the presence of *Aspergillus* sp. mold. If the *Aspergillus* spores are inhaled into the lungs, a serious, chronic respiratory or sinus infection can result. If mold is visible, the cannabis should be treated as a biological and respiratory hazard.

It is impossible to determine the prevalence of infectious or communicable diseases in the environment in which forensic practitioners work. Consequently, practitioners should adhere to recommended procedures for handling biological material and adopt an approach known as the "standard precautions." This approach requires practitioners to assume that all biological material is a potential source of infection, independent of diagnosis or perceived level of underlying risk.

Vaccinations should be offered for practitioners. The types of vaccinations given may depend on whether work is confined to the laboratory or whether work is performed in the field, as well as whether forensic practitioners are likely to be deployed overseas where other diseases may be more prevalent.

Firearms

Forensic practitioners may retrieve firearms from crime scenes. All personnel who may be required to handle firearms, either in the field, in the laboratory, or in support roles such as property or exhibit stores should be trained in how to render a firearm safe. As with the "standard precautions," it is important to consider all firearms as potentially loaded and adopt the practice of never pointing a firearm in the direction of another person, even after it has been rendered safe.

Firearms examiners, who undertake firearms investigations including test firing and bullet recovery, will be exposed to hazards such as noise and lead. They should have their hearing and blood lead levels monitored on a regular basis, to ensure that hearing protection is being worn and is functioning correctly, and any exposure to lead from the firearms is quickly identified and addressed.

Computer Forensics Laboratory

Computer forensic examiners specialize in obtaining, analyzing, and reporting on electronic evidence stored on computers and other electronic devices. Crimes involving a computer can range across the spectrum of criminal activity, from child pornography to theft of personal data to destruction of intellectual property. Potential hazards involve static postures, occupational overuse, and stress from viewing graphic images.

Some suggestions to minimize the stress from viewing graphic images are as follows:

- psychological assessment before and after viewing graphic material, and periodically;
- exposure to only one medium, for example, visual material only, rather than examining both sound and visual material simultaneously;
- specifying limits as to the amount of time spent examining explicit material in a day; and
- ceasing any examination of explicit material the end of their shift, to allow themselves time to refocus attention away from this stressor.

Electrical/Machinery

Forensic laboratories use a wide range of electrical equipment and machinery. Practitioners need to ensure that any inherent risk from electric shock is mitigated. The use of residual current devices (safety switches) is an appropriate strategy, as is visual inspection and periodic testing and tagging of power cords, to detect obvious damage, wear, and other conditions which might render it unsafe by a person qualified to do so under the legislation in effect in the jurisdiction.

Fume Cupboards

Fume cupboards are integral to minimizing the risk of exposure to chemical and biological hazards. Not all fume cupboards are suitable for all hazards. Fume cupboards should be maintained and inspected periodically. During maintenance, attention should be given to:

- The fume cupboard itself, including flow rates and replacement of absorbents or filters.
- In the case of externally vented fume cupboards, the ductwork and location of external vents. This is particularly important during any building maintenance or refurbishment.
- Fume cupboards must be used for all operations that have the potential to release hazardous fumes, mists, or dusts.
- Before commencement of work, ensure that the fume cupboard is clean and free from contamination.
- Ensure the minimum of equipment is stored in the fume cupboard and is placed toward the back of the cupboard to reduce disturbance to the air flowing into the fume cupboard.

- Lower the sash as far as practicable during use to improve fume containment.

Recirculating fume cabinets rely on filtration or absorption to remove airborne contaminants released in the fume cabinet before the exhaust air is discharged back into the laboratory. They are suitable for light-to-moderate use with a known range of substances. The range of substances for which each cabinet can be used is limited by the need for compatibility with the chemicals in use as well as with the particular type of absorbent or filter fitted to the cabinet.

Robotics

The introduction of automated robotic platforms has significantly enhanced the efficiency of forensic analysis. The use of robotics is becoming more common and is very useful for a range of repetitive laboratory tasks. Besides saving time, robotics overcomes the need for repetitive work involved in pipetting, eliminating musculoskeletal injuries.

Hazards associated with robotics include the risk of exposure to the chemicals used in the work, electrocution, and cutting, stabbing, or shearing from the moveable parts of the robot. The interlocks on the robots should not be bypassed.

X-rays

X-rays are used in analytical and imaging instrumentation. Potential exposure to X-rays is generally localized to specific parts of the body, usually the hands or fingers. Depending on the X-ray energies delivered, effects may range from erythema (redness) at point of exposure, blood changes, cancer through to death. Depending on the legislative requirement in each country, practitioners working with X-ray equipment may be required to use dosimeters to assess radiation dose.

Lasers

Lasers span the visible and nonvisible electromagnetic spectrum and have many applications in forensic science, including Raman spectroscopy. Lasers are generally classified according to the level of risk they represent. Damage from laser beams can be thermal or photochemical. The primary sites of damage are the eyes and skin. Hazards associated with laser work may include:

- fire,
- explosion,
- electrocution, and
- inhalation of contaminants from laser interactions.

Precautions for use of lasers include:

- Display the class of laser in use.
- Appropriate protective eye wear with side protection and appropriate attenuation for the wavelength(s) in use must be worn.
- Interlocks on the laser should not be bypassed.
- Keep the laser beam path away from eye level whether one is seated or standing.

High-Intensity Light Sources

High-intensity light sources such as the Polilight® provide a range of colored light bands and white light for forensic work.

- Care should be taken that high-intensity white light is not directed onto any object at short distances from the end of the light guide, as this can cause severe heat damage to the object and may result in a fire.
- The light beam should never be directed at eyes as the light can cause permanent damage.

Manual Handling

Manual handling refers to any activity that involves lifting, lowering, carrying, pushing, pulling, holding, restraining, or the application of force. Only a very small number of manual handling injuries are caused by the lifting of heavy weights alone. Actions such as reaching, twisting, bending, or maintaining static postures contribute to injury affecting the muscle or skeletal systems of the body. These musculoskeletal injuries predominantly involve the neck, back or shoulder or arm muscle, tendon, ligament, or joints.

Injuries may be caused from activities such as maintaining static postures while working at fume cupboards, repetitive keyboard and mouse work, pipetting, prolonged use of comparison microscopes.

Some preventative strategies include:

- Seeking further assistance to have the activities assessed to minimize the manual handling risks inherent in the activity.
- Planning tasks so that rest breaks are scheduled.
- Choosing the best tools for the tasks.
- Alternate hands while using a mouse, if possible.

There is a move to make instruments smaller and more portable for use at crime scenes. While this has significant benefits, including potentially reducing the number of exhibits collected, moving equipment can also raise manual handling concerns.

General Laboratory Management

Housekeeping is important in laboratories. It is important to maintain clear passageways, proper labeling of chemicals, clean and uncluttered work areas, and appropriate storage. The handling of powders is a potentially hazardous operation, and good housekeeping can help minimize airborne contamination from spilled materials. Having a planned preventative maintenance program and regular inspections of the workplace, plant, and equipment are essential for the smooth running of the laboratory.

Handling of Exhibits in Court

Each evidential item must be appropriately packaged and sealed, if this is not already the case, before it is exhibited in court. Items such as clothing which are normally stored in paper may need to be repackaged in clear plastic allowing the item to remain sealed, and minimizing the risk of cross contamination when handled in court. Caution should be exercised against opening exhibits in court, in case any hazards such as mold or irritant fumes are released.

Hazards in the Field

Forensic practitioners are often required to work or train in the field. Consideration should be given to managing hazards which may affect practitioners, including:

- environmental hazards such as heat, cold, humidity or wet weather, the terrain, and fauna or flora at the scene;
- the type of operation, for example, working in a clandestine laboratory often involves quite specific hazards;
- the possible presence of offenders or other security risks such as booby traps at a scene; and
- the availability of first aid and emergency response domestically and overseas.

  The risks from these hazards should be considered within the scope of the exercise or operation. Some possible responses to hazards, which may be considered in a dynamic risk assessment, include:
- Designating a location for emergency equipment, such as a crime scene vehicle, and ensuring that disinfectants, antiseptics, and a first aid kit are easily accessible;
- Planning an emergency exit from the scene and ensuring that this is communicated to all personnel present;
- Establishing a decontamination point if there is exposure to chemical or biological material;
- The use of appropriate PPE including sunglasses, sunscreen, and hats when working outdoors;
- Depending on the external temperature, work activity, duration, and PPE worn, practitioners should have access to shade for rest and adequate fluids if required during hot weather to prevent heat stress. The wearing of PPE including chemical suits and respirators requires longer and more frequent periods of rest break for recovery in hot temperatures and humid environment;
- In cold weather, provision should be made to have adequate warm clothing and a sheltered area;
- The risk of animal or dog bites while attending a crime scene should not be discounted. If practitioners are searching in vegetated areas, the risk of snake or tick bites should be considered, along with possible exposure to plants such as poison ivy or stinging nettles.

Confined Spaces

Forensic practitioners may have to enter confined spaces. Due to the high risks associated with entering the confined space, many jurisdictions mandate that entry into a confined space must not be made until a confined-space permit has been issued. Practitioners must receive specific training before work or entry into confined spaces.

Chemical Biological and Radiological and Nuclear Incidents

Forensic practitioners may be required to attend a chemical biological and radiological and nuclear (CBRN) incident. CBRN incidents where forensic practitioners may attend and conduct examinations include:

- chemical (warfare agent, toxic industrial chemical);
- biological (weaponized agent, natural disease);
- radiological (discrete, or wide area contamination); and
- nuclear.

Depending on the response agency protocol in place, forensic practitioners may be working closely with the Fire Brigade and other emergency first responders. Entry must not be made into the "warm" or "hot" zone of the scene without consultation with the other emergency first responders.

Clan Labs

Clan labs pose a significant threat to the health and safety of police officers, forensic practitioners, the general public, and the environment. There are many hazards associated with clan labs including:

- flammable materials and/or explosive atmosphere;
- acutely toxic atmospheres;
- leaking or damaged compressed gas cylinders; and
- traps and hazards deliberately set to cause injury or death to police and other responders.

As a result of the frequency at which clan labs are encountered and the severe and variable risks associated with the investigation, many jurisdictions have developed specific policies and procedures concerning clan lab investigations.

For forensic practitioners to deal with clan labs requires a high level of fitness as well as technical expertise. Practitioners have to understand:

- illicit drug chemistry;
- how to neutralize the risks of explosions, fires, chemical burns, and toxic fumes;
- how to handle, store, and dispose of hazardous materials; and
- how to treat medical conditions caused by exposure.

Practitioners must also wear full protective equipment including respirators and may be required to move equipment at the clan lab in the process of collecting evidence. The storage and handling of unknown chemicals from clandestine laboratories or seizures should also be considered. Preliminary identification should take place, before its storage or disposal.

When unknowns such as "white powders," chemicals (in liquid, solid, or gas state), or biological materials are encountered in the field, it is prudent to be cautious and obtain up-to-date intelligence to shed more light on what is at the scene. It may be an explosive material or contain anthrax spores or ricin or something as innocuous as talc.

Some precautions include:

- wearing the appropriate level of protective clothing/equipment for the activity;
- avoiding direct contact with the substance, even if only in small quantities;
- not smelling or tasting anything from the scene;
- noting physical characteristics such as color, form, and consistency;
- where it is safe to do so, looking for hazard symbols on packaging or labels if available; and
- seeking specialist advice if unable to identify the substance.

Potential Hazards during an Overseas Deployment

Forensic practitioners can be required to work overseas to assist with large-scale disasters. An example was the Thailand Tsunami Victim Identification process involving forensic practitioners from 30 countries working to recover and identify bodies. Forensic practitioners need to be mindful of hazards likely to be encountered during an overseas deployment depending on the location, magnitude of the operation, and how many practitioners are deployed. Some hazards to be considered include:

- climatic demands;
- remote and sometimes dangerous terrain;
- different cultural sensitivities;
- security requirements;
- different levels of infrastructure support at the locality;
- logistics, including the transport of large quantities of equipment, manual handling, setting up, and packing up;
- different hygiene levels;
- diseases that can be transmitted by insect and or animal vectors;
- the possibility of infectious diseases; and
- asbestos and other hazards in buildings.

Work-Related Stress

Practitioners at work may experience work-related stress. There are some specific stressors unique within forensic work. Forensic practitioners may experience workplace-related stress due to their attendances at morgues, violent crime scenes, Disaster Victim Identification or from requirements to view explicit or graphic material or images.

Indicators of stress include changes in eating habits, tiredness due to changes in sleep patterns, frequent absences from work, reduced productivity, concentration, motivation, and morale. Physical symptoms may include headaches, abdominal pains, diarrhea, constipation, high blood pressure, insomnia, anxiety state, and depression.

Many organizations offer programs to provide assistance to employees, including counseling to help practitioners to deal with work-related stress or resilience training to manage work-life balance.

See also: **Management/Quality in Forensic Science:** Principles of Quality Assurance; Risk Management; Principles of Laboratory Organization.

Further Reading

Clancy, D., Billinghurst, A., Cater, H., 2009. Hazard identification and risk assessment – understanding the transition from the documented plan to assessing dynamic risk in bio security emergencies. In: World Conference on Disaster Management, Sydney, Australia. http://www.humansafety.com.au/getattachment/da338cb7-29b0-4d3a-8a06-d7dc0b569a87/C20.aspx.

Furr, K., 2000. Handbook of Laboratory Safety, fifth ed. CRC Press, Florida.

Green-McKenzie, J., Watkins, M., 2005. Occupational hazards: law enforcement officers are at risk of body fluid exposure. Here's what to expect if it happens to you. Law Enforcement Magazine 29 (9), 52–54, 56, 58.

Hanson, D., 2007. Hazardous duty training officers to tackle hazmat emergencies. Law Enforcement Technology 34 (4), 80–85.

Haski, R., Cardilini, G., Bartolo, W., 2011. Laboratory Safety Manual. CCH Australia Ltd, Sydney.

Horswell, J., 2000. The practice of crime scene investigation. Florida. CRC Press.

Jackel, G., 2004. The high cost of stress. AUSPOL: The Official Publication of the Australian Federal Police Association and ALAJA 1, 4–37.

Mayhew, C., 2001a. Occupational health and safety risks faced by police officers. Australian Institute of Criminology Trends and Issues in Crime and Criminal Justice 196, 1–6.

Mayhew, C., 2001b. Protecting the occupational health and safety of police officers. Australian Institute of Criminology Trends and Issues in Crime and Criminal Justice 197, 1–6.

Rothernbaum, D., 2010. Exposed: an officer's story. Clan Lab Safety Alert 7 (2), 1–2.

Smith, D., 2005. Psychosocial occupational health issues in contemporary police work: a review of research evidence. Journal of Occupational Health and Safety, Australia and New Zealand 21 (3), 217–228.

Tillman, C., 2007. Principles of Occupational Health and Hygiene: An Introduction. Crows Nest: Allen & Unwin.

Whitman, M., Smith, C., 2005. The culture of safety: no one gets hurt today. Police Chief LXXII 11, 20–24, 26–27.

Winder, C., 2011. Hazard Alert: Managing Workplace Hazardous Substances. CCH Australia Ltd, Sydney.

Witter, R., Martyny, J., Mueller, K., Gottschall, B., Newman, L., 2007. Symptoms experienced by law enforcement personnel during methamphetamine lab investigation. Journal of Occupational and Environmental Hygiene 4, 895–902.

Relevant Websites

http://www.ccohs.ca/oshanswers/occup_workplace/labtech.html—Canadian Centre for Occupational Health and Safety (CCOHS).

http://www.cdc.gov/niosh/—Centers for Disease Control and Prevention (CDC).

http://www.forensic.gov.uk/html/company/foi/publication-scheme/health-and-safety/—Forensic Science Service, Health and Safety.

http://www.hse.gov.uk/services/police/index.htm—Health and Safety Executive (HSE).

http://www.police.qld.gov.au/Resources/Internet/rti/policies/documents/QPSForensicServicesHealth_SafetyManual.pdf—Health and Safety Manual, Police Forensic Services, Queensland Police.

http://www.londonhealthandsafetygroup.org/archive.html—London Health and Safety Group.

http://www.osha.gov/—Occupational Safety & Health Administration.

http://www.ccohs.ca/oshanswers/occup_workplace/police.html—What Do Police Do?.

Measurement Uncertainty

Ted Vosk, Criminal Defense Law Firm, Kirkland, WA, USA

Glossary

Bias The quantitative characterization of systematic error.

Combined uncertainty The standard uncertainty associated with the final measurement result determined by "adding" up the standard uncertainties associated with each of the individual sources of uncertainty.

Coverage factor A positive, real number that when multiplied by a measurement's combined uncertainty yields the expanded uncertainty. The coverage factor determines the level of confidence associated with a coverage interval.

Coverage interval An interval about the best estimate of a measurand's "true" value that will contain those values believed to be attributable to the measurand with a specified level of confidence.

Expanded uncertainty Measure of uncertainty obtained by multiplying a measurement's combined uncertainty by a coverage factor. It defines the half width of a coverage interval.

Level of confidence The probability, defined as a degree of belief, that the "true" value of a measurand lies within the range defined by a coverage interval.

Measurand The quantity whose value is sought to be determined by a measurement.

Measurement function A function that describes the relationship between the measurand value and those quantities required to determine it.

Quantity Physical properties subject to measurement, such as length, time, weight, and concentration.

Random error The inherent unpredictable fluctuation in measured values under fixed conditions.

Sensitivity coefficients The partial derivatives of a measurement function that describe how the measurand's value varies with changes in the values of the input quantities.

Standard uncertainty Measurement uncertainty expressed as the standard deviation of a frequency- or belief-based probability distribution.

Systematic error The tendency of a set of measurements to consistently (on average) underestimate or overestimate the "true" value of a measurand by a given value or percentage.

Uncertainty The quantitative characterization of the dispersion of values that, based on one's universe of information concerning a measurement, are believed to be reasonably attributable to a measurand.

Nomenclature

b_{ias} Bias

$\bar{y}_c$ Bias corrected mean measured value

Y_b Best estimate of "true" measurand value

μ_c Combined uncertainty

k Coverage factor

U Expanded uncertainty

X Input quantities

ε_m Maximum total error

$\bar{y}$ Mean measured value

$f(X_1,X_2,\ldots,X_N)$ Measurement function

ε Measurement error

y Measured value

$Y_{99\%}$ Measurand value with 99% level of confidence

ε_{ran} Random error

μ_r Relative standard uncertainty

$\partial f/\partial x_i$ Sensitivity coefficients

σ Standard deviation

μ Standard uncertainty

ε_{sys} Systematic error

Y "True" measurand value

$\boxplus$ Unspecified method for combining ε_{sys} and ε_{ran}

 http://dx.doi.org/10.1016/B978-0-12-800573-6.00023-9

Measurement

Measurement constitutes a specific category of scientific investigation. It is an empirical process whereby a researcher seeks to determine the numerical magnitude attributable to some physical/phenomenological quantity of interest referred to as the "measurand." Many naively consider measurement to be a mechanical process whereby the quantity of interest is sensed/probed by a measuring instrument yielding directly the value attributable to the measurand. This mechanical activity is simply one step in the overall measurement process, however. Alone, it does not tell us what we want to know about the value(s) attributable to a measurand. Rather than a passively mechanical process of probing and discovery, measurement is more completely understood as an empirically grounded, information-based inference requiring active input from the researcher before any value can be attributed to a measurand. Measurement uncertainty identifies in an explicit, quantitatively rigorous manner the limitations governing the rational inferences that can be made concerning the value(s) attributable to a measurand based on the results of measurement.

Measurement to Meaning

Measurement Error and Error Analysis

What does a measurement result mean? In other words, given a measured value y, what value(s) can actually be attributed to a measurand. Lay people often interpret the value reported by a measurement as representing the singular "true" value attributable to a measurand (**Figure 1**):

$$Y = y \quad [1]$$

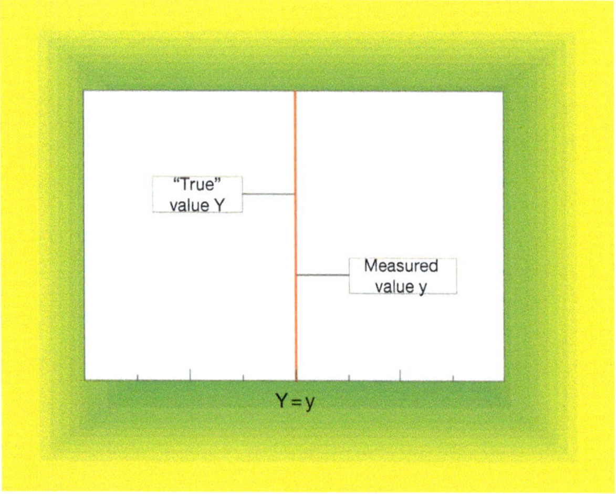

Figure 1 Measurement as singular "true" value.

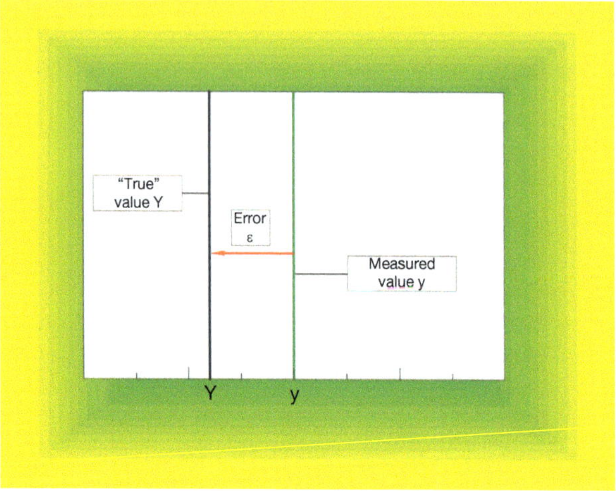

Figure 2 Measurement in reality inherent error.

Science has long realized, however, that "error" is an inherent characteristic of measurement distinguishing measured values from the "true" quantity values sought to be determined (**Figure 2**).

Error analysis is the traditional approach to the interpretation of measurement results. It is based on the premise that if the error associated with a measurement can be determined, then a measurand's "true" value can also be determined:

$$Y = y - \varepsilon \quad [2]$$

There are two types of errors associated with every measurement: random and systematic. Systematic error is the tendency of a method/instrument to yield values that are consistently (on average) artificially inflated or depressed with respect to the "true" values of the quantities being measured. It is quantitatively characterized as bias (**Figure 3**).

The identification of systematic error can be one of the most difficult aspects of the measurement process. The reason is that if one is measuring an unknown quantity, the measured values themselves provide no basis for concluding that they are systematically offset from the measurand's "true" value. Thus, one can never know whether all systematic errors associated with a measurement have been identified. Some sources of systematic error can be identified and quantified through measurement of reference materials. Even when rigorously determined in this manner, however, the magnitude of the bias can never be exactly known.

Random error is the unpredictable/random fluctuation in measured values under fixed conditions. It introduces inherent variability into the measurement process placing a fundamental limitation on the repeatability of measured results. For many common situations, the random variation in a measurement's results can be approximately characterized by a Gaussian (normal) distribution (**Figure 4**).

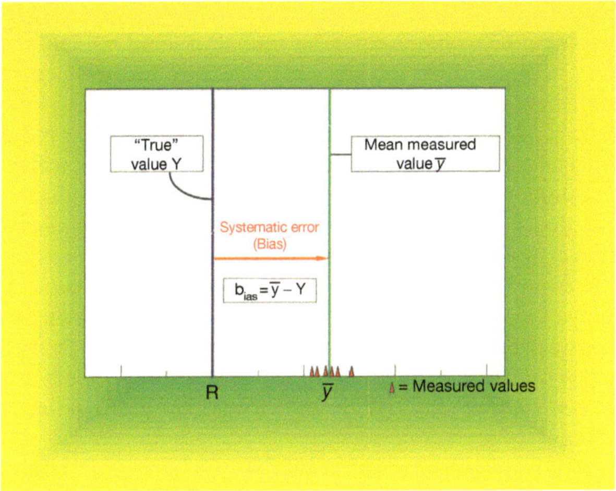

Figure 3 Systematic error and bias.

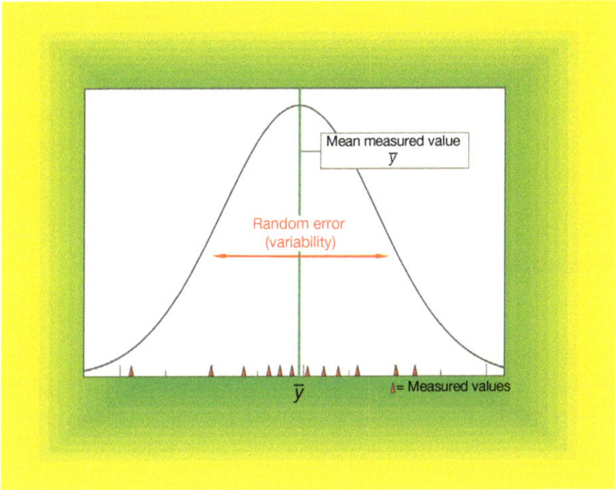

Figure 4 Random error and variability.

Random error is quantitatively characterized by a set of measurement's standard deviation:

$$\sigma_y = \sqrt{\frac{\sum_{i=1}^{n}(y_i - \bar{y})^2}{n-1}} \qquad [3]$$

The standard deviation provides a measure of the variability of individually measured values about their mean. If there is significant variability, the standard deviation will be large. If variability is slight, the standard deviation will be small.

Systematic and random errors describe aspects of the *physical state of a measurement*. It is not always clear whether an error should be categorized as systematic or random, and the determination may be context-dependent. Taken together, they constitute what is formally known as "measurement error" (**Figure 5**).

The total error associated with a measurement can never be absolutely determined; that is, it is unknowable. As a result, error analysis can never supply a measurand's "true" value. Instead, the goal of error analysis is to identify, minimize, and eliminate *as best as possible* all identifiable sources of error so as to provide an estimate of a measurand's value that is *as close as possible* to its "true" value (**Figure 6**).

This requires some method for combining systematic and random components of error to obtain a characterization of a measurement's total error:

$$\varepsilon = \varepsilon_{sys} \boxplus \varepsilon_{ran} \qquad [4]$$

To understand where this leads, one must have an idea of the mathematical underpinnings of error analysis. Error analysis is ground in frequentist statistical theory. Frequentist theory defines probability in terms of relative frequency of occurrence. This means that the probability that a particular condition will be found to exist is determined by how frequently it occurs within the universe of all possible events. Although these probabilities can seldom be known because the universe of all possible events can seldom be completely known, they can be "objectively" estimated as the relative frequency of occurrence over sample data sets. What is critical is that in error analysis, the estimation of probabilities is "objectively" based solely on statistical sampling according to the frequentist paradigm.

The analysis of random error fits well within the frequentist paradigm. On the other hand, except in limited circumstances, the evaluation of systematic error does not. Because systematic and random errors are different in nature, each requires distinct treatment. There is no rigorously justifiable manner within the

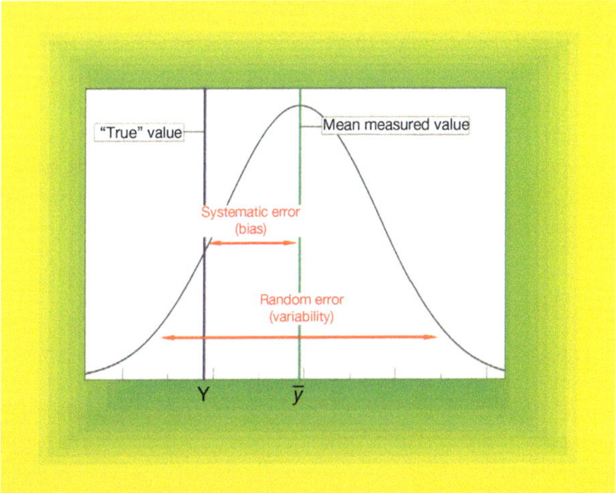

Figure 5 Measurement error.

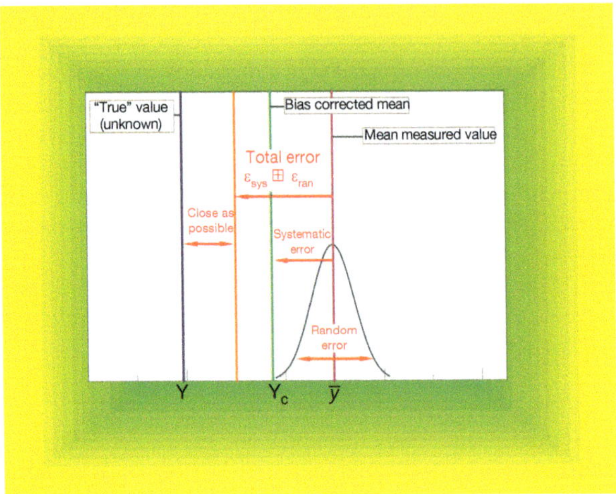

Figure 6 Error analysis estimate as close as possible.

frequentist paradigm by which systematic and random errors can be combined to yield a statistically meaningful estimate of a measurement's total error.

Due to the frequentist underpinnings of error analysis, the best it can provide is an upper limit on a measurement's total error. This bounded error is often expressed as some linear combination of the bias and standard deviation associated with a measurement:

$$\varepsilon_m = b_{ias} + 3\sigma \quad [5]$$

This places a bound on the maximum separation expected between a measured and "true" value. It does not, however, denote how close together the two values are *actually* expected to lie. In other words, it tells us the worst a measurement result could be without any indication of how good it actually is. Moreover, the meaning of this bounded error is vague as it fails to tell us how probable it is that a measured value lies within the prescribed range of the measurand's "true" value. Given a measured value y, the best error analysis provides is an incompletely defined estimate of the maximum separation between a measured value and a "true" value. It cannot tell us the values that are likely to be attributable to the measurand given a particular measured value.

The Meaning of Meaning

A significant epistemological question surrounds any scientific proposition: Is a scientific proposition intended to describe some physical state of the universe itself or simply to describe our state of knowledge about such a physical state? If it is the former, the direct object of the proposition is an external fully independent reality. If it is the latter, the direct object of the proposition is an internal cognitive position that is information-dependent. Many claim that if scientific propositions are to be objectively meaningful, they must fall into the first category. Others counter that regardless of the objective content of scientific propositions, they necessarily reside in the second category as all we can ever actually claim to know is our internal cognitive state, not some independent external reality.

Although seemingly esoteric, the position adopted can have practical implications. It may change not only the interpretation of scientific statements but also the manner in which they can be investigated. And so it is with scientific measurement. When a measurement result is reported, is it to be interpreted as a statement about the physical state of a measurand? Or, is it simply an expression of our state of knowledge about the measurand's physical state? And what are the practical implications of the choice made?

Measurement error is an aspect of the *physical state* of a measurement. It is related to a measurand through error analysis that purports to convey the bounds of its actual *physical state* through the determination of a bounded error. Where a precise estimate of a measurand's actual value is not critical, the bounded error may provide a result with sufficient meaning to be useful. Where a measurand's actual value is important, however, this level of meaning may be inadequate. If possible, one would like to understand the meaning of a measured value in terms of how it maps into those values that are *likely* to be attributable to the measurand.

Measurement Uncertainty

The New Paradigm

Measurement uncertainty addresses the shortcomings of error analysis by fundamentally redefining the way measurement is interpreted and providing a quantitative metric for mapping measured values into those believed to be reasonably attributable to a measurand. In this new paradigm, error is replaced as the focus of analysis by a new entity: uncertainty. This is not a matter of mere semantics. Uncertainty and error are completely distinct concepts. While measurement error concerns the actual *physical state of* a measurand, measurement uncertainty relates to the *state of knowledge about* the measurand.

This does not mean that those phenomena formerly understood as systematic and random errors are ignored. To the contrary, they are fully encompassed within the uncertainty framework. What they represent, however, has been reconceptualized to overcome the limitations inherent in frequentist philosophy. Central to the uncertainty paradigm is the alternative Bayesian notion of probability as a degree of belief. That is, probability is defined by how strongly one believes a given proposition. This formulation permits consideration of information about a measurand beyond that cognizable in frequentist theory and provides a common basis for its analysis whether statistically or nonstatistically based.

In the uncertainty paradigm, as in error analysis, a measurand's "true" value is unknowable. However, this is not due to the physical phenomenon of irreducible error, but due to the impossibility of our ever-possessing perfect knowledge concerning a measurand's state. Uncertainty focuses on this limitation interpreting a measurement result as a probability distribution that characterizes one's state of knowledge about a measurand's value. While measurement error as a physical phenomenon is as unknowable as a measurand's "true" value, the characterization of a result as a probability distribution in this manner permits a result's uncertainty to be rigorously determined.

When a measurement is performed, it always takes place against a backdrop of existing information about the measurement to be made and the measurand itself. Some of this information may be in the form of statistically obtained data, while some may be based on other sources such as general knowledge of the behavior and properties of relevant materials, methods, and instruments. When a measurement is performed, the discrete value obtained adds to our universe of information and updates our state of knowledge concerning the measurand. Because our information is necessarily incomplete, our knowledge concerning the measurand remains fuzzy. Given the information possessed, the discrete value obtained represents a packet of values dispersed about the measured result, all of which are believed to be attributable to the measurand with relative degrees of conviction (**Figure 7**).

It is the identification of probabilities as degrees of belief that transforms this packet of values into a probability distribution. In this context, the meaning of a measured value corresponds to a probability distribution characterizing the relative likelihood of the values believed to be attributable to a measurand based on the totality of currently available information (**Figure 8**).

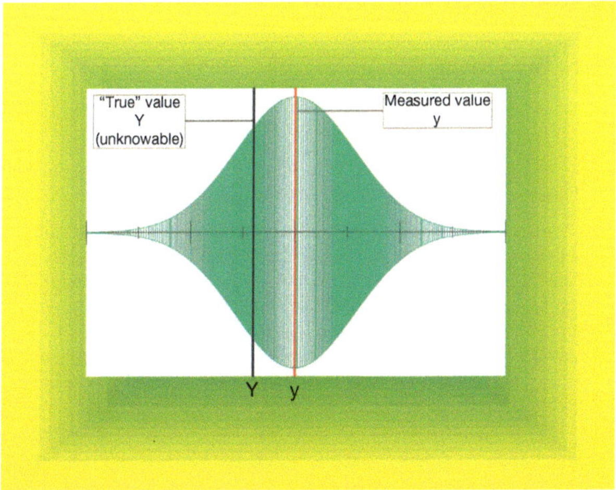

Figure 7 Measurement as packet of values.

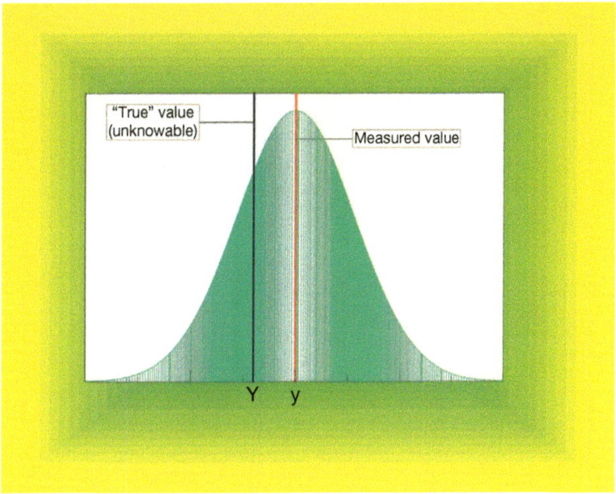

Figure 8 Measurement as probability distribution.

This distribution completely specifies our state of knowledge concerning the values attributable to a measurand. Moreover, it delineates in a mathematically rigorous manner how a measured value, y, maps into those values believed to be attributable to a measurand. By doing so, it also determines the inferences that can be made concerning a measurand's value based on the values measured.

As an example, given a measured value, the distribution permits one to determine the probability that a measurand's value lies within any given range of values. In this context, one can think of the probability associated with the distribution as being equal to the area under the curve representing it. The probability that a measurand's value lies within a specified range is given by the proportion of the area under the curve spanning the range in question to the total area under the curve (**Figure 9**).

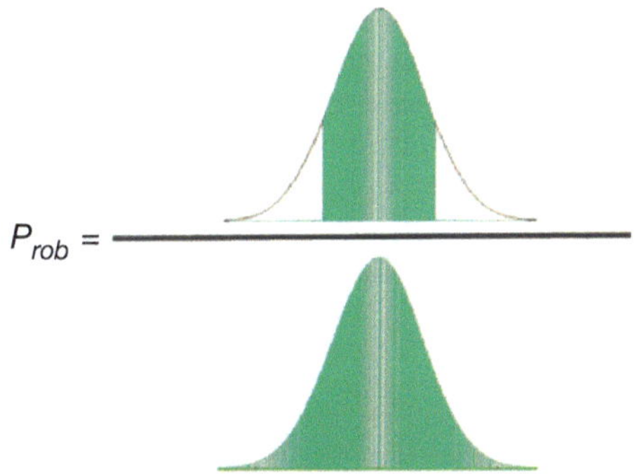

Figure 9 Probability = ratio of areas under curve.

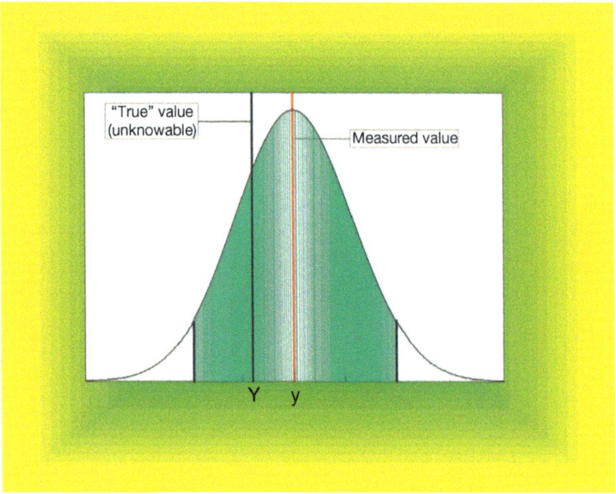

Figure 10 Values reasonably attributable to a measurand.

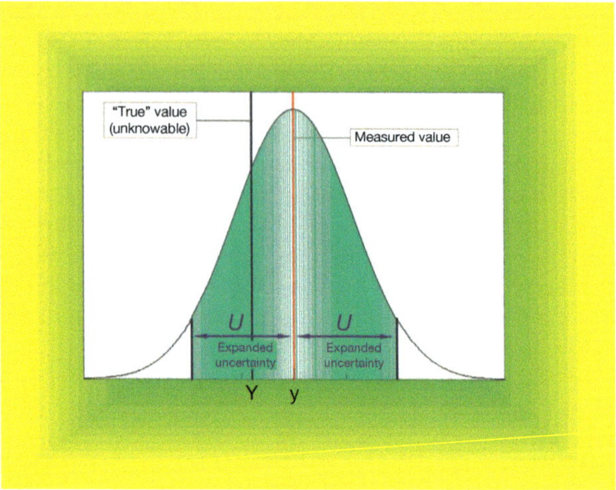

Figure 11 Expanded uncertainty.

Given a measured value, y, the question of what values can *reasonably* be attributed to a measurand involves two competing considerations. First, we want to exclude values that, although possible, are highly improbable. Second, we need to include enough values so that there is a significant probability that the measurand's value is actually among those considered. The measurement's probability distribution provides a conceptually straightforward way of accomplishing this. Simply slice off the tails of the distribution while including enough of its middle so that the area of the remaining region represents a significant probability that the measurand's value lies within it (**Figure 10**).

From this, we can obtain a range of values reasonably attributable to a measurand, along with an associated probability that the value of the measurand lies within it. This defines the uncertainty of a measurement. Measurement uncertainty is the quantitative characterization of the dispersion of values that, based on the universe of information concerning a measurement, are believed to be *reasonably* attributable to a measurand. The half width of this range of values is known as a result's expanded uncertainty, U (**Figure 11**).

The expanded uncertainty defines what is known as a "coverage interval" about a measured value. The coverage interval conveys the set of quantity values reasonably attributed to the measurand along with the specific probability that its "true" value actually lies within this range. The probability is referred to as the interval's associated "level of confidence." Coverage intervals having an associated level of confidence between 95% and 99.7% are typically selected (**Figure 12**):

Coverage interval

$$y - U < Y_{99\%} < y + U \quad [6]$$

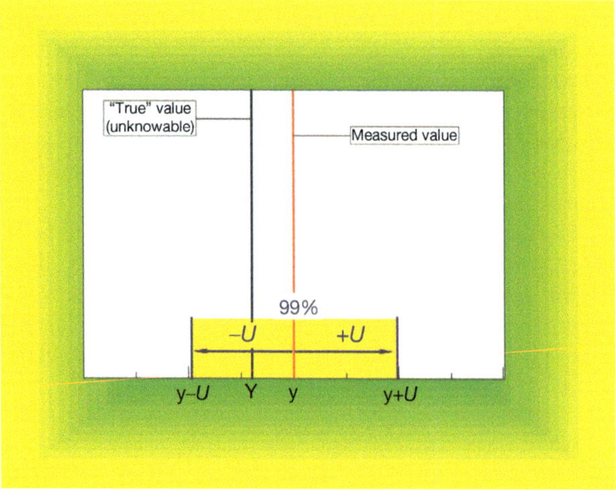

Figure 12 Coverage interval.

Coverage Interval versus Confidence Interval

Coverage intervals and confidence intervals are distinct tools and should not be confused. A coverage interval is a metrological concept based on Bayesian analysis. In this framework, parameters of interest can be treated as random variables so that they can be the subject of probabilistic statements without logical inconsistency. The level of confidence associated with a coverage interval refers to the probability, understood as a degree of belief, that a measurand's value lies within the interval.

A confidence interval is a statistical concept based on frequentist methodology. In this framework, the stochastic nature of the investigation lies entirely in the sampling process, not the parameter value. Accordingly, the level of confidence associated with a confidence interval does not associate a probability with the measurand value. Rather, its object is the interval itself. If one were to conduct multiple sets of measurements and generate a confidence interval for each set, the level of confidence tells you the proportion of these intervals that would be expected to cover/overlap a measurand's value (**Figure 13**).

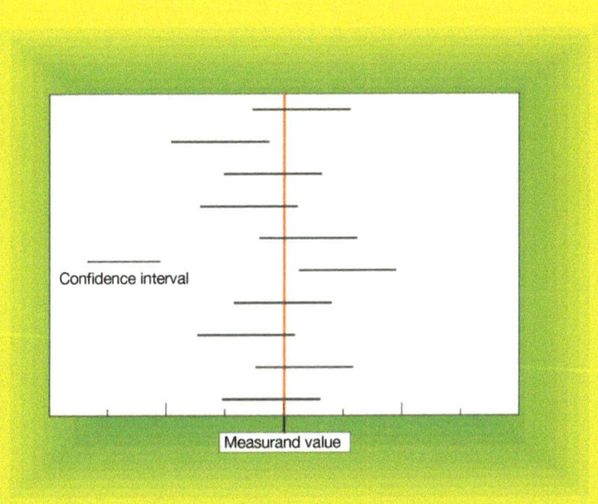

Figure 13 Interpretation of a confidence interval.

There are two types of uncertainties: type A and type B. Unlike the two types of errors, type A and type B uncertainties are not distinguished by the nature of their source. Instead, they are defined by the manner in which they are determined. Type A uncertainty refers to the uncertainty that has been determined by statistical (frequentist) methods utilizing observed frequency distributions. Type B uncertainty refers to the uncertainty that has been determined by nonstatistical means relying on knowledge, experience, and judgment to create belief-based a priori distributions.

Type A evaluations are often referred to as "objective" and type B as "subjective." However, this does not mean that type B evaluations are any less real or valid than type A. Both evaluations rely on accepted notions of probability. Nor is one approach necessarily superior to the other. Whether type A or type B analysis yields better results is context-dependent.

Regardless of the approach employed to determine them, a foundational tenant of this paradigm is that the uncertainties themselves do not differ in nature. Once determined, all distributions are interpreted in the Bayesian manner, representing models of our state of knowledge quantified according to degree of belief. This permits type A and type B uncertainties to be treated on equal footing as standard deviations of the distributions they are based on, providing rigorous justification for their combination into a "combined uncertainty" using traditional methods of analysis.

The importance of this lies in the fact that a measurement's uncertainty is usually made up of the combination of uncertainties from several distinct sources. To understand the significance, recall the inability of error analysis to combine systematic and random errors in a rigorously justifiable manner to determine a measurement's total error. To avoid confusion, in the context of uncertainty, systematic errors are referred to as "systematic effects." For pedagogical purposes, systematic effects were not included in the above discussion. Nonetheless, the determination of uncertainty assumes that every measurement has been corrected for significant systematic effects.

What the uncertainty paradigm permits us to do, regardless of the nature of a systematic effect or how it has been quantified, is to treat it as a probability distribution. When this is done, the distribution's expectation yields the required systematic correction (hereinafter referred to as bias) and its standard deviation characterizes the uncertainty associated with the bias. Treated in this manner, systematic effects and their associated uncertainties are placed on equal footing with measured values and their associated uncertainties, so that those phenomena formerly understood as systematic and random errors can now be combined in a logically consistent and rigorously justifiable manner. In general, the evaluation of the uncertainty arising from systematic effects may be either type A or type B.

Returning to the above discussion, it can now be seen that the uncertainty paradigm naturally incorporates systematic effects into the mapping of measured values to those believed to be attributable to a measurand (**Figure 14**).

The correction shifts the position of the probability distribution along the axis of values while the uncertainty associated with the correction will modify the shape of the distribution. As would be expected, this will shift the coverage interval in the direction of the correction as well.

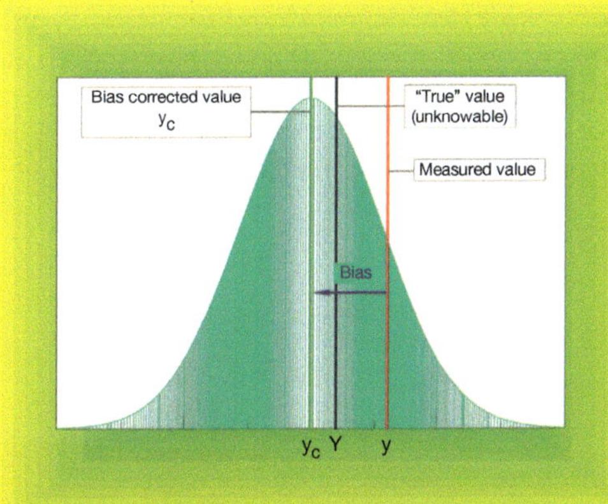

Figure 14 Mapping measurement to "reality."

Something that must be considered at this point is that given the inherent variability of measured values, it is seldom acceptable to base the determination of a measurand's value on a single measurement. Good practice requires acquisition of multiple measured values combined to determine their mean. The *best estimate* of a measurand's "true" value is then given by the *bias corrected mean* of the measured values:

$$\begin{aligned}\text{Best estimate} &= \text{bias corrected mean}\\ Y_b &= \bar{y}_c\end{aligned} \quad [7]$$

It is a fundamental principle of measurement that where the actual value of a measurand is important, a result is not complete and cannot be properly interpreted unless it has been corrected for bias and is accompanied by a quantitative statement of its uncertainty. Accordingly, a complete measurement result consists of the best estimate of the measurand's "true" value accompanied by its uncertainty:

$$\begin{aligned}\text{Measurement result} &= \text{best estimate} \pm \text{uncertainty}\\ Y_{99\%} &= Y_b \pm U\end{aligned} \quad [8]$$

$$\begin{aligned}&\text{Coverage interval}\\ &Y_b - U < Y_{99\%} < Y_b + U\end{aligned} \quad [9]$$

Measurement Uncertainty: A Forensic Example

The value of a measurand can be critical to the determination of certain criminal matters. For example, some states define the offense of driving under the influence of alcohol (DUI) by an individual's "true" breath alcohol concentration (BrAC). The measurement of BrAC, like any other scientific measurement, is accompanied by uncertainty. Thus, by themselves, the values reported by a breath test machine tell us little about an individual's "true" BrAC and whether they have actually committed a crime. Consider tests administered to two different individuals on different instruments in a state where DUI is defined by a BrAC of 0.08 g/210 l (**Figures 15 and 16**).

Each test reports identical BrAC values in excess of the state's per se limit with a mean value of 0.0825 g/210 l. Without more, these "breath test tickets" clearly seem to indicate that the BrACs in question exceed the legal limit. Moreover, given that the external standard readings are both reading true, there is actually no way to distinguish between these two tests.

The two tests' uncertainties reveal a different picture though. Despite identically measured values, the uncertainty of each, expressed as coverage intervals, is different (**Figures 17 and 18**).

Blank test	.000
Internal standard	Verified
Subject sample	.084
Blank test	.000
External standard	.082
Blank test	.000
Subject sample	.081
Blank test	.000

Figure 15 Identical measurement results, different measurement meaning: breath analysis.

Blank test	.000
Internal standard	Verified
Subject sample	.084
Blank test	.000
External standard	.079
Blank test	.000
Subject sample	.081
Blank test	.000

Figure 16 Breath analysis.

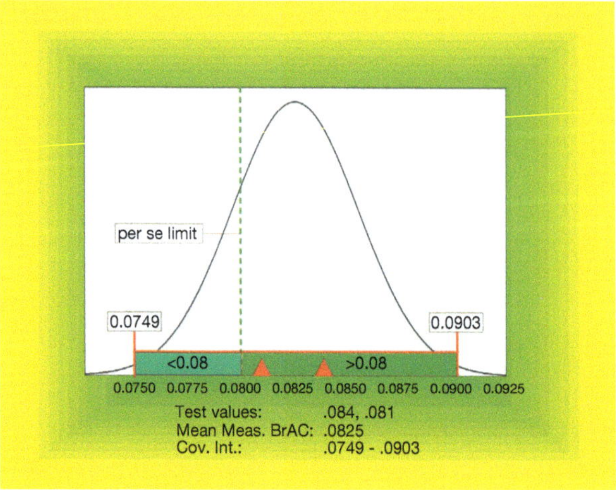

Figure 17 BrAC test 1.

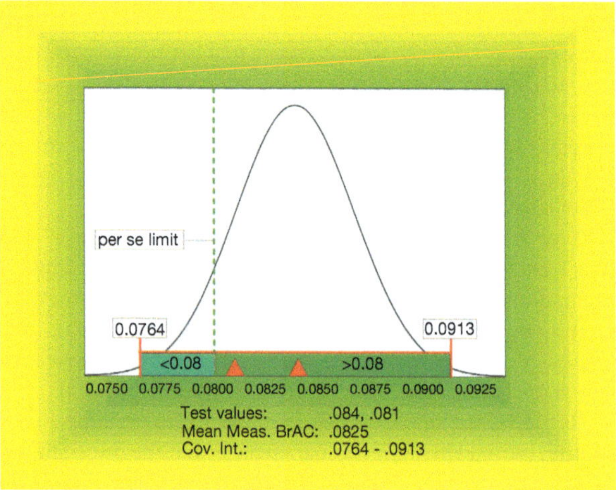

Figure 18 BrAC test 2.

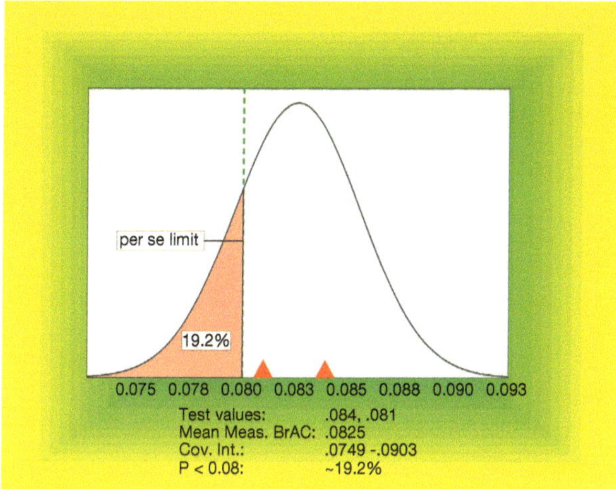

Figure 19 BrAC test 1.

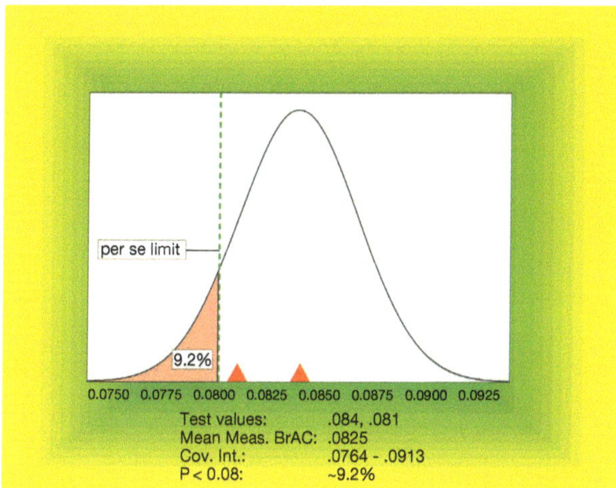

Figure 20 BrAC test 2.

Clearly, the computed uncertainty associated with test 1 is greater than that associated with test 2. Moreover, further examination reveals that the likelihood that each individual's BrAC is actually less than 0.08 g/210 l is nearly 20% and 10% for tests 1 and 2, respectively (**Figures 19 and 20**).

Thus, not only do these "identical" tests not have identical meanings, but each represents a sizable likelihood in the context of reasonable doubt that the BrACs in question are less than the relevant limit. Proper interpretation of these results clearly requires knowledge of their uncertainty.

Determining Measurement Uncertainty

There are several different methods for determining a measurement's uncertainty. The first step in each is to identify and quantify all systematic effects and appropriately correct for each.

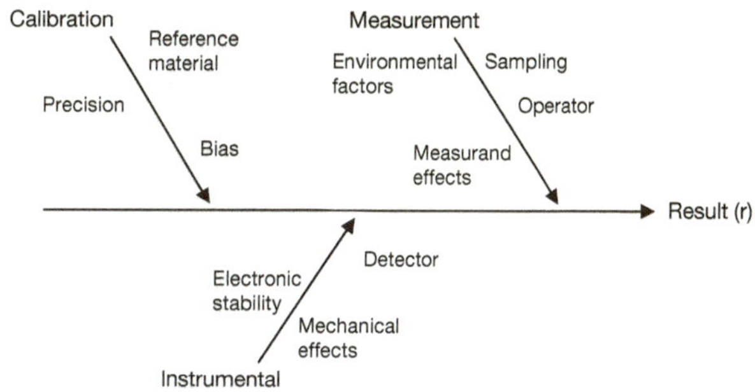

Figure 21 Cause and effect diagram.

The second step is typically the identification of relevant sources of uncertainty. A common way to document these is through a cause and effect diagram, which depicts each source of uncertainty and their relationship to each other and the final result (**Figure 21**).

When all the quantities on which a measured value depends can be varied simultaneously, a result's uncertainty can be determined, directly using statistical methods. Except for simple measurements, however, this approach is typically not practical.

Generally, then, the next step is to determine the magnitude of each of the relevant uncertainties. Each is quantified as a standard deviation and referred to as a "standard uncertainty":

Standard uncertainity

$$\mu \equiv \sigma \qquad [10]$$

The relative standard uncertainty is the ratio of the standard uncertainty to the best estimate of the measurand value. It can be useful when combining or comparing uncertainties of separate measurements:

Relative standard uncertainity

$$\mu_{r_y} = \frac{\mu_y}{|Y_b|} \qquad [11]$$

For some measurements, each source of uncertainty may be associated with the measurement as a whole and manifest itself independently as a direct effect on the final result. Such is the case with direct measurements. In these circumstances, a result's "combined uncertainty," μ_c, is given by the root-sum-square of the standard uncertainties:

$$\mu_c = \sqrt{\sum_{i=1}^{n} \mu_i^2} \qquad [12]$$

Most measurements are indirect in nature, determining a measurand's value through its relationship to other measured quantities. The most common method of determining uncertainty in these circumstances is discussed in the *Guide to the Expression of Uncertainty in Measurement* (the *GUM*). Application of the *GUM* requires that a measurement be modeled as a mathematical function, referred to as the measurement function:

$$\text{Measurement function} \quad Y = f(X_1, X_2, \ldots, X_N) \qquad [13]$$

This function describes the relationship between the measurand value and those quantities required to determine it. For example, if the measurand is the volume of a cylinder, the measurement function might be given as

$$V(r,h) = \pi r^2 h \qquad [14]$$

The combined uncertainty of the measurand is determined by "adding" up the individual standard uncertainties using the method of "propagation of uncertainty":

$$\mu_c = \sqrt{\sum_{i=1}^{N}\left(\frac{\partial f}{\partial x_i}\cdot\mu_{x_i}\right)^2 + 2\sum_{i=1}^{N-1}\sum_{j=i+1}^{N}\frac{\partial f}{\partial x_i}\cdot\frac{\partial f}{\partial x_j}\cdot\mu_{x_i x_j}} \qquad [15]$$

If each of the input quantities is independent, the expression simplifies to

$$\mu_c = \sqrt{\sum_{i=1}^{N}\left(\frac{\partial f}{\partial x_i}\cdot\mu_{x_i}\right)} \qquad [16]$$

For the volume of a cylinder, the combined uncertainty would be given by the expression

$$\mu_{cv} = \sqrt{(2\pi rh\mu_r)^2 + (\pi r^2\mu_h)^2} \qquad [17]$$

Propagation of Uncertainty: Applied to Measurement Functions with Independent Input Quantities

1. Measurement function:

$$Y = a\cdot X \qquad [18]$$

$$Y_b = a\cdot x_b \qquad [19]$$

$$\mu_y = a\cdot\mu_x \qquad [20]$$

2. Measurement function:

$$Y = X^n \qquad [21]$$

$$Y_b = x_b^n \qquad [22]$$

$$\mu_{r_y} = \frac{\mu_y}{|Y_b|} = |n| = \frac{\mu_x}{|x_b|} \qquad [23]$$

3. Measurement function:

$$Y = X - W + \cdots + Z \qquad [24]$$

$$Y_b = x_b - w_b + \cdots + z_b \qquad [25]$$

$$\mu_y = \sqrt{\mu_x^2 + \mu_w^2 + \cdots + \mu_z^2} \qquad [26]$$

4. Measurement function:

$$Y = \frac{X \times \cdots \times W}{Z \times \cdots \times Q} \qquad [27]$$

$$Y_b = \frac{x_b \times \cdots \times w_b}{z_b \times \cdots \times q_b} \qquad [28]$$

$$\mu_{r_y} = \frac{\mu_y}{|Y_b|} = \sqrt{\left(\frac{\mu_x}{x_b}\right)^2 + \left(\frac{\mu_w}{w_b}\right)^2 + \cdots + \left(\frac{\mu_z}{z_b}\right)^2 + \left(\frac{\mu_q}{q_b}\right)^2} \qquad [29]$$

k	:	%
1	:	68.27
1.645	:	90
1.96	:	95
2	:	95.45
2.576	:	99
3	:	99.73

Figure 22 Coverage factors and levels of confidence: Gaussian distribution.

The expanded uncertainty is obtained by multiplying the combined uncertainty by a coverage factor, *k*:

$$\text{Expanded uncertainty} \quad U = k\mu_c \qquad [30]$$

The coverage factor determines the coverage interval's level of confidence. It is commonly based on a *t*-distribution.

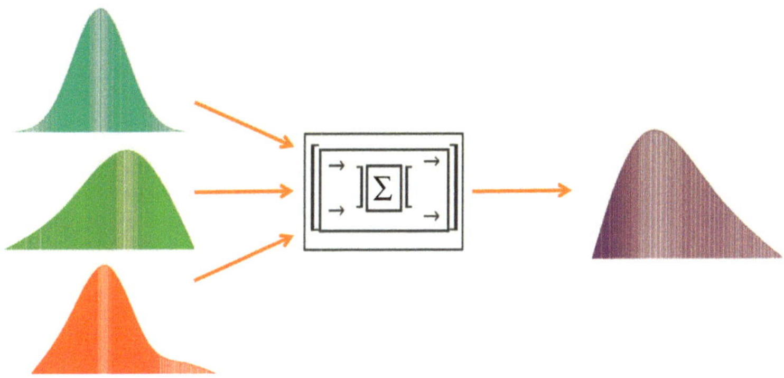

Figure 23 Propagation of distributions.

Where a measurement's degrees of freedom are sufficiently large, the level of confidence bestowed by a given coverage factor is approximately that associated with a Gaussian distribution (**Figure 22**).

The coverage factor is typically chosen to yield a level of confidence of 95% or greater. For the volume of a cylinder, the expanded uncertainty yielding a 99% level of confidence would be given by the expression

$$U = 2.576\sqrt{(2\pi rh\mu_r)^2 + (\pi r^2\mu_h)^2} \quad [31]$$

For the *GUM* to apply, the distribution characterizing a final result must not depart appreciably from normality. Where this is not the case, or where a measurement function is complicated or unknown, a more general approach to the determination of uncertainty is based on the *propagation of distributions*. Instead of determining the standard uncertainty of each input quantity and combining them, the distributions characterizing the quantity value of each input quantity are directly combined to construct the distribution characterizing our state of knowledge of the measurand's value (**Figure 23**).

The standard deviation of the final distribution yields a result's standard uncertainty. It should be noted that the resultant distribution and, hence, its uncertainty (coverage interval) need not be symmetric about the mean. The Monte Carlo method, a computer-based iterative simulation process, is an example of this approach.

A final approach to the determination of uncertainty is the top-down method, so-called because it focuses on the measurement process as a whole instead of its detailed breakdown into distinct sources of uncertainty. It utilizes overall reproducibility estimates, based on measurement trials, as a direct estimate of the uncertainty associated with a measurement method. This approach is often utilized where a measurement function is complicated or unknown. Although each has its advantages, in certain circumstances, the *GUM* and top-down approaches can be used together to determine the uncertainty of a measurement where desirable.

Meaning Requires Uncertainty

Scientific measurement provides a powerful tool for investigating physical phenomena. No matter how good a measurement is, we can never know the "true" value of the quantity of interest. Error analysis focuses on the measurand itself, with the intent of providing a value that is as close as possible to its "true" value. What it actually provides is an ill-defined upper limit on a measurement's total error, revealing the worst a measured value might be without conveying how good it actually is. Uncertainty analysis focuses on our state of knowledge about a measurand, providing a quantitative mapping of measured values into those values believed to be actually and reasonably attributable to the quantity of interest. This conveys the meaning of a result by rigorously defining and constraining the inferences that can be drawn from it. Accordingly, where the actual value of a measurand is important, a result is not complete and cannot be properly interpreted unless it is accompanied by a quantitative statement of its uncertainty.

See also: **Foundations:** Statistical Interpretation of Evidence: Bayesian Analysis; The Frequentist Approach to Forensic Evidence Interpretation; **Legal:** Legal Aspects of Forensic Science; **Methods:** Chemometrics; **Toxicology:** Interpretation of Results; **Toxicology/Alcohol:** Breath Alcohol.

Further Reading

Ehrlich, C., Dybkaer, R., Wöger, W., 2007. Evolution of philosophy and description of measurement. Accreditation and Quality Assurance 12, 201–218.

Estler, W.T., 1999. Measurement as inference: fundamental ideas. CIRP Annals 48 (2), 611–631.

EURACHEM, 2000. Quantifying Uncertainty in Analytical Measurement (2000). QUAM:2000.1.

EURACHEM, 2007. Measurement Uncertainty Arising from Sampling: A Guide to Methods and Approaches.

ISO, 2004. Guidance for the Use of Repeatability, Reproducibility and Trueness Estimates in Measurement Uncertainty Estimation. ISO/TS 21748.

JCGM, 2008a. Evaluation of Measurement Data – Guide to the Expression of Uncertainty in Measurement (GUM). JCGM 100.
JCGM, 2008b. Evaluation of Measurement Data – Supplement 1 to the 'Guide to the Expression of Uncertainty in Measurement' – Propagation of Distributions Using a Monte Carlo Method. JCGM 101.
JCGM, 2008c. International Vocabulary of Metrology – Basic and General Concepts and Associated Terms (VIM). JCGM 200.
JCGM, 2009. Evaluation of Measurement Data – An Introduction to the 'Guide to the Expression of Uncertainty in Measurement' and Related Documents. JCGM 104.
Kacker, R., Sommer, K., Kessel, R., 2007. Evolution of modern approaches to express uncertainty in measurement. Metrologia 44, 513–529.
Kirkup, L., Frenkel, B., 2006. An Introduction to Uncertainty in Measurement: Using the GUM (Guide to the Expression of Uncertainty in Measurement). Cambridge University Press, New York.
NIST, 1994. Guidelines for Evaluating and Expressing the Uncertainty of NIST Measurement Results. NIST 1297.
Vosk, T., 2010. Trial by numbers: uncertainty in the quest for truth and justice. The NACDL Champion 56, 48–56 (reprinted with permission in The Voice for the Defense 40 (3), 24–33 (2011)).

Key Terms

Bayesian, Best evidence, Bias, Brady material, Confidence interval, Confrontation, Coverage interval, Degree of belief, Discovery, Ethical considerations, Forensic, Forensic laboratory report, Frequentist, GUM, Hazard, Health, Holistic approach, Integrated case management, Investigations, Measurement, Measurement error, Occupational health and safety (OHS), Probability, Probability distribution, Propagation of distributions, Propagation of uncertainty, Random error, Risk, Safety, Strategy, Submissions, Systematic error, Testimony, Type A uncertainty, Type B uncertainty, Uncertainty.

Review Questions

1. Are the models offered for forensic service provision suggested by Ramsey and Burton the only ones available? What other models might there be?
2. What is a "forensic strategy"? What questions are part of developing one? Why is it important to a case and to a laboratory?
3. Why is integration of forensic cases "the single biggest challenge to the forensic science community"?
4. What is currently in forensic reports? How do these differ from other scientific reports? How do they differ from published articles in peer-reviewed journals? What *should* be in forensic reports? Make a table listing each component and compare.
5. Who is the "audience" of forensic reports? The police using the technical information to investigate the case or other scientists who must review the technical information? Is it both? How does this affect the content of forensic reports? Should it?
6. How do the legal requirements of the contents of a forensic report differ between the UK and the US?
7. Can forensic reports stand on their own (that is, without an expert's testimony)? What determines this?
8. Are there ethical obligations to the format and content of a forensic report? If so, what are they?
9. What is "Brady material"?
10. What is "OHS"? What should this policy articulate?
11. What is a risk, in OHS terms? How is it prevented or mitigated? What is the hierarchy of control measures?
12. Why is stress a health and safety issue? What types of analysis are particularly prone to mental or stress issues?
13. Why is good housekeeping important in a forensic laboratory?
14. What is a "measurand"? What does error mean in the context of measurement?
15. What are the two types of error associated with every measurement? How are they identified and dealt with?
16. What is measurement uncertainty? What are the types of uncertainty? How are they different than "errors"?
17. How does measurement of uncertainty tie into other forensic statistical methods, like the frequentist approach?
18. Is the true value of a measurement ever known?
19. What types of measurement uncertainty are there in firearms examinations? Why are they relevant?
20. Should firearms reports contain measurement uncertainty (like a +/− on trigger pull measurements)? Why or why not?

Discussion Questions

1. How should forensic examinations and analyses be "integrated"? With laboratory specialization, how can cases move through a forensic laboratory in an integrated fashion? What are the benefits to doing this? What are the problems?
2. Why are forensic reports formatted they way they are? Is there a better way to present this information? Who are they written for and who *should* they be written for?

3. Why would police and prosecutors be unwilling to consider a wrongful conviction? What professional or social pressures might be at play? What is the role of forensic science in these cases, especially if science was used to prosecute the person in the first place?
4. Why is uncertainty of measurement analytically important to forensic science? Is it important ethically? Why or why not?
5. Are some types of forensic science more prone to hazards and health risks than others? If so, list them and explain why they are; if not, why not?

Additional Readings

Cole, S.A., 2014. History of forensic science in policing. In: Encyclopedia of Criminology and Criminal Justice. Springer, New York, pp. 2153–2158.

Howes, L., Kirkbride, K., Kelty, S., Julian, R., Kemp, N., 2014. Forensic scientists' conclusion: how readable are they for non-scientist report-users? Forensic Science International 231 (1–3), 102–112.

de Keijser, J., Elffers, H., 2012. Understanding of forensic expert reports by judges, defense lawyers and forensic professionals. Psychology, Crime & Law 18 (2), 191–207.

Roland, M.C., 2009. Quality and integrity in scientific writing: prerequisites for quality in science communication. Journal of Science Communications 8 (02), A04.

Siegel, J., King, M., Reed, W., 2013. The laboratory report project. Forensic Science Policy & Management 4 (3–4), 1–11.

INDEX

Note: Page numbers followed by "f" indicate figures and "t" indicate tables.

A

B

E

F

G

H

I

P

Q

R

S

Kolibri 360 GmbH
Ferdinand-Jühlke-Straße 7
99095 Erfurt, Deutschland
produktsicherheit@kolibri360.de